Runes and Magic

Runes and Magic

Magical Formulaic Elements in the Older Runic Tradition

Third Revised and Expanded Edition

Stephen E. Flowers

Copyright © 2014
LODESTAR

All rights reserved. No part of this book, either in part or in whole, may be reproduced, transmitted or utilized in any form or by any means electronic, photographic or mechanical, including photocopying, recording, or by any information storage and retrieval system, without the permission in writing from the Publisher, except for brief quotations embodied in literary articles and reviews.

For permissions, or for the serialization, condensation, or for adaptation of this book write the Publisher at the address below.

Published by
LODESTAR
P.O. Box 16
Bastrop, Texas 78602

www.seekthemystery.com

Table of Contents

Acknowledgments..vii
Abbreviations Used in the Text and References........................ viii
Transliteration of the Runes...xi
Note on Translations...xi
List of Figures, Tables and Maps.. xii
Preface to the Second Edition..xiii
CHAPTER ONE: Introduction... 1
CHAPTER TWO: Theoretical Problems....................................9
   1. Introduction...9
   2. Magic...9
   3. Traditional Societies... 18
   4. Symbol Systems and the Communicative Process............ 21
CHAPTER THREE: Previous Scholarship................................31
   1. Introduction.. 31
   2. Cultic Aspects.. 31
   3. Magical Aspects... 33
CHAPTER FOUR: Social Aspects of Operant Runic Practice........ 47
   1. Introduction.. 47
   2. The Runic System... 47
   3. "Pre-Runic" Period... 48
   4. Runic Origins..48
   5. Runic Data and Analysis...50
   6. Development of the System... 51
   7. The Social Matrix..52
   8. Conclusions on Runic Origins....................................... 54
   9. Höfler's Theories.. 54
   10. Diffusion and Maintenance of the Older Fuþark................ 56
   11. The Older Runic System..57
   12. Conclusions on Diffusion and Maintenance..................... 59
   13. Social Aspects... 59
   14. Individual Rune-Carvers.. 62
   15. Decline of the Runic Tradition in South Germanic Culture. 63
   16. Wōðanaz...64
   17. Runic Reform..66
   18. Social Developments...67
   19. The Younger Runic System... 69
   20. Social Context... 70
   21. Óðinn..72

22. Medieval Period (after 1150).. 72
23. Conclusion.. 73
CHAPTER FIVE: Runes and Germanic Magical Practice............... 85
  1. Introduction.. 85
  2. Power Concepts.. 85
  3. Dynamistic... 86
  4. Animistic.. 88
  5. Extra-Human Entities... 89
  6. Non-Runic Magic.. 91
  7. The Magician... 92
  8. Magical Procedures.. 94
  9. Substances... 96
  10. Signs and Symbols.. 97
  11. Magical Tools... 98
  12. Amulets.. 98
  13. Runic Practice: Lexical Evidence.................................... 99
  14. Technical Terminology... 103
  15. Operative Runic Formulas in Written Records............... 106
  16. Runic Ritual... 111
CHAPTER SIX: Corpus of the Older Operative Formulas............ 127
  1. Introduction... 127
  2. Rune-Master Formulas: Introductions............................. 127
  3. Rune-Master Formulas: Criteria...................................... 128
  4. Rune-Master Formulas: Types... 128
  5. first-person Formula.. 129
  6. "I N.N. color the runes" (Type I)..................................... 129
  7. Corpus of I.A... 130
  8. Corpus of I.B.. 132
  9. Corpus of I.C.. 133
  10. "I N.N. colored" (Type II).. 134
  11. "I, the rune-master" (Type III)....................................... 136
  12. Corpus of III. A.. 137
  13. Corpus of III. B.. 138
  14. Corpus of III. C.. 140
  15. Corpus of III. D.. 141
  15b. I, the rune-master am called the crafty one.................. 141
  16. Survey of Viking Age and Medieval Material................ 143
  17. first-person Type A.. 143
  18. first-person Type B.. 144
  19. first-person Type C.. 145

20. Third-Person Formula: "N.N. carved (the runes)"............ 145
21. Corpus of Type I... 145
22. Corpus of Type II. A.. 147
23. Corpus of Type II. B.. 149
24. Corpus of Type II. C.. 150
25. Survey of Viking Age and Medieval Material................ 151
26. Appendix: Personified Object— "N.N. made me"............ 154
27. Ambiguous Restricted Proper Names........................... 155
28. Isolated Proper Names: Manufactured Objects............... 156
29. Isolated Proper Names: Natural Objects....................... 158
30. Proper Names in Elaborated Context............................159
31. Typology of Rune-Master/Carver Names...................... 165
32. Female Rune-Masters.. 169
33. Word Formulas: Introduction......................................170
34. **alu**.. 170
34b. Appendix on **medu**.. 174
35. **ota**.. 175
36. **auja**.. 175
37. **laukaR**..176
37b **līna**...178
38. **salu**..178
39. **ehwa-**...178
40. **laþu**..179
41. *Nomen agentis* Spear Names..................................... 180
42. Unique and Ambiguous Word-Formulas....................... 182
43. Rune-Formulas.. 182
44. Sequential Fuþark Inscriptions..................................... 183
45. Survey of Viking and Medieval Fuþark-Formulas........... 184
46. Isolated Non-Sequential Formulas................................ 185
47. Appendix on Old English Amuletic Rings..................... 186
48. Contextual Non-Sequential Formulas........................... 187
49. Survey of Viking Age and Medieval Rune-Formulas....... 190
50. Operative Syntactic Formulas......................................192
51. Appendix on Christian Formulas.................................. 200
52. Speculatively Operant Inscriptions...............................201
53. Survey of Viking Age and Medieval Syntactic Formulas.... 203
CHAPTER SEVEN: Magical Formulaic Analysis................ 229
  1. Introduction... 229
  2. Rune-Master Formulas.. 230

3. Word-Formulas.. 239
   4. Rune-Formulas... 243
   5. Syntactic Operative Formulas.. 248
   6. Auxiliary Elements: Concealment.................................. 252
   7. Auxiliary Elements: Runic Logographs.......................... 252
   8. Auxiliary Elements: Number Patterns............................ 253
   9. Auxiliary Elements: Ideographic Signs.......................... 253
   10. Auxiliary Elements: Pictographic Signs........................ 254
   11. Auxiliary Elements: Color... 255
CHAPTER EIGHT: Summary.. 259
REFERENCES..263
FUÞARK FIGURES... 299
MAPS... 305

Acknowledgments

I would like to give thanks to Prof. Dr. Edgar Polomé for the many years of inspiration and special insights he gave me during my entire course of graduate studies at the University of Texas at Austin. Special gratitude also goes to Prof. Dr. Klaus Düwel for the many hours of patient discussion of concepts used in this work, for his indispensable guidance of my runological studies, and for his kind personal hospitality in Göttingen during the 1981-82 academic year. Without certain viewpoints that he was able to convey, and his careful reading of the manuscript, this study would have been impossible. Beyond this time his continued help and guidance through the years has been indispensable to my research and development.

Further I would like to thank Profs. Drs. Erhard Schleisier and Peter Fuchs of the Seminar für Völkerkunde and Prof. Dr. Heike Sternberg of the Seminar für Ägyptologie in Göttingen for their helpful guidance in the most recent theories concerning magic and the theory of magic, and Prof. Dr. François-Xavier Dillmann for his help, stimulating conversation, and hospitality in Copenhagen.

Special thanks also go to the staffs of various museums in which some of my research was carried out: Dr. Michael Gebühr of the Schleswig-Holsteinisches Landesmuseum für Vor- und Frühgeschichte, Drs. Erik Moltke, Maria Stoklund, and Elisabeth Munksgaard of the National Museum, Copenhagen, Dr. Jan Peder Lamm of the Statens Historiska Museum, Stockholm, Sigrid Kålund of the Bergen Museum, and Jane Floor and Lillian Myrvold of the Stavanger Museum.

In addition, I would like to thank the DAAD for its support of my work in Göttingen during 1981-82.

For this third edition of the text a very special thanks go to Michael Moynihan for his scholarly reading and editing of the text and to Lothar Tuppan for his thorough corrections of the copy.

Despite the guidance which I received for many learned persons throughout my research in this field, any mistakes or errors in judgment that might be found in this study are entirely my own.

Abbreviations Used in the Text and References

Standard abbreviations for Eddic poems are those used by Neckel-Kuhn (1962).

AAWG	Abhandlungen der Akademie der Wissenschaften in Göttingen
acc.	accusative
Alem.	Alemannic
ANF	*Arkiv för Nordisk Filologi*
ANO	*Aarbøger for Nordisk Oldkyndighed og Historie*
APS	*Acta Philologica Scandinavica*
BCE	Before the Common Era (= B.C.)
BGDSL	*Beiträge zur Geschichte der deutschen Sprache und Literatur*
br(s).	bracteate(s)
CE	Common Era (= A.D.)
cent(s).	century/centuries
crem.	cremation
dat.	dative
DBG	*De bello gallico*
DR.	*Danmarks Runeindskifter*(cf. Jacobsen-Moltke 1942)
EGmc.	East Germanic
ES	*Egils saga Skallagrímsson*
ESS	*Edda Snorra Sturlusonar*
fem.	feminine
Flb.	*Flateyjarbók*
Frühmast.	*Frühmittelalterliche Studien*
Fv.	*Fornvännen*
G.	*Gotlands Runinskrifter* (cf. Jansson-Wessen 1962)
gen.	genitive
Germ.	*Germania*
GGA	*Göttingische Gelehrte Anzeigen*
G-H. s.	*Göngu-Hrólfs saga*
Gk.	Greek
Gmc.	Germanic
Go.	Gothic
GRM	*Germanisch-romanische Monatsschrift*
Gr.s.	*Grettis saga*
Gylfa.	*Gylfaginning*
HDA	*Handwörterbuch des deutschen Aberglaubens*

Heimsk.	*Heimskringla*
Hist.	*Historia/Historiae*
Hitt.	Hittite
IK.	See Hauck (1985-1989)
JEGP	*Journal of English and Germanic Philology*
JIES	*Journal of Indo-European Studies*
KHNM	*Kulturhistorisk Leksikon for Nordisk Middelalder*
KJ	*Die Runeninschriften im älteren Futhark* (see Krause 1966)
Lat.	Latin
Lex. Poet.	*Lexicon Poeticum* (cf. Egilsson-Jonsson 1931)
M.	Marquardt 1961
masc.	masculine
MHG	Middle High German
MLN	*Modern Language Notes*
MM	*Maal og Minne*
MQ	*Mankind Quarterly*
MSca.	*Medieval Scandinavia*
MS(S)	manuscript(s)
MWel.	Middle Welsh
NAWG	Nachrichten der Akademie der Wissenshaften in Göttingen
NE	New English
NGmc.	North Germanic
NHG	New High German
NIæR	*Norges Insdskrifter med de ældre Runer* (Bugge-Olsen 1891-1924)
nom.	nominative
NoR	*Nytt om Runer*
NTS	*Norsk Tidskrift for Sprogvidenskab*
ODan.	Old Danish
OE	Old English
OFranc.	Old Franconian
OFris.	Old Frisian
Ög	Östergötlands Runinskrifter (see Brate 1911-18)
OHG	Old High German
OIce.	Old Icelandic
OInd.	Old Indic
OIr.	Old Irish
Öl.	Ölands Runinskrifter (see Söderberg-Brate 1900-06)
ON	Old Norse
ONorw.	Old Norwegian

Op.	See Opitz 1977
OPers.	Old Persian
OSwe.	Old Swedish
PGmc.	Proto-Germanic
PIE	Proto-Indo-European
pl.	plural
PMLA	*Publications of the Modern Language Association*
PN	personal name
PNor.	Primitive Norse/Nordic
p.p.	past participle
pret.	preterite
r.	rune (when cited in an ordinal series)
RGA[1]	*Reallexikon der germanischen Altertumskunde* (first edition, see Hoops 1911-19)
RGA[2]	*Reallexikon der germanischen Altertumskunde* (second edition)
s.	saga
SGmc.	South Germanic
Skalds.	*Skáldskaparmál*
Skj.	See Jónsson 1908
Skt.	Sanskrit
Sö.	*Södermanlands Runinskrifter* (see Brate-Wessen 1924-36)
SS	*Scandinavian Studies*
st(s).	stone(s)
subj.	subjunctive
subst.	substantive
U.	*Upplands Runinskrifter* (see Wessen-Jansson 1940-58)
Vat.s.	*Vatnsdœla saga*
Vg.	*Västergötlands Runinskrifter* (see Jungner-Svärdström 1940-58)
voc.	vocative
VS	*Vǫlsunga saga*
WGmc.	West Germanic
Wulf.	Wulfila's Gothic translation of the Bible
ZDA	*Zeitschrift für deutsches Altertum*
ZDP	*Zeitschrift für deutsche Philologie*
ZfV.	*Zeitschrift für Volkskunde*

Transliteration of the Runes

The transliteration of the runes generally follows the standard set in the works of modern runologists. Runes are transliterated as lowercase bold Roman letters, e.g., **alu**. Supplied characters are placed between parentheses ( ), and those reconstructed from damaged or problematic forms are placed between square brackets [ ]. Otherwise ambiguous forms have a single point placed below them, e.g., **alu̇**. Indefinite and unreconstructed characters are represented by an x, while sections that are broken off or completely defaced are rendered by ellipses . . . An arch over two or more characters indicates a bind-rune made up of those runes. For transliterations of individual runic characters, see Figures I-III. Latin letters are represented by Roman capitals.

A Note on Translations

Unless otherwise noted, translations of runic texts, and those of written Germanic or Latin texts, are those of the author.

List of Figures, Tables and Maps

Chart I.	Literary Operative Formulas, maximum criteria	109
Chart II.	Literary Operative Formulas, medium criteria	110
Chart III.	Literary Operative Formulas, minimum criteria	110
Figure IA.	Older Fuþark	299
Figure IB.	Older Fuþark Inscriptions	300
Figure II.	The Old English Epigraphical Fuþorc	301
Figure IIIA.	The Younger Fuþark	302
Figure IIIB.	The Gørlev Fuþark	302
Figure IV.	Ætt-arrangement of the Runes	303
Figure V.	Runic Alphabets	304
Map I.	Older Runic Inscriptions before ca 250 CE	305
Map II.	Older Runic Inscriptions between ca. 250 and 350	306
Map III.	Older Runic Inscriptions between ca. 350 and 450	307
Map IV.	Older Runic Inscriptions between ca. 450 and 550	308
Map V.	Older Runic Inscriptions between ca. 550 and 650	309
Map VI.	Older Runic Inscriptions after ca. 650	310
Map VII.	Areas of Early Germanic Cultic Leagues	311

Preface to the Second Edition

This work was first written as a dissertation for the University of Texas at Austin in 1984. It was subsequently only slightly edited for publication by Peter Lang in 1986. It has therefore been a quarter of a century since this work was first composed. Only 250 copies of the published work appeared, and most of these found happy homes in various academic libraries around the world. This new edition corrects the technical problems with the original and makes, I hope, an overall better impression on the eyes of potential readers of this often difficult material.

The conceptualization of *Runes and Magic* took place during the year I studied with Klaus Düwel in Göttingen (1981-82). The main impetus for its theoretical background was simply this: that if one were to study the concept of *magic* in any scientific context, one would have to come to terms solidly with the general scientific theory of magic (as worked out by specialists in anthropology and folklore) and apply it to any specific cultural material in question. Any other approach would be unscientific.

In this new edition I have only added a few new inscriptions to the catalog and updated the bibliography and other apparatus to bring the contents into line with the current state of runology. Additionally I have made minor changes to the text and corrected errors. However, as the work is essentially one of applied theory, and these theories have not fundamentally changed in the academic community, the main thrust of the argument of the work remains now as it was then.

The first edition of *Runes and Magic* met with a mixed reception. This was mainly due to the prevailing academic atmosphere of the times, which was one decidedly skeptical about the magical functions of the fuþark. However, the work was often generally acknowledged as the "only comprehensive attempt to survey runic magic." (MacLeod and Mees 2006: 2) In other words, the work was widely cited as a source, but its theoretical components and their scientific application to other materials have, to date, found less traction.

In the first edition I made the provocative statement to the effect that no single older runic inscription could definitely be shown *not* to have some magical function. In other words, the entire corpus of the runic inscriptions in the older fuþark could be interpreted from a magical, or *operative*, perspective. This is because during this older period (ca. 100-800 CE) the Germanic peoples were only literate in a specifically restricted way, and so their attitude toward the whole process of writing was fundamentally different than it was to the widely literate Greeks or to our contemporary experience of this activity. This statement of mine was specifically cited as being absurd by one critic, (McKinnell 2004: 31) who counters that the inscription on one of the horns of Gallehus is clearly simply a maker's mark ('I, Hlewegast Holtsson made the horn') and could have nothing to do with "magic." I would argue that since the horn is decorated with a rich cultic iconography it is this to which the "maker's mark" refers and that the "*ek-formula*" must be understood in the greater semiotic context of the older runic inscriptions. Such an understanding, coupled with the poetic form of the formula and the obvious religious function of the horn, have led generations of scholars to see something in this object, viewed as a *whole*, which is heavily endowed with symbolic and cultic content.

The basic approach I used was to look at every older runic inscription, it the context of the object and what we can understand of the cultural milieu which produced these artifacts and apply the current scientific semiotic theory of magic (or operative communication) to these artifacts to see what emerges. This method seems sound and to be one that can be applied not only to a larger body of runic evidence but to a whole range of ancient artifacts. This method was also (independently, as far as I know) discovered by one other scholar, John G. Gager, professor of religion at Princeton University, who used a similar semiotic theoretical framework (including utilization of the work of Tambiah, *et al.*) to examine the meaning of ancient Greek and Roman "curse tablets" in his book *Curse Tablets and Binding Spells from the Ancient World* (Oxford, 1992).

The main shortcoming of recent efforts to study runes and magic (e.g., MacLeod and Mees 2006 and McKinnell and Simek 2004) is that the authors claim in the titles of the works to be concerned with "magic" yet nowhere do they provide a viable scientific theory or framework of understanding for this concept. This leaves the reader free to fill this gap in theory with a layman's level of understanding of the topic of magic. All of this simply leads to misunderstanding of the whole field of study.

The semiotic theory of magic could be summarized: Through willed communicative operations an operator (magician) is able to modify the symbolic universe in which he lives in ways which harmonize with his own will. Because the frame of reference for such operative acts ascribes a responsive quality to the object of such communications, this object in turn is seen to become an active agent capable of responding to the operator in the form of symbols or phenomena.

The very act and presence of writing in a cultural context of restricted literacy by itself constitutes a powerful operative *sign*. When we speak of the semiotic theory of magic in connection with runes it is easy to focus only on the content and form of the inscriptions—the meaning and interpretation of the text itself. Although this is the primary focus of this present study, it should not be forgotten that other components of the runic tradition also constitute *signs* each of which play a part in the overall semiotics of rune-magic. These include the very presence of the written text, the act of writing, the act of coloring, the choice of substance into which the inscription is made, the location of the artifact, and even the act of reading itself.

Writing is more permanent (eternal) than speech, the world of the gods is more permanent than that of humanity, therefore writing (especially when executed in stone or other *hard* substances) reflects a semiotic quality similar to that of the gods and their world—writing has higher *prestige* than mere speech.

A more holistic approach is necessary to help the current analyst of these ancient artifacts actually understand the meaning of them. This requires us to understand as far as possible the mind-sets of those who produced these objects and to make the effort to understand their cultural frame of reference. Viewing these linguistic artifacts in a cultural and intellectual vacuum in which modern attitudes and prejudices are allowed free reign creates just one more avenue for the advent of wild speculation. It is perhaps a greater exercise in pure speculation to imagine that a rune-master living in the year 500 CE thought of himself, his world and his work in the same way as a modern person might, than it is to assume that he thought of these things differently than the typical modern man might, and that by studying the whole of the culture of which the rune-master was a part and by applying comparative evidence we can come to a greater understanding of the meaning of the artifacts in question. Some runologists are only interested in specific things the inscriptions might illuminate, e.g., historical linguistic phenomena or techniques of rock-carving, whereas others are interested in the overall meaning of the artifacts and their places in the spiritual life of the ancient people who made them.

In the context of the foregoing discussion, the by now familiar proposed distinction between "speculative" or "imaginative" and "skeptical" runologists must, I believe, be modified. More precisely it does not seem that the difference lies so much in the respective runologists' indulgence in speculation, but rather it lies in the scope of that speculation. One school tends to look at the runes as part of a larger, more culture-wide phenomenon, whereas the other tends to see runic evidence in a more restricted way—usually relevant almost exclusively to historical linguistics. Therefore, I propose that the previously named "imaginative" runologists should be redefined "holistic runologists," whereas the "skeptical" ones should be designated as "specialized runologists."

It is my hope that future runologists will continue to make use of every scientific tool available to them in order to make true scientific progress in the understanding of these artifacts which allow us to hear the words of the ancient rune-masters and even to understand their mysteries.

Stephen E. Flowers
Woodharrow Institute
February, 2009

Chapter I

Introduction

For most runologists at the beginning of the scientific study of runic writing and its attendant cultural features, there was little doubt as to the essentially "magical" nature of the runes.(1) However, since the middle of the twentieth-century serious objections to this general assumption have often been raised,(2) and never has the questioning of the magical nature of the runes and of runic inscriptions been as strong as in the last few years.(3) For this reason, the times demand a new, more critical examination of the whole question of the connection between the older runic tradition and the practice of magic by the Germanic peoples during the first millennium CE.

One of the principal deficiencies in the study of runes and magic has historically been the routine neglect of the complex problem of *magic* in ethnological and religious-historical terms and the possibility of linking it with runological study. In this regard, a singular shortcoming has been the lack of a comprehensive (or even of a limited, heuristic) definition of the concept "magic" and the contextual placement of that idea within the runic tradition. Although this topic receives extensive discussion in ch. II, at this juncture a preliminary definition may be offered from the *Encyclopedia of Anthropology*:

> Magic supposes a set of beliefs and techniques designed to control the supernatural or natural environments for specific purposes. The element of control helps analytically to distinguish it from religion (more propitiatory) and the empirically untested belief in magic distinguishes it from science, but the frontiers dividing the three are not always clear.
>
> (Hunter and Whitten 1976: 254)

When we seek to understand these concepts in the runological context, it seems prudent to distinguish carefully between the idea of "rune-magic" (magical operations in which the runes themselves are considered agents of some extraordinary force, or the force itself) and the more neutral "runes *and* magic" (which leaves the question as to the ontological relationship between the runes and the magical element open).(4)

In this study, the data is approached from essential two viewpoints: 1) the runological (i.e., the philological study of the runes and the attendant disciplines of archeology and art history),(5) and 2) the ethnological and religious-historical. It is necessary to deal exhaustively with the concrete runological problems of the inscriptions in question in order that the interpretive comments concerning their supposed magical functions rest on as firm a foundation as possible. Various readings of inscriptions from the extensive secondary runic literature are referred to, as it is often a mistake of those who deal with this topic to accept the readings of particular scholars too easily, or to ignore basic runological problems. For the sake of convenience the reader is usually referred to readings found in Krause (1966)—which are not necessarily those of Krause himself—as this is the only edition which approaches completeness,(6) and one which is easily available.

Additionally, the religious-historical approach is also influenced by an anthropological or ethnological viewpoint. The runic data are studied as the primary traces of an intellectual or spiritual world, which, if properly and carefully dealt with, reveal some of this archaic inner world to us today. There are significant difficulties with the study of historical materials in a way similar to that of living traditional societies— the limited and often disparate data demand a methodology of their own. Unfortunately, no such coherent methodology has yet been developed. However, this problem has been kept in mind throughout the course of this work.

Much of the religious-historical approach is drawn from ethnological work done in the field of magical theory. More recent studies which recognize the essential wholeness and non-evolutionary nature of the concepts "magic," "religion," and "science"(7) (Wax and Wax 1962 and 1963, and van Baal 1971) and ones which have begun to develop a fresh approach to magic as a system of *communication* between perceived realms of reality (cf. Finnegan 1969, van Baal 1971, Tambiah 1973, Grambo 1975) have been keystones of the anthropological considerations. Furthermore, special attention has been given to the history of Germanic religion and its attendant magical or "operant" aspects. Of paramount importance is the placement of the runic phenomenon firmly within a more comprehensive Germanic magico-religious world-view(8)— based upon literary and archeological evidence.

Perhaps a word should be said on the temptation to use (or over-use) comparative evidence in a study of this kind. In theoretical and methodological constructs (ch. II) topological analogies with exotic cultures (contemporary and historical) can be of some heuristic value. However, we can not be sure, that although a given practice or institution may appear to be similar or identical to one found in the Germanic world, that the *attitude* of the subject toward that practice and its aim and context (or "frame of reference")(9) are not in fact radically different. For this reason, the preponderance of any comparative evidence is kept as far as possible within the Germanic cultural context, with a secondary emphasis on the wider Indo-European world, and the exotic cultural features are placed in tertiary position.

A methodology which combines inductive and deductive reasoning has generally been employed in the development of the research. Various categories of inscriptions and formulaic elements within the texts of the inscriptions were obviously developed only after the runic corpus had been analyzed, while advantage was taken of past scholarship to establish the basic categories, e.g., rune-master inscriptions or word-formulas. In the area of magic itself, general ideas synthesized from common theories used by anthropologists and ethnologists (ch. II) govern a basic approach to the data (a necessary first step); however, this theoretical base is modified according to specific data gathered from the runic corpus (chs. VI and VII), so that a more accurate picture of the "magical thinking" involved with the runes may be gained.

After a theoretical groundwork for magic, the problems of traditional (or pre-literate) societies, and useful theories of symbol systems as well as their use in magic among various peoples have been discussed (ch. II), previous scholarship concerning the whole problem of rune-magic, and the runes and magic is briefly surveyed (ch. III). A pivotal problem in the question of any magical aspects that were possibly involved with the runes revolves around the nature of the society in which those concepts would have flourished. In ch. IV some of the socio-cultic features of early Germanic society are examined in the context of the historical development of runic systems. Before the epigraphical corpus itself is treated, the role and nature of magic (both runic and non-runic) and the basis for customary magical thought in the Germanic world is discussed (ch. IV) to provide a context for the inscriptional evidence presented in ch. VI. Material in ch. VI is arranged according to a formulaic typology intended to articulate evidence in a new way, conducive to the examination of runic inscriptions in the contexts of their basic linguistic or communicative units. The last major chapter forms an interpretive analysis of the formulaic elements deduced from the older runic corpus and in this an attempt is made to establish a case for the operant function of these elements.

Evidence considered includes both the epigraphical corpus itself(10) and the important, but problematical, literary and historical references to runes and runic practice, and attestations of lexical items relevant to runic problems.(11) Runic epigraphy is considered on a contextual level—for the actual linguistic information imparted by the inscription—and from a structural point of view. This structural data includes the juxtaposition of the formulaic elements to one another, as well as the structure of the runic system (shape, order, phonology, articulation into groups of eight), both of which can impart significant information on the nature and development of the traditions.

Archeological data are sometimes employed in the discussion of individual inscriptions (e.g., rune-stones and grave finds), as well as whole classes of inscriptions (e.g., bracteates), when such evidence provides significant information about the possible function of the inscription. In the case of rune-stones, it is helpful to know whether the stone was most probably found within a grave-mound or nearby one (which is not always that easy to determine).(12) With grave finds, other information about the grave (cremation or inhumation, man or woman, etc.)(13) can be important, while the general placement of the bracteates, and the typology of their finding circumstances may be informative.

Art-historical problems, such as the iconography and style of the bracteates(14) and of the few older rune-stones with pictographic representations, as well as information which art historians can provide concerning the technique of executing a runic inscription (carving techniques, pigmentation, etc.) can be useful in the establishment of the technical and symbological knowledge of the early rune-carvers. Such information may be useful for both a better understanding of the craft of carving runes and for the light it might shed on technical aspects of *operative* runic practices and beliefs.

Comparative evidence of essentially two types is introduced at various relevant points: 1) the intercultural—the problems of which have been briefly discussed, and 2) the inter-epochal evidence found within the Germanic tradition. This latter category presents a host of special problems. The principal questions for this study in the older tradition are: 1) to what extent can medieval written sources be used as evidence for runic practices in the Migration Age and before, and 2) what is the value of the younger epigraphical material in the investigation of the older inscriptions? Any general conclusions reached on the nature of the older tradition may not rest too heavily upon either of these types of evidence. However, when the literary historical problems of Eddic sources and the saga literature and the possible cultural influences surrounding the younger runic tradition are kept in perspective, comparative evidence of this nature, when corroborated by the older epigraphy, can be helpful in reconstructing significant technical, and procedural aspects of the older period.(15)

The purpose of this study is manifold. First, it represents an attempt to place the problem of rune and magic in the context of the most recent ideas on the problem of magic in general. Here, magical theory will be approached from the viewpoint of a *semiotic* model and as a representation of a communicative relationship, rather than from what have become barren ideas of nebulous numerological computations and the like. The possible relationship between runes and magic is evaluated on the foundation of linguistically and formally based formulaic models, all of which have been material problems of runology over the past hundred years. Sound runological evidence has been the standard basis through which magical or operant aspects have been approached. Second, any rune-magic which might be deduced is placed, as far as possible, within the context of a general understanding of "magical thought" in the Germanic world. Third, an attempt has been made to develop an explanation of the runic phenomenon which takes into account the social realities of those times. The social context of the runic tradition—as nearly as we can determine it—may yield information which is useful in order to ascertain the nature of that tradition, as well as that of the society in which it thrived. Fourth, I have made an effort to evaluate the possibilities for the establishment of a general theory of the use of runes in magical operations.

The extent to which anyone can be successful in the exploration of this topic, and in finding solutions to those problems, remains somewhat doubtful. Because "magic," "religion," and even language are so much an expression of some psychic reality, they represent extremely difficult objects for study by means of the human intellect. No scientific "mirror" has yet been devised by which this subject may reflect upon itself and become its own object— and it seems certain that this paradox will endure all scientific efforts to resolve it. Probably no single comprehensive theory will be able to account for all variations given such a model. However, it is precisely for this reason that the universal fascination endures, and the absolute necessity and responsibility for the continuing exploration of the possibilities of "understanding" these phenomena remain. This study is an attempt to come a step closer in this process, or at least to frame the questions in a more revealing manner than has heretofore been the case.

Notes for the Introduction

1. The common assumption that the runes were first and foremost used by "priests" of some kind in divinatory rites plus the etymology of the word "rune" led to the conclusion that the runes were essentially "magical" (see ch. V). Editions such as Bugge-Olsen (1891-1924) and Krause (1937) emphasized magical interpretations of various inscriptions, while special studies in rune-magic were produced by Olsen (1916), Agrell (1927a, 1927b, 1928, 1931, 1932, 1938), and Brix (1928, 1929, 1932)— all of which were in one way or another based on numerical formulaic theories.

2. Quite early Neckel (1928: 31-32) raised some objections to the unquestioned magical interpretations. It was not until Bæksted (1952) that this was built into a comprehensive thesis. Other important studies which sought to reduce the credibility of magical interpretations are Morgenroth (1961), which is principally directed against the numerical methods of Olsen, and Page (1964), which focuses on the Anglo-Saxon tradition.

3. Most recently, works by Antonsen (1980a, 1980b) and by Moltke (1976, 1981a) call the magical nature of the runes into question anew.

4. Cf. Thompson (1977) for a survey of the history of the word "rune," the original sense of which ("mysterium") would seem to place it in the magico-religious semantic field (see ch. V), but there have also been objections raised by Bæksted (1952) and Page (1964: 14ff.).

5. For a discussion of basic problems in runology, see Düwel (2001: 15-22), and Page (1999: 1-15).

6. Krause's (1966) edition contains discussions on 222 older inscriptions. The actual number of known older inscriptions now stands at around 400— many of the additional inscriptions are on bracteates, of which Krause merely discusses one example of an inscriptional group-type and mentions others in notes only. For this reason the more complete numbering system of the comprehensive bracteate edition by Hauck, *et al.* is used (see note 10 below). There have been more recent additions to the runic corpus from the South Germanic tradition, see Opitz (1977). Other more recently discovered inscriptions not found in Krause (1966) are referred to by their initial publications.

7. For purely heuristic reasons, I have generally used the term "magic" in most contexts, see ch. II.

8. This topic has too often been ignored, however, studies by Höfler (1970; 1971) and Dillmann (1981) have dealt with this problem in some detail.

9. This term "frame of reference" proceeds from the idea that a magico-religious act takes place and is effective within a given set of specific cultural circumstances, see Grambo (1975: 77-81).

10. The entire runic corpus is not contained in any one edition. For the period of the older fuþark (to ca. 750 CE) Krause (1966) is the most complete (see ch. I n. 6 above). Krause is supplemented by older editions limited to Scandinavian material, e.g., Bugge-Olsen (1891-1924), which concentrates on the Norwegian inscriptions but in which almost all older runic epigraphy known at the time is discussed. Jacobsen-Moltke (1942) is concerned exclusively with Danish inscriptions. This is supplemented by Moltke (1976) and Marstrander (1952), which concentrates on inscriptions found in Denmark and Sweden. Then there is the important *Ikonographischer Katalog* of the gold bracteate

inscriptions edited by Hauck *et al.* (1985-1989), in which the runological questions are dealt with by Klaus Düwel. Editions limited to older South Germanic runic epigraphy are Arntz-Zeiss (1939) and Opitz (1977). A comprehensive edition of the Old English runic inscriptions is still lacking. A concise edition for students is presented by Flowers (1999). A bibliography of the Old English inscriptions is provided by Marquardt (1961), see also Elliott (1989) and Page (1999). The younger runic corpus is still a relatively rapidly growing one, but the majority of its inscriptions is contained in the Swedish series *Sveriges Runinskrifter* (since 1900), or for Norway in Olsen (1941-1960), or for Denmark Jacobsen-Moltke (1942) and Moltke (1976), or for the British Isles Olsen (1954), and more recently Barnes and Page (2006).

11. Besides various standard reference works on the literary language of old Germanic dialects, i.e., lexicons and etymological dictionaries for Go., ON, OHG, OE, OFris., the major literary texts for the history of runic practice are the *Codex Regius*, or *Poetic Edda* (see the edition by Neckel-Kuhn 1962), and some sagas, e.g., the *Völsunga saga* (*VS*), the *Egils saga Skallagrímssonar* (*ES*), and the *Grettis saga Asmundarsonar* (*Gr. s.*), among several others. The vast topic of runic tradition in Old Norse literature has been extensively dealt with by Finnur Jónsson (1910: 283ff.) and by Dillmann (1976).

12. This is a question that has been made complex due to the inexact nature of early archeological reports. It has been widely assumed that a whole class of rune-stone inscriptions were housed entirely below ground within the burial mound. Bæksted (1951: 63ff.) raised objections to this assumption. Stones were originally not placed on top of grave-mounds, however, in modern times farmers attempting to replace stones to their "rightful place," after having displaced them perhaps generations earlier, often thought it fitting to place them in such a high place of apparent honor.

13. For inscriptions discovered before the introduction of rigorous archeological methods (the majority of the major older rune-stones) the exact circumstances of the finds are often difficult to establish. Some objects were moved about before they were found by academics, while for others the reports made by the archeologists may be lacking or vague. The most convenient source of archeological evidence is Krause (1966) in which such data are usually included for each inscription, also Bugge-Olsen (1891-1924) and Marstrander (1952) often contain detailed archeological data.

14. Bracteate studies have been extensively pursued by Hauck (1957, 1969, 1970a, 1970b, 1972, 1977, 1980, 1981a and 1981b). These works deal for the most part with iconographical analyses within the framework of art history and the history of religion in the Germanic Migration Age.

15. The literary evidence is discussed and its problems dealt with exhaustively in ch. V, while in ch. VI each discussion of the various types of inscriptions in the older period is followed by a brief examination of comparative material (or lack of it!) in the younger tradition. Related cultural historical problems are also touched upon in ch. IV.

Chapter II
Theoretical Problems

1. Ultimately, three major areas of study, each of which involves special theoretical problems, must be at least briefly discussed in order to provide a proper context for any interpretations of the runic tradition and of individual inscriptions which might seem "magical." These areas are: 1) "*magic*" itself— as discussed in the ethnological disciplines, 2) traditional societies and their common characteristics, and 3) the usual nature of graphic symbol systems— especially those used for both linguistic and magical communication. A general understanding of these areas is of considerable aid in any attempt to arrive at a comprehensive interpretation of the runic system as a whole, its individual inscriptions, and in the possible development of a general theory of "rune-magic."

Magic

2. Over the years numerous scientific theories concerning magic have been forwarded in the ethnological literature. These are too disparate to be delineated in their entirety here. Our purpose is to present an overview of some major concepts and to synthesize them into a view consistent with the latest academic theories on the topic, theories which we will later be able to apply to runic data.

Perhaps the first great theoretical synthesis of the study of magic was provided by Sir James Frazer.(1) Although his overall view of magic as a form of "erroneous thought" as a product of primitive man's lack of knowledge concerning causal relationships, and his *evolutionary* model in which he saw "magic" as the first stage in a development in which the second stage is "religion," and the third stage is "science" (Frazer 1890: I, 220-43) have been generally rejected,(2) his ideas concerning the sympathetic basis for magical thinking (Frazer 1890: I, 219) have fallen on more fertile ground.

In magical theory, the law of sympathy states that "like attracts like." It presupposes a hidden link between things, and most especially between concrete *things* and *symbols* of them— both of which are seen as sharing in a single unity in the magical universe. Therefore, through the manipulation of the symbol, its corresponding object may be similarly manipulated (see

Frazer 1890: 55ff., Bertholet 1926-27: 110ff.). However, as we shall see, this may be a rather gross oversimplification.

Important to any theory of magic have also been various "power concepts." These fall into essentially two categories: 1) the dynamistic and 2) the animistic. This dichotomy, although perhaps overemphasized for heuristic reasons, does seem to have solid foundations in the magical models of traditional peoples.(3) Dynamistic is that magical power which is manipulated, gathered and dispensed as if it were a concrete force of nature— almost as a type of "electricity." This dynamistic force is perhaps best known by the Polynesian word *mana*.(4) However, many peoples know similar forces, see the Iroquois *orenda*, the Algonquin *manitu*, the Dakota *wakan* of the American Indians, the *numen* of the Romans, the δυναμις(5) of the Greeks, and even the *hamingja* of the Scandinavians (to which could also be added perhaps *máttr* and *megin*).(6) there are many terms for this multifunctional concept in some languages, but the basic concept remains one which is essentially *impersonal*.

Conversely animism lends itself to a more personalized conceptualization. The analytical idea of animism was introduced by Tylor (1871) as an explanation of the belief in spirit-beings among "primitive" peoples. It is certain that a belief in psychoid beings—which may be seen as great gods or goddesses, or as lesser divinities, or very commonly as ancestral spirits—is an important aspect of any magico-religious world-view. Both dynamism and animism are involved with the idea that "everything is alive," but dynamistic force remains a relatively rare thing— something which is possessed by certain objects, persons, or even numinous (animistic) beings themselves—and not by others. On the other hand, animistic thinking posits that everything has a life somewhat akin to human or animal life, or that the mode of dealing with such psychoid entities is analogous to dealings with living things. Rocks, streams, and trees have "spirits"— all of which may be manipulated if the proper procedures are carried out by the proper person (see Wax and Wax 1962: 180-82). With an animistic model, it is always possible that the "spirit" will resist efforts to manipulate it, or to refuse attempts to communicate with it. This is not possible with a dymanisitc model, however, and so the burden of the correct performance and use of proper materials become more important. Both dynamism and animism seem to co-exist as magical views among most peoples, and in fact they appear to complement one another.(7)

Besides the "law of sympathy" and these two objective magical force modalities, another pivotal aspect is that of the human will or consciousness— the subjective element. First of all, it is essential to point out that, for example, among the Germanic peoples the human being is thought to be composed of what might best be described as a psychosomatic complex (see ch. V). Certain elements of such a complex could give special personas active access to both dynamisitc and animistic force-modalities. In any case, the primary element would be that of the will, the faculty of desire, which is the motivating agent in any magical operation (see Bertholet 1926-27: 110ff., Ehmark 1956: 2-3, Pettersson 1957: 109ff., Tambiah 1973: 209-12).

    man   sympathy   causal forces
    (will)

This general model of man and his will on the one side (to be sure, often in possession of various personal spirit beings and powers), and a world filled with both dynamistic and animistic forces (with routinely causal functions) on the other side, has been a common understanding for some time. However, the mode by which the "law of sympathy" in all its permutations is able to transfer the willed effect thought these forces has remained rather vague.

Before we discuss the possible nature of the connection between the will (operator) and the causal forces, it is necessary to include the sociological factor in magical theory. This generally proceeds from the school of Durkheim,(8) and would state that magic is an anti-social form of religious practice— a viewpoint which was subsequently for the most part abandoned.(9) However, certain other models from this sociological school remain of vital importance to our work. As Mauss (1972: 40) points out, the attitude of a given society toward the magician and his powers forms a critical factor in the exercise of magic in a culture. "Public opinion" is for Mauss, and those of the sociological school, the creator of the magician and his power. The sociological position of the magician, both within the larger culture and within the society of magicians—that he is at least for the duration of the performance of magical rites qualitatively set apart from the community, and that he finds special identity within a specialized community of magicians—also becomes a source of "socio-magical" power (see Mauss 1972: 25ff.). These sociological sources of power may not be ignored in any attempt toward a comprehensive theory of magic.

A kind of "missing link," which seems to have been implicit in models of magic all along, but which has only been explicitly formulated since the late 1960s, might best be described as the semiotic theory or model (see Grambo 1975). Basic to this theory is the idea of *communication*, and the model is most clearly understood as a meta-linguistic one.(10)

Fundamental to the work of van Baal (1971) is man's ability to effect communication with his universe and to "think ascriptively," i.e., hidden meaning is *ascribed* to the phenomena of the universe and it becomes a partner in communication. This model of communication implies the real existence of two subjects: 1) man and 2) the hidden other side of the universe (van Baal 1971: 240-41). The "other side" is the indirect object of man's magical message, and in turn becomes the subject of an action to which man becomes the indirect object (see below).

```
subject ————————> direct object ——————————> indirect object
(man)                 (symbol-symbolized)         ("other reality")

indirect object <—————  direct object <—————  subject
(man)                    (phenomenon)              ("other reality")
```

In his analysis of the nature of a magical spell, van Baal summarizes his ideas on this communicative relationship and places it in a certain perspective:

> The formula takes its origin from the discourse between man and his universe, in the case of a particular formula a discourse concerning a certain object and the fulfillment of a desire. In this discourse man feels addressed or singled out by his universe, and he endeavors to address it in turn, trying to discover the kind of address to which his universe will be willing to answer, that is, willing to show itself communicable. The formula he finally discovers in answer to his quest is not really man's discovery but a gift, a revelation bestowed upon him by his universe. The formula is the outcome of an act of communication in which man's universe reveals to him the secret of how it should be addressed in this or that circumstance, a secret which is at the same time a revelation of its hidden essence in that particular field.
>
> (van Baal 1971: 263)

Van Baal's views emphasize a causal function within the "hidden other reality," with which man communicates with his equally real volition, and from which he receives responses in the form of phenomena (van Baal 1971: 264-66).

The strict case/effect model is somewhat called into question with the new emphasis on the idea of "analogical thinking" in the magical model proposed by Tambiah (1968; 1973) and Finnegan (1969). For both Tambiah and Finnegan, the ideas drawn from Austin (1962) on "performative speech,"(11) are fundamental: "...ritual acts and magical rites are the 'illocutionary' (see Austin 1962: 98ff. on 'illocution') or 'performative' sort, which simply by virtue of being enacted (under appropriate conditions) achieve a change of state or do something effective..."(Tambiah 1973: 221). For Tambiah, magical acts are "'performative' acts by which a property is imperatively transferred to a recipient object or person on an analogical basis" (Tambiah 1973: 199). The idea of magical analogy could quite easily be understood in terms of what Frazer and others called "sympathy." However, "analogy" has the advantage of being in the context of this perhaps more comprehensive "linguistic model" of magical theory. In the model posited by Tambiah, the idea of *appropriateness* within an entire "frame of reference" (much as Grambo [1975] understands it) is the basis for magical effectiveness, and thereby the mechanistic cause/effect model is ameliorated.

A semiotic theory, or model, in which magic is seen as a message of sorts, is discussed by Grambo (1975). This study is especially valuable because in it use is made of historical Scandinavian sources, and the author advocates a restriction of magical definitions to limited cultural areas. According to Grambo (1975: 81), the first step in understanding how a magical act works is the comprehension of the "frame of reference" in which the act takes place. This is of both an objective (environmental) and subjective (psychological) category (see Newcomb 1952: 94ff.), and Grambo further analyzes the factors as 1) the social group to which one belongs, 2) the private experiences of each individual, 3) the psychological condition of each individual, and 4) the sex of the individual. This "frame" would then seem to act as a matrix, a kind of underlying meta-semantics or grammar in which magical messages are encoded. The magician is then able to use this common, culturally conditioned code (made up of various symbols) to transmit the magical message. Grambo's model would then appear:

```
                      ┌──────── frame of reference ────────┐

transmitter              message              recipient
(magician)               (magic)              (human victim,
                                              supernatural being,
                                              object, etc.)
```

This semiotic theory contains much in common with the ideas of van Baal, Tambiah, and with some sociological aspects of Mauss, and it would seem that a synthesis of these essentially similar models could provide a more comprehensive theory of magic.

A further basic element with which the semiotic model must come to terms is that of magical symbols and symbol systems. In magical operations, these symbol systems are extremely complex and manifold in nature (see sect. 3. below). In function, however, they all would seem to share two fundamental aspects: 1) magico-analogous unity with the object of the symbol,(12) and 2) the symbol is capable of manipulation through the agency of the human will. To a certain extent these symbols may be considered the equivalent of lexemes in the semiotic scheme. Whole systems of these symbols could then constitute a sort of magical lexicon, and this within the psycho-cultural frame of reference composes the semantics of magic over which the trained magician has at least partial command. The exact ontological relationship between the symbol and the thing symbolized remains ambiguous, but essentially it would appear to oscillate on a continuum between the two poles of 1) symbol/numinous object identity, and 2) the independent existence of the symbol in its own right which might possess the power to attract or repel a secondary numinous force or being. Thus, I would cautiously suggest 1) a direct, and 2) and indirect mode of operative (= magical) symbolic communication.

A synthetic view of the semiotic theory of magic might be summarized as follows: By means of willed performative or operative acts/speech, the operator/magician (subject) is able to manipulate, or to participate in, a complex of symbols which have an analogical ("sympathetic") connection to the indirect object of these acts. Because the psycho-cosmological and social frame of reference for such operative acts ascribes a grammatically subjective nature to this indirect object of the action, it is considered a partner in a phenomenologically communicative process, and it in turn becomes the subject/agent of an action of which the magician or some other person(s) or thing(s) become the object.

The articulation of a comprehensive theory, or even complete definition of "magic," is a daunting task. That which is presented here should be understood in a heuristic framework, and should not be considered a comprehensive, universal representation. From the most recent scientific work done in the field of magico-religious theory, it is clear that the process variously known as "symbolist," "operative," "instrumental," or "semiotic," in which the magician is able to communicate by means of symbols with a wider reality (of which he himself is also an integral part), provides the best general theory for examining data such as the runes represent. Complexities arise when this process is seen within the manifold holistic context or frame of reference (which would include components which we might be tempted to analyze as "social," "psychological," "cosmological," "theological," etc.), which give it its potency. At risk of oversimplifying the actuality of magical thought, the process may be conceptualized as a mode of operative communication with a "causal reality"(13) which utilizes the whole environment. As far as a working definition of "magic" is concerned, I would like to suggest: a technique by which the human being is able, by the power of volition, to affect events in subjective and/or objective(14) reality. Any further refinements of such a definition must be culture specific, and perhaps even tradition- or technique-specific (see ch. VII on specific theories of magic with runes).

As far as a typology, or classification of magical procedures or techniques is concerned, Frazer (1880 I: 52-219) made a useful beginning with his analysis of the "law of sympathy" into the two classes of homeopathic and contagious, i.e., that which works on the basis of similarity or imitation in the former, and that which works because of a substantial link with an object or person to be affected (*pars pro toto*) in the latter. The Frazerian theories and models were subsequently synthesized with other late 19th and early 20th-century ethnological ideas and theories(15) and expanded into a more comprehensive system by van Gennep (1960: 1-14), who analyzed the whole question into two aspects: 1) a theoretical frame (which he would call "religion") and 2) an operational frame (which he would call "magic"). This latter category is analyzed in terms of binary oppositions, which were also generally implicit in Frazer's discussions. Van Gennep's model would appear:

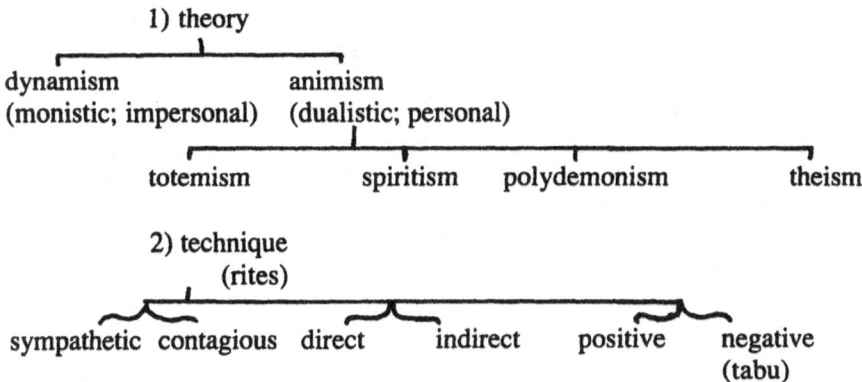

The structural content of operative rituals themselves must also be considered. Such operations may consist of either non-verbal or verbal content, but more often than not these are combined into a more complex combination of verbal and non-verbal elements.(16) This synthesis of verbal and non-verbal elements is perfectly illustrated in most descriptions of the ways in which runic inscriptions were executed for operative purposes. (See V.15.) From a semiotic perspective both verbal acts and non-verbal object-manipulations are seen as belonging to a single field of communicative theory. The relationships between the verbal component and the non-verbal elements remain significant, however.(17)

It must be emphasized that the semiotic model of magical theory focuses on the idea of how languages (i.e., symbolic systems) first structure reality for given cultures and then can be utilized within their own set of "logical" principles to restructure it at critical junctures under the proper conditions.(18)

The semiotic model does not entirely *replace* the intellectualistic "cognitive model," but rather reorients and essentially expands it. However, along with this shift comes a fundamental re-evaluation of the nature of magical thinking from one considered to be "pre-logical,"(19) or "pre-scientific," to one which is positively symbolic or metaphorical and which functions by means of analogical processes within an established psycho-cosmological frame of reference.

Besides these often nebulous *modes* of magical effectiveness, there is a sometimes more easily classified set of common magical *motives*, i.e., reasons why magical operations are undertaken. These are often reported in historical, literary, or scientific depictions of magical acts, or can sometimes be deduced from relics of the operation left in the archeo-linguistic record (e.g., talismans, inscriptions, implements, etc.). The most common general motive of a magical act "is to modify a given state" (Mauss 1972: 61), but this may also include the idea of preserving a given state which might otherwise deteriorate.(20)

The question of motive is also important to the analysis of typically "magical" as opposed to "religious" acts.(21) From the viewpoint of a communicative or semiotic theory of magic/religion, it would seem that the motive underlying a "religious" act would be to bring as aspect of *this* reality (phenomenological, psychic, etc.) into harmony with a traditional archetypal paradigm in *that* reality.(22) The process is essentially the same in a magical act, except that the will of the magician chooses the nature of the symbolic communication, and thus elicits from *"that"* reality the willed result from a wide range of critically determined possibilities. Both motives can be viewed as equally "magical," or equally "religious"; the main distinction would seem to be that religious acts are often more calendrically and traditionally bound in their form and result, and magical acts *can* be more original and freely performed with a wide range of resultant possibilities. However, no universal distinction between "magic" and "religion" can be drawn.

Here is a list of common categories of "magical motivations" which can be applied to aid in the analysis of magical behavior and, it is hoped, to help in the classification of possible magical paleolinguistic artifacts and epigraphic evidence. A primary aspect of this categorical structure may be conceptualized as a triad:

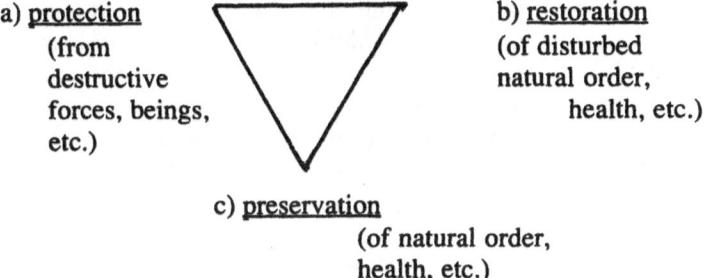

a) protection
   (from
   destructive
   forces, beings,
   etc.)

b) restoration
   (of disturbed
   natural order,
   health, etc.)

c) preservation
   (of natural order,
   health, etc.)

To this must be added a list of further categories:
d) attraction (of desired forces, beings, persons— invocations, evocations, love-magic, etc.).
e) destruction/dissolution (of forces, beings, persons— curses, etc.)
f) transformation (of forces, beings, persons— initiation, shape-shifting, etc.)
g) perception (of hidden reality— divination)

It is clear that these classifications do not constitute isolated and exclusive categories. For instance, (d) attraction of an apotropaic being may be used to ensure (a) protection from destructive force— or (d) attraction may be utilized in its own right to draw a lover, etc. These categories are, however, convenient handles for use in more specific analyses.

Before I leave the topic of "magic" itself and begin to explore the role of magic and cult and the use of scripts or symbol systems in *traditional societies*,(23) it is important to re-emphasize the importance of the social aspect of what Grambo (1975) calls the "frame of reference." The cultural context in which magical acts take place may indeed be the chief factor in the actual working of magical phenomena (see Mauss 1972: 40ff.). Here, a certain "psychological" aspect may be inferred, but in traditional societies this would probably seem to be a gross misapplication of the term "psychological" as commonly understood in Western scientific terminology.(24) It comes closer to simply being a common set of far-reaching assumptions about reality, and possibilities within that reality, which facilitate rather than impede the effectiveness of magical acts. One of the most dramatic and well-documented phenomena which apparently functions within such a set of assumptions is that of so-called "voodoo death," i.e., actual death induced through a magical rite of *destruction*, or "curse." Cannon (1942: 169-81), based on evidence from South America, Africa, the Caribbean, the Pacific, and Australia, explains in medical terms how death can be induced through profound emotional stress which leads to prolonged and intense action of the sympathico-adrenal system. Apparently, this causes the blood pressure to drop to such a degree that death ensues from a lack of oxygen supply to the essential organs. The key element in this process is a kind of social conditioning which includes in its frame of reference the belief that if x happens (e.g., a bone is pointed at someone by a shaman) then that one is doomed to die.

> This is a belief so firmly held by all members of the tribe that the individual not only has that conviction himself but is obsessed by the knowledge that all his fellows likewise hold it. Thereby he becomes a pariah, wholly deprived of the confidence and social support of the tribe.
>
> (Cannon 1941: 175-76)

Traditional Societies

3. Since the social contexts for magical acts are so important to their interpretation, and since we especially want to deal with some of the social factors in the development and maintenance of what were possibly magical characteristics in the runic tradition, it seems first necessary to discuss these ideas on a more theoretical basis and come to terms with certain aspects of "traditional societies"(25) in the scientific context of ethnology/sociology. Here, we briefly address three topics pertinent to our study: 1) cultic social structure, 2) the role of magic in traditional societies, and 3) the role of nascent writing in cult and magic.

It seems best to take a balanced approach to these concepts which takes into account the often persuasive arguments of the "Vienna School" of ethnology, which posits that religious beliefs develop within the context of material, social, and economic change (i.e., in accordance with an external level of material culture),(26) but which is also cognizant of what may be fundamental underlying distinctions in the attitude of the religious subjects toward their numinous objects.(27)

No culture of which we have any even moderately detailed information, either ancient or contemporary, archaic or modern, can be said to be without a cultic life of some sort. Most often this cult is conducted by members of a larger society, who for a variety of purposes set themselves apart from the rest of society to one degree or another.(28) This "setting apart" may be as extreme as that of a hermit or monk, or as situational as that of the some shamans or priests who, when not performing sacro-magical acts, have nonsacral professions or crafts in the society. The nature of the relationship of any cultic body to its host culture would seem to be partially dependent upon the level of social stratification in that culture. Also, we might expect that the degree of hierarchical arrangement would tend to influence the degree of complexity of the lore preserved by the cult.

Typically, cults are characterized by a dynamic inner social structure into which an individual from the extra-cultic society is initiated into the cultic body by means of a rite of transformation.(29) Once within the socio-cultic structure, the initiate can be taught the creed and lore of the cult by the elders or masters of the cultic society. For most traditional societies with no "secular schools," this process would be the most efficient and plausible way to transmit complex lore of any kind from one person to another, and from one generation to the next.

As with cultic life, the often related practice of magic of some type is found in every culture of which we have extensive historical or contemporary reports. It would seem that its practice is virtually universal among pre-literate peoples but that it is no less prevalent in newly literate cultures.(30) Even "advanced" societies retain vast reservoirs of magical thought both within established religious practice, as well as in heterodox institutions.(31)

For our study, it is most important to focus on the influence of *writing* in the shaping of these institutions of cult and magic in "traditional societies." As Goody (1968: 1-26) and others analyze it, one may never draw a clear distinction between "pre-literate" and "literate" peoples because for a period after its introduction, literacy is always limited by various factors, and therefore we may speak of protoliterate or better yet of oligoliterate societies as those in which literacy is *restricted* to a small group of specialists (see Goody-Watt 1968: 36). One may then, as Parsons (1966) does, begin to classify societies based upon their level and type of literacy. In such a scheme, the class of society which would most interest us would be classified as "archaic" by Parsons (1966: 51); characterized as "possessing an esoteric craft literacy confined to a small, highly specialized group, usually of *religiosi* or magical practitioners" (Gough 1968: 72). Factors which could limit literacy are: 1) secrecy: purposeful limitations on literacy by socio-cultic interests, 2) complexity: limitations due to difficulties in learning the system, and 3) material: difficulties caused by the writing technology, e.g., exclusive epigraphy, absence of paper, etc. (see Goody 1968: 11ff.). In societies with restricted literacy, writing may still be used for a wide range of purposes, religious and non-religious(32) But as Goody (1968: 16) points out: "In certain ways writing encouraged the growth of magico-religious activity. The priest was a man of learning, the literate, the intellectual, in control of natural as well as supernatural communication." It appears that in many societies of an "archaic" type, this restricted literacy is chiefly the possession of an elite, which is very often religious in nature.

It is virtually impossible to predict what effect the introduction of writing will have upon a culture. Goody (1968: 1) indicates that a script facilitates the organization of dispersed parties, religious sects, and kinship groups. While writing may have a profound influence upon the way a culture functions, and perhaps even the way people think and reason which can lead to fundamental questioning of tradition,(33) there seems to be as much, and perhaps even more, evidence which indicates that the introduction of writing has little disruptive effect on traditional ideology. Moreover, the script may be largely adopted into the service of tradition.(34) The possible deciding factor is the existence of a well-developed aristocratic social order, the elite of which is invested with a magico-religious function.

Walter Ong (1982: 78-116) and others have claimed that writing "restructures consciousness." But because of the restricted nature of runic literacy in the early period, and because of the particular nature of the runic system which incorporated many extra-linguistic features, this "restructuring" may not have been as profound as one might expect in the early Germanic world.

It seems relatively safe to say that the Germanic world around the beginning of the present era was of an archaic type, large portions of which were dominated by aristocracies of one kind or another; aristocracies which would seem to have often had a socio-cultic importance (see ch. IV). From what we know about the Germanic world at the most probable time for the origin of runic writing (100 BCE -100 CE)(35) we could suppose that the restricted oligoliteracy represented by the runes most probably had some religio-magical significance in the culture. To suppose otherwise would seem to be an attempt to argue a special case for the Germanic peoples.

Symbol Systems and the Communicative Process

4. Basic to our discussion is the idea of *communication*. All types of linguistic and meta-linguistic communication depend upon some kind of interactions between at least two poles. This may be unilateral (but this would concern us little here) or be characterized by an "action-reaction interdependence" (Berlo 1960: 106ff.). This implies a *discourse*. Fundamental to this process is a certain level of *empathy* (i.e., a similarity between systems or ability of one system or project itself into the other system) between the source and the receiver (Berlo 1960: 116ff.). Our magical model is dependent upon this type of communicative relationship between the human and the numinous worlds.

A convenient model of the communicative process is provided by Berlo 1960: 30-38), which may be tailored to the magical theory and summarized:

1. communication source — person/group with ideas to be communicated (= *communicator*-magician)
2. encoder — motor skills by which the ideas are translated into meaningful messages (= *encoding faculty*,(36) means by which the communicator encodes ritual speech/action)
3. message — translation of ideas into an encoded set of symbols in physical form
4. channel — medium which carries the message (= *medium* - soundwaves, paper/pen, etc.)
5. decoder — sensory skills by which the message is translated into meaningful ideas (= *decoding faculty*, means by which the receiver decodes)
6. communication receiver — person/group/(numinous entity) as target of the communicator's message (= *receiver* - numinous being/force, human psychic aspect, etc.).

The major difference between interpersonal and "magical" communications is that the form or medium of the *feedback*, or response, from the receiver would usually be in a non-verbal form of actual phenomena or events (although it may be "translated" into a verbal form, e.g., when the gods speak to men in oracles, etc.). In magic we are dealing with a kind of "inter-reality communication."

An important factor in this process, and one which principally interests us in the present study, is that of the symbolic message(37)— the encoded form of the magical (operative) communication. In written forms, this has two essential aspects: 1) the verbal formula for which the written form stands, and 2) the physical form of the written formula. The role of language is central to the semiotic model of magic, but it is only one among several symbolic categories by which operative communication may be effected, (e.g., gestures, natural substances, colors, spatial and temporal circumstances, non-semantic sound-formulas,(38) and graphic representations). This latter category would include not only pictographs and ideographs, but could also include the graphemes of a writing system themselves— perhaps embellished through secondary symbolization.

The two aspects of written forms have two main functions: 1) the visible, physical manifestation of the invisible verbal formula (thus projecting it into a special status beyond the limitations of time and space with more permanent and real effect),(39) and 2) the representation of the formula by means of a symbol system of (secondary?) magical importance. The first function (which would belong to the language isomorph category)(40) is relatively clear, with its only special characteristic being that of making the invisible visible— the potentialities for the uses of such a process in magical belief systems should be obvious. However, the second function (which would belong to the language extension category) does not necessarily follow. The symbolic value(s) of a graphemic or ideographic system may be quite complex, and may be due to an accretion of values over a period of time. In most cases, including that of the runic system, the possible iconic or extensive symbolic values attached to each runestave could be construed as secondary constructions— but that would not lessen their importance in a syncretic traditional magical system in which "secondariness" would be irrelevant and unconscious. An essentially *non-iconic* symbol system may also be secondarily invested with *iconic*(41) properties.

The semiotics of magical symbolism function on a variety of levels simultaneously. The nature of this symbolism at the graphemic level, and its relationship (for simplicity's sake) to the lexical level, might be formulated:

Integral level: I. xyz = (a lexical sememe), e.g., "ale."
Analytical level: II. x.y.z. = (three graphic sememes), i.e., "x" + "y" + "z"

At the integral level, the lexeme may have several ideolectal or sociolectal contextual significances, while at the analytical level each of the visible signs may carry independent iconic and/or extensive meanings (semes).(42)

Scripts have been used for magico-operative purposes by many peoples throughout history. The following brief survey of these culture-specific examples, with the often attendant mythic explanation for the "divine origins" or writing,(43) is intended only as a collection of comparative data to demonstrate the rather common idea that writing and operative acts were often originally connected in a fundamental way. Dornseiff (1922: 1-2) notes that there seem to be two kinds of alphabetic mysticism: 1) when the script is a mysterious novelty, and 2) in a post-rationalist "universalism" when familiar things (here "letters") are turned into symbols of the mysterious. In any event the presence of myths with regard to the origins of writing in a culture seems to be the best indicator of the attitude of that culture toward the act of writing itself, which inevitably demonstrate metalinguistic characteristics.

In non-Indo-European cultures we find a historically and culturally diverse body of evidence. Both Sumerian and Egyptian traditions have a high level of iconic graphs which could lead to the concept of a "magical link" between the graphic form and the thing represented. Therefore, the conceptual link between "writing" and "doing," especially in ceremonial, hierophantic contexts, could be relatively closer.(44) In Babylon, Nabu was held to be a divine scribe who determined the fates of men,(45) while in Egypt, Thoth (*Dḥwtj*) was the god of the word, the inventor of magical formulas and other intellectual features.(46)

The Hebraic tradition also contains a mythic paradigm of a celestial scribe or "divine writing,"(47) but furthermore it refers to human or proto-human inventors of the script, i.e., either Adam(48) or Moses (Exodus 34:18). The Hebrew alphabet has been used throughout history as a "magical script," especially since the formulation of Kabbalistic doctrines from the third to sixth centuries CE.(49) This Hebrew tradition contains one striking similarity to that of the Germanic-runic, i.e., the use of lexes as *names* for the various graphs or letters (this is not the case in Greek, Latin, etc.).

Operative beliefs are also strongly held in connection with Chinese calligraphy in Taoist traditions (Legeza 1975: 8ff.). In this tradition, the execution of Chinese ideograms, normally governed by strict formal rules, seems to be opened to an otherworldly influence; and talismanic, operatively functional versions of the ideograms are produced by the magician. The resulting forms are virtually illegible to the non-initiate, but for that reason are perhaps thought to be even more effective forms in the process of magical communication with the spirit world.

In Indo-European cultures we are faced with equally divergent models of "scriptural operancy." the development of writing in the Greco-Latin world seems to have been generally one in which the magical was a secondary accretion (see Dornseiff 1922: 5ff.; Goody-Watt 1968: 36ff.). However, these mystico-magical secondary (post-rationalist) developments were extensive and complex. They include numerical and phonic formulas, *ephesia grammata* or *voces magicae*, alphabetic series, etc.(50) At first, there was no mythic framework for writing, and only through more extensive contact with the Orient and Egypt did myths concerning Hermes-Thoth or Hermes-Moses, etc., develop according to a syncretic scheme. It is clear that in these later stages, the magical-operative nature of the script had been firmly established; however, it is equally certain that these represent post-literate and post-rationalist manipulations, which would seem somewhat removed from the type of cultural setting in which we find the early runic tradition.

In India, writing appears to have been slowly incorporated into an already developed and pre-existing phonic mysticism. It is clear that an iconic interpretation of the devangari script,(51) for example, is a secondary, or even tertiary accretion. Writing was apparently initially shunned by, and then later incorporated into, the theocratic systems of India.(52) Eventually, what seems to be an isomorphic employment of the script to represent *mantras* (seed-syllabic or versified forms) in the constructions of *yantras* ("instruments")—purely abstract operative diagrams(53)—may be found.

A great ideological gulf might seem to exist between the realm of tantric mysticism and that of the runic tradition, but closer parallels are perhaps provided by the oghamic traditions of the Celts. Generally unsatisfactory attempts have been made to link the runic and oghamic traditions historically;(54) however, these questions will occupy us more in ch. IV. Ogham is a curious epigraphical "script" (ca. 360 known inscriptions) based on a binary code which was used in the British Isles from about 400 to 650 CE—although the tradition must have been slightly older, and memory of it was preserved in manuscripts well into the Middle Ages. The fifteenth-century *Book of Ballymote* (308 B44) recounts that the script was invented by Ogma mac Elathan, who has been connected to the Celtic Heracles, Ogmios, reported by Lucian (see Arntz 1935b: 366-69). Arntz (1935b: 349ff.) points out what he considers to be at least four similarities between the oghamic and runic traditions: 1) magical employment, 2) division of script into groups, each of which is called a "family" (OIr. *aiccme*, ON *ætt*),(55) 3) possibility of being written right to left or left to right (boustrophedon), and 4) a certain similarity in the *names* of the letters. To this could be added the tradition of giving lexemic names to the graphs in the first place.

But was the oghamic script used for operative ("magical") purposes? There is a good deal less hard evidence in this direction for ogham than for the runes, but circumstantial and later literary evidence would tend to suggest that there was some meta-linguistic dimension to the ogham tradition.(56) Arntz (1935b: 373-74) considers three inscriptions to be doubtlessly magical in character: 1) Glenfahan, which reads **BMCBDV**—evidently "non-sense," 2) the amber pearl of Ennis, which is dextroversely transcribed **MTBCML** (read in reverse it is quite similar to Glenfahan), and 3) the now lost stone of Clonmacnoise, with the macaronic inscription +COLMAN ⳵⃫ ⃪⃧ ⃫⃫⃫ ⃫⃫ ⃫⃫ **THCOB/BOCHT**?) is also interpreted as a proper name plus an *ephesion grammaton*.(56) However, the vast majority of the oghamic monuments are memorials, and pose the same problem as many Viking Age and medieval runic memorials when their "magical" significance is considered.

Scripts are widely employed in the execution of magical operations, but it is never clear in the most archaic stages to what extent they are pure abstractions for the *sound* which is believed to contain the power. In syncretic magical thought this distinction is probably irrelevant or becomes so in secondary symbolizing processes. The best indicator that some kind of iconic function is present in the letter-symbol complex is probably the existence of lexical letter names, as we find in early Semitic, as well as in the oghamic and runic traditions.

Notes for Chapter II

1. Frazer was preceded by Tylor (1871), however, his treatment incorporates more disparate elements than that of Tylor.
2. See Wax-Wax (1963) for a history of these thoughts and a summary of ideas against the evolutionary model.
3. Not only does this dynamistic/animistic dichotomy seem to be present in Germanic evidence (although the terminology is sometimes confused), e.g., between concepts of concrete powers— *hamingja, máttr* and *megin* (see ch. V.2 and note 5 below), and personified or zoomorphic powers—*fylgja, vörðr*, etc.—but similar concepts are present in other traditional systems, e.g., among the Aztecs the dichotomy between *tonalli* and *nahualli* seems instructive (see Foster 1944: 85ff. and Soustelle 1964: 196).
4. For a study of this sometimes over-used word see Lehmann (1966). The term was first introduced in a study by R. H. Codrington (1891) who challenged the animism of Tylor (1871), but whose theories did not replace those of Tylor but rather supplemented them, see also Mauss (1973: 108-121).
5. On Greek dynamism, see Nilsson (1941: I, 41ff.; 200ff.), and Benveniste (1973: 346-56) on Gk. κυδος.
6. It has been suggested that these terms connote a supernormal power (Grønbech 1931: I, 248ff. *et passim*) and de Vries (1956: I, 276-79) beyond the sense of simply "might, strength; health, etc." (see Cleasby-Vigfusson 1957: 419, 421). Ström (1948: 29-76) presents a study of the terms *máttr* and *megin* in the religious historical context of Scandinavian outlaws, of whom it is said that they worshipped no gods but *trúði á mátt sinn ok megin* ("trusted in their own might and main"). He concludes that these terms must be understood in the archaic linguistic context, which shows them to be expressions of dynamistic force, with magico-religious overtones of the "luck-concept."
7. It would probably be an error to see the dynamism : animism contrast as a model for the distinction between magic : religion (as do scholars such as Bertholet 1926-27: 128ff. and Jensen 1950: 248ff.), see below on the semiotic magical theory.
8. See Durkheim, *The Elementary Forms of the Religious Life* (1947), in which he stresses the dichotomies between social : anti-social (individualistic), and sacred : profane. Mauss (1975: 89-90) maintains a similar position of religion as a "collective phenomenon," and that magic is the appropriation of this collective force for individual purposes.
9. Wax-Wax (1963) present a summary of ideas to oppose the magico-cosmological theories of Durkheim, and a series of discussions by various scholars on this question. With the general shift toward an emphasis on the psychological attitude of the celebrant of a given rite, Durkheimian sociological theories lose much of their value, since collective rites are often performed in an operant attitude (e.g., the Vedic sacrifice), while individual rites may also be suppliant in character (e.g., certain Christian prayer formulas).
10. Linguistically based models of magical operations began in earnest with Finnegan (1969), who combined the ideas of Austin (1962) on performative speech with a magical thought mode. Over the following decade, a series of studies appeared, most of which developed independently of the Austin-inspired model (e.g., van Baal 1971 and Grambo 1975), and some of which further elaborated the performative nature of magical speech and acts (e.g., Tambiah 1973 and Kippenberg 1978: 49ff.).

11. In his series of lectures, *How to Do Things with Words*, Austin outlines a theory of linguistic acts "in which to *say* something is to *do* something" (1962: 12). These utterances he calls "performative speech," or simply "performatives." To be effective, these utterances must be made in a conventional procedure ("certain words, by certain persons, in certain circumstances"), and with the proper attitude or felicity (e.g., "I do" in a marriage ceremony). Although Austin's work is not primarily devoted to magic, his concentration on ceremonial and formalities of speech are potent as elements in a linguistic model for magic.

12. This "symbolic" or "mimetic identification" is exhaustively outlined by Skorupski (1976: 116-53).

13. The "causal" aspect of magic has been questioned by Wax-Wax (1962: 182-83, 1963: 501-02), Tambiah (1973: 204ff.), and Skorupski (1976: 102-115), in favor of an analogical or metaphorical model in which cause-and-effect are replaced by a participation in a traditional pattern of correctness. So magic would only seem to be a manipulation of a "causal reality" from a hypothetical objective viewpoint.

14. From the perspective of the magical point of view, the terms "subjective" and "objective" would seem to have little validity, since it appears that the operative viewpoint proceeds from the concept of a holistic reality (which would fundamentally connect the magician and his will to the supposedly causal reality in which a way that they participate in the same whole). Thus the "objective" man: nature dichotomy and the "subjective" isolation are negated in favor of an *omnijective* attitude in which the observer and the observed, the "manipulator" and the "manipulated" are parts of the same reality.

15. That is, those who followed Tylor (1871) and Codrington (1891) in the "animistic" and "dyaamistic" schools.

16. These are discussed by Mauss (1972: 50-60), and are further elaborated in a South Germanic context by Hampp (1961: 110ff.).

17. See Tambiah (1973: 223) for an analysis of typical distribution of symbolic ritual action and ritual speech in given magical operations. He recognizes four categories of the interaction between these media: 1) equal-redundant, 2) unequal-subsidiary, 3) complementary (words : metaphorical / action : metonymical), and 4) separate and discontinuous.

18. Problems of the development of the theories and the shift in emphasis to the study of magical acts are discussed by Kippenberg (1978: 9ff.).

19. See Goody-Watt (1968: 43, n. 2) for a bibliography and criticism of this idea.

20. Mauss (1972: 61) goes on to state: "We are prepared to claim that all magical acts are represented as producing one of two effects: either the objects or beings involved are placed in a state so that certain movements, accidents or phenomena will inevitably occur, or they are brought out of a dangerous state."

21. Although actual distinction between these two analytical categories remains in doubt, they provide us with limited heuristic value in specific cultural contexts.

22. According to Titiev (1960: 431) religious acts tend to be calendrical (i.e., performed on a more regular, predetermined basis), while magical acts would tend to be performed on a "critical" basis (i.e., upon the demand of circumstances).

23. For a general discussion of the position of writing in societies that possess only limited literacy, see articles edited by Goody (1968).

24. The concept of "suggestion" might be partially relevant here, see Seabrook (1940: 11ff.), who especially considers curses as examples of "induced autosuggestions." Such a

psychological model also seems implicit in Cannon's work on "voodoo death" (1942: 169-81), see above.

25. The technical term "traditional society" must remain somewhat ambiguous, since the most common deciding factor, non-literacy *versus* literacy, is usually not clear cut, see Parsons (1966) and the various articles presented by Goody (1968).

26. Outlines of those theories may be found in Graebner (1911), Schmidt (1931 and 1939), and more recently, if more superficially, in a study by Lincoln (1981). Studies typical of the Vienna School approach which deal specifically with Germanic material have been offered by Closs (1936, 1952a, 1961).

27. This subject/object relationship should be understood in the context of all that which has been said in ch. I and above in ch. II.

28. For general discussions of the cult and its role in traditional societies, see Eliade (1958: 41ff.), and within Germanic society, see Höfler (1934 and 1952), and Ström (1954).

29. A treatment of such rites in traditional societies is contained in the classic study by van Gennep (1909). There, he analyzes each of those rites of transformation, or "passage," as consisting of three ritual stages: 1) rites of separation, 2) rites of transition, and 3) rites of incorporation. For a more recent study of this pattern, see Motz (1973: 91ff.).

30. The apparent universality of some phenomena which religious science is prone to designate as "magical" is constantly commented upon by scholars, and in fact this constitutes one of the principal problems in the study of magic: How can these virtually identical external processes be accurately understood from a subjective point of view? (See Kippenberg 1978.)

31. For example, in modern western society there exist both forms of "religious magic" (operant behavior within established; orthodox religions — (e.g., Catholic votive masses, Protestant healing rites, etc., see Kriss [1968: 69-84]), and various forms of magical activity in subcultural heterodox groupings.

32. Greece of the sixth and fifth centuries stands out as an example of a society in which alphabetic writing was relatively quickly adopted by a wide range of social classes and utilized for a wide variety of purposes, see Jeffery (1961: 46, 63) and Goody-Watt (1968: 42ff.). This came after a slower, more restricted development in the eighth and seventh centuries.

33. This is the primary analysis of Goody-Watt (1968) concerning the effect of literacy in Greece, and they seem tempted to expand the validity of this argument to other cultures.

34. Traditional adoption, in fact, would seem to be the more common pattern, see Gough (1968a: 69-84), Tambiah 1968b: 85-131), and Gough (1968b: 133-60).

35. From sources such as Caesar *De bello gallico* VI, 11-20; IV, 1-19 and Tacitus *Germania* we know that Germanic society was characterized by a tribal-aristocratic social order, with an emergence of extra-tribal warrior bands and an apparent strengthening of sacerdotal functionaries (Tacitus *Germ.* chs. 7-15).

36. The magical encoder may also include the necessary (psychic) qualities, powers, or secret knowledge possessed by the magician which enable him to encode the message into symbolic forms of speech, gesture, graphic manipulations, etc.

37. Grambo (1975: 92-93) goes as far as to equate the "message" with the "magic."

38. Into this category would fall the non-semantic magical utterances of shamans (cf. Eliade 1964: 93-99, 440) and the well-known phenomenon of glossolalia in pagan Greek

and Judeo-Christian tradition (cf. Williams 1981: 125-212, and Goodman 1972). This aspect is reviewed with reference to runic "non-sense" inscriptions, or *ephesia grammata*, in chs. VI and VII.

39. As far as interpersonal communication is concerned, Goody (1968: 1) noted this aspect of writing: "Its essential service is to objectify speech, to provide language with a material correlative, a set of visible signs. In this material form speech can be transmitted over space and preserved over time; what people say and think can be rescued from the transitoriness of oral communication."

40. See Chao (1968: 194ff.), who defines the category of "language isomorph" as a system which reflects natural language, while that of "language extension" is seen as an abstraction beyond natural language, with the most common example being that of scientific formulas.

41. Chao (1968: 198-99) defines *iconic* symbols as those which share some common property with the symbolized object, and *non-iconic* symbols as those which are "purely" symbolic (abstracted).

42. See Mammarström (1976: 2-3, 11ff.) for an outline of the terminology for linguistic units and items.

43. Here again we are reminded of van Baal's (1971: 263) statement that magical spells are always thought to have a divine, or other-worldly, origin, and to be a "gift" to mankind. See also Dornseiff (1922: 2-3).

44. Since these were both originally, at least partially, pictographic (iconic) systems, it is easy to see the close thing/word symbolic connection. The idea that there is any ontological *identity* between the "word" and the "thing" has been rejected.

45. Besides Nabu, the culture hero Oannes (HA-NI) was held to be the inventor of writing.

46. For a general treatment of the god Thoth, see Bonnet (1952: 805ff). It is clear that Thoth's primary power is that of magical *speech*, and that of writing is secondary.

47. See Dornseiff (1922: 3-4, 89ff.). It is for the most part clear that these are borrowings from Babylonian and/or Egyptian sources.

48. Adam as the inventor of writing is also an Islamic motif, see Dornseiff (1922: 3-4). In Judaic myth, this would seem to be a later development.

49. This is the time period assigned by Scholem (1974: 23-30) to the composition of the *Sepher Yetzirah* ("Book of Creation") which contains magico-cosmological speculations on the nature of the Hebrew letters. See also descriptions of the Greco-Judaic letter-magic and the magical power of "divine names" by Blau (1898: 93-146). It has been generally concluded that most of those practices in Judaic tradition stem originally from that of the Greeks— especially of Gnostic and Neo-Platonic circles.

50. See Dornseiff (1922) and Dieterich (1901: 77-105) for numerous examples of these practices in the Greco-Italic traditions. The edition of the Greco-Egyptian magical papyri by Preisendanz (1973-74) contains hundreds of these *ephasia grammata* or *voces magicae* (magical letter-formulas) in the context of specific magical operations.

51. See Shamastastry (1906), who presents what can only be taken as a relatively modern interpretation of the *devanagari* letters as derivatives of ancient tantric symbols.

52. Gough (1968: 73-74) notes that writing was probably initially introduced into Aryan India by merchants around 700 BCE, but was rejected by the Brahmans. Sacred texts, or commentaries on them, only began to appear after the fourth-century CE.

53. Mookerjee-Khanna (1977: 49-62, 132-35) provide a brief discussion of the use of *yantras* and seed-syllables in *mantras*. "In some *yantras*, the sound equivalents of the deities are symbolically represented by the Sanskrit seed syllables inscribed in the spaces within the geometric pattern... The mantric syllable symbolizes the essence of divinity." (p. 51). Avalon [Woodroffe] (1913: xciv) relates: "The *yantra* when inscribed with *mantra*, serves the purpose of a mnemonic chart of the *mantra* appropriate to the particular Devata whose purpose is to be invoked into the *yantra*."

54. Pedersen (1920-25: 135 *et passim*) and Marstrander (1928: 125ff.) speculate that the oghamic tradition played a formative role in the development of the runes (which is impossible for chronological reasons), while Arntz (1935a: 277ff. and 1935b: 321-413) argues the reverse. Damian McManus (1991: 9-11) provides a useful overview of the theories.

55. It is possible that the ON runic *terminus technicus* "*ætt*" originally denoted "(a group of) eight," but that it later fell together with the word for "family" or "class" and was borrowed into Irish in that meaning.

56. See also Ferguson (1887: 54), who reads the ogham levoversely as **BOCHT**: "pauper," as a "designation of humility."

Chapter III

Previous Scholarship

1. The study of "rune-magic" has sometimes been characterized by pendular swings in the scientific attitude toward the relationship between runes and magical practice. On balance, this relationship has been viewed as a close, even integral one (probably due to factors outlined in chs. IV and V, 12-18). But recently, some scholars have chosen to concentrate upon distinctions between the runic tradition and magico-cultic activity or practice. In this chapter, a brief historical survey of 20th-century scholarship on this subject, and on that of the possible social structure which might have supported the runic tradition, are presented to establish points of reference for the often divergent interpretations and assumptions(1) in the present study.

Cultic Aspects

2. It seems reasonable to assume that runic writing and its attendant traditions were not originated, diffused, and maintained in a social vacuum, but rather they were facilitated and supported by an institutional framework of some kind—relatively informal though it might have been. Unfortunately, this has been one of the least-studied aspects of the runic tradition. An abortive attempt was made in the copious works of Sigurd Agrell (1927a: 56ff.; 1928a, b; 1931: 7ff., and 1937/38) to link the runes with late antique alphabetic magic and the Greco-Roman cult of Mithras.(2) Agrell argues that Germanic soldiers in Roman service (especially at the time of the Emperor Commodus 180-192 CE) came into intimate contact with mystical alphabetic traditions rooted in symbolism perhaps ultimately inherited from the Persians and based upon the 24-letter structure of the Greek alphabet. To some extent, the Germanic soldier-cultists would have established an *interpretatio Germanica* for symbolic elements in the system without altering its structure. This structure and the mystico-numerical practices connected with it were, according to Agrell, adopted by the Germanic auxiliaries and exported from the *limes* northward. Although he gives a good picture of the Mithraic beliefs, Agrell's discussion of any

historical relationship between the Germanic cult (of Wōðanaz?) and the Mithraic cult, and of the nature of the receivers of this lore on the Germanic side (and how they would have been able to develop, diffuse, and maintain this radical cultural innovation)— is left virtually undeveloped. This is not to suggest that such a process might not have taken place secondarily (see ch. IV. 8). Agrell's views, although rather popular and not unprecedented when they first appeared,(3) have been totally abandoned principally because his technical argumentation proceeded from his universally rejected "Uþark-Theory."(4)

In two studies Höfler (1970, 1971) extensively discusses the rule of cultic institutions in the development and spread of the runes for the first time.(5) His investigations center primarily on the *Eruli* or *Heruli*, whom he sees not as a "tribe" but as a *kultischer Kriegerverband*,(6) which eventually became a vast network of cultic bands spread over a wide geographical expanse (1970: 118). Höfler strongly maintains that the fuþark-system was invented by a single man, and that by virtue of his prestige, or that of this students, the system was able to spread intact through this network which would have provided the necessary *traditionswillige Schüler* for such a diffusion (1970: 117). According to Höfler (1971: 146-49) the cult of the Eruls is best identified with that which was later to be known as Oðinn, which was sociologically concentrated in aristocratic warrior bands and which was concerned with the magical and the intellectual generally. The theories of Höfler and those of Elgqvist (1952) will be further discussed in ch. IV.

Thompson (1972) presents a smaller, less comprehensive, yet highly suggestive study in which he sheds light on the institutional nature of the system of education and organization for rune-carvers in eleventh-century Uppland. He discusses the idea of "schools" of rune-masters set up according to a master-apprentice relationship—but does not attempt to project this into more archaic times. Thompson speculates that in some inscriptions, the OSwe. term *lið*: "troop, retinue, body of men," might also have the significance of a school of rune-carvers (e.g., U. 1161: Altuna church *en þæiR balli, Ffoystæinn lið Lifstæinn(s ristu)*: "and Balli and Froysteinn of the 'school' of Lifsteinn carved (the runes)," and U. 479: Aliske parish *Ulfkell Higo rū(naR), Lofa liði*: "Ulfkell, follower (pupil?) of Lofi, hewed the runes.").

A more systematic beginning for inquiries into possible socio-cultic aspects of the runic phenomenon is forwarded by Dillmann (1981), who raises a series of fundamental questions:

a) Was the runic art exclusively exercised by men, or did women also practice it?
b) Was the rune-master distinguished from his surroundings by special psychological characteristics, for example, by the gift of extra-ordinary inspiration?
c) Did the rune-masters think of themselves as exclusive, or in a social elite?
d) Were the rune-masters made a part of a more-or-less secret and cultic "league," for example dedicated to one of the great Germanic gods?
e) Did the rune-masters transmit their knowledge in schools?(7)

Höfler's initial bold strokes, coupled with the systematic approach of Dillmann, have just begun to open this area of runology to scientific study. In ch. IV of the present work, I hope to supplement ideas forwarded by Höfler, and address some fundamental issues raised by Dillmann. Until we know more about the social setting in which the runes were produced, it will remain difficult to understand many of their baffling technical features.

Magical Aspects

3. Although the assumed magical characteristics of the runes and runic writing have received much more attention over a much longer period than the more recently recognized socio-cultic aspects, in point of fact a good deal of it has been unsystematic and/or devoid of any methodological constraints. The single most conspicuous defect in the history of rune-magical studies has been the lack of even a heuristic understanding (or of a debate upon the understanding) of "magic" itself in the context of the runic tradition or phenomenon (see ch. II).

Two trends are evident from the earliest independent studies of rune-magical questions: 1) a symbolic (extra-linguistic or graphic) interpretation, and 2) a numerological interpretation. The interpretation of rather complex supposed numerical patterns in the Rök st. (Ög. 36), essentially based upon the number of runes in a given row or line, became the foundation for a series of studies by Pipping (1911, 1912, 1919, 1921, 1929/30). At approximately the same time, Olsen (1916) produced the first exclusive study of magic and runes in which he attempted to give a comprehensive view of this phenomenon. For Olsen, *runene er først or fremst trolldomsskrift* (p. 230). He considers the presence of certain elements, or inscriptions types, as criteria for considering a given inscription as "magical," i.e.: 1) fuþark-inscriptions (in which the rune-row is represented as a whole or in part), especially when they are *in* graves or on (talismanic?) bracteates; 2) individual runic signs, alone or in various combinations; and 3) linguistically clear magical formulas. Olsen sees the fuþark-inscriptions as concentrations of collective magical power in the runes, and compares their prescribed order to medieval magical formulas (pp. 3-4). According to him, the Lindholm amulet (KJ 29, see ch. VI) would be an example of a combination of magical formulas with linguistic sense and with exclusively magical signs. Also, rune-stones *inside* graves, or stones outside the mound that do not name the dead are considered magical by Olsen (p. 6).

Besides this symbolist approach, Olsen also indulges in magico-numerical analyses, and the authority of his study became an influential part of the way rune-magic was judged for almost forty years. The technique is essentially the same as that found in Pipping's sign-counting method, and even goes so far as to transliterate some of Egill Skallagrímsson's poetry into runes (in which he thinks they were originally composed) and to analyze them according to numerical patterns. All half-strophes are supposed to contain 72 runes (pp. 12ff.).(8) Essentially, for Olsen, the writing of runes was tantamount to an invocation of the hidden powers contained in them (p. 5).

The numerological interpretation of runic inscriptions reached its first peak with the studies of Sigurd Agrell (1927a, 1927b, 1928a, 1928b; 1931, 1932, 1934, 1935/36 and 1938), whose uþark-theory, as noted above, brought the runic tradition into correspondence with Mithraic numerology; and of Hans Brix (1927, 1928, 1929 and 1932), who carried the computations and the discovery of "inner" and "outer" systems (see Brix 1932), etc., to a level of extreme complexity.(9) While Brix remained with the common rune-count system (in which he includes word counts and sign-counts, e.g., dividing marks), Agrell introduces the concept of *gematria*(10) into runic studies. According to this practice, each rune is thought to stand for the numerical value of its position in the cardinal series 1-24, i.e., (in Agrell's Uþark-theory $u = 1$, $þ = 2$, $a = 3$, etc. Thus, the conspicuous runic formula **alu** works out to 3.20.1, which are then added together to render the runo-numerical sum of 24, i.e., a *pars pro toto* runic formula.(11)

Another group of investigators confined themselves to the articulation of certain aspects of the symbolic, grapho-linguistic interpretations expressed by Olsen. In a general study of early Germanic magic, Linderholm (1918) extensively discusses the uses of runes in magic (esp. 46-107). he divides magic into dynamistic (*dynamiska naturmagi*) and animistic (*demonistik*) types, and further analyzes the dynamistic as basically either *verbal* or *material* magic. The runes form the basis for his evidence concerning this verbal form of magic, and they represent *en fullt utbildad värbal magi i ordets egentligaste mening, en magi som räknar såväl med ordens som med bokstävernas, runornas, hemliga trolldomskraft* (p. 46) For a matrix for runic magical beliefs and practices he resorts to Greek evidence (pp. 58-66), which is to be expected.

Lindquist (1923) examines the rule of metrics and poetic style in the composition of runic magical formulas during the older period. He concludes that the *galdr*-meter (ON *galdralag*), present in the *Merseburger Zaubersprüche*, as well as OInd. magical formulas for the *Atharva Veda* (pp. 6-52),(12) is an archaic style (p. 91ff.), which he is able to detect in the Stentoften st. (KJ 96), which is the focus of his study. Lindquist emphasizes poetic form as the source of magical power, and that the "mystery" (*rūnō*) of a formula is its magical effect, which lies in the hidden meaning of what seem to be straightforward words (p. 167ff.).

Not all scholars were unanimous in their judgment of the existence of rune-magic. Neckel (1928: 31-32) claims that the great majority of inscriptions have nothing to do with "magic," and sees such interpretations as a "romantic notion." However, his personal bias that the heathen Germanic people had no special *Hang zum Übersinnlichen, geschweige magisierenden Raffiniertheiten*(!), is also critical.

Erik Moltke (1934) presents a study concentrated on Viking Age and medieval evidence in which the magical effect of the runes and/or the words and names they portray is not doubted,(13) and they are seen as tools *at opna kontakt med høyere væsener* (to open contact with higher entities), etc. (p. 42). He judiciously avoids the topic of numerical magic, which had already been rejected in his studies of 1928. In contributions on individual inscriptions or in survey articles of this period, Moltke (1929, 1932, 1936a, 1936b, 1938a, 1938b) also often indicates magical interpretations for various inscriptions or types of inscriptions, e.g., fuþarks and *ephesia grammata*, or "non-sense" series. Lis Jacobsen (1935) produced a work which focuses on the "curse-formula" in the runic corpus. Besides the Blekinge stones (Stentoften and Björketorp), she discusses the later Saleby st. (Vg. 67), Glavendrup (DR. 209), Tryggevælde (DR. 230), Glemmings (DR. 338), Sønder-Vinge 2 (DR. 83) and Skærn (DR. 81) stones. The nature of these curse-formulas is discussed (pp. 58-62) and it is maintained that they have the effect of *transforming* the victim into an accused state. (p. 59).

In a series of studies Nordén (1941, 1934a, 1934b, 1936) developed the theory that Iron Age runic inscriptions served essentially the same magical function that pictographic rock-carvings had served in the Bronze Age; he also produced two important articles which survey several magical Swedish inscriptions (1937) and a collection of medieval amuletic tin, bronze or copper rune-plates (1943).

Wolfgang Krause contributed to the study of the magical aspects of certain runic inscriptions and of characteristics within the runic tradition throughout his career. He investigated the magical formulaic and ideographic aspects of the Kylver stone (KJ 1), (1932: 53-71), and of the fibula of Soest (KJ 140), (1932: 77-81). The identification and interpretation of the *laukaR*-formula on bracteates (1934: 5-17) was also forwarded.(14) But one of Krause's most intriguing general contributions is a methodological development of the notion of *Begriffsrunen* ("ideographic runes"), or more aptly "logographs." This is the idea that isolated runes can represent their traditional names, e.g., ᛟ = *opila*: 'property' (see Krause 1938).(15) Magical interpretations also predictably figured prominently in Krause's more popularized general survey treatments of the runic tradition (1935, 1943a) as well as in the first edition of *Runeninschriften im älteren Futhark* (1937), in which certain inscriptions are classified according to such categories as *magisch-poetische Speernamen, magische Wortformeln, der Runenmeister* and *Beschwörung und Ritus*.

Helmut Arntz, in his *Handbuch der Runenkunde* (1935a: 230ff., 1944: 233ff.), also contributed favorable surveys of the question of the use of runes in magic to express magical formulas and for divinatory purposes. In the first edition, a whole chapter is devoted to rune-magic, which he sees as related to, but distinct from, Mediterranean alphabetic practices (p. 232). It also seems clear that he favors a secondary magical function for the runic script itself and that for him the primary magical function lies in the spoken word (pp. 244-45). The second edition contains somewhat condensed and rearranged material on magic, and is generally more cautious. The Arntz-Zeiss edition of *Die einheimischen Runendenkmäler des Festlandes* (1939) often includes considerations of magic in the interpretations of individual runic inscriptions. For example, the "pre-Christian" corpus is classified into the following categories: 1) amulets, 2) consecrated weapons, 3) consecrated knives, and 4) other consecrated objects (pp. 468-69).

A synthesis, and brief but comprehensive treatment, of the questions surrounding pre-Christian rune-magic is presented by Sierke (1939). The runic evidence is arranged according to a typology of the physical objects upon which the inscription appears, which he then correlates with a rudimentary typology of magical intent, e.g., grave/death and weather magic on stone, apotropaic magic on personal jewelry, fertility/love magic on bone. He is able to identify some seven basic magical motivations in the runic corpus: 1) protection of graves and the dead from plunder, 2) protection of the living from the walking dead, 3) protection from an attack by enemies, 4) protection from sickness, 5) production of fertility and prosperity, 6) promotion of good weather, and 7) instilling of love.(16) Also, Sierke seems prepared to identify at least three modes of magical effect: 1) execution of ideographic runes to invoke the power or meaning of that sign (fuþark inscriptions = apotropaic series of ideographs), 2) use of (*völlig unmagische!*) letter-runes to portray a magical word or sentence to give it permanence, and 3) employment of magico-formulaic words (*laukaR, alu,* etc.) which exist independent of syntactic context (pp. 121-23).(17)

In the late 1930s and early 1940s, the National Socialist regime in Germany had a large measure of control over scientific investigations of German antiquities. The essential result of this was the co-existence of lay-runology (represented by those such as Theodor Weigel, H. Schilling, etc.) and perhaps a certain degree of compromise among scientific investigators.(18) Popularized discussions of the runes also began to appear in greater abundance, and magical aspects drew some attention (e.g., Krause 1939, Harder 1943). This peculiar era in the history of runology is the subject of Ulrich Hunger's *Runenkunde im Dritten Reich* (1984).

The most serious and comprehensive objections to the overwhelmingly magical interpretation of the runic corpus were raised by Anders Bæksted (1952). He is principally concerned with casting doubt on the magical view in three areas of investigation: 1) the link between epigraphic and literary/historical runic traditions, 2) the rune-row and alphabetic magic, and 3) numerological rune-magic. Bæksted calls into question the idea, which had become entrenched by 1952, that the runes were primarily a script used for magical purposes, and that a principal technique of the runic magician was the employment of numerical patterns or formulas. This articulated a new phase in runic investigations because the idea of rune-magic could no longer be taken as self-evident. Bæksted has the most difficulty with the first category, due to the numerous direct references to the mytho-magical nature of the runes and their origins in both epigraphic and literary sources. As far as the fuþark-inscriptions are concerned, he seems to be put in the position of having to plead an exceptional case for the Germanic peoples, since he admits that similar "ABC-inscriptions" from Mediterranean cultures may have magical import, but objects that this does not mean that the typologically identical fuþarks had a similar function (pp. 118ff.). One of Bæksted's most astute general analyses is that the runic tradition seems to have been a partially abortive (*delvis mislykket*) attempt to imitate the Mediterranean script (pp. 138-39). In the area of numerical formulas, he is most able to cast doubt upon the schools of Pipping, Olsen, Brix, Agrell, et al., and his fundamental objection lies in the *fuldkomne mangel på sammenhæng og system i helheden af de talmagiske fænomener* (p. 185).

Two important studies of runic word formulas also appeared in this period. Edgar Polomé (1954) provides convincing (if controversial)[19] etymology for the difficult runic formula **alu**, which he identifies with "ale,"[20] and connects to the Hitt. *alwanzḫḫ*: 'to enchant.' Thus according to Polomé, the common root meaning of the term would have been 'ecstasy (→ magic)', and subsequently reflected in Hitt. *termini technici* for "magic," and transferred to "the drink which brings ecstasy, the cultic drink" in Germanic. (See ch. VI.34 and ch. VII for a more detailed discussion of the possible operative functions of the runic term.) Another runic word-formula (*līna*) *laukaR* is the subject of Winfred Lehmann's 1955 study in which he concludes that *līna* ("flax") primarily deals with characteristically feminine, and *laukaR* ("leek") with masculine attributes. Furthermore, he speculates that their function in fertility magic is based upon this sexual polarity (pp. 163ff.).

The as-yet-unsurpassed history of Germanic religion by Jan de Vries (1956/57) contains an invaluable treatment of the runes within the context of a general survey of Germanic magical conceptions and practices (1956: I, 307ff.). De Vries takes it for granted that the runes were originally a *Zauberschrift*. Although this discussion admirably fulfills its intended purpose as an overview of the possible conceptual framework(s) for runic practice, de Vries often perhaps unavoidably deals less than critically with some questions, e.g., runic *gematria* (pp. 312-15) and the routine projection of conceptions and practices found in medieval Iceland into the older period.

A new, if controversial,[21] theory concerning the magical functions of the runes is forwarded by Karl Schneider (1956).[22] His theories are based upon the representation of a cosmological scheme in the names, shapes, and order of the runes. The names are grouped in categories, e.g., agricultural/ cyclical, cultic, cosmogonic/mythological, theogonic (and the divine family), and finally that of "fate." The runic shapes assume the level of "hieroglyphics" with each shape developed from pictographic representations of the name. His conclusions led to the reconstruction of an *Urfuthark* in which the order is altered to accommodate his cosmological scheme. In the realm of magic itself, Schneider sees the ideographic use of runes as the primary magical agent (as magical symbols to be manipulated for desired effects). He then applies his theories to several older runic inscriptions and Old English *runica manuscripta* (Anhang, 495-574). Schneider brings a vast amount of learning to bear on certain questions, and many of his views on the runic system articulate valuable possibilities. However, the whole study is flawed by the tendency to over-systematize, to re-arrange data based on his own conclusions, and to fail to distinguish between historical periods and traditions.(23)

The runologist Ralph Elliott (1957) presents a study of the magical associations of the yew tree with the runes—especially in the Anglo-Friesian tradition, where he detects considerable Celtic influence. Although interesting, in this contribution Elliott can do little more than compare Germanic and Celtic yew-lore and suggest that the English syncretized and exported elements indigenous to the Celts to the Friesians and thence to the rest of the Germanic territories (although he does not deny the existence of some indigenous Germanic and Indo-European yew-lore, see pp. 251ff.). In 1959 (second edition 1989), Elliott also produced an introductory text of runology in which magical criteria are considered (esp. pp. 41-42, 66-72 *et passim*). Another English philologist, Wrenn (1962), non-dogmatically suggested a sometimes-naive magical interpretation of the Caistor-by-Norwich astragalus(24) in which he makes use of some of Schneider's methodology (pp. 314ff.).

A more critical note was sounded by R. I. Page (1964) in an excellent study in which he concentrates on the Old English tradition, and especially on its manuscript tradition. It seems he wrongly tries to generalize the lack of magical associations in Old English epigraphy to that of Scandinavia (pp. 25ff.).(25) However, Page identifies some eight Old English inscriptions as ranging from undoubtedly magical to possibly so—these are the four amulet rings,(26) 1) Kingmoor (M. pp. 84-85); Bramham Moor (M. pp.26-27); and 3) England C (M. pp. 43-44) and England D (M. p. 44); the Thames scramsax (M. pp. 127-29); the Thames "fitting" (M. p. 127); the Holborough spear (M. p. 52); the Caistor-by-Norwich astragalus, and the Lovden Hill urns (Page 1999: 180 *et passim*). These, along with a few others, will be discussed according to their inscriptions in ch. VI of this study. Later, Page (1973) presented a general study of Old English runes in which he briefly approaches the problem of runes and magic from the viewpoint of the history of its scholarship (pp. 13-14). In this significant passage for the history of runic scholarship, Page identifies two qualities present and necessary in the runologist: imagination and skepticism. When one or the other quality is highly developed in an individual investigator, Page can speak of "imaginative" and "skeptical" runologists, e.g., Schneider would fall into the former category; Bæksted into the latter. These labels can occasionally prove valuable when analyzing the scholarship of runologists. In the preface to the present work I have endeavored to take this dichotomy into a more productive direction.

In 1968, Niels Åge Nielsen presented two studies of importance to the investigation of formulaic aspects of runic inscriptions. The first of these deals with apotropaic formulas on South Scandinavian rune-stones, and significantly updates scholarship on several inscriptions(27) and suggests that the formulas are not ones of "cursing" (*formandelseformler*) strictly speaking, but rather ones of protection (*værnformler*)— i.e., *bot et ønske om, at den person, som eventuelt engang i fremtiden forstyrrer mindesmært, må regnes for at være et individ, der socialt set står lige så lavt som troldmænd...* (p. 47).(28) The Eggjum stone (KJ 101) is the subject of Nielsen's second 1968 study, in which the inscription is analyzed according to its various formulas, i.e.: 1) the protective formula, 2) the warning formula, 3) the memorial formula, and 4) the Odinic invocation.

During this general period, three important introductory books on runology first appeared, each of which touches on the magical problem. The French historiographer Lucien Musset (1965) presents a cautious and objective study, which includes sections on magic and divination (pp. 141-55), in which he generally concludes *les runes ne sont pas magiques, elles ont seulement partfois servi à la magie*. In Germany, Klaus Düwel (1968, fourth ed. 2008), in the best short introduction to runology available, gives a brief and moderate account of the idea of rune-magic (pp. 208-11), while Krause (1970: 46-63) attempts to provide a rudimentary typology for "cultic" and "profane" inscriptions. As belonging to the cultic sphere, he would classify all those 1) with apparently profane texts but which appear on "cult-objects" (e.g., Piatroassa, KJ 41; Gallehus, KJ 43); 2) with overt formulas of blessing, curse, invocation, etc., 3) with assertive statements (e.g., Strand, KJ 18; Viborg, DR. 100b; Vetteland, KJ 60); 4) with certain formulaic words (*alu, laukaR*, etc.); 5) with the **fuþark** (whole or in part) in some cases, and 6) those which have the classic rune-master formula. Krause often considers grave-inscriptions to be in the magical area, but in general this material is held to be of a borderline type between the magical and the profane. (See further criteria for these questions in ch. VI.)

In 1973 two problematic studies gave new impetus to magical interpretations. Becker (1973) offers a learned evaluation of the Franks Casket (M. pp. 10-16), which is concentrated on the magical relationship between the runic inscriptions and the iconographical representations on it. He bases his theory on the mutual function of object- and epigraphical (word)-magic, and posits the cultural context for such practices as a syncretism of pagan magical belief and similar practices in "Christian magic" (pp. 153ff.).(29) The principal objection Becker's thesis appears to be its dependence upon the unique evidence of the Franks/Auzon Casket itself, which prevents it from being applied elsewhere.(30) (But it should be admitted that the Franks Casket is indeed a unique object!) Heinz Klingenberg (1973) argues for a numerological interpretation of the runic inscriptions (focusing on the Gallehus rune-horn, KJ 43) based upon a gematric system in which rune-sums are reduced through a factoring process.(31) Furthermore, he claims to be able to discern a constant numerical pattern based on the number thirteen in the body of older inscriptions. In the art of writing runes (i.e., "secrets"), Klingenberg sees *die Kunst des Verbergens* (pp. 111ff.). To some extent, this work represents a further refinement of the kind done earlier by Agrell and others, but it remains flawed by the fact that the institutions which might have enabled such complex patterns to develop and spread, and most importantly the practical (operative) reason for their use, are not addressed. His calculations seem almost to float in a cultural, historical, and theoretical vacuum, although he does again apparently connect the runic traditions with those of late antique Greece (pp. 62-70). An important review of Klingenberg's work is offered by Düwel (1979b: 240-43), who brings four arguments to bear against Klingenberg's interpretation of the Gallehus horn, two of which seem pertinent to the whole idea of gematria ("number magic") in runic studies. These points are: 1) that Klingenberg arbitrarily chooses one of the three extant graphic representations of Gallehus B(32) as a model although the other two sometimes show variant readings; 2) that there is not one attested instance of a rune standing for a numeral in the epigraphic or manuscript traditions; 3) that the gematric theory presupposes a single and constant order for the fuþark, which cannot be *proven* to such an extent to make such precise computations plausible; and 4) that the readings of a good percentage of the inscriptions upon which the computations rely are questionable and often reconstructed. A further problem with numerological interpretations which might be mentioned here is that they never take into account the special archaic Germanic number-system (see Meyer 1919: 576-77 and Ulff-Møller [1993]).

As a material-type, bracteates have long been generally recognized as having a primarily "amuletic" function, and no corpus of scholarship has contributed more to the understanding of these objects than that of the art-historian Karl Hauck (e.g., 1969, 1970, 1972, 1977, 1980, 1981a, 1981b). Although not a runologist, Hauck is able to provide valuable insights into the iconography and function of the bracteates, which he sees as of an Odinic nature, and either purely amuletic (see 1969, 1970, 1972, 1977) or more recently (1981a: 4ff.) perhaps also as *teure Seelenmedizin von grossen überregionalen Kultstätten. . . vertrieben*, which he compares to devotionals sold at places of pilgrimage, or similar practices in pagan Mediterranean cultures.

In the last few years, some of the most important contributions to runology have been made by the Göttingen scholar Klaus Düwel. Since the first edition of his *Runenkunde* (1968), he has produced a vast and ever-growing body of research, which has often touched upon matters of runes and magic in a critical and objective manner—that earlier leaned toward the "skeptical," but in more of his later work a more moderate position has been evident. Besides his already mentioned 1979 review of the Klingenbergian methods, a few of Düwel's notable contributions have been ones (1970b: 219ff.; 1971: 200ff.) in which formulaic words (e.g., *laukaR*) are examined, (1974), on *Begriffsrunen* and their problematic role in magic, one (1976: 321ff.) on the possibly magical function of the Beuchte brooch inscription (KJ 8), and another (1978) on the use of rune-stones in grave-magic or as a means of sanctifying a location. In a subsequent work concerning the function of runic inscriptions on weapons, Düwel (1981a: 146) seems to suggest that the formulas/names on the weapons of attack and defense actually represent a kind of inter-weapon communication—which is both provocative and significant for the present study. In a series of important studies (1988, 1992, 1997a) Düwel focused his attention mainly on incontestably magical runic inscriptions on bracteates and elsewhere.

If we focus on the late 20th-century trend against regarding the runes as primarily a "magical" or "cultic" script, the two most prominent scholars were the senior runologist Erik Moltke (esp. 1976; 1981a) and the linguist Elmer Antonsen (esp. 1975, 1980a, 1980b). Although Moltke had earlier expressed his disagreement with the numerological school (1928, 1934), his later criticisms stem from his idea that the runes were invented as a practical script, probably for mercantile purposes (for which there is no early epigraphical evidence), and were based on the Latin capitals (see Moltke 1976: 51-58). He would therefore view it as "foolish to ascribe a magical character to the runes" (1981a: 4).(33)

Antonsen's main motivation seems to be the establishment of the runic corpus as a reliable source for historical linguistic research—and certain "magical interpretations" (i.e., that criteria other than purely phonological ones might have been used in the graphic composition of an inscription) tend to compromise such reliability (see Antonsen 1972, 1980a: 1ff.; 1980b:

129ff.). Unfortunately, in his inclination to push back the dating of Nordic inscriptions to bring them closer to PGmc. he often ignores archeological data (Høst 1977b: 151ff.) and in his approach he commonly discounts cultural data of any kind. One of Antonsen's legitimate objections is that runologists often tend to rely too heavily on Old Norse cultural material when interpreting inscriptions from the older period. His general refusal to view the runes in and of themselves as "magical" is well taken (but still debatable), however, he always seems to be working with an ambiguous and unscientific idea of what might be considered "magical" when dealing with specific inscriptions. Sometimes even his own readings appear to fit current ideas concerning magical or operant behavior, but he nevertheless asserts them to be "non-magical." The enigmatic inscription on the Torsberg shield boss (KJ 21) is a conspicuous example of this type which Antonsen analyzes as the name of the shield: *aisgz-h(agla)*: 'the seeker of hail (i.e., of the shower of spears and arrows).'(34) He follows this reading with the statement: "It may well be that weapon-names could represent a pious wish on the part of the owner, such as 'I hope this shield will seek out spears and arrows (and keep them away from me),' but I see no reason to assume that they are 'magic formulas'. . ." (Antonsen 1980a: 4).(35) Here, Antonsen has at once both defined the essence of operative communication and denied its existence in one statement. That such a statement was possible to make is perhaps a testimony to the lack of interdisciplinary rigor among the current school of runologists.

Until runologists arrive at a view, at least the rough outlines of which are held in common, concerning both the general *nature* of Germanic society and psyche during the first millennium CE, as well as the basic characteristics of magical behavior as defined by academic specialists in this field of study, there will always be strong disagreements on the interpretation of the epigraphic data. It seems clear that there have been excesses among both "imaginative" and "skeptical" runologists. It may also be that those with "imagination" have often merely tried to apply, with little real imagination, ready-made magical thought from extra-Germanic traditions (e.g., that of late antique Greece) to the runic evidence, while those "skeptics" have sometimes over-actively *imagined* that a member of an archaic, tribal, oligoliterate society would have one and the same attitudes and rationale with respect to "writing" and to "magic" as they do as members of contemporary Western society.

Notes for Chapter III

1. These "assumptions" are essentially those for which theoretical background is established in ch. II, and for which the original rationale is provided in chs. IV and V.

2. The originally Iranian cult of Mithra(s), although it had been known in Rome at least from the time of Pompey (ca. 67 BCE), began to spread more vigorously throughout the West from the time following Trajan's conquests in Armenia, Assyria and Mesopotamia (97-117 CE), and its influence remained strong throughout the Empire until the end of the fourth-century, see Cumont (1911: 139-42) and Ulanasey (1989: 3-14). The cult was common along the Rhineland *limes* throughout the second and third centuries CE (see de Vries 1937: I, 157ff and Ristow (1974: 1-5). Agrell (1927: 56ff.) also points to the eastern *limes* of Dacia and Moesia as a likely locale for any Germano-Mithraic syncretism.

3. V. Friesen (1913: 4ff.) posits a transfer of a practical script among auxiliary troops in the region of the lower Danube, ca 200 CE.

4. Agrell's so-called "Uþark theory" states that the original order of the runes did not begin with /f/ but rather with /u/, with the /f/ positioned at the *end* of the entire sequence. The resulting alteration in the supposed numerical values of the runes, and the new general structure brought the runic inscriptions and the runic tradition into an apparent close correspondence with Mithraic formulas and lore (see also Agrell 1935-36); however, there is simply no attestation to substantiate this modification. Even Turville-Petre–Ross (1936), who see a strong probability of the existence of numerical "magic" in runic inscriptions, consider Agrell's late antique connection and Uþark theory doubtful.

5. These studies have never been followed by "Eruler, Runen und die Edda" announced by Höfler (1971: 146). However, they were preceded by a detailed study, ignored by Höfler, by Elgqvist (1952: 100ff.) in which the author connects the aristocratic class of Eruls with the Jutlandish cult of Nerthus, and sees their involvement with runic writing as possibly secondary.

6. The Lat. term *(H)eruli* (also Gk. ἐρουλοι) is most probably reflected in the runic corpus as *erilaR* (see Elgqvist 1952: 117-35). Although its full and original significance remains obscure, it indeed seems to indicate more a designation of social class or function (e.g., "high-born man") than an ethnic name.

7. Dillmann (1981: 27) articulates these critical points of inquiry, but takes no unequivocal positions on them.

8. This rather dubious method is criticized by Morgenroth (1961: 279ff.), who shows that Olsen's rules for runic transliteration are designed to fit stanzas 28-29 in the *ES*, and that the pattern with seventy-two runes is due more to the traditions of *syllable* counting than to that of rune-counting. Morgenroth does not, however, totally deny the importance of numerical magical formulas in the runic tradition.

9. Moltke-Jacobsen (1928), rightly it seems, reject the numerical theories of Brix as falacious (its complexity and flexibility invites manipulation). For Moltke, one must combine a linguistically interpretable magical formula with a possible numerical pattern before the numerical pattern can be considered magical. He cites the Trondheim weaving reed (*NIyR*. n. 461) and the Lund weaving temple (DR. 311) as examples for true *talmagi*.

10. This procedure, the *terminus technicus* for which is derived from Gk. γεωμετρια, was probably devised in eighth-century (BCE) Greece for the alphabetic

system. A similar system for ideograms was also known in Babylon at least from the time of Sargon II (727-707 BCE). In its simplest and most original form each of the 24 letters of the Greek alphabet was assigned a numerical value 1-24 (cf. Dornseiff 1922: 11-14, 91-118; Scholem 1974: 337-43).

11. For criticisms of this evaluation or runic data, see Moltke (1928: 90-96), and see the discussion of Klingenberg's theories below. The magico-theoretical basis for Agrell's views are clearly outlined: (1927: 145ff., 16667; 1931: 233ff.; 1936: 36-37, 109-110).

12. See Kuhn (1864) who compares the second Merseburg charm (along with related Scandinavian and English material) with *Atharva Veda* IV, 12, as well as the Old Saxon *contra vermes* spell and *Rig Veda* X, 163 (and *Atharva Veda* XX, 96, 17-22).

13. Later Moltke (1976, 1981a) would take a more critical view of magical interpretations, see below.

14. Krause (1946/47) attempts to identify *laukaR*: 'leek (= increase)' as the most archaic name and sense for the l-rune (which is more usually reconstructed **laguz*: 'water'), which he speculates was altered in later Christian times due to its heathen "culto-magical character."

15. A more critical stance has been taken in recent times toward the possibilities of this notion (see Düwel 1974: 150-53), and in later years Krause himself (1966: 1970, 1971) became more doubtful of the consistent application of the ideographic interpretation of isolated runes.

16. This does not represent an exhaustive classification of the data presented in his own study, e.g., rune-master formulas, martial objects.

17. Sierke's 1939 work, although extremely valuable, is sometimes perhaps unavoidably superficial. Marquardt (1941: 302-04) presents some objections to Sierke's interpretation of rune-stones as "*Verbotstafeln*" (since only a fractional minority could actually *read* them), to his idea that stones buried *within* the grave-mounds could be memorials, and to the generalization that rune-magic was always "selfless" and noble (as opposed to medieval magic in Christian times).

18. See Hunger (1984) and Losemann (1977). Contrasts between certain views concerning runic origins and other remarks, when one compares, for example, the 1935 and 1944 editions of Arntz' *Handbuch* or the 1935 and 1944 editions of Krause's *Was man in Runen ritzte*, might be taken as typical.

19. This etymology is accepted by de Vries (1961a: 7), but is questioned by Neu (1974: 77) who maintains that the verbal form **alu- ~ *alua(i)-* is actually unattested in Hittite, and that its IE origin is also uncertain. Polomé later refined his views (1996: 99-105).

20. The identification of runic *alu* with Gmc. **alu(þ)* had already been made by Bæksted (1945: 88), and was supported by Marstrander (1952: 80). See Høst (1980) for a survey of various interpretations of this formula.

21. Cf. negative review by Lange (1957) and Derolez (1959b: 1-4).

22. Following this major study, Schneider continued to develop his ideographic theory in later works (e.g., 1968, 1972, 1980).

23. Much of the most controversial content of Schneider's discussion would, I think, be less so if he had ascribed it to secondary development rather than to primary or original conditions of the tradition.

24. See Page (1964: 29; 1999: 19-21, 179-80, 228-29 *et passim*).

25. It is recognized that Page's primary intent was the preservation of the reverse, i.e., to prevent the generalization of Scandinavian evidence in the OE tradition.

26. These had earlier been the subject of brief studies by Dickins (1935) and Harder (1931, 1936).

27. Nielsen discusses all those previously analyzed by Jacobsen (1935), plus the Sparlösa st. (Vä. 119).

28. To a limited extent, Nielsen tries to understand these inscriptions in terms of what seems to be nascent shamanism (*sejd*) in the region (pp. 48-52).

29. Becker (1973: 143ff.) also presents a general examination of the possibilities of rune-magic in Anglo-Saxon culture, in which he agrees with Page (1964) that there is no compelling proof for magic in the Old English corpus; however, he sees the probability as a strong one.

30. Cf. rev. by Hauck (1976)

31. Elsewhere, Klingenberg (1969) also uses an iconic method similar to that employed by Schneider (1956), and a phonemic method in which a secondary, hidden linguistic sense is imparted in runic inscriptions. Unfortunately, these methods were not further developed in his 1973 work.

32. This golden horn (B), along with a similar one without runes (A), were stolen from the National Museum in Copenhagen in 1802 and melted down, so that we are now dependent upon three drawings made from the originals, see Krause-Jankuhn (1966: 97-103).

33. In 1982 Moltke was still willing to concede that there are secondary magical elements connected with the **fuþark** (personal correspondence March 12, 1982 and 1976: 57-58).

34. Problems with this reading include the absence of a thematic vowel in *aisgz*, which is most unlikely at this early date (ca. 200 CE).

35. The *værneformler* ("protection-formulas")—a term which Antonsen ambiguously translates as "warnings" (1980: 11)—on the Stentoften and Björketorp stones (KJ 96 and 97) *et al.* are also treated in a similar manner by Antonsen (1980b: 133ff.).

Chapter IV

Social Aspects of Operant Runic Practice

1. Although it is possible that magical elements may have been secondary accretions in the runic tradition, it is impossible to speculate on the degree to which these elements were only remotely important and removed in time from the origins of the runic system or writing itself. It is equally difficult to determine to what extent these magical ideas were simultaneous with—and of critical importance for—the origin of the runes, without some knowledge of the type of society in which these cultural events occurred. Here we can only offer a brief historical outline of some of these factors, and suggest further avenues for investigation, with a constant focus on the social aspects of the ongoing process of runic origins and reformations, their dissemination and distribution, as well as the maintenance of those systems throughout various historical periods.

The Runic System

2. The single most remarkable feature of the runic tradition is what has aptly been called the *runic system*. Derolez (1981: 19) defines this complex as:

> ... (1) the order of the runes in the futhark, (2) the division of the futhark into three groups of runes, (3) the acrophonic names of the runes, (4) and whatever explanatory text accompanied these names, (5) the general ductus and style, (6) the direction of the writing, as well as, most important perhaps, (7) the "perfect fit" between graphemes and phonemes...(1)

With respect to the first point, the order of the runes, it might be added that the total number of graphs seems to have been fixed at 24. What makes this system so remarkable is not so much its complexity alone as its durability over a millennium in a society of restricted literacy. But herein probably lies the reason for its durability.

The "Pre-Runic" Period

3. During the first half of this century, a good deal of work was done on the possible origin of the runes in Bronze Age graphs or ideographic petroglyphs (see Nordén 1934a, 1934b, 1936, 1941, Arntz 1944: 125-67, and Altheim 1938) or at least on the functional correspondence between these petroglyphs and later runic inscriptions. Such a theory would suggest that the runes were influenced in their development by "pre-runic" signs or symbols(2) (commonly thought to be of a cultic or magical character), and that runic inscriptions began to be used in situations in which iconic rock carvings had previously been employed.(3)

Another supposed "pre-runic" attestation of graphic symbols among the Germanic peoples is offered by Tacitus *Germ.* ch. 10 in which he reports on the divinatory practices of the Germans(4) and mentions that the strips of wood (*surculi*) were scored with signs (*notae*). It has always been considered possible that these *notae* were actually runic in character —despite the gap between the composition of the *Germania* (98 CE) and the first positively runic artifact, the spear-head of Øvre-Stabu (KJ 31) from the mid-second century. This has been made somewhat more certain by the discovery of the Meldorf brooch (ca. 50 CE, Schleswig) which bears an inscriptions of probable runic character.(5)

What seems certain is that there was an ongoing use of graphic signs among the Germanic peoples from an early date, and that these signs were employed for cultic and/or magical purposes—beyond this we can speculate little. It is tempting to assume that the presence of runic inscriptions and pictographic carvings in graves, or on freestanding rocks or slabs somehow represents a continuity in practice if not actual function. As far as the Bronze Age carvings are concerned, the relationship between the ideographic signs and pictographic figures in rock-carvings remains obscure.(6)

Runic Origins

4. Düwel (2008: 90) poses the three major questions of runic origins as: 1) which alphabet is the basis for the runic row, 2) when were they developed, 3) in which locality, 4) and by whom or within which Germanic tribe were the runic signs developed, and 5) for what purpose were the runic characters created? On the second question there seems to be some general, if tentative, agreement. According to common principles of alphabetic development, the period of genesis is most often placed some 100 to 200 years prior to the date of the first concentration of attestations of the script.(7) Although the spear-head of Øvre-Stabu (KJ 31, ca. 150 CE) was long thought to be the oldest runic inscription, the first great concentration

of finds from south Scandinavian moors dates from ca. 200 CE—which would indicate that the developmental period was between 50 BCE and 50 CE, or perhaps later (cf. Krause 1966: 7ff.). If the Meldorf inscription is runic, it could *theoretically* push the date back some 100 years, but it is also possible that it is exceptional with regard to the hypothetical 100-200 year period, or that it even represents "proto-runic" epigraphy.(8) There have been attempts to push the date well back into the latter centuries BCE (see Kabell 1967: 94ff.), partly on the theory that the first inscriptions were carved exclusively on perishable objects. In any case, the extant inscriptions from the latter half of the second century CE constitute the only reliable *post quem*.

With regard to the other questions, there is no conclusive agreement. There have been three credible theories as to the alphabet which served as a model for the runes—the Greek theory, the North-Italic theory, and the Latin theory. The hypothesis that the 24-letter Greek alphabet was the model for the 24-rune older fuþark was popular in the early 20th-century, principally due to the work of von Friesen (1904 and 1918-1919) and before him that of Bugge (1874). They would have placed the development in the Balkan region where the Goths first made contact with the Hellenistic culture. But since the oldest runic evidence is now known to date from a time before this initial contact was made (ca. 200 CE), this theory has been largely abandoned. Possible secondary influences from the Greek world cannot be as quickly discounted.(9)

The North-Italic, or Etruscan, theory (see Marstrander 1928: 5-179; Mammarström 1930; Krause 1937: 29ff.; Altheim-Trautmann 1939; Krause 1966: 7; Höfler 1970 and 1971) states that the runic signs were developed in the Alpine or sub-alpine region from various extant Italic scripts(10) (with no single alphabet serving as the model for the entire fuþark). This theory has met with the greatest acceptance over the years perhaps due to the close typographical resemblance between the Italic and runic signs, and because a famous Germanic inscriptions, the Negau helmet B (and A?) is written in one of these scripts(11) (see note 27 below). Objections to the North-Italic theory include the chronological gap between possible Germanic-North-Italic contacts and the manifestation of the runic tradition in the North, the lack of a uniform model for the runes among the known North-Italic alphabets, and the absence of phonemic : graphemic correspondence in some cases of formal similarity, e.g., runic M /d/ : Italic M /š/; runic X /g/ : Italic X /t/; runic Γ /l/ : Italic Γ /p/, etc. (see Marstrander 1928: 99).

More recently, the previously well-supported Latin theory (see Wimmer 1874; Pedersen 1920; Askeberg 1944: 85) has found vigorous new support with a few innovations in the work of Erik Moltke (1976: 51-55; 1981). The Latin theory has two decided advantages: 1) the on-going contact between Romans and Germans gave ample opportunity for extended cultural exchange, and 2) the relatively high rate of graphemic-phonemic correspondence or relationship between the two scripts (e.g., ᚠ : F; ᚢ :V; ᚨ: a; ᚱ: R; < : K; ᚺ : H; | : I; ᛋ : S; ᛏ : T; ᛒ : B; ᛗ : M; ᛚ : L; ᛟ : O).(12) But neither do these capitals solve all the formal problems of runic origins.

The development of the runic signs: ᚦ /þ/, ᚷ /g/, ᚹ /w/, ᚾ /n/, ᛃ /j/, ᛁ /i/, ᛈ /p/, ᛉ /z/, ᛖ /e/, ᛜ /ŋ/, ᛞ /d/ remains problematical, and it would seem that the best solution is that suggested by Krause (e.g., 1948/50: 33-35) that at least some of these signs are developments from indigenous Germanic symbology. He also speculated (as late as 1970: 43) that the original forms of *jēra and *iŋwas were circular ᛜ and ᛜ, and represented aspects of the agricultural cycle. It must be emphasized that these ideas are conjectural.

There can be no final conclusions on the possible alphabetic model of the fuþark. But based purely on the material evidence that we do have, it would seem most reasonable to assume that the originator(s) of the fuþark were familiar with a *variety* of scripts and symbol systems and employed them freely—with substantial additions of their own lore or inventive urges (see Höfler 1970, 1971; Moltke 1981a: 607).

As to the questions of the location of the tribe in which this cultural innovation took place—there are even more diverse answers. Some suggestions have been: the Goths on the Vistula (Askeberg 1944) or on the Black Sea (von Friesen 1933), the Cimbri and Teutones in the Transpadana region (Baesecke 1934: 413-17; Altheim-Trautmann 1939), or the Marcomanni in Bohemia (Marstrander 1928: 95ff; Krause 1964: 312). Two more interesting ideas identify the human matrix not as a *tribe* but as a social niveau or functional stratum of society. Moltke (1976: 57-58 and 1981a) sees the runes as having their origins among *merchants*(13) concentrated in Denmark, while Höfler (1970; 1971) views bands of elite warriors (the *Eruli?*) as the social context for runic origins in the Alpine region.

Runic Data and Analysis

5. We are severely limited in what we are able to offer here since the period of actual runic generation is largely undocumented due to normal conditions of script development. Therefore, we must make observations in which a broader view of runic history is taken in order to allow for some

general conclusions as to the probable institutional framework(s) active in the process of runic genesis.

The history of the entire *runic system* would seem to suggest that its features were present in the tradition, if not from its beginnings, certainly from an early period of sweeping reform or codification (cf. Derolez 1981). For our purposes, we will consider four points in the system, i.e.: 1) graphic style, 2) name, 3) order and total number, and 4) tripartite division of the system. With regard to the style or form of individual runic characters, if we assume for the moment that a given form has been patterned on a Roman original (e.g., F → ᚠ), the possibility always remained to alter the shape at any time during the long historical process of runic development which took place in Scandinavia—a cultural environment largely isolated from direct Roman influence. However, any formal alteration rarely occurred.(14) The acrophonic names, which admittedly are directly known to us only from manuscript traditions dating from as early as the 8th-century (OE MS Salis, 140),(15) seem to have also been an established and archaic tradition at that time. Again there existed ample opportunity to use any one of hundreds of nouns with the appropriate initial phoneme, but we find that the same name (with a few notable and perhaps explicable exceptions)(16) is used throughout. The fixed order and the total number of graphs in the system are also generally constant, with only apparently regular inversions in the orders of the 13th/14th and 23rd/24th runes. The Kylver stone (KJ 1) is the earliest attestation of a complete fuþark (ca. 400). While the tripartite division of the fuþark is documented from as early as ca. 450 (on the Vadstena/Motala brs.), its later vigor, shown in the devising of runic codes, would seem to indicate that even at that time it was no mere isolated or sterile practice.

This historical situation is rendered more remarkable when we consider that this unified system was instituted and maintained among several distinct tribal groups. In such a complex and technical lore we might normally expect more divergence among tribal and/or regional traditions (cf. the similar situation among the North-Italic tribes with their wide variations in alphabetic types, Jensen 1958: 478ff.).

Development of the System

6. Possible motivations for such complex traditions will be discussed in chapters V, VI and VII, but at this point the important question would be: How did this complex and uniform system develop and thrive in the vast pluralistic world of the Germanic tribes during the early centuries of our era? The possible permutations of the elements of the runic system in a

society of restricted literacy are staggering. In the absence of a written tradition, the most reasonable and simplest solution would appear to be that "apprentices" were taught this system by "masters"(17) in some sort of *traditional* framework, and in some sort of *traditional* way, i.e., orally (with the secondary aid of the runic characters). This transmission of lore from teacher to pupil is obviously the social phenomenon at the root of the runic tradition. To suggest that the runes spread by means of "alphabetic rune sticks" (Haugen 1976: 120) or other models, is problematic without the added element of the *teacher* and the *prestige* of the school which the teacher represented.

Regardless of whether the graphemic origin of the runes is to be found in the Roman, Greek, North-Italic or some other alphabet, the entirety of the system does not appear to be derived from any of them. Furthermore, it is most unlikely that the purely graphemic use of the runes, not to mention the complex auxiliary system, could have spread throughout such a vast territory and crossed dozens of tribal boundaries without some social support system. It would seem most reasonable to suppose that this teaching institution pre-existed the introduction of runic writing.(18) If this were indeed true, then the runes would have to be considered another element of lore injected into a traditional network, which also bore certain religious practices or beliefs, mythic and epic material, as well as other cultural and economic features.

The Social Matrix

7. Before the first two centuries of our era, it is difficult to establish with any certainly the existence of the social matrix necessary for the maintenance of such a traditional network.(19) Common elements in Germanic religious and epic tradition point either to their existence in a Proto-Germanic period, or to their mutual diffusion from one region to another, or as is most likely, to a combination of both processes. More central to the period in question are the relevant reports of Caesar(20) and of Tacitus.(21) Between the time of Caesar's reports concerning the Germans along the Rhine (ca. 55 BCE) and the *Germania* of Tacitus (98 CE), we may observe a trend which gives a concrete clue to the social context in which this traditional network cold have developed. Caesar explicitly states that the Germans had no private property, that they were constantly moved from one plot of land to another by what he calls *magistratūs* and *principes*, and that there was no difference between the holdings of the "most powerful" and the "common man" (*DBG* IV). Tacitus, on the other hand, portrays a society characterized by powerful and wealthy *principes* who have permanent bodies of retainers. Archeological evidence corroborates this

differentiation process and further points to a uniformity among funeral goods in the graves of leading families throughout the Germanies (Krüger 1976: I, 521ff., Brønsted 1960: III, 123-79; 413; Hedeager 1978b: 217-23). Intertribal communication lines must have been well developed along with long established contacts with Mediterranean cultures throughout the Roman Age. Such socio-economic conditions seem conducive to the establishment of a medium for the spread of any cultural feature such as the runes represent.

Without doubt, the cultures bordering the Germanic peoples during the Roman and Migration Ages were significant for the formation of certain socio-cultic, as well as socio-economic institutions and customs. As for religion, societies tend to be conservative in the area of public cult and underlying creed. However, in the realm of magical technique and lore, many peoples tend to be quick to assimilate foreign models, as it is sometimes believed that the magic of neighboring strangers is endowed with special powers (Mauss 1972: 31).

Neighboring populations which seem to have had the greatest direct influence on the Germanic peoples are the Lapp and Finno-Ugric populations in the eastern Baltic, the Celts, and Romans. Certain correspondences between north Germanic "shamanistic"(22) practices and those of the Lapps or "Finns"(23) have been noted by several scholars (e.g., de Vries 1956: I, 129ff. and Buchholz 1968: 14-21 and 1971: 7ff.). Although the cultural connections between the Celtic and Germanic peoples have been the subject of several important studies (e.g., de Vries 1960; Hachmann-Kossak-Kuhn 1962; Birkhan 1970; and Evans 1981), the relationship between the runes and Irish *ogham* (or any other script) remains controversial,(24) and no clear case can be made for Celtic borrowings in Germanic religious life. Roman influence is certainly the best documented. Trade appears to have been vigorously pursued by the Romans(25) from the time of Augustus (Krüger 1976: I, 300ff.), and it is noteworthy that this commerce was generally carried out by Romans (or their agents) traveling in Germania. The directly commercial activities of the Germans seem to have been limited to the *limes* regions. Moreover, Germans, some of whom were originally prisoners of war, began to join the Roman army.(26) The results of these socio-economic trends have already been noted—class differentiation, development of standing retinues, and increased inter-tribal communication.

One important possible influence, directly applicable to the question here, is that of Mithraism. This element was certainly overemphasized by Agrell (see ch. III.3), who wanted to demonstrate a direct and comprehensive borrowing of Mithraic doctrines into runic practice. There is, however, evidence to show that there was at least some degree of religious syncretism, and perhaps socio-cultic influence, at work within Mithraism between Roman and German adherents. for example, Behn (1966: 48ff.) cites this syncretism of Mithras-Mercurius-Wodan along the Rhine-*limes* among the Mithraic populus, and even shows a sculpture of Mithras (from the Mithraeum at Dieburg) which depicts the god riding a horse armed with a spear. This seems to be an imitation of typical portrayals of Wodan—and one that is at variance with Mithras' usual attributes of chariot with bow and arrow. It would also appear that, if nothing else, the exclusively male and militant Roman Mithraism could have had some influence on the shaping—or subsequent reformation—of the Germanic retinue system as Germanic auxiliaries returned home after having served in the Imperial army (and perhaps having been initiated into the Mithraic mysteries). Mithraism was widespread throughout the region of the Rheinland-*limes* (de Vries 1937, 157ff.). Ristow (1974: 1-5) demonstrates the well established nature of this cult in Cologne during the second and third centuries CE from archeological evidence. Clemen (1937: 221ff.) rightly criticizes Agrell's theories in this area, and indicates that the influence of Mithraism could have only been slight in the North Germanic realms.

Conclusion on Runic Origin

8. The extant runic data does not allow final conclusions on the origin of the writing system, or on the socio-cultic elements which might have attended or aided its development. The earliest grouping of runic artifacts occurs in the Danish isles, Jutland and in southern Norway, with isolated finds in Scania (Skåne), on Gotland, and in eastern Europe. It seems most probable that these brooch and spear-head inscriptions represent only a small portion of the corpus, both numerically and typologically. There appears to be general agreement that the majority of inscriptions were executed on wood or other perishable materials and simply did not survive. However, it is tempting to think that the extant artifacts provide a reliable indication of the *distribution* of runic activity in the early centuries of the tradition. Recent archeological analysis, however, places the points of origin for the objects found in the sacrificial bogs of Thorsberg and Moosgård elsewhere in Scandinavia from invading tribes whose homelands were to the north and east of Denmark. It must be emphasized that this is of little help concerning the original phase—since it may be totally undocumented. The evidence at this juncture will not support any firm conclusions about the geographical region in which the runes had their origin.

Höfler's Theories

9. Höfler (1970 and 1971) presents a plausible theory concerning the social dynamic of runic origins. It is his contention that a Germanic auxiliary (an "Erulian") in the Roman army (at the beginning of the Common Era) came into contact with the North-Italic scripts of the Alpine region, and from a combination of these the Erulian formulated a fuþark for writing the Germanic dialect.(27) This auxiliary was apparently an influential man of great cultural authority—at least within the network of his fellow warrior-cultists—since the radical innovation of writing and his system, or that of his early "pupils," was adopted on a broad basis and used throughout this culture. The social dynamic of Höfler's theory seems fundamentally sound. Its historical accuracy may be more questionable. It appears equally plausible that the mere idea of writing was brought northward by wandering warriors of the kind identified by Höfler as Erulians, and that the runic tradition was formed in the north (e.g., among the Danish isles or somewhere else in southern Scandinavia) based on Roman and North-Italic models (with a certain amount of innovative additions, see 12 below). Whatever social phenomenon was responsible for the origin of the runes, it seems clear that it must have been an *intertribal* organization of some sort. A tradition of such complexity would be accepted only slowly and reluctantly by given tribes if the innovation originated from within a foreign grouping—no matter how great its temporary prestige might have been. However, an intertribal "network"(28) generally responsible for the transmission of lore and mythic material (and perhaps even trade goods)—as informal as all this process might have been among the Germanic peoples at this time—(29) would have already been established and predisposed toward the utilization of such intellectual and symbolic material. Also, the network's intertribal structure would have facilitated a rapid dissemination of any material properly injected into its body of lore.

It would be difficult positively to identify this network with the *Eruli*, since we do not have reports of this group before 267 CE,(30) but it seems probable that this *Kriegerverband* at least became heir to the rune lore,(31) and perhaps to some extent became identified with it by other uses of the tradition (see ch. VII, 11, on the term *erilaR*). The network that I would propose as responsible for the early runic tradition would have certainly been less specialized than these later *Eruli*—and probably quite diverse with regard to the tribal cultures to which individuals of this network might have belonged.

More difficult still is the determination of possible religio-cultic characteristics of such a social stratum or network. It is always tempting to see in this obscure early phase of the tradition (between 100 BCE and 200 CE) characteristics which could later legitimately be called "Odinic," i.e., associations with poetry, "shamanism" and magic—as well as commerce and the political structure of the warrior-band. But this has little other then typological evidence to support it.

Diffusion and Maintenance of the Older Fuþark

10. To a large extent the origins and spread of runic writing are impossible to separate due to the lack of an early body of evidence and perhaps also because under optimal conditions the actual diffusion of this cultural feature theoretically may have reached an advanced stage in a matter of weeks or months. The period between 150 and 750 CE contains virtually the entire body of some 250 inscriptions in the older fuþark found to date,(32) with around 160 additional runic impressions on bracteates, and thus comprises the bulk of epigraphical evidence used in this work.

If we roughly divide this period of six centuries into segments of 100 years and show the distribution of the runic finds throughout the European territory (see Maps I-VI), an approximate impression may be developed concerning the chronological(33) and geographical distribution of the older fuþark inscriptions.

Map I (ca. 150-250) shows the relatively early record of widely distributed runic finds. The principal area of concentration is the Danish archipelago, Scania and southwestern Norway—with the highly dispersed spearheads on the continent and on Gotland to the east. This eastern group dates from the latter part of the period (ca. 250). The historical data between 150 and 250 is particularly sparse (see Schwarz 1956: 11-12) and the north remains especially obscure since most even tangentially relevant historical material deals with the regions of the *limes* (e.g., Tacitus *Germ.* 98 CE).

In the case of each map, we generally assume that 1) only an extremely small fraction of the inscriptions survived, but 2) the present distribution of the finds *may* be approximately equivalent to the relative distribution of the tradition in the given historical periods.(34) It can not be too strongly emphasized that this analysis is tentative and mainly heuristic. Given the small number of total finds in the early period, additional finds could, and we hope will, substantially alter the interpretation of such distributive analyses.

Map II (ca. 250-350) demonstrates a marked decline and geographical restriction in runic activity (with a total of five inscriptions from southern Norway and the Danish archipelago). Reasons for this apparent inactivity are unclear,(35) but it seems that the tradition was conserved and again became vigorous over the next 100 years (350-450), as Map III shows. Continental inscriptions reappear in southeastern Europe and northern Germany, and activity expands in Norway, central Sweden and Gotland—with a continuance of activity in the Danish region.

The next 100 years (450-550) demonstrate an intensification of activity in Norway and central Sweden—which continued sporadic finds on the continent (Map IV). The Danish area again seems to form the epicenter of innovation represented by the bracteate inscriptions. This trend is carried further in the next hundred years, as Map V shows, with the development of concentrated south Germanic activity in the Alemannic and Frankish territories, and in Friesia and England. Activity continues in Norway and Sweden, but seemingly at a diminished level, while it has virtually disappeared from the Danish region. There were doubtlessly historical and socio-cultural reasons for these shifts, but they have left no trace that we can unequivocally connect to phenomena in the runic record. Map VI (650-750) shows a drastic reduction throughout the Scandinavian peninsula, and despite this some of the most remarkable inscriptions of the older period come during this time, i.e., the stones of Stentoften (KJ 96), Björketorp (KJ 97), Eggjum (KJ 101), and Roes (KJ 102).

The Older Runic System

11. This chronological-geographical treatment demonstrates the history and relative vigor of the tradition. Beyond this, there are considerations of elements of the *runic system*. It is commonly suspected (see Derolez 1981: 19ff.) that these elements have been with the tradition from its inception and contributed significantly to its maintenance of internal integrity through sometimes drastic geographic shifts and migrations.

With only slight, and strangely consistent, variations it is clear that the original fuþark consisted of 24 characters arranged in a certain and thoroughly unique order. The oldest attestation of the fuþark is on the Kylver stone (KJ ca. 400)—on which the 13th and 14th runes are perhaps reversed. There is a total of nine inscriptions from between 400 and ca. 850 which show a high level of traditional integrity for the fuþark order and number.(36)

The tripartite division of the row of 24 characters into groups of eight is first attested on the Vadstena/Motala and Grumpan brs. (KJ 2; 3. ca. 450-550), and that this was an integral part of the archaic tradition is supported by the indication of these divisions in an 11th-century Old English manuscript Cotton, Domitian A9 (see Derolez 1954: 10). The Latin "is-runa tract" in five manuscripts from the 9th-11th centuries (see Derolez 1954: 89ff.) provides an explicit technique for using the divisions in runic code forms (see VII.6). Because the younger fuþark tradition not only shows the three-fold division,(37) but also demonstrates a rich variety of runic codes (Page 1999: 80ff.), we would suspect that the tripartite division was an integral part of the continuous underlying runic tradition.(38)

Acrophonic rune-names are not attested before the Old English manuscript Salis 140, which dates from between 750 and 850. However, corroborating Scandinavian and independent continental evidence,(39) would indicate that the rune-names again represent a part of an integral and archaic system.(40)

Related to the acrophonic names, and perhaps composed as traditional "exemplary texts" (cf. Derolez 1981: 19ff.) for those names, are the rune-poem stanzas. Four distinct rune-poems survive. The Old English "Rune Poem" of 29 stanzas dates form at least the 10th-century,(41) but probably goes back to the 9th or 8th-century. From the 9th-century comes the *Abecedarium Nordmannicum* (St. Gall 878), which is a dialectic mixture of Old Norse, Old English and Low German and which contains the 16 runes of the younger fuþark. This later 16-rune system is also the basis of the Old Norwegian (late 12th/early 13th cent.) rune rhyme and the Old Icelandic (15th cent.) rune poem. The Old English, Old Norwegian, and Old Icelandic texts all conform to a common style in which the acrophonic rune name becomes the theme of a poetic stanza. Furthermore, the Old Norwegian and Old Icelandic poems are clearly based on the same tradition.(42) It is interesting to note that by the time the Old Icelandic poem is recorded, the common mode of runic writing has again been radically reformed by the addition of dotted-runes (*stungnar rúnar*) and new characters to account for Latin letters. Moreover, the order of the runes had been generally modified into an alphabetic one.(43) The fuþark had been replaced by a true *runic alphabet*. Despite this, the poem reflects only the older tradition, which gives some indication of the possible level of continued knowledge and prestige of the fuþark-system.

From the beginning, the runic tradition demonstrated a consistency in the style and shape of individual runic forms. It certainly seems that by ca. 200 CE, the correspondence between shape and phonetic value was firmly established,(44) and that it was conserved with a high degree of integrity.

If we use the typological classification system introduced by Antonsen (1975a: 6-10, 1975b: 129-32) and apply it to the older corpus, we see that the majority of runic forms have their typological variation restricted to such an extent that they always keep their predominant and distinctive features and show little variation typologically. A more refined stylistic typology(45) reveals that many forms demonstrate minor variations of several features within the bounds of major typological distinctions, while very few have typologically variant forms. As Antonsen points out (1975b: 130), the minor variations may be due to local traditions rather than actual chronological development. (This would then be evidence for the existence of "schools" of writing, perhaps with their roots in some social complex with concerns beyond that of mere epigraphical stylistics.)

Now, the direction of the writing alternates from dextroverse (158 inscriptions in the older tradition) to levoverse (73 inscriptions), with a combination of the two, *boustrophedon*, in 9-13 inscriptions. In addition, some 64 inscriptions are ambiguous as to the direction of the script. This seems to indicate that this extra-linguistic feature was also part of the archaic level of the system.

Conclusions on Diffusion and Maintenance

12. Based upon runological data, it seems most straightforward to assume that runic writing of the traditions represented in the epigraphical evidence had its origins in the Danish archipelago or seacoast regions of southern Scandinavia sometime between 100 BCE (or earlier) and 100 CE, and that the social matrix responsible for its development and spread was highly mobile and probably of a special, functional type rather than a "tribe" in the usual sense. That this society possessed a high degree of self-consciousness and a fairly sophisticated organization, is indicated by the remarkable preservation of the complex (and for the time rather novel) runic tradition. Furthermore, the runic data suggest that shapers of the tradition were not exclusively concerned with representing a natural language for inter-human communication, since such extra-linguistic features unnecessary to these ends (e.g., tripartite divisions, acrophonic rune names, peculiar order, variable writing directions) play such a prominent role in the continuity of the system.

Social Aspects

13. Two functionally distinct, but in a historic sense apparently not totally unrelated, social institutions seem to have been present and vital during the periods of runic origins and dissemination: 1) the men's society (*Männerbund*),(46) and 2) the cultic league. Associations of men for a variety of cultural purposes (religious, political, economic, military, etc.) is

indeed an old, and apparently virtually universal phenomenon.(47) While the basic traditional *Männerbund* or *Altersklasse* seem to have been mainly intra-tribal or intra-clanic institutions, other types of associations in the Germanic world which appear to have been structured along the lines of the men's societies (i.e., the warrior-band and ultimately the *comitatus*) soon became inter-clanic and inter-tribal institutions. The warrior-band might be brought together for a certain campaign and dissolved upon completion of that action, while the *comitatus* signifies a lasting contractual relationship between a lord and his standing retinue.(48) On the other hand, the cultic league (*Kultverband*) had a primarily religious *raison d'etre* with secondary political, military and economic functions. They constituted natural alliances and provided close trading relationships. Although the men's societies present in Germanic culture between the time of Caesar's account and those of Tacitus were probably distinct from the cultic leagues themselves, it seems reasonable to suppose that they had some effect on the formulation of such leagues and/or that they were affected by the cultural associations made through the leagues.

The amphictionies as described by Tacitus (*Germ*. Chs. 39, 40, 43 and *Annali* I, 51) seem to have found their main expression in seasonal assemblies, but any other supporting infrastructure (e.g., unified priesthoods) remains obscure. However, in the institutions of the *Altersklasse* (initiatory age-group distinctions) and the *Männerbund*, as well as the warrior-band and its formalized version, the *comitatus*, we find a social organization with the capacity for the establishment of complex and ongoing traditions. The youths of the social elite received training in matters necessary to their functioning as leaders within the clanic or tribal structure (Tacitus *Germ*. chs. 13, 24, 31, 32). We would suppose that this took various shapes, but that its basic form was that of the master/apprentice arrangement in which the youth was assigned to a mentor (perhaps sent into fosterage with a maternal uncle, etc.)(49) to be trained. The inter-clanic and inter-tribal institutions of the warrior-band and *comitatus* could have cleared the channels for the transmission of knowledge of the type which the runes represent. The *comitatus* was an organization in which a man could serve among a foreign tribe, assimilate various cultural features, and after a time return to this native tribe, and there pass on these newly learned features. Wandering poets (who may have also functioned as merchants, entertainers, magicians, etc.) could have also played an active role in the spread of lore of this type. We have no direct evidence for these wandering poet-magicians among the Germanic peoples in this early period, but it is not unreasonable to assume that such an institution was known among them.(50)

Archeological evidence shows that during the later Roman Age there was an increasing socio-economic class differentiation in Germania. Grave goods indicate the development of an intra-tribal elite, and inter-tribal correspondences in these goods show the presence of close cultural contacts (Krüger 1976: I, 521ff.). In this social context it would be quite natural for networks of persons responsible for cultural traditions of the kind the runes represent to be strengthened.

The antiquity of such institutions as the men's societies/warrior-bands and the cultic leagues is impossible to determine, which is unfortunate since conditions during the last centuries BCE are critical for a complete examination of likely social contexts for runic origins. However, if we assume that the period of origin pre-dates the first attestations of the system by 100-200 years,(51) and we place the period of first concentrated attestations at ca. 200 CE, it becomes apparent that the most critical period for such an examination is the first century of our era. Fortunately, we are relatively well-informed on this epoch by Roman historians and ethnographers.(52) We know, for example, that there existed at least three great amphictionies throughout the first century.(53) They were: 1) the Nerthus-cult on Jutland (and perhaps in the Danish archipelago) among the Reudingi, Aviones, Anglii, Varni, Eudoses, Suarnes and Nuitones (Tacitus *Germ.* ch. 40); 2) the cult of the Semnones-grove(54) among the Swabian tribes, e.g., Langobardi, Semnones, Marcomanni and Quadi (Tacitus *Germ.* ch. 39); and 3) the Alcis-cult among the tribes between the Oder and the Vistula, i.e., the Lugii- (or Vandali)-group, with their cultic center among the Naharvali (Tacitus *Germ.* ch. 43). A fourth center known in the early first century is that of the Tanfana in the Marsi territory among the Sugambri-group of tribes east of the lower Rhine. However, this alliance was short-lived, ca. 12-14 BCE, when the sanctuary was destroyed during a raid by Germanicus (Tacitus *Annali* I, 51). See Map VII.

Hachmann (1971: 106) writes concerning the broader social implications of these cultic leagues:

> We are stuck by the general cultural concordances within the cult leagues, extending far beyond the religious field. Much of the secular material associated with a particular cult league shows specific features found throughout the whole area. This may be to some extent due to the fact that cult leagues were at the same time economic associations through which, by contacts between one settlement and another, particular products became generally known and imitated, so that they took on similar forms throughout the area. But there is also another, deeper, reason: many objects of everyday use had a religious significance in addition to their primary social or economic function.

As Map VII shows, the territory of the Swabian cultic league would seem to form a suitable north-south bridge for the transmission of cultural features during the period in question. But in the absence of contemporary runic attestations among the Marcomanni and related tribes, this linkage remains speculative.(55)

Both the cultic league and the *comitatus* seem to be cultural responses to similar social conditions, and it appears that each would have complemented the function of the other. The lines of communication opened through the establishment of inter-tribal alliances of chieftains' families and their *comitati* are simultaneously broadened through the development of a common cult, the festivals of which also serve as the basis for regular cultural, economic and political activity and exchange.

Individual Rune-Carvers

14. In general terms, we have some idea of what groups might have had a motivation and opportunity to develop and/or spread the runic tradition—but who might the *individuals* have been? What might have been their function in the society otherwise, and what could have been their motivations for the use of writing at all? Any answers to such questions must remain speculative, especially for the earliest period. Of some 30 inscriptions which date from around 200 CE or earlier, only two positively reveal anything about the carver: 1) KJ 13a Nøvling brooch: 'Bidwar cut ([the runes] into wood),' and 2) KJ 12 Gårdlösa clasp: 'I, the one free from rage.' While three others seem to refer to the carver: 1) KJ 10 Himlingøje II brooch '... Wood-hound (= wolf),' 2) KJ 11 Værløse brooch (vocative PN) 'Alugod!'—or—'*alu* God(ag)!' and 3) KJ 13 Næsbjerg clasp: 'one who guards against idle talk(?).' Other epigraphical evidence from the period(56) shows the use of runic dedicatory formulas and owners' or makers' marks (which may contain the name of the carver) and weapon names. Although this evidence is slight, it is possible to conclude that from the beginning, both the activity of carving and the personality of the carver/master(57) were important, and that in the earliest period the martial aspect was emphasized.

The rune-carvers must have represented a part of a social elite, concerned with matters of military and religious importance. The earliest group of inscriptions(58) contain five or more terms which might be construed as bearing a religious connotation: i.e., (KJ 20) *Wu(l)þuþewaR*: 'servant of *Wulþuz* (→ ON Ullr), (KJ 24) *a(n)sula*: 'the little god,' and *wī(h)ja*: 'I consecrate,' (KJ 11) *alu* (see ch. VI), and (KJ 12)— *wōð*— 'inspired psychic activity, rage.' These men probably did not represent a 'professional priest-class,'(59) but rather were more likely members of a large network of military elite, whose specialties might have included magic, poetry, medicine, etc. Although these bodies and these individuals were probably engaged in trade as well, the absolute lack of any indication of a runic function connected with commerce throws doubt on the idea that the runes were developed in a primarily mercantile setting.(60)

Throughout the rest of the older runic period, there occur several inscriptions which give us some insight into the cultural context and role of the rune-carvers. Primary among these are the eight examples of *erilaR ~ irilaR* (KJ 16, 27, 29, 56, 69, 70, 71 and 128), which, regardless of the interpretation of the word (see VI.11), certainly seems to give a special name or title for those capable of carving runes. Also interesting is the identification of the rune-master with the possible religious office of *gudija* (ON *goði*) on the Nordhuglo stone (KJ 65, ca. 425). Numerous apparently functional bynames used by the rune-masters also point to a religious or magical sphere of activity (see VI.31). A few others indicate a martial context, i.e., KJ 53: *baijǫR*: 'warrior' (cf. Krause 1966: 119), KJ 55: *hagustaldaR þewaR*: 'the young warrior, retainer,' and possibly KJ 27: **(ga-)mūha*: 'one belonging to the same group → retainer' (Krause 1966: 66). Several inscriptions refer to familial relations, most typically either by identifying the carver with an ancestor (KJ 43, 69 [?], 71, 96 [?], 98), or indicating the relationship of the carver to the deceased, i.e., KJ 60: *magōR mīnas* ... 'my son's ...,' KJ 75: *magu mīniō* '(acc.) my son,' KJ 76 *swestaR mīnu* 'my sister.' And others reveal a specific service relationship in which the rune-master seems to have performed his craft for the sake of a non-relative, e.g., KJ 17a, 24, and 71. A most interesting relationship is demonstrated in the inscription on the tune stone (KJ 72, ca. 400), where the rune-master *WīwaR* 'worked' (the runes?) in memory of his lord (*wit(n)da-halaiba*) named *WōdurīdaR* (see Grønvik 1981). This appears to indicate a lord/retainer relationship in a possibly Odinic-religious context (see VI.31).

This small body of inscriptions demonstrates the social context of the rune-masters through 1) identification of carver with functional or 'official' titles, 2) indications of institutions or service relationships with others, and 3) stated familial relationships. The evidence seems to show the rune-master in a society dominated by the warrior-band or retinue, but one in which the family, especially in southwestern Norway) was not forgotten.

Decline of the Runic Tradition in South Germanic Culture

15. While the runic tradition in Scandinavia thrived into the 8th-

century, and subsequently underwent an indigenously engineered reformation, runic practice died out on the Continent at the end of the 7th-century except in Friesia. However, as Map V shows, the end of the tradition saw a flurry of activity. Runologically, this activity remained a part of the older fuþark tradition, but the contents of the inscriptions betray a social revolution. All of the inscriptions (see Opitz 1977) are on loose objects from between 500 and 700 CE, most of which seem to be dedicatory formulas (Arntz-Zeiss 1939: 468-69) and to be composed in a cultural framework dominated by Christianity. The formulas executed in these inscriptions also appear to have been determined by Latin models, and as such generally fall outside the scope of this work. What is interesting is that the demise of traditional Germanic forms seems to have been precipitated by the disruption of the culture which supported the older tradition by Christian-Antique traits (see Opitz 1977: 214-28; Düwel 1982: 84-86). Perhaps the best evidence of the depth of the revolution in 'rune-using' society is the clear indication of female rune-carvers (Op. 53/KJ 164: Weingarten I and the more recently discovered Neudingen/Baar, see Opitz 1981 and the ivory ring of Pforzen. All of these inscriptions are from the 6th-century) which throws open new possibilities for the interpretation of ambiguous South Germanic inscrioptions.(61) The presence of female rune-carvers throws open new possibilities for the interpretation of some ambiguous SGmc. inscriptions.(61) The epigraphical co-existence of the runes alongside the Latin script (see Düwel 1982, Oomen 1971: 404-07) and the persistence of the runic tradition in this context does appear to have some underlying significance of a possibly "magical" or operative nature. Therefore, certain individual inscriptions from this milieu are discussed in ch. VI.

*Wōðanaz

16. The god *Wōðanaz has often been directly connected with the *Männerbund* and related institutions (see Höfler 1934: 323ff., 1971: 146ff., de Vries 1956: I, 494ff.). Details concerning the cult of this god and his connections with the runic tradition are difficult to demonstrate before the Viking Age. The name indicates a primary link with numinous-operative matters: *wōð-an-az: 'master of inspiration or ecstasy,'(62) but the antiquity of this god, especially in the north, has sometimes been questioned. Although it is impossible to know for certain whether the cult of this god played a role in the formation of the runic tradition, we can be quite certain, for reasons mentioned below, that the cult was known during the first century CE.

It has been held that the cult of Wodan had its origins outside Scandinavia and that it migrated there from either the eastern Gothic realms(63) or from the Rhine region.(64) However, others would support the idea that *Wōðanaz represents a common Germanic god, and that although certain functions might shift, his basic function remains that of a deity presiding over numinous activities.(65) This latter view appears to be correct. It also seems that the runic tradition has caused some confusion in this matter. At one point, Wodan was thought to be so strongly connected to the runes that he and they were practically considered a unit *sine qua non*.(66) Therefore, since the runes may be comparatively late, and since they migrated from the south to the north in some way, these must also be characteristics of the development of Wodan and his cult. In this whole question, it seems most reasonable to conclude with Dumézil:

> If Odin was first and always the highest magician, we realize that the runes, however recent they may be, would have fallen under his sway. New and particularly effective implements for magic works, they would become by definition and without contest part of his domain. (1973: 34)

An attempt to trace the existence of a cult of *Wōðanaz in the first centuries of our era is almost totally dependent on Roman literary/historical and indigenous epigraphical and archeological sources. It is generally acknowledged that the *interpetatio Romana* for *Wōðanaz was Mercurius.(67) Tacitus (*Germania* ch. 9) reports: 'Of the gods they worship Mercury above all, (and) they consider it right to offer him human sacrifice on certain days. They appease (Hercules and) Mars with the ordinary animals.'(68) In his *Annali* (XIII, 57) we read that 'a battle, which went in favor of the Hermunduri, was very disastrous for the Chatti since in the event of victory both sides had consecrated (the enemy) to Mars and Mercury...'(69)

Other Roman accounts of certain Germanic sacrifices, e.g., when the Cimbri and Teutones offer all the Romans defeated in the battle of Arausio (105 BCE) by hanging them in trees (Ososius *Historia* V,16,5), or the description of the cult of the grove among the Semnones where human sacrifice is made (Tacitus *Germania* ch. 39), are strikingly similar to later Odinic practices (see de Vries 1957: II, 28ff.).

Votive stones in the Rhineland region (in both Germania inferior and superior) often bear the name MERCURIUS; however, we can only suppose that this refers to *Wōðanaz when it is within a Germanic linguistic or archeological context— which seems quite rare. From this problematic evidence it can only be inferred that the 'Germanic Mercury' was known and honored in a ruling capacity among the Germans along the Rhine within the Empire (see de Vries 1957: II, 29-32 and Betz 1957: 158ff.).

It is not until the late Migration Age and early medieval period (between ca. 600 and 1000) that we have substantial written evidence on the nature of the cult of Odin in Germania. Before that time, however, there is important and widespread evidence of a cult of *Wōðanaz with magical (some say "shamanistic") characteristics. This is found around the North and Baltic Seas and especially throughout the Danish archipelago in a form recorded in the iconography and runic epigraphy of the bracteates, which were manufactured between 450 and 550. (See Hauck 1969, 1970a, 1970b, 1972, 1980.) Besides this bracteate corpus (much of which includes runic material, see ch. VI), there is a more questionable Germanic sculpture motif which shows a warrior on horseback carrying a spear— an image often connected to Wodan.(70) The only direct runic evidence for Wodan comes from the Alemannic brooch of Nordendorf (KJ 151; Op. 33, from ca. 600-650). This, regardless of its interpretation,(71) is primary evidence for the existence of the cult of Wodan in South Germanic territory.

In the literary/historical accounts of the late Migration and early Middle Ages, Wodan is presented in various aspects. He may have been the divine ancestor of the Goths(72) and to the Angles and Saxons,(73) but to the Langobards he is rather a divine and heavenly patron of their victories.(74) There is also evidence of diverse kinds for the actual practice of a cult of Wodan. In the Anglo-Saxon *Vita S. Kentigerni* (from ca. 600) Woden is said to be the principal god of the Angles,(75) while Ionas Segusiensis, in the *Vita Columbani* (I, 27) from 642, relates a report of some Swabians in the Danube region who were holding a sacrifice to *Vodano, ... quem Mercurium, ut alii aiunt autumant* (see Clemen 1928: 32). A later source, the *Indiculus superstitionem et paganarium* (ca. 743) includes injunctions against 8. *de sacris Mercurii et Jovis* and 20. *de feriis quae faciunt Jovi vel Mercurio* (see Clemen 1928: 43). In these cases we are dealing with late *interpretationes Romanae* for Wodan and Þunar. These gods are directly mentioned in the Low German baptismal vow (from ca. 825-50). (See Braune-Ebbinghaus [1969: 39] and Foerste [1950: 90ff.]).

Outside Scandinavia, attestations of Wodan's magical activity are rare. Two prime examples are the *Merseburger Zauberspruch II* (see Braune-Ebbinghaus 1969: 89), in which Vuodan heals the hoof of a horse with an incantation,(76) and the later Old English "Nine Herbs Charm" (11th-century), in which Woden strikes a serpent with nine *wuldortānas* ("glory twigs") such that it flies into nine pieces (see Storms 1948: 189).

Two other possible, but questionable, references to Wōden occur in Old English literature; one in a gnomic verse which says *that Woden weorhte weos* ('Woden made sacred images'),(77) the other in a prose version of a dialog between Solomon and Saturn in which Solomon asks: *Saga mē hwā ǣrost bocstafas sette?*—to which Saturn replies: *Ič secge Mercurius sē gygand.*(78)

The Runic Reform
The Early Younger Period (ca 750-1000 CE)

17. Before any conclusions on the socio-cultic aspects of the older runic period can be drawn, we must look at the transformation of the traditions into the shorter, younger fuþąrk (Fig. III). This process can reveal much concerning socio-cultic organization at the dawn of the Viking Age, but we can only briefly touch on it here— with our view always turned toward the latter part of the Migration Age and the older runic period.

Runologically, the period between about 600 and 800 is curious. With the cessation of the bracteate school (around 550), the runic tradition seems to have all but disappeared from the Danish region (see Map V); however, it is from Denmark that the intense runic activity in the younger, "Danish" fuþąrk (Fig. III) following about 800 proceeds.(79) This situation is somewhat misleading since it seems that this form of the fuþąrk was actually developed in southern Norway and/or the Swedish districts of Blekinge and on Gotland—where runic activity remained strong during the last phase of the older period. It is most probably from these districts that a form of the younger fuþąrk came to Denmark where it fell upon very fertile ground.(80) That this process was actually a reform of a living tradition and not the revival of a dead one is not only shown by the continuation of extra-linguistic structural features (see below in section 19) but also by the existence of the Sparlösa stone (Vg. 119, ca. 780-800) which has typologically older runes next to younger ones (e.g., ᚳ:ᛏ or ᛘ:ᛦ), see Arntz (1944: 100ff.). Also, formal knowledge of the older fuþąrk apparently continued for some time to come, since the Rök stone (Ög. 136, ca. 850) contains cryptic uses of forms such as ᚱ,ᚷ, and ᚺ.

As far as the systems are concerned, the younger row represents a contraction of the older one—both stylistic simplification of some individual runic forms and the reduction of the total number of runes from 24 to 16. This reduction in the number of total available graphemes oddly enough occurred at a time when the Scandinavian dialects were undergoing changes which significantly increased the number of phonemes to be represented.(81) This runs counter to all norms of alphabetic historical development where graphemes are usually *added* to account for new phonemes.(82) Oddly, the question as to whether this reform took place for essentially linguistic or extra/non-linguistic (perhaps 'magical' or otherwise symbolic) reasons has most commonly been answered to the detriment of the latter.(83)

Social Developments

18. The time around 800 also saw great social change. From the late 8th-century to the mid-9th-century, Denmark was ruled on a virtually national scale by the powerful war-kings Godfred (died 810) and his son Horik. This rulership was apparently accomplished along a retinue-system model. After the death of Horik (ca. 853) the Danes turned to more individualistic viking raids, and it seems the Danes were always able to raise sizable and well-organized armies. In Norway, the situation was quite different. From there leaders or chieftains led small bands on numerous viking raids. The organization of these raids was probably on a rather loosely based warrior-band model. The Swedish region of Uppland and the island of Gotland were powerful and wealthy areas, and had been from around 600 CE. Uppland was a kingdom dominated by royal families, while Gotland was a "peasant republic" (Stenberger 1962: 157ff.)—both utilized a combination of selective raids and well-organized trade along the "eastern roads."

We are faced here with a wide variety of social organizations—but in each we see: 1) the growth of wealth and power in a certain leadership-class and 2) the increase of inter-regional communications between members of this 'class.' To some extent, conditions similar to those which existed during the period of runic origins in the first century seem to have again been prevalent in Scandinavia around 800. These conditions could have provided a suitable matrix for the re-invigoration of a continuous runic tradition, along with the growth in the status and role of that group within the society which had preserved a knowledge of the runes.

Danish inscriptions of the earliest Viking Age (ca. 750-900, DR period 2.1) give an insight into familial and institutional relationships present in the rune-using society. They show a definite family tradition. Six of the nineteen early Viking Age Danish inscriptions bear explicit formulas which indicate the stone was at least commissioned by a surviving family member;(84) however, three others bear similar formulas in which no familial relationship is stated (e.g., DR 221 Vordingborg st.—"Þjodver made (the monument) after Adils + *ephesion grammaton*").(85) There are also certain persons who have apparently official or functional titles. The *goði* ("heathen priest") *RólfR* is mentioned in DR 190 and 192, while the þulaR ("cultic speaker")(86) *GundfaldR* appears on the famous Snoldelev st. (DR 248). From the Glavendrup st. (DR 209, ca. 900) we get a tentative picture of complex interpersonal relationships in which the wife and sons of a dead thegn ("retainer," runic þiakn) *Alli* commissioned a stone which was executed by the rune-carver *Soti*, who refers to *Alli* as his lord (*dróttinn*, runic **trutin**).(87) The rune-carver or master possibly also appears on four other of these nineteen stones (see sect. 20 below).

The Younger Runic System

19. Characteristic structural features of the runic tradition (see sect. 11 above) are not lessened in the period of the younger fuþark and some of them are emphasized to a new degree. The reformed fuþark of 16 runes seems to have kept its sequence firmly intact, along with a tripartite division, coupled with an essentially pagan system of rune-names (with subsequently attested explanatory poetic texts, i.e., the "rune poems"). The style of individual runic characters was, however, subject to radical alterations even throughout the some 400 years of uncontested younger fuþark tradition before the introduction of a "runic alphabet" in the 13th-century (Fig. V).

Fuþark inscriptions become more numerous in the later periods (around 100 total have been found from the Viking and Middle Ages)(88)—most of these date from the 11th-century and many are in abbreviated form. The oldest of these is found on the Gørlev stone (DR 239, ca. 800, see Fig. III) which occurs in an overtly pagan and magical context. Later, a large number of fuþark formulas appear in churches. From ca. 800 to 1200 those fuþark inscriptions demonstrate a continuous internal structure, i.e., they retain 16 typologically similar runes in an established order with consistent phonetic values.

Another integral part of that structure, the tripartite division into *ættir*, which now consisted of three groups of 6/5/5 runes (see Fig. IV), was exploited for runic codes (see sect. 11 above) on a much wider scale (see Arntz 1935: 272-77, Düwel 2008: 182-188, Page 1999: 80-88). The Rök stone (Ög. 136, ca. 800-850) is a virtual catalog of these cryptographic techniques which includes five different methods of runic encoding. The numerous medieval finds from the Bryggen district of Bergen (see Liestøl 1963: 16-18) attest to the fact that this complex, extra-linguistic, underlying tradition was a vital part of the repertoire of rune-masters—both ancient and medieval.

Rune-names and poetic stanzas (or lists of poetic kennings) which correspond to them are considerably less problematic in the younger tradition than in the time of the older one. The two medieval Norse rune poems (see sect. 11 above) certainly reflect older material. The later Old Icelandic poem has been said to have the Old Norwegian poem as a prototype (see Dickins: 1915 7), however, it seems more probable that both are simply different expressions of a common underlying tradition (Düwel 1968: 105). Furthermore, it should be noted that this common basis remained the old form of the Viking Age 16-rune fuþark—despite the fact that these poems were composed at a time after the "runic alphabet" had been introduced and many aspects of older cultural structures had been dissolved.

As Fig. III shows, the several fuþarks in use from ca. 800 onward evidence wide stylistic, and sometimes typological, variations—from the "Danish" to the "Norwegian-Swedish" fuþarks to the most radically reduced version: the Hälsinga runes (11th-century). Yet the underlying phonemic correspondences and extra-linguistic structural features (order and total number: 16) held the tradition intact. As a matter of fact, it seems that these characteristics provided the primary cohesion for the whole system.

From this evidence we can see that the idea that the runes first fell into total disuse and that the younger fuþark is a purely new creation (Bæksted 1952: 140ff.) is quite fantastic—and untenable. Besides, in a society of radically restricted literacy, as 8th- to 9th-century Scandinavia represented, complex traditions of this kind would have had to be kept alive by oral means. Since no written, non-personal, sources would have been available, the only possible repository for the complex features of the tradition (especially the extra-linguistic ones) would have been *living persons*. The vigor of precisely these features would suggest that the socio-cultic network of men with runic knowledge not only survived, but flourished in the Viking Age.

Social Context

20. The only possible institution which could have provided a matrix for the runic tradition was the retinue or warrior-band (see 13. above). There remains some controversy as the exact nature of 9th-century military associations in Scandinavia.(89) It would seem that the Nordic societies contained a latent potential for two types of institutions: 1) the *warrior-band* (formed on a non-standing basis with egalitarian and intra-clanic organizational characteristics), and 2) the *retinue* (a standing institution, in war- and peace-time, maintained in the vicinity of a permanent leader, and formalized by mutual trust and obligations between that leader and his men).(90) As socio-economic factors in a given society dictated, one or the other type of institution might be formed to meet the need of the situation.

Archeological and art-historical evidence would seem to suggest that there was continued a growing inter-Germanic cultural exchange among increasingly wealthy groups (especially among the England-Denmark-Uppland/Gotand sea-lanes).(91) Gotlandic pictorial stones of the 8th-9th centuries often seem to represent the war-leader surrounded by his band.(92) The evidence of 9th-century runic inscriptions (see sect. 18. above) and early skaldic poetry also tend to portray a close-knit elite society. In any case, there appears to have been at least three specialized functions within the typical *drótt* or *líð*: 1) leader, 2) skald, and 3) warrior.(93) It is most likely that the rune-carvers would be classified in the second group. Although these underlying functions seem to have been present from the beginning, we only get positive evidence for the specialization of individuals in these roles in historical times.

The earliest Viking Age runic inscriptions show the continued importance and apparent exclusivity of runic knowledge. Several 9th-century Danish stones bear certain rune-master formulas—DR 190 Helnæs st.: **auaiR faþi**: 'Afer colored (the runes).' DR 209 Glavendrup st.: ... **in suti. raist. runaR þasi . . .** : 'but Soti carved these runes...,' and DR 230 Tryggevælde st.: **iak sata ru[na](r) ri[t] kuni armutR . . .** : 'I set the runes rightly. Gunni ArmundR . . .' Two others probably have similar formulas which Moltke-Jacobsen reconstructed—DR 188 Ørbæk st.: **[k]uþ(u)friþR : (r)a[i]st** or **(ri)st: aft: þiaubur(k)**: 'Godfred carved (the runes) after (= in memory of) Thjudborg,' and DR 192 Flemløse st. I which probably ended with the same formula as DR 190—'Afer colored.' The Rök st. also tells us that: **uarin faþi**: 'Warin colored (the runes).'(94) while the Sparlösa st. (Vg. 119, ca. 800) informs us that **ukraþ runaR þaR rAki-ukutu iu þar suaþ Aliriku lubu fAþi**: 'and read the runes there, those which stem from the gods, which Alrik [lubu] thus colored there.'

This evidence viewed in context suggests that runic activity continued among an elite stratum of society and that the rune-masters were members of this stratum. The position of *Soti* (in Gavendrup) as the thegn of *Alli* and the apparent service rendered by *Afer* to the family of *RōlfR* (DR 190 and 192) show the close relationship between the rune-masters and those whom they served. But we know nothing further about his position in this culture. By the 11th-12th centuries (especially in Sweden), the mass of evidence enables us to determine that there were indeed "schools" of famous rune-masters.(95) Despite the proliferation of runic evidence in the later period, the formulas are such that little more can be ascertained as to the relationship between the rune-master and the rest of society.

As far as the function of the rune-master in this early Viking Age society is concerned, it is certain that it was not exclusive, but manifold. From the few 9th-century inscriptions, we could conclude that the rune-masters were also men-in-arms, and the magico-religious contents of the inscriptions demonstrate their interests in this field.

Óðinn

21. From the preponderance of literary evidence it is clear that the god Óðinn must have held a special place in the religious outlook of the rune-masters in the Viking Age—at least in western Scandinavia (see V.5). Although this is probably a continuation of an older association as seen above, the Viking Age evidence gives us new material with which to deal—and new problems. It is generally thought that the Odinic cult is an aristocratic one—mainly practiced by royal warrior societies—and that magico-poetic traditions are an integral part of the cultus.(96) The runic evidence of the 9th-century contains several direct religious references, but many of them refer to gods other than Óðinn (e.g., Vg. 119 Sparlösa—with possible references to Freyr and Ullr,(97) and DR 209 Glavendrup, DR 110 Virring, and DR 220 SønderKirkeby—all of which contain some form of the formula *Þōr vīgi þasi rūnaR!*: 'Thor consecrate these runes!'), cf. Marold (1977). However, it is still possible to assume that these stones were executed by *Óðinsmenn* since although the historical Odinic cult seems to have been exclusive from a sociological perspective, it appears to have been equally all-inclusive from a theological viewpoint.(98)

Medieval Period
(After 1150)

22. As early as the 10th-century (ca. 980-1000) the 16-rune fuþark system developed isolated special forms (so-called pointed- or dotted-runes, *stungar runar*) in Denmark(99) (i.e., ᚽ /ü/, ᛔ /g/, ᛂ /e/—cf. Arntz 1944: 108). In many cases these accounted for phonemes lost during the transition from the 24- to the 16-rune fuþark. Despite this, the structure of the 16-rune row was not compromised at that time. However, by 1200 the fuþark-system was being disrupted by the alphabetic, Latin one (see Wimmer 1887: 252ff.). The oldest attestation of this new tradition is on the church bell of Saleby (ca. 1228; see Fig. V), cf. V. Friesen (1933: 232). As similar runic reforms came to Iceland in the 13th-century, an attempt was made to preserve the integrity of the unique runic system—an attempt which ultimately failed.(100) It is clear that the cultural stream concurrent with the influx of Christianity, and the resultant disruption in the indigenous culture

and social organization, effectively dissolved the complex runic system at its most sophisticated levels. This is to be expected, since the guardians of the tradition were to be found in archaic native institutions of religion and the retinue—which were the most drastically affected by the initial Christian cultural wave. It is therefore remarkable that the use of runic forms continued in a wide variety of contexts—sacred and profane—for many centuries to come in Scandinavia.(101) It should be noted that although an alphabetic reform took place during the Middle Ages, the use of fuþark inscriptions, i.e., inscriptions in which the fuþark order was represented, persisted throughout the age.

The Middle Ages saw a great proliferation in the types of inscriptions commonly executed. It is not until this period that we have any evidence of casual interpersonal communications ("runic correspondence"), or extensive use of runes for commercial purposes, i.e., owners' labels (*merkelappar*) or bills of sale. Such inscriptions are often found among the Bergen finds (cf. Listøl 1963). However, magic is also well represented here as well. It is significant that in this time magical inscriptions are often executed in runes with Latin texts (Listøl 1963: 19ff.). It seems that once the Christian religion was established in certain quarters of society, at least some of its clerical representatives turned to the use of runes for magical purposes (cf. Moltke 1938a: 116ff.). In this medieval period there were two streams of apparent magico-runic practice: 1) the clerical (characterized by the use of Latin texts and Christian or originally Mediterranean magical formulas)(102) and 2) the secular (distinguished by archaic runic formulas and references to heathen deities).(103) From a sociological viewpoint, the new runic tradition represents a pluralization—what had formerly only been available to an elite, official and established group now became the possession of a wide spectrum of social levels. But the uniquely runic, and rather sophisticated levels of the tradition appear to have been lost in the process as institutional repositories of that tradition were compromised or destroyed.

Conclusion

23. Throughout the history of runic practice it seems that members of an elite, militaristic, usually cultic and inter- or extra-tribal—but apparently unofficial—network conserved the tradition. The degree to which this tradition was an agent of social change is unclear. It seems to have been a conservative force in the restricted society in which it was intimately known. Yet as a possible solidifying factor, it could have also indirectly affected society in general. Although the tradition appears to have been periodically forced by conditions to conform to changing social realities, the

continuity of technical features reflect an internal integrity within the social institutions, which supported that tradition. Typically, the niveau interested in such arcane matters would most likely see the tradition as having an operative function. As far as the role of the Odinic religion is concerned, we may conservatively assume that only in Scandinavia did the magical aspects of this cult become integrally linked with the runic tradition. Further investigations of archeological and art-historical data, as well as a complete typological survey of all runic material (especially that of the various "stave types") must be completed before these conclusions can be extended.

Notes for Chapter IV

1. Numbering not in original. Nr. 5 refers to the consistency in the style or shape of the individual runic graphs, e.g., that the general shape ᚠ would represent the phoneme /f/. The "direction of writing" (6) refers to the dextroverse/levoverse alternations—sometimes called "boustrophedon."

2. For example, Krause (1943a: 3ff.; 1948/50: 33-35) pursued the idea that runic forms without clear models in Mediterranean alphabets might be reflections of pre-runic ideographs. Although this aspect was not energetically developed in his later work, this possibility is still suggested (1970: 43) for the *jēra- and *ingwaz runes.

3. This line of reserch was most enthusiastically pursued by Nordén in a series called *Från Kivik till Eggjum* (1934a, 1934b, 1936) and in a separate report (1941).

4. Cf. Much (1967: 189ff.). *Auspicia sortesque ut qui maxime observant: sortium consuetudo simplex. Virgam frugiferae arbori decisam in surculos amputant eosque notis quibusdam discretos super candidam vestem temere ac fortuito spargunt. Mox, si publice consultetur, sacerdos civitatis, sin privatim, ipse pater familiae, precatus deos caelumque suspiciens ter singulos tollit, sublatos secundum impressam ante notam interpretatur. . .:* 'They have the highest regard for divination and casting of lots: the custom of lost casting is uniform. From a nut- (or fruit-) bearing tree a twig is cut which they divide into strips; these are marked with certain signs and they throw them at random onto a white cloth. Then, if it is a public consultation, the priest of state, or if it is a private one, the father of the family himself, after prayers of the gods and while looking up to the sky, picks up three strips (one at a time) and interprets them according to the signs cut on them. . .'

5. The brooch is positively dated by Gebühr *"vor der Mitte des ersten Jahrhunderts nach Christus"* (Düwel-Gebühr 1981: 167) and is tentatively read by Düwel as a fem. i-stem **hiwi**: *Hīwi*—'for Hiwi (mistress of the household),' cf. Düwel 1981d: 12) and Düwel-Gebühr (1981b: 171ff.), but also the non-runic reading by Odenstedt (1983) as a dat. or gen. fem. PN IDIN < *Idda*.

6. It is interesting to note that runic inscriptions are more often juxtaposed to pictographic material following the 5th-century. Two inscriptions, KJ 53: Kårstad rock-wall, and KJ 54 Himmelstalund rock-slab, are actually executed within the context of older Bronze Age carvings, while other inscriptions (e.g., KJ 99: Mjöbro, 100 Krogsta, 101 Eggjum, and 102 Roes) and all the runic bracteates (ca. 450-550 CE) juxtapose an inscription to a pictorial representation.

7. This is basically analogical to the history of the Greek script, cf. Krause and Düwel (1968: 95).

8. Düwel (1981d:13; 1981b: 173) speculates on the possibility that the Meldorf runes are "pre-runic" and perhaps related to the *notae* of Tacitus. Cf. also Odenstedt (1983).

9. Certain elements of the runic system (i.e., the set number of 24 characters, their division into three groups of eight, and the practice of boustrophedon) are possible examples of such secondary influence. But if they are indeed borrowings from Greek tradition this would indicate an extremely well-developed institutional framework capable of rapid and widespread adaptations of complex and technical features from an exotic source.

10. For a general description of the Italic scripts, see Jensen (1958: 478ff.) and Whatmough (1933: II, 501ff.). The earliest Italic script, the proto-Tyrrhenic, was probably

developed during the 8th-7th centuries BCE under the influence of the Greek alphabet. By the 1st century BCE the later Etruscan and Alpine systems has been supplanted by the Latin script.

11. Tables of correspondences between runic and Italic forms are presented by Elliott (1989: 8) and Jensen (1958: 486), cf. also Marstrander (1968: 99). A more recent study by Bonfante (1981) would support a pre-200 origin of the runes based on the Etruscan alphabet. She supports this theory with archeological data which indicates an archaic Etruscan-Germanic connection, and with the etymology of Germanic *erz*: 'metal, bronze' < *erissi*, *Aresso*—an Etruscan metallurgical center especially in the 5th-4th centuries BCE (p. 127).

12. Cf. Moltke (1981a: 7) for a systematic treatment of these correspondences. Moltke emphasizes the aspect of originality in the genesis of the runes, and that the tradition was only "freely molded" on the Latin alphabet—with a variety of indigenous modifications and innovations. This aspect clearly distinguishes Moltke's theory from that of previous adherents of the "Latin Theory."

13. The main problem with this idea is that there are no extant examples of runic epigraphy which would indicate the use of runes for such purposes, and besides such records would probably be unnecessary in the type of trade conducted by the early Germanic peoples—it would have been the Roman tradesmen who would have kept records of this kind (in their own Roman script).

14. It has been noted by Höfler (1970: 124ff.) that certain graphic forms, most conspicuously ⟨ ⟩ (*kēnaz*), ⟨ ⟩ (*jēra-n*), ⟨ ⟩ (*sowilō*), and ⟨ ⟩ (*ingwaz*) were subject to radical alterations in the older period—while many other graphs remained typologically stable throughout runic history.

15. These are often recorded in alphabetic lists found in Britain and on the Continent (e.g., those attributed to Hrabanus Maurus), all of which were usually made under the influence of the Anglo-Saxon tradition. The four rune poems, the *Abecedarium Nordmannicum* (St. Gall MS 878, 9th-century), the Old English Rune Poem (10th-century), the ONorw. Rune Rhyme (13th-century) and the OIce. Rune Poem (15th-century), also give a *generally* consistent form of the tradition.

16. The OE tradition contains some names which appear to have been altered due to a combination of sound changes and possible editing by Christian clerics (see V.14.).

17. This relationship need not always be an instutionalized one, and could also be understood as a natural mode of transmission of cultural information from one person to another.

18. Höfler (1970, 1971) certainly suggests this, and such a supposition seems to be borne out by the complex runic record.

19. Inter-tribal networks may be established on the level of material culture through an examination of grave goods and other archeological data. This is valuable as supporting evidence, but obviously cannot alone suffice to trace the development of intellectual traditions.

20. *DBG* (ca. 52 BCE) IV, 1-15; VI, 21-28.

21. *Germ.* (98 CE), as well as the *Hist.* and *Annali*.

22. For a discussion of this concept, see Buchholz (1968: 8ff. and 1971).

23. Ellis Davidson (1973: 38-39) astutely surmises that the Finns so often mentioned in shamanistic contexts in Icelandic sources are most probably a Finno-Ugric group, e.g.,

the Biarmians, who lived east of the Baltic. The speculation is chiefly backed up by the lack of the drum (central to Lappish shamanism) in Germanic *seiðr* (usually connected to shamanism, cf. Ström 1935). Also, the prevalence of the horse in Germanic magical practice would be another feature presumably evident in the shamanism of the horse-riding Finno-Ugric steppe-culture (cf. Eliade 1964: 127; 151; 173ff.; 246ff.).

24. It has been suggested that the runes are derived from ogham (Marstrander 1928) or from an ogham-like proto-alphabet (Hammerström 1929) and to the contrary, that the runes were a determining factor in the development of ogham (Artz 1935a: 277ff., 1935b). Since runes and ogham represent two different kinds of script, it is impossible to determine any genetic relationship. Historical data would suggest that the runes are substantially older than ogham, as the oldest ogham inscriptions date from the 4th-century CE. See McManus (1991: 9-11).

25. The general case seems to have been that non-Germanic Roman merchants traveled deep into Germania in order to conduct trade, although goods were also transferred within Germania by other means as well, see Eggers (1951: 72-77), Mildenberger (1977: 58-62).

26. While serving with the Romans, Germanic soldiers were sent to rather exotic locations, e.g., as early as 55 BCE Caesar indicates the presence of *Germani* in Syria and Egypt, cf. Grimm (1969: 110-111). It may be presumed that a number of such men eventually returned to their homeland.

27. Höfler (1970: 111ff.) injects the highly controversial bronze helmets of Negau A and B (3rd-1st century BCE?) into his argument. Both helmets bear inscriptions in North-Italic script—one (B) records a levoverse Germanic text HARIGASTI TEIVA, perhaps to be translated 'to the god Harigast (= Wodan),' (cf. De Tollenaere 1967 for a range of possibilities)—while on the other (A) is inscribed an obscure levoverse sequence:

which Höfler takes to be an attestation of the term *erul*-, i.e., C. ERUL = C(*enturio*) Erul(*i*). The alternate dating of these inscriptions to the first decade CE is historically attractive (time of the Pannonian revolt), and since the North-Italic scripts seem to have been in use until the end of the first two decades CE, this is quite plausible.

28. As used here, the term "network" need signify nothing more than a geographically dispersed number of individuals known to one another either personally or by some other link (familial, religious, political, etc.) who are in the habit of orally sharing intellectual material among themselves in the course of their travels.

29. Caesar (*DBG* VI,12) reports that the Germans *neque druides habent*. However, it seems likely that Caesar's statements on the religion of the German are colored by his constant attempt to contrast the culture of the Gauls with that of the peoples east of the Rhine. Tacitus, only 150 years later, describes several religious offices carried out by Germans, (e.g., divination by the *pater familiae* or the *sacerdos civitatis*, *Germ*. ch. 10, the priest of the Nerthus cult, Germ. ch. 40, and the legislative function *Germ*. chs. 7 and 11). Descriptions of female priestesses or seeresses from this period (see Tacitus *Germ*. ch. 8, *Hist*. IV, 61, 65; V, 24) and Strabo's report *Geogr*. VII,1, 4.292) on the Chatti priest Libes also tend to indicate that Caesar is less than reliable in his matter. A survey of the sparse

early evidence for a Germanic priesthood shows that it is most likely that offices such as sacrificial priest/augur, poet, and cultic orator (cf. ON þulr, OE þyle) were present for an early stage (see de Vries 1960: 89-90). It could also be assumed that some of these persons (especially the poets) enjoyed rights of free passage between tribal or clanic groups, as did the Celtic bards (see note 50 below).

30. Schwarz (1956: 104-07) provides a brief history of the apparent movements of this *merwürdiges Volk*, as Schwarz calls them, on the Continent.

31. Cf. Höfler (1970 and 1971) for arguments for defining the Eruli as a "warrior-band" rather than as a "tribe." Most evidence for the cultic features of this society is circumstantial. However, accounts of the Euli given by Procopius and other ancient writers (cf. Summary provided by Chadwick 1899: 32ff.) clearly demonstrate certain socio-cultic characteristics, e.g., conservative preservation of their heathen faith (Procopius *de bello Goth.* II,14), a berserkr-like mode of fighting without protective armor (Jordanes *Getica* chs. 23; 50; Paulus Diaconus *Hist. Langobardi* I,20 and Procopius Persian War II,25), and the practices of sacrificing the old and of *sutee* (Procopius *de bello Goth.* II,14).

32. A few inscriptions are discovered every year; some of them have been very significant, e.g., the Meldorf brooch (Düwel-Gebühr 1981), the Neudingen/Baar loom fragment (Opitz 1981: 29ff.), the Illerup spear-heads (Moltke-Stoklund 1981; Düwel 1983: 124) or the foot stool of Wremen but most are difficult to interpret either due to the terseness or to the poor condition of the inscription.

33. The dating system used here is generally that suggested by Krause and Jankuhn (1966). Of course, these dates can only be approximate, and perhaps their chief value is their placement of the data in a relative chronology, cf. also Roth (1981) on the systematic dating of inscriptions from southern Germany.

34. A certain exception might be the case of the East Germanic spear-heads which were perhaps fashioned in the Scandinavian or Baltic homelands and deposited during migratory expeditions—but nevertheless they indicate the presence of rune-using societies in those eastern regions.

35. It is tempting to speculate that social upheavals in the southern regions contributed to disruptions in Scandinavia and that only in certain stable, perhaps culturally conservative, locations or ethnic groupings was the delicate tradition able to be maintained.

36. These will be treated in ch. VI. Besides these clear epigraphical sources, there are also two bracteates from the same stamp from Jutland (Lindkær/Overhornbæk III, KJ 4). These appear to be botched copies of the fuþark. Later Old English manuscript attestations (see Derolez 1954: 1ff.) show that the tradition was entrenched as late as the 12th-century.

37. According to 17th-century Icelandic sources, these divisions were called *ættir* (sg. *ætt*). 'family, *genus*.' However, it has also been suggested that the term originally referred to "an eight" (i.e., a division of eight runes in the older row). If this is the case, it would mean that an archaic *terminus technicus* continued in use—preserved orally—for some 800 years after the reduction of the fuþark to rows of 6/5/5. It may also be significant for possible cosmological associations that the eight-fold division of the heavens are also called *ættir* in Icelandic (Cleasby-Vigfusson 1957: 760 and de Vries 1961a: 682), see also ch. II, note 55.

38. Page's (1999: 83) assertion that the "cryptographical system is obviously a secondary development, something of an antiquary's toy" is probably true in the instance he is discussing—but it would seem that the system had some use antedating the later

antiquarian manuscript traditions, which although perhaps secondary was nonetheless archaic. Certainly most surviving material comes from post-Christian traditions, either Old English manuscript usages or medieval Scandinavian practices (see Derolez 1954: 89ff. and Liestøl 1963: 16ff.). However, numerous examples do indicate a more operative function, e.g., the cryptic runes on the Rök st. (Ög. 136, ca. 850), the description of the use of "secret runes" (ON *launstafir*) in *Egils saga* (ch. 72), and perhaps the Körlin ring (KJ 46, ca. 550-600) with the sign ᛌ which could be at once a bind-rune ᚨᛚ and a cryptographic representation of u = 2:1—so that the whole reads *alu* (see ch. VI.34).

39. The most systematic later evidence is provided by the Norwegian and Icelandic rune poems, and by the *Abecedarium Nordmanicum* (see below in this section)—which reflects the Nordic and on the OE tradition.

40. Blomfield (1942: 209ff.) maintains that the peculiar, apparently Gothic, letter names contained in the 9th-century Salzburg-Vienna Codex 795 fol. 20 have their origins in the OE manuscript tradition and do not represent a survival of the possible 4th-century Gothic rune-names, cf. also Krause (1968). However, if she is correct this too could be considered as East Germanic evidence for the archaism of the rune-names.

41. The time of the Cotton MS Otho BX in which the poem was discovered. This MS was destroyed in the Cottonian fire of 1731, but it has been previously transcribed and printed in Hickes' *Thesaurus* (1705).

42. Of the 16 stanzas in each of the ONorw. And OIce. Rune poems, then (stanzas 1, 2, 5, 6, 7, 8, 10, 12, 13 and 14) indicate common textual or traditional archetypes through similar or identical formulas or lexical items. This is most probably due to an older tradition common to both (cf. Düwel 1983: 105). It is also possible that there was an original, common Germanic poem, but it cannot be reconstructed with any certainty based on extant texts (cf. Halsall 1981: 33-38).

43. This process had begun as early as 1100 in Iceland where Ári inn fróði and Þoroddur rúnameistari created an expanded "fuþorkh" to compete with the Latin script, while in Norway during the reign of Valdemar (1202-41) a true runic *alphabet* was formulated.

44. Düwel (1981d: 13) mentions the slight possibility that the Meldorf brooch (ca. 50 CE) represents a proto-runic stage in which phonetic values had not yet been fixed.

45. As contained in the author's private notes made in the Fall of 1981. There is also a system referred to by Höfler (1970: 125ff *et passim*) constructed by H. Mittermann.

46. The term "men's society" (*Männerbund*) seems most neutral with regard to possible connections with the cultic league. However, in the usual martial sense, the "warrior-band" or *comitatus* are perhaps sometimes to be preferred. The old Germanic *Männerbünde* are most thoroughly studied by Höfler (1935) and Weiser (1927) in two informative but highly controversial works. For criticism of these views, cf. Baetke (1964) and von See (1972).

47. Old but still fundamental works on the institution of the *Männerbund* in archaic societies are provided by Schurtz (1902) for traditional societies around the world, and by Wikander (1938) for Indo-Iranian society.

48. Cf. The critical study by Kuhn (1956) and the indispensable contribution by Lindow (1975: 19-21).

49. In Nordic society it seems common that youths has a close relationship with the maternal uncles and that the young men were often trained by them or received secret

teachings from them, cf. Tacitus *Germ.* 20, *VS* ch. 16, Grípisspá, Háv. 140.1-3. With respect to the institution of fosterage, it seems likely that it was known in early Germanic times, and to some extent it may have functioned together with the exchange of hostages. It appears unlikely that these institutions could have had much effect on the original *dissemination* of the runic tradition. This view is due to the fact that the fuþark spread so quickly—and the slow and intrinsically conservative educational process implicit in the fosterage model could not account for it fully, and due to the circumstance that children were often fostered to persons of lower social prestige than the father (cf. Neckel 1944: 191-92 and Barlau 1975: 134ff.). However, these institutions may have played an important role in the *maintenance* of the tradition in later times.

50. The Celts, for example, had laws which gave the wandering intelligentsia (OIr. *aes dana*) safe passage between often hostile tribal regions, cf. Chadwick (1970: 112-13).

51. This is a general assumption use by Krause (most recently 1970: 35). In the cases of the Meldorf brooch and even the Øvre-Stabu spear-head (KJ 31) we could be dealing with anomalous survivals.

52. The 200 years between ca. 100 BCE and 100 CE are principally documented by Julius Caesar (*DBG* I, 30-54; IV 1-15; VI, 21-44), Strabo (*Geographikon* VII, 1-3) Cornelius Tacitus (*Germ., Annali, Hist., passim*), with shorter, but nevertheless important passages in the works of Valleius Paterculus (*Hist. Romanae* II, *passim*) Iulius Frontius (*Strategematon, passim*), Suetonius Tranquillus (*De vita caesarum, passim*). Many of these passages are conveniently collected by Woyte (1916), Clemen (1928), and translated into English by Chisholm (2002).

53. For a general discussion of these groupings, see Hachmann (1971: 86ff.) and Hachmann-Kossak-Kuhn (1962: 53ff.), and for the socio-historical functioning of these cultic leagues, see Wenskus (1961: 246ff.).

54. Cf. De Vries (1957: II, 32-34), who identifies the *regnator omnium deus* with *Wōðanaz—although the cult has also been connected with *Tiwaz (cf. e.g., Helm 1946: 26-34). The identification with *Tiwaz essentially issues from the historicist notion that at this early stage the sky-god was still "all-powerful" (cf. Tacitus *Hist.* IV, 64), and perhaps also that *Tiwaz-Mars received at least some form of human sacrifice (see e.g., Tacitus *Annali* XIII, 57; Jordanes *Getica* V, 41). However, more specific evidence again seems to point to an identification with *Wōðanaz. The designation *regnator omnium deus* seems too vague, while the reception of human sacrifice would narrow the choice to either *Wōðanaz or *Tiwaz (the ritual form in question would seem again to favor *Wōðanaz). Two other elements: 1) the *binding* of worshippers, and 2) the way in which the cult of the god serves to form an inter-tribal synthesis, also seem to point more to *Wōðanaz than to *Tiwaz.

55. Marstrander (1928) emphasizes the role of the Swabian culture as the medium for the spread of a central European Celto-Roman culture—of which the development of the runes was a part. According to him: *Runeskriften er opstaat hos sveberne, høist sandsynlig i Marobodvus rike blandt kvader og markomanner, og spredte sig herfra til goter og nordgermaner* (p. 97). Krause (1970: 44) seems to see these Marcomanni as possible transmitters of runic knowledge to the North.

56. Cf. KJ 20, 21, 24, 31 and the recently found Meldorf brooch (see Düwel-Gebühr 1981) and the Illerup finds (see Düwel 1981a: 138-39; 1981b: 81; Ilkjær-Lønstrup 1977a and 1977b; and Moltke-Stoklund 1981).

57. See ch. VI for a more complete description of these terms.

58. From this early corpus (ca. 200 and earlier), over fifty percent are found on weapons, while for the entire older tradition (pre-800, including the OE inscriptions), this category represents about seven percent.

59. Caesar's report (DBG VI, 21,1) that the Germans *neque druides habent* seems to be a self-serving negative comparison to the well-organized professional judiciary/priest class present among the Gauls (see note 29, above). Jordanes (*Getica* V, 40-41; X, 65; XI, 71-73) reports on a strong priest class developed under direct Roman influence. Although details of his account are suspect, it seems plausible that, given the nature of East Germanic societies, a strong sacerdotal function could be present. It is my guess that for most Germanic tribes, the sacerdotal function was never monopolized by a professional class, but nevertheless has always been present at least in the personals of the *matres* and *patres familiae*. The most notable exception to this would be the apparently official seeresses active in Germanic society at least from the first century CE into the Viking Age.

60. Cf. most recently Moltke (1976a: 57-58; 1981a: 4ff.).

61. Among runologists, the general tendency has been to interpret isolated masc. PNs on women's objects as the benefactor or donor of the object, or as the rune-carver, and isolated fem. PNs as perhaps indicating the benefactor or owner (cf. Arntz-Zeiss 1939: 332-33). But the idea that there were female rune-carvers has been generally, if not emphatically, rejected (cf. Bruder 1974: 15ff.). See also ch. VI.32.

62. Cf. de Vries (1961a: 416), Polomé (1969: 268), and Höfler (1971: 147; 1973b: 133ff.). The possible connection between PGmc. *wōð- and *wind- seems unlikely (PIE *wāt- ~ *wēt- > PGmc. *wōð- : PIE *we-nt- > PGmc. *wind-). *Wōð- seems to belong primarily to the psychic realm with cognates in other IE languages (e.g., Lat. *vātēs*: 'seer,' OIr. *fáith*: 'prophet,' MWel. *gwawd*: 'panegyric poem') which point in this direction. The nasal suffix *(a)n- indicates 'one who has power over something, or manages it in an official capacity.'

63. Cf. Pedersen (1876) also Salin (1903: 133ff.). This view was later supported by the theories of von Friesen who saw a Gothic origin for the runes (see 4.).

64. Cf. Mogk (1925: 258ff.), Helm (1913: I, 259ff.; 1946; 1953: II/1, 251ff.) and Schröder (1929: 45ff.).

65. Cf. Neckel (1925: 49, 1926: 139ff.), Dumézil (1973: 31ff.), and Polomé (1970: 59ff,; 1974: 60ff.).

66. This problem is discussed by Dumézil (1973: 34). Such thinking resulted in the illogical conclusion that Wodan must be a foreign god, since as a *schreibender Gott* he would have to have had his origin among a literate people (!), cf. Schröder (1929: 48).

67. This can be inferred from the earliest historical sources of Tacitus (*Germ.* 9, *Hist.* 13, 57) and Orosius (*Hist.* V, 16, 5), and is made more clear by the apparent translation, or *interpretatio Germanica*, of the late Roman week-day name *Mercurii dies* (cf. Strutynski 1975: 364ff., who sees the various week-day name equations as having taken place in the Roman Age for mercantile reasons, p. 372). Migration Age and medieval sources clearly reflect these associations, cf. the phrase *Vodano, quem Mercurium . . . autumant* from Ionas Seguiensis *Vita Columbani* I, 27 (ca. 642 CE).

68. Cf. Much (1967: 171ff). *Deorum maxime Mercurium colunt, cui certis diebus humanis quoque hostiis litare fas habent. (Herculem et) Martem concessis animalibus placant.*

69. Cf. Clemen (1928: 12) *sed bellum Hermunduris prosperum, Chattis existiosius fuit, quia victores diversam aciem Marti ac Mercurio sacravere, quo voto qui viri, cuncta viva occidioni dantur.*

70. Images of this type are known from at least the 6th cent. and apparently divine figures with a spear date from as early as the Bronze Age rock carvings (see de Vries 1957: II, 36-37; 44-46). Gotlandic sculpture (especially 9th-11th cent.) portrays more explicitly Odinic images in similar contexts (cf. S. Lindqvist 1941: I, 95ff., *et passim*). This complex appears to be old iconographical material, as it seems to have influenced the depiction of Mithras at the Mithraeum at Dieburg (see Behn 1966: 46ff.).

71. The inscription is a definite indication of heathen elements in 7th cent. Alemannic culture; however, it may be interpreted as invocatory (see Arntz 1939: 277-300; 462) or as apotropaic (see Düwel 1982: 85-86).

72. Cf. Jordanes (*Getica* XIV, 79, ca. 550), who sets a certain Gapt—read by most scholars, after Wessén (1924: 18ff.) as Gaut, cf. ON Gautr ~ Gauti and Gautatýr as *Óðinsheiti* (Falk 1924: 11-12) and OE Geat— at the head of the Ostrogothic royal line. For a study of the Getae/Geatas in ethnography, see Leake (1967). On the linguistic derivation of Gapt from Gaut, see Birkhan (1965).

73. Of the eight Anglo-Saxon royal genealogies, seven record Wōden as the ultimate ancestor (cf. Grimm 1888: IV, 1709-36; Philipson 1929: 152; and also Chaney 1970: 29ff.). Bede (*Hist. Eccl.* I, 15) is the earliest reporter of this tradition (ca. 731).

74. Cf. the *Origo Gentis Langobardorum* I (ca. 670-700) and Paulus Diaconus *Hist.* I, 8 (ca. 787) where the legend of how Gōdan ~ Wōdan was tricked into granting victory, and a new name, to the Winnili— who thus became the Langobardi ("Long-beards") although his allegiance belonged to the Wandali.

75. *Acta Sanctorum* I, 820.

76. This verse: *ben zi bena / bluot zi bluoda // lid zi geliden / sose gelimida sin* is extremely archaic (see Kuhn 1864: 49-63 and Murdoch 1983: 47-48), and this charm's mythic context may also be common to a group of Migration Age bracteates (see Hauck 1970b; 1977).

77. From the Exeter MS, cf. Grein-Wülcker 1881: 348. *Wēos* OE *weoh* (*wīh ~ wīg*): 'idol'— but originally 'sacred object, or divinity (?).'

78. Text from Cottom Vitellius A XV, cf. Thorpe 1868: 115. The text goes back to a Latin original, so the *interpretatio Romana* becomes more understandable. Although we can not be sure that Wōden is intended, the fact that this Roman deity is inserted among Judeo-Christian mythological figures would seem to indicate that it is a native interpolation.

79. Chiefly in the form of barrow- and memorial-stones, cf. DR. 9, 17, 144, 188, 189, 190, 193, 211, 221, 239, 248, 250, 323, 333, 356.

80. It is generally held that there were two slightly different forms of the younger fuþark: 1) the Danish (or Common Norse), and 2) the Swedish-Norwegian, and that the latter developed from the former (cf. Arntz 1944: 100ff.).

81. A convenient survey of this situation is offered by Haugen (1976: 142-150).

82. This, of course, did not take place in the Anglo-Friesian runic reform, where at least five new runes were simply appended to the 24-rune system, see Elliott (1989: 42ff. and Page 1999: 38ff.).

83. e.g., Quak (1982: 150-51) uses linguistic criteria to analyze the development of voiced stops in NGmc. (ƀ, đ, g- > b, d, g; e.g., initially and after nasals), resulting in a

system with primary distinctions between ± fricative and ± voice. However, Quak does not totally reject "magical" considerations in the formulation of the final shape of the system (pp. 145ff.). Conversely, H. Andersen (1947: 219ff.) sees the reform as more a technical rather than linguistic matter; the purpose of which was to simplify and standardize the system, to facilitate and standardize learning, and to create a more suitable epigraphical script.

84. DR. 144, 190, 192, 209, 230, and 356.

85. The other two from this period are DR. 188 and 189.

86. Polomé (1975: 660-62) connects ON *þulr* to a Hitt. verb form *tallia*-: 'to solemnly call upon the god (to do something).'

87. Cf. Aakjær (1927) on the terminology and institutions of the old Danish retinue.

88. Cf. Sierke (1939: 109-114), Moltke (1976a: *passim*), and the continuing "Runfynd" series in *Fornvännen* and after 1986 the contents of the annual newsletter *Nytt om Runer*. Also Liesøl (1963: 15) reports that around 50 inscriptions from Bergen's Bryggen district contain the fuþark formula.

89. Kuhn (1956) believed that the retinue or *comitatus* (as defined in sect. 13. above) was not present in 9th cent. Scandinavia. However, Green (1965: 270-77) and Lindow (1975: 19-21) present effective counterarguments which show the possible existence of the retinue-like nature of the 9th cent. *drótt*.

90. It must be emphasized that these "types" are to some extent merely convenient heuristic models.

91. This is clear from the presence of Swedish goods in Anglo-Saxon graves (Bruce-Mitford 1978) and Anglo-Saxon objects in Swedish graves (Stenberger 1962: 152ff.).

92. See especially the Lärbro Tängelgärde sts. I and II (S. Lindqvist 1942: II, 92-94).

93. It is attractive to see in such a structure the first two Dumézilian functions, i.e., binary Function I—leader (judge/king) skald (poet/magician), and Function II— warrior.

94. The Rök st. may also contain a reference to a certain wise 'rune-man' (**runimaþR**), Vari, who has a sacred enclosure (**ui**: OSwe. *wē*), cf. Brate (1911: 248ff.).

95. See Thompson (1972; 1975 *passim*). The survey of Swedish rune-carvers' names (cf. Brate 1925) demonstrates the "professional" nature of their work in the 11th-12th centuries and also the existence of certain "schools" around them.

96. This aspect is copiously discussed in the handbooks, e.g., by Helm (1953: II, pt. 2, 251-68), de Vries (1957: II, 27-106), Turville-Petre (1964: 35-74), and Dumézil (1973: 26ff.).

97. As interpreted by N. Nielsen (1969).

98. This all-inclusive or synthesizing function is most clearly demonstrated in the mythic religious controversy between Othinus (= Óðinn) and Mithothyn (Saxo *Gesta* I, 25) in which Mithothyn (< *Mjǫtuð-inn: 'the measurer, orderer' = Týr) tried to forbid collective sacrifice to the gods and attempted to institute specialized cults. Othinus, however, was able to overcome Mithothyn and preserve the common cultus, cf. de Vries (1957: II, 103-04). It is therefore not inconceivable that an *Óðinsmaðr* could, for magical purposes, henotheistically employ other god-forms for special functions (here apotropaic?).

99. Perhaps this practice began in Norway under the influence of the OE tradition where ᚼ /y/ seems to be the oldest example of this type of practice (cf. Krause 1970: 23ff. and Arntz 1944: 108).

100. Cf. Olsen in von Friesen (1933: 100ff.).

101. For example, in the culturally conservative areas of central Sweden and Gotland where runic forms continued to be used into the 19th-century, cf. von Friesen (1933: 234ff.), and Arntz (1944: 112-14), and Krause (1970: 121-23).

102. See examples in VI. Most common of these are the *Ave Maria* prayers, the magical formulaic word *agla*, and the *sator*-square formulas.

103. See the discussion in VI.53. Although displaced for conventional purposes, knowledge of the fuþark system was preserved throughout the medieval period for magical or encoding purposes.

Chapter V

Runes and Germanic Magical Practice

1. Runes were probably closely associated with some kind of religious, and perhaps operant, practices from at least the time when the technical term *rūnō* was attached to them (see sect. 13). In order to understand how the Germanic peoples might have comprehended the nature of these "mysteries," how they became associated with a writing system, and how this complex might have been used for operant, or "magical," ends we must address certain issues. Initially we must review some of the concepts fundamental to Germanic "magical thought," as well as some basic material on Germanic operant behavior, and essential evidence for the nature of runic practice. We cannot hope to give a complete outline of the whole of Germanic magical thinking, so our discussion here is limited to that which is of direct aid to the understanding of possible runic practices.

GERMANIC MAGIC

Power Concepts

2. Generally, there may be said to exist two types of magical power, or means by which to operate: 1) the dynamistic, and 2) the animistic (see II.1)(1). In the Germanic model, the dynamistic aspect has a side which humans can manipulate, but which they do not seem to be able to possess ("the holy," etc.), and a second side which men may possess and wield as a concrete force (i.e., personal dynamism).

A conceptual framework for the means by which events or conditions might be brought about or affected is contained in what is certainly a common Indo-European idea of the "dichotomy of the holy."(2) In Germanic, this dichotomy is expressed by the two terms *wīhaz* and *hailagaz*.(3) *Wīhaz* seems to indicate the awesome aspect of the holy— that which is "wholly other"—apart from the profane world, and the exclusive possession of the numinous. It characterizes something separate, or verbally, the act of separating something from the mundane so that it enters into a numinous state.(4) This concept and operation are fundamental to the Germanic "technology of the sacred"—in such endeavors as sacrifice,(5) and magical communication. *Hailagaz* describes the condition of wellbeing and invulnerability—the attractive side of this dual-aspected holy. That which is **hailagaz* reaches out and penetrates into the world of men, is a part of it, and expresses the concept of a "wholeness" of the divine or numinous and the human or mundane worlds.(6) Verbal constructs reflect the idea of "making whole" (Go. *hailjan*, OE *hælan*, OHG *heilan*, OS *helian*: 'to heal'), or of somehow binding the profane with the sacred or of communication with the sacred realm (e.g., OHG *heilison*: 'to observe signs and omens;' OE *hilsian*, ON *heilla*: "to invoke spirits; enchant").

These two concepts must be understood as an organic whole. A thing is **wīhaz* insofar as it belongs to, or has been made a part of, the numinous, "otherly" realm (in a state of sacrality), and it is **hailagaz* as far as this power resides in it and streams forth from it (for human benefit, etc.). So something would have to be **wīhaz* before it becomes **hailagaz*—the two seem to be functions of the same state or process.(7) Although **wīhaz* and **hailagaz* are used adjectivally and nominally to describe a state of being, it is their use in connection with verbs which is of greatest interest to the study of magic. It is clear that certain persons were believed to be able to operate these concepts "to make things sacred" (**wīh-jan*) and thus "to fill things with holy power" (**hailagon*).

Another concept similar to **wīhaz* and **hailagaz*, but which appears less malleable, is contained in the root **gin-*: 'magically charged.'(8) This is decidedly super-human and cosmic in proportion. In North Germanic it is found as a prefix for cosmological conceptions, e.g., ON *ginn-unga-gap*: 'magically charged space, or void, or as a description of numina, e.g., ON *ginn-heilog goð*. (Vsp. 6, *passim*; Ls. 11) and *ginn-regin* (Hav. 80, 142; Hym. 4; Alv. 20, 30)—both as designations for the gods. It is also attached to the runes in the curse formulas of Stentoften (KJ 96) and Björketorp (KJ 97) where *gino-rūnoR* or *gina-rūnaR* are mentioned. This root is perhaps contained in the South Germanic verbal form **bi-ginnan*: 'to begin,' in which case it might have originally had some causal force, and had some connection to ON *gandr*.(9)

Dynamistic

3. In the specifically Germanic cultural context there seem to be concepts which form a bridge between the strictly dynamistic and animistic. The most purely dynamistic forces are those of **mah-tiz* and **mag-ena* (ON *máttr*: 'might' and *megin-*: 'main'), which are both derived from PGmc.

mag-: 'to be able, have power.' These can be understood in a physical, or in a numinous or psychic sense (cf. de Vries 1956: I, 275ff.; Strom 1948: 29-76).(10) Other dynamistic aspects of the human psychophysical complex such as PGmc. *wōð-*: 'excited mental activity' (Go. *woþs*: 'angry, possessed,' OE *wōd* and OHG *wuotig*: 'mad, furious,' ON *óðr* (adj.): 'mad, frantic,' ON *óðr* (noun): 'mind [as a faculty of inspiration]; song, poetry),'(11) and *mōð-*: 'furious, forceful will' (Go. *wōþs*: 'anger,' ON *móðr*: 'excitement, anger,' OHG *muot*: 'soul; mind; mood; excitement,' OE *mōd*: 'spirit, courage, power, violence,' OS *mōd*: 'soul, will') indicate emotive faculties essential to the perception and expression of the numinous experience.(12)

More "magical" perhaps are the various concepts of "luck," e.g., ON *gæfa* and *gipta*: 'luck' or NGmc. *auja*: 'good fortune' (on two bracteate inscriptions IK. 161: Skodborg and IK 98: Sjælland).(13) The substantive **hailaz*: 'luck, omen.' (OE *hæl, hælo*: OHG *heil*; ON *heill*) provides a more common root conception, which connotes "luck" as a result of a holistic relationship with the numinous. Another term often associated with "luck" is ON *hamingja*: 'shape-shifting force; luck; guardian spirit' poses a complicated problem. It seems to have originally been a purely dynamistic concept,(14) which became animized and anthropomorphized in later lore. The equally complex ON term *gandr* must have at first been an expression of some kind of "magical power" (perhaps connected with **gin-*)(15) but one which became zoomorphicized in the practical symbology so that it became synonymous with malevolent animal-shaped "sendings."(16)

The name of a person (or even a thing)(17)—either his proper name or some byname—appears to be considered a concrete entity which is a power in its own right and one subject to direct linguistic manipulations. The name also serves a synthetic function for other aspects of the psychophysical complex. This is shown in the psychological framework of Germanic name-giving practices wherein it is clear that those who receive the names of dead ancestors inherit their powers and characteristics.(18) Names given at birth may be seen not to fit a person (de Vries 1956: I, 181), which necessitates a name change. Also bynames could be added to the birth-name. The sources of these bynames are manifold, but in order for them to be valid a gift should be given to 'fasten' the name to the person (ON *nafnfestr*).(19) It would seem that each of these changes or additions of names either effect or formalize a transformation in the person on social or psychological levels (cf. W. Schmidt 1912: 21ff.). Here we may even be dealing with the vestiges of an initiatory naming system which is perhaps better reflected in the more archaic runic records.

As an external manifestation of an unseen essence, the name can be used to gain a certain power over the bearer. It seems that the name has a power of attraction over the entity to which it is attached, to other aspects of the soul, etc.(20) This appears to be the underlying conception for the magicians' prohibitions against the pronouncing of their names while they are on a *gandreið*, 'magic-ride' (cf. Ellis Davidson 1973: 32, n. 39; 36), since such an utterance would call them back from their shamanistic wanderings. The name may also be used, especially by dying men, in powerful curse formulas.(21) The practice of harming or healing a person by means of his written name is also widely known (cf. W. Schmidt 1912: 28-29, 31). At the root of all these conceptions is the idea of an analogical relationship between the name as an operative symbol and the being of which it is a part. The most comprehensive study of these conceptions in Germanic within a general framework is offered by Bach (1953: I, 240ff.).

These power concepts are generally attached to persons. They usually indicate a state of being of some kind, but are capable of being manipulated or stimulated in certain ways. More commonly, however, these seem to constitute one of the agents by which magical operations are effected.

Anamistic

4. Besides these dynamistic entities, there exist several types of animistic conceptions (see ch. II), usually either with anthropomorphic or zoomorphic characteristics, but what is most essential is their psychoid and sometimes autonomous nature. In Germanic lore, these have a broad range of functions, as bearers of fate or wisdom, or as apotropaic or aggressive magical entities.(22) One class of such entities is dependent upon living persons or groups of persons (although they may be transferred from one person to another, etc.). This includes the ON *fylgja*: 'guardian, following spirit' and *ættarfylgja*: 'clanic guardian spirit'—usually in human (female) or animal form.(23) The English "fetch" seems to be originally related to a similar conception (cf. Philippson 1929: 68). In medieval Iceland the cognitive-synthetic soul conception *hugr* also took on many of the characteristics of the *fylgja* (cf. Strömbäck 1975: 5ff.). The ON *mara* (OE *mere, mære*) seems to be a demonic (aggressive) soul aspect in gynemorphic shape which especially female sorceresses are able to send out to attack certain persons (cf. Strömbäck 1976/77: 282ff.), and which seems related to the *gandr* and *gandreið* concepts mentioned above. To this might be added Germanic *wardaz* found in ON *vǫrðr*, OE *weard* (*Bēowulf* 1741), and OHG *wartil* ("Muspilli" 66), which might indicate a guardian aspect of the soul (cf. de Vries 1956: I, 221). The other class of animistic beings

comprises independent, or semi-dependent entities that are often perceived as demigoddesses. The ON *valkyrjur* (sg. *valkyrja*, cf. OE *wælcyrie*) were apparently originally demonic gynemorphic beings which attacked one's opponents and defended one's own war-band,(24) while the ON *dísir* (cf. OHG *idisi*, OE *idesa*?) and *nornir* were also conceived of as protective, power or fate-bearing entities. Members of this second group might attach themselves to an exemplary individual and function in a way analogous to the *fylgja*. All of these beings serve both as sources for magical power and as expressions or tools of that power conceived of as being "projected" to do the magician's will—a messenger or agent in the magico-communicative process.

Extra-Human Entities

5. A wide variety of entities also stands largely outside the psychological sphere of living human beings—and as such are potential objects of human communication of an exceptional sort. These range from walking corpses to the great gods of high mythology.

The re-animated corpse—a common motif in Old Norse literature from the oldest period to modern times(25)—is of two types: 1) one which remains in the grave or burial mound (usually called a *draugr*),(26) and 2) one which leaves the house and walks abroad (sometimes termed an *aptrgöngumaðr*). This entity is in fact the physical corpse of a dead man which remains animate and usually retains, in an intensified mode, the personality traits or characteristics of the individual.(27) The *draugar* are extremely powerful and strong, and guard their graves against would-be robbers.(28) When these *draugar* leave their howes they always exercise a malevolent influence. The most usual way to prevent such instances of *aptrgöngumenn* is to destroy the body by fire, staking it down, beheading, or binding it in the grave (cf. de Vries 1956: I, 232).

The dead play an important and complex role in the magical outlook and practices of the Germanic peoples. According to H. R. Ellis (Davidson) (1943: 165ff.) the dead are employed in three distinct ways: 1) as a channel for the reception of hidden knowledge or wisdom,(29) 2) as direct sources of inspiration to the living in cultic practices (e.g., *útiseta*, "howe-worship," etc.), and 3) as raised corpses directed by magicians for military and/or malevolent purposes.(30) There appear to have been magical steps which could be taken to prevent such use of corpses, e.g., the whispering of a formula into the ear of the corpse (see de Vries 1956: I, 300) or the performance of a more complex ceremonial (*G-H s.* ch. 32):

Möndull gengr tysvar rangsælis kringum valinn. Hann blés ok blistraði í allar ættir ok þuldi þar forn fræði yfir ok sagði þann val þeim eigi at meini verða mundu.(31)

The entry of a man into the howe and struggle with a *draugr* in order to win its treasure seems also to have some initiatory function.(32)

Considerable but disparate evidence shows that the Germanic peoples had what might be called a manifold "ancestor cult," or at least a cult of the dead.(33) One manifestation of this is the common Germanic belief in divine progenitorship — that the gods are the ultimate ancestors of men.(34) The famous example of worship at the burial mound of Óláfr Geirstaðaálfr(35) is perhaps late, but nevertheless it reflects a deep-rooted belief which involves both re-birth and something like the *ættarfylgja*. In fact the apparent links between such lore concerning the dead and "ancestral spirits," and the cults of the important lesser divinities (*dísir, álfar, dvergar*, etc.) has often been noted (cf. e.g., Falk 1926: 172; Turville-Petre 1963; 1964: 221ff.).

These so-called lesser divinities hold an important place in the magico-religious world-view of the Germanic peoples.(36) It seems that they are collective bodies individuated not so much according to "personality" as to function. There are the predominately masculine types, i.e., elves (ON *álfar*). who are rather atmospheric, and the dwarves (ON *dvergar*), who are conversely chthonic. Elves often receive sacrifice (ON *álfablót*, cf. de Vries 1956: I, 258) and are connected with fertility and magic. They are sometimes benevolent and allied with the Æsir and Vanir, but are also on occasion involved in malevolence (cf. Turville-Petre 1964: 231). The dwarves rarely, if ever, receive sacrifice (see Turville-Petre 1964: 233) but are more usually regarded as tutelary beings, who teach men certain skills, etc.(37) The feminine genus, the *dísir* (perhaps related to OE *idesa* and OHG *idisi*) also receive sacrifice (ON *dísablót*, cf. de Vries 1956: I, 455ff.) and are protective, fertility-bestowing beings. They would appear to be active in magic as well (cf. *Merseburger Zauberspruch* I). But it seems that their negative action of withholding their protective powers (or being forced to do so by a magician, cf. *ES* ch. 57) is a more usual role for them in a malevolent context. This can also be said of the *landvættir*, (cf. Turville-Petre 1963; 1964: 222ff; 232ff.). Etins (ON *jötnar*, OE *eotenas*) or giants are not always the adversaries of gods and men and they also enjoyed a cult.(38) It seems that the elves, dwarves, and *dísir* at least partially had their origins in beliefs in ancestral spirits, while the etins may represent autochthonous populations or their gods. However, manifold conceptions are simultaneously active here.

At least in the North, as is well known, the greater gods are divided into two generations — the Æsir and the Vanir. The former are more concerned with law, magic, and war, while the latter generally rule over matters of fertility, material well-being, and eroticism (cf. Dumézil 1973). These gods do not always figure in magic the way, for example, god-forms of Mediterranean origin do in Continental magical grimoires from the Middle Ages onward.(39) Certainly sacrifices to the gods or dedicatory oaths made to them must have had an operative effect. The report by Tacitus (*Hist.* XIII, 57) concerning the dedication of the Germans' enemies to Mars and Mercurius (*Tiwaz and *Wōðanaz) betrays an operative motivation.

Some of the functions of Woden have been mentioned (IV.16). In an operative sacrificial formula (*Heimskr., Hákonar s. goða* ch. 14) Óðinn is said to receive a ritual toast *til sigrs ok ríkis konungi* ('for victory and power to the king'). Various *heiti* and *kenningar* of Óðinn also show his intimate relation to technical aspects of magic, e.g., *Gǫndlir*: 'bearer of the magical staff (< *gandr*),' *Fjǫlnir*: 'the concealer' (< *fela*: 'to conceal, hide'),(40) *Báleygr*: 'fiery eyed,' or the kenning, *galdrs fǫðr*: 'father of magical incantations.' The *Merseburger Zauberspruch* II shows the use of Woden in a mythic/epic context serving as a framework for operative activity.(41) Þórr is similarly used in two runic formulas, the Kvinneby copper plate, ca. 1050-1100, and the MS Canterbury formula (for both see VI.53).

Among the Vanir, Freyja is also known to have magical functions, and it is she who taught Óðinn the type of magic known as *seiðr* (*Heimskr., Ynglinga s.* ch. 7, see 6. below). Njǫrðr and Freyr were also recipients of an operative sacrificial formula (*Heimskr. Hákonar s. góða* ch. 14) *til árs ok friðar* ('for good harvest and peace').

It seems that the greater gods figure in magic in at least three ways: 1) as receivers of sacrificial gifts for which they must reciprocate,(42) 2) as idealized models for the behavior of the magician, and 3) as figures the myths of which are used as analogous paradigms for operative aims.

Non-Runic Magic

6. The possible use of runes for magical ends is perhaps most clearly understandable in the context of operative techniques generally employed by the Germanic peoples. Our data for the formulation of this context are again severely limited and disparate. It is my intention simply to give a modest idea of the magico-technical framework into which any operative runic tradition would have had to be integrated.

Our sources are basically archeological data (which is sometimes subject to wide variations in interpretation), indirect reports of non-Germanic writers concerning the customs of the northern peoples, and historically diverse but direct Germanic sources (chiefly medieval ON, OE, and OHG documents). A special sub-group of this latter category is constituted by references to various magical practices in the laws of the Germanic peoples (cf. Kiessling, 1941).

It is perhaps most convenient to classify non-runic magical behavior according to technical criteria, i.e., according to the *means* by which operant ends are effected. A rough and ready list of these means would include: 1) oral formulas (incantations), 2) glyphic devices (non-runic ideographs), 3) iconic talismans (representations of symbolic natural objects, e.g., axes, hammers, etc.),(43) 4) elemental substances (physical materials with innately magical qualities, e.g., blood, ale, mead, herbs, etc.), and 5) the complex "shamanistic" (cf. Strömbäck 1935: 191ff.; Buchholz 1968: *passim*; Ellis Davidson 1973: 20ff.) tradition (trance inductive), which appears to form a special category of its own.

What seems clear is that the runic tradition supplemented and expanded the scope of the categories above — oral formulas became graphically represented, often in ideographic or iconic contexts. Some of the most conspicuous formulas verbally stand for "magical" substances, e.g., *alu*, *medu* (?), *laukaR*. It is unclear the degree to which runic tradition (which seems analytical, intellectual, and linguistic) might have found a place in apparently emotive and trance-inducing shamanism. The commonly held *galdr/seiðr* antagonism may be present here. This dichotomy, although real at one level, may be a secondary or later development. The oldest runic record appears to contain shamanistic traits, e.g., ego-alteration (see VII.2.), metamorphosis (bracteate iconography, et al.), emotive non-semantic formulas, etc. Also could the **ehwaR* formula have a shamanistic background? This coupled with the definite shamanic character of much of the Óðinn-mythology (including the rune-winning initiatory myth, see 16. below) renders the conventional dichotomy ambiguous.

The incidence of magic in the archeological and written records is difficult to assess due to the wide disparity in the types of behavior indicated. Perhaps the only statistically relevant body of data is offered by Old Icelandic literature. There we see that magic of one sort or another is portrayed as an element of everyday life in the historical sagas, as well as an important part of the mythical world of the *fornaldarsögur* (cf. Eggers 1932, Jaide 1937). From the survey of Jaide (1937), which is by no means exhaustive with regard to magical motifs, it is apparent that the majority of sagas contain examples of operant acts. What is by no means clear is the extent to which literary invention has played a role in the incidence of these magical motifs.(44)

The Magician

7. The function and position of the magician him/herself within society is an important one, but so complex that it only allows a brief sketch here,(45) since the majority of the material would fall outside the references to runic operations. Basically the magician seems to have either one of two functions in society: beneficial or maleficent. This dichotomy is an ancient one and pre-dates the introduction of Christianity.(46) It also seems worthwhile to note the social class and gender of northern magicians.

Both beneficial and maleficent magic are recorded for most epochs of early Germanic history — although the first Roman reports contain no references to harmful (from the Germanic viewpoint) sorcery.(47) As time progresses, and the vantage points of the reporters change, more malevolent forms of magic are depicted. In the typically sparsely documented Migration Age, most references are of a negative sort, e.g., the famous account of king Filimer driving out the demonic *magas mulieres* (Go. *haljarunae*, Wulf. *haljarūnos*) from his Gothic population.(48) The majority of these references in the Migration Age are from decidedly Christian sources.(49) With the Viking and Middle Ages, the available material expands and a more balanced picture emerges.(50) To be sure, the image of the maleficent sorcerer or sorceress continues, but more often than not he or she is countered by the magic of a beneficial magician.(51) This tendency is ultimately expressed in the figures of late Middle and early Reformation Age Icelandic magicians, e.g., Sæmundur, Gottskálk, etc. — who were at once Christian priests and powerful magicians.(52)

It is sometimes impossible to determine the social group to which an individual magician might belong. Unfortunately, this is especially true during the late Roman and Migration Ages. Roman historians report on Germans of exclusively high social status —the *patres* or *matres familiae* (e.g., Tacitus *Germ.* 10; Caesar *DBG* I, 50) and the various holy women or seeresses mentioned must have been of noble class. The less explicit sources between ca. 100 and 1000 CE are difficult to interpret in this regard, although it seems that magic or sorcery might be practiced by free-born or noble persons.(53)

During the Viking and Middle Ages in Scandinavia we can make better judgements concerning the class of individuals depicted as being involved with things magical, but an ambiguous pattern emerges. Magic is often practiced by persons or families of the lower classes or foreigners ("Finns," etc.),(54) but there are many instances of similar operative behavior by persons of the higher classes.(55) Some types of magic might carry a degree of social stigma (e.g., *seiðr* — although the specifics of why this is so are never entirely clear), while some figures seem to have had a personal aversion to magicians in general.(56)

Both men and women engaged in magical activity; however, there was some distinction in the type of operant role they might have. For example, the *Ynglinga s.* ch. 7 explicitly contrasts the use of *galdr* by men with that of *seiðr*(57) by women.(58) In the Roman Age, we see both men and women performing divinatory functions — but the famed Germanic seeresses certainly held an exalted role.(59) Migration Age laws give us some information on the existence of female "witches" (Lat. *stigia*) and their practices.(60) The ancient role of the female seeress is well attested in the figure of the Viking Age *vǫlva* (cf. e.g., *Eiríks s. rauða* ch. 4).(61) At the same time, it must be said that men participate in various magical activity with equal frequency. In the Middle Ages, men seem to dominate the magical tradition (especially in Iceland). These may be priests who dabble in *fornfræði* or laymen who also make use of "runes" and magical signs.(62) Gender appears to have been significant, but not always a determinative factor in the practice of Germanic magic.

Magical Procedures

8. General, non-runic operative procedures for the time span 100-800 CE are virtually impossible to establish, and therefore we are uncomfortably dependent upon later Viking Age and medieval sources — which are usually far too unsystematic and incomplete. In order to build up a context for runic operations, however, some framework of common non-runic magical behavior must be briefly established.(63)

The *location* in which an operative action takes place is often explicitly prescribed. In the performance of *seiðr* a special high platform (ON *seiðhjallr*) is often employed (cf. Ellis Davidson 1973: 34ff.), while a cross road, a grave mound or other high ground is necessary for the practice of *útiseta*.(64) For the most part isolated and lonely places seem to be preferred — but many descriptions also show an almost casual attitude in this regard.(65)

Overt operative behavior in the Germanic evidence is too manifold to be comprehensively discussed here, but some of the most outstanding features of apparent relevance to the runic tradition must be touched upon. We can at least partially classify those observable actions in four categories: 1) verbal, 2) graphic, 3) projective, and 4) demonstrative.

Magical spells or incantations are a primary operative behavior— as performative speech (see II.1). This may be semantically formulated in poetic spells(66) or devoid of semantic content as with *ephesia grammata* or *xenoglossia*(67) — but in either case the speech would seem to be highly structured and formulaic. The original, and in certain contexts continuing, meaning of a term such as ON *kraftaskáld* or *ákvæðaskáld* would be "magical, shaping power" (cf. Almqvist 1965; 1974 *passim*). Furthermore, it has long been supposed that Germanic alliterative verse had its origin in divinatory or magical practices.(68) In the Germanic lexicon, terms for magic often indicate an utterance of some kind, e.g., ON *galdr*; OHG *galdar ~ galstar*, OE *gealdor*: 'incantation, magical song,' or OHG *spell*, OE *spell*: 'recitation (sometimes in magical contexts), magical formula'.(69)

The execution of graphic signs or plastic images is also extensive in Germanic magic. Besides the making of ideographic signs (see 10. below), patterns may be made on the ground which have apparently cosmological significance, cf. the *hólmganga* rite described in detail in *Kormaks s.* ch. 10 and a form of the *útiseta* rite in the *Maríu s.* (cf. Simpson 1973: 176-77). Also, iconic images, or sculptures, are employed for magical ends, e.g., the *tréníð* in which carvings or actual objects are placed on the *níðstǫng* to help effect the spell (cf. Ellis Davidson 1973: 34).

A projection of power over distance through what are conceived of as expressive physical organs seems to be at the root of the frequently mentioned "magical gaze" of Germanic magicians (cf. Háv. 150; *Heimskr. Ynglinga s.* ch. 7, *Haralds s. hárfagra* ch. 32; *Vatnsdœla s.* ch. 26, 29; *Laxdœla s.* ch. 38; *Gull-Þoris s.* ch. 17, *Gunnlaugs s.* ch. 7). Furthermore, the use of a "magical breath," which the magician breathes or blows onto the object of his magic, or onto a symbol of it, or even into the air in various symbolic directions, is not uncommon.(70) Two of the most conspicuous demonstrative actions used in magical operations are 1) dance (especially circumambulations) and 2) the throwing or shooting of some magical object (spear, arrow, "shot," etc.). The idea of shamanistic dance depicted especially on the B-type bracteates is discussed by Hauck (1969: 33ff.; 1977), also the Old English terminology for operative behavior seems to emphasize this aspect, cf. OE *wicca/wicce*: 'sorcerer/ess' (<*weik- ~ *weig-*: 'to turn, twist').(71) The use of magical projectiles of one kind or another is a constant feature of Germanic operations. The most noteworthy example is the casting of a spear over one's enemies in order to "consecrate"(72) them to a god — most typically Óðinn in the Old Icelandic sources. The mythic account of the first battle between the Æsir and Vanir (Vsp. 24) attributes this action archetypically to Óðinn himself, while most historical reports(73) also connect the act to the Geirtýr: 'spear-god' (cf. Falk 1924: 12-13). This whole complex is perhaps related to the magico-legal procedure for taking possession of territory in which an arrow is shot over the land.(74) Magical "shots" (ON *gand, gandfluga*: 'magic fly;' OE (*ylfa ~ esa*) *gescot*: 'shot of elves or æsir') are also often actually thrown in the course of an operation, although their function is substantially different from that of spears or arrows.(75)

It is also common that direct contact between the physical extremities (hands and feet) of the magician and the object of his or her operation effects the desired results — this apparently due to the amassed dynamistic force present in the person of the magician.(76)

Substances

9. There are essentially two types of substances with intrinsically magical power used in operations: 1) naturally occurring substances, e.g., certain plants, woods, rocks, stones, blood, etc., and 2) manufactured substances, i.e., those compounded artificially by the magician or others, such as magical drinks, salves, etc.(77)

Herbs are often mentioned in magical formulas, some of which seem deeply embedded in an indigenous Germanic tradition, e.g., the various types of leek (ON *laukr, ítrlaukr, geirlaukr*) and appear to have a definite magical quality.(78) Often formulaically related to the leek is flax or linen, e.g., in the preparation of the *Vǫlsi* and in the poetic formulas concerning it:

(4)   Aukinn ertu Vǫlsi   ok upp um tekinn
       líni gœddr,   en laukum studdr...(79)

There are a variety of other herbs with Germanic names in a number of magical and/or therapeutic formulas, e.g., ON *friggjargras*: 'Frigg's herb,' ON *baldrsbrá*: 'Baldr's brow,' ON *mistilteinn* and OE *misteltān*: 'mistletoe,' OHG *alrūna*: 'mandrake,' etc."(80)

The use of various woods is also conspicuous in Germanic magical practice. Besides the general terminology connected with the runes, i.e., *stafr*: 'stick → secret lore' (see sect. 14.), there are specific directions on what types of wood to use in magical operations in later sources, cf. e.g., the *Galdrabók* nos. 9 and 36 (*hriseik*: 'shrub-oak'), 29 (*reynir tré*: 'rowan-wood'), 32 (*elri*: 'elder'), 33 (*askr*: 'ash'), and 47 (*eik*: 'oak').(81)

Certain stones, both large (e.g., *jarðfastir steinar, merk-steinar, áfsteinar*, etc.) and small (e.g., *lýfsteinar*, cf. Moltke 1938: 139-147) play a large role in Germanic magical thinking, and seem to be both the dwelling places of numina and containers of dynamistic force itself (cf. Reichborn-Kjennerud 1923: 39ff.).

Blood, be it human or that of a sacrificial animal (ON *sónardreyri*), is certainly thought to have magical effect. Not only is it used in rune magic (see 16. below), but it is also seen to have therapeutic (cf. Reichborn-Kjennerud 1923: 46) and transformative properties.(82)

Although various salves and balms made by ancient Germanic "leeches" were thought to contain magical powers, the most potent, complex, and apparently also sometimes toxic(83) substance was the ale, beer, or mead used in religious rituals and feasts.(84) Storms (1948: 69-70) collects several examples of therapeutic magical recipes from the Old English *Leechbook* and *Lacnunga* MSS which make use of ale, wine, or mead.(85) It is probably the "internal application" of this substance as an ecstasy promoting, transformative agent which reflects its true importance in operative acts (see VI.3.).

Signs and Symbols

10. Non-runic signs, characters, and even pictographic sculpture are sometimes used in isolation for an apparently magical effect—but occasionally also in the context of a runic inscription (see VI). These elements fall into one of two categories, either 1) ideographic, or 2) pictographic.

Ideographic signs such as the swastika ᛡ (ON *sólarhvel*), or the so-called triskelion ᛢ may have originally been symbols of the sun, fire, or thunder, and seem to have had an apotropaic function (cf. Helm 1913: 169ff.). Nordland (1951) speculates that the later runic ᚼ shape was originally a sign of lightning or thunder and that it fell together with the concept **hagalaz*: 'hail' embodied in the ᚺ rune. This type of conjecture has often surrounded the ideographic use of runes themselves as "magical signs" or as graphs with a magical function.(86) In the medieval period, certain magical signs (ON *galdrastafir*) begin to appear which some have derived from runic combinations or bind-runes (ON *bandrúnar*).(87) The actual derivations of the various shapes is a topic far too complex to enter into here; however, it does seem most probable that these characters have three aspects which relate to the runes: 1) stylized bind-runes (relatively rare, cf. Árnason 1954: I, 432 *et passim*), 2) signs possibly re-interpreted as "runic" (especially in 16th- to 17th-century Scandinavia, e.g., the famous *ægishjálmr* sign: ᛯ), and 3) non-runic magical *sigilla* of Mediterranean origin.(88)

The use of sculpture for magical purposes has already been noted above in the case of *tréníð*. The most notable other example of pictographic images used to convey some operative communication is provided by the bracteate-amulets (from ca. 450-550) of which there have been some 800 found to date (Hauck 1981a: 4).(89) It would also seem that the mythic iconography displayed for example on the Gotlandic memorial stones has something other than a "decorative" function (cf. S. Lindqvist 1941-42 and Buisson 1976, but also Düwel 1981c).

Magical Tools

11. Objects utilized to effect magical ends fall into one of two categories, either 1) they are objects with a singularly operative function (magical wands, etc., see also sect. 12.), or 2) they are otherwise utilitarian tools with secondary operative functions (e.g., weapons, clothing, etc.).(90)

The most noteworthy single type of object used for magical purposes is the "wand" or "staff" (ON *gandr, vǫlr, stafr, kefli*) —generally of wood and apparently anywhere from a few inches to several feet in length. Sometimes it seems that the wand serves as a "sign of office,"(91) or it may have a specific operative function, e.g., the staff called *Hǫgnuðr* in the *Vatnsdœla s.* ch. 44 which had the power to cause memory loss, or the one mentioned in the *Landnámabók* (*Sturlubók* 225) which could cause water to flow.

Magical "shots" were also made especially for various operations (cf. Honko 1959: 96-97). Certain pieces of cloth were also used for special operative acts, e.g., the *gizki* mentioned in *Vatnsdœla s.* ch. 47 (cf. also Ellis Davidson 1973: 35ff.), and we should not forget the use of a white cloth in lot-casting rituals (*Germ.* ch. 10).

Weapons, especially swords, were often thought to possess magical characteristics, e.g., they could "fight by themselves," cut through anything, protect the owner, give certain victory, etc.(92) Swords, and sometimes spears, were also given proper names, especially when they were thought to have some special power (cf. Falk 1914: 47-65, 83). Certain other household, utilitarian items are also known to have been used in occasional magical acts, e.g., boxes used to keep magic shots (cf. Ellis-Davidson 1973: 31), bowls used for divinatory gazing (cf. N. Lindqvist 1921, the *Galdrabók* nos. 33; 45, and Strabo *Geographia* VII, 2, 3, who reports on the divinatory release of blood into kettles), and weights (ON *met, hlutir*) used for a divinatory operation in which objects were dropped into water and omens taken from the sound they make (cf. *Flb.* I, 152).

Amulets

12. An amulet or talisman (ON *hlútr, taufr ~ tǫfr, heill*, OHG *zoupargascrip*, OE *lybb, lyfesn, healsbōc, þweng*) is a concrete object somehow endowed with the power to ward off malevolent influences or to

attract beneficial ones, and which can usually be carried or worn on the person.(93) For our purposes we may divide these objects into two categories: 1) natural objects (of stone, wood, bone, etc.), and 2) manufactured objects (generally of metal).

Stones which have the power to heal or as protective amulets (ON *lýfsteinar*: 'healing stones') are known in Old Norse literature,(94) Besides these apparently amorphous, naturally shaped stones, miniature carved stone axes or hammers are also common from the Bronze Age onward. These probably had a apotropaic function.(95) Wooden amulets must have also been widely used; however, few have survived which can be distinguished as such.(96) Various organic and inorganic materials are often found in small bags or lockets which must have also served amuletic purposes.(97) Curved claw- or tooth-shaped amulet pendants are also known from early times.(98) Human skull plates with holes bored in them (to be used as pendants?) could apparently serve an operative function as well.(99)

Metal objects in the shape of (finger, arm, or neck) rings also serve amuletic purposes and other operative functions.(100) Bracteates are essentially talismanic (see sect. 10. above), and their power surely comes from the fact that they are made of gold and from the images struck upon them. Amulets similar to bracteates — but not necessarily used as pendants — are miniature sculptures of divine beings, which are widely known in the archeological record.(101) The operative function of those is corroborated by literary-historical sources, e.g., the small image of Þórr which Hallfreðr is found to carry in a leather bag (*Hallfreðar s.* [= *Flb.* I, 274]) and the *hlútr* with an image of Freyr given to Ingimundr by Haraldr *hárfagri* (cf. *Vatnsdœla s.* chs. 9, 7, 10, 12).

RUNIC PRACTICE

Lexical Evidence

13. Terms which denote operative acts or imply their performance are rather sparse in the actual epigraphical record. Such terms would have to convey an operative mode etymologically or appear in contexts which lead one to conclude that an operative act is intended or reflected. These fall into two main categories: 1) the abstract (sometimes verbal), and 2) the concrete-symbolic, i.e., lexemes which directly represent concrete but symbolic things.

The clearest representative of the abstract class is the PGmc. fem. ō-stem *rūnō-* (pl. *rūnōz*): 'secret, mystery, written character, letter.' Although the etymology of this word is not completely certain, it is clear that it belongs to the magico-religious semantic field. The word is attested in all Germanic dialects — Go. *rūna*: 'secret, mysterium;'(102) OHG *rūna*: 'religious mystery, secret;' OE *rūn*: 'mystery, secret council,' ON *rún*: 'secret, secret lore, wisdom; magical sign; letter.' The term may represent a Germanic/Celtic isogloss which appears in OIr. *rūn* and MWel. *rhin*; both meaning 'secret.'(103) Most scholars ultimately connect *rūnō- with some vocal activity, e.g., 'whispering, roaring, singing, chanting, etc.' (cf. Pokorny 1959: 867, Falk-Torp 1960: II, 921; 925, Johanesson 1951-56: 705; Jente 1921: 332-33). This is by no means certain, however, and it might be most prudent to allow it to remain without etymology outside Germanic with the basic abstract meaning "mystery."(104) The term *staƀaz: 'staff' (cf. KJ 95 Gummarp) seems to have semantically fallen together with *rūnō- at some point, so that we have ON *stafr* (esp. the pl. *stafir*): 'staff; written character; lore, wisdom.' Presumably, this represents a semantic transfer from the abstract meanings behind the "runes" to the material medium upon which they were often carved. Furthermore, there are often compounds with *rūnō- which demonstrate its place in a cosmic and/or magical world-view, i.e., *haidR-rūnō* (cf. KJ 96 Stentoften and 97 Björketorp): 'bright or shining runes' and *gina-rūnaR* (also KJ 96, 97): 'magically powerful runes.'(105) In the younger epigraphical tradition we find the conspicuous adjectival forms **rynasta** ON *rýnnasta* (Fyrby st., Sö 56), **runstr** → ON *rýnstr* (Maeshowe 18) both meaning 'most skilled in runes, secret lore,' and the positive form **ryn** → ON *rýnn* (Ågersta st.: 'with knowledge of runes, secret lore' (Olsen 1932a: 167ff.), or the nominal compound *rūnimaðR* (Rök st.), all of which refer to the rune-carvers themselves.

Several bracteates have the formula **laþu**: *laþu* (cf. IK. 13, 42, 58, 83, 149, 163[?], 189, and 305[?]) which is glossed as 'invocation, invitation' — which is presumably a verbal declaration of the purpose of the formula and/or object upon which it is executed. Similarly, the word *ūƀarba-spā*: 'prophesy of doom' stands in isolation on the Björketorp st. (KJ 97). Both the terms *laþu* and *-spā* ultimately refer to an act of oral performance.

The verb *wīhjan: 'to hallow' is perhaps used in three older inscriptions (KJ 24, 27 and the Nydam ax-handle) with indirect reference to the runes themselves; however, in the younger tradition, the four inscriptions with the formula *Þórr vígi þasi rúnaR* (see IV.21.) clearly show that the runes might be "consecrated," made holy or powerful through the agency of an operative act. Most of the numerous verbs used in connection with the actual execution of the runes (cf. Ebel 1963: 14ff.) tell us little concerning any magical attitude toward this act. The notable exceptions are *faihjan (ON *fá*): 'to color' (cf. KJ 60, 63, 67, 73, IK 11, 340) and ON *rjóða*: 'to redden' (cf. Ebel 1963: 36-37).(106) The latter may refer to an archaic concept of contagious magic in which blood, or its symbolic substitute, is applied to an object in order to sanctify or vivify it, or to endow it with magical powers.(107) It is attractive to connect this practice with an etymology of OHG *zoubar*: 'magic' and ON *taufr*: 'magic; talisman' which links them to OE *teafor*: 'red ochre; minium',(108) This would then imply that "to endow with magical power" is operatively derived from "to make red."(109)

Of course the most common verbs in runic technology are ON weak *rista* ~ strong *rísta*: 'to carve, cut' — of which only the strong alternate is *writan is found in the older corpus — (cf. KJ 17a, 70, 74, 98, 144, 164, IK 156[?]). In operative contexts the idea of "carving runes" can assume the character of a magical formulaic action in and of itself. The verb *felhan: 'to hide, bury' (cf. Go. *filhan*: 'to conceal') is found on the two explicitly operative formulas of Stentoften (KJ 96) **felAhekA**: *felh-eka*: 'I hide (the runes)' and Björketorp (KJ 97) **fAlAhAk**: *falah-ak*: 'I hid-(the runes).' This may be used in a specialized technical sense.(110) A verb derived from *rūn-* is also perhaps found on the cryptic Kingigtorsoak st. **rydu** ← *rý(n)du* 3.-pers. pl. pret.: 'used runes (i.e., magic),' (cf. Olsen 1932a: 199-200).

Among the concrete symbolic terms, the most conspicuous and most problematic is *alu* (which may appear on some 32 older inscriptions, see VI.34.). Since it is most probably identical with ON *ǫl* and OE *ealu*, *ealoð*(111) it should be classed as a concrete symbol-word which may represent the substance itself. Perhaps to be understood as a parallel to *alu* is the formula **medu** (OE *medu*: 'mead') on the recently found Undley bracteate. Other symbolic words of this kind are *laukaR*: 'leek,' which may appear on as many as 18 older inscriptions (cf. Krause 1966: 246-52 and see VI.3.), and *līna*: 'flax, linen' (cf. KJ 37).(112) A new etymology for the bracteate formula *salu* (PGmc. **salwu-* > PNord. *salu > ON *sǫl*: 'samphire' [a valuable edible and therapeutic red sea alga]) would also place it in this category (Lundeby 1982). Besides these substances which have innate magical power, an animate being, the horse (*ehwaR) seems also to appear as a concrete word-symbol on up to eight bracteates (cf. Krause 1966: 242-46).(113) All of these terms, if interpreted correctly, demonstrate an interface between the runic formulaic repertoire and the broad, non-runic, mytho-magical lore.

Later written sources may also be used to some extent to reconstruct earlier practices, but we must not rely on them too heavily except where they find correspondence in the older runic corpus itself. A survey of the occurrence of terms such as *rúnar*, *stafir*, compounds made with them, and adjectives attached to them—especially in the Old Norse poetic records(114) — may indicate some archaic attitudes toward the whole concept *rūnō-. The Old Norse runic terminology is comprehensively dealt with by Dillmann (1976).

The isolated term *rūnō-* (and in ON also *stafr*)(115) appears in texts of all the major Germanic dialects with the basic meaning of secret or (religious) mystery, e.g., ON *rún*: 'secret lore; written character' (but perhaps also even "words" or "songs"),(116) OE *rūn-*(117) 'a whisper, secret, mystery, secret council' (which often alternates with *rǣd*: 'council'),(118) OHG *rūna* (~*girūni*) glosses *sacramentum, mysterium*,(119) Go. *rūna* glosses μυστηριον ('mystery'), βουλη ('will'), and συμβουλιον ('council').(120) It is clear that the word refers to a concretized abstract or collective concept. In ON the terms *rún* and *stafr* usually appear in plurals (i.e., *rúnar* or *stafir*) in their more abstract meanings. However *ES* ch. 44 gives an example in which run is used as a collective:

    Ristum rún a horni,   *rjóðum spjǫll í dreyra* etc.

The verb **rūnan* is relatively rare, and may be secondary (cf. Wilbur 1957: 13ff.). In OHG *rūnen* glosses *susurro, murmurare,* and *auricularis*,(121) while in Old English we find the perhaps more archaic *rȳnan*: 'to roar,' and secondarily formed verbs *rūnian ~ reonian*: 'to whisper.' Only in ON *rýna*: 'to inquire, conduct secret conversations, practice (rune) magic'(122) do we get possible connections. It is quite feasible that this term was originally parallel with the *gala* : *galdr* complex and indicated "to whisper magical formulas," etc.

The ON adjective forms *rýnn ~ rýninn ~ rýndr* 'with knowlege of secret lore'(123) are reflected in the epigraphical tradition (see sect. 13. above; Olsen 1932a). Adjectival compounds *fullrýninn* (Am. 11): 'with complete knowledge of secret lore' and *glǫggrýnn* (*VS* ch. 34): 'clever at interpreting secret lore' are also known. At one time such terms might have functioned in a manner similar to various adjectival appelations in rune-master formulas (see VI.2.).

Numerous compounds in **rūnō-* and various adjectives attached to the term give a rich context for possible further understanding. These modifiers fall into essentially four categories: 1) technical terminology, 2) terms which seem to indicate something beneficial and 3) something detrimental, and 4) neutral terms, often of a magical, cosmological, or psychological nature. It should not be assumed that this colorful and rich runic vocabulary was invented by later medieval writers, as many examples of it exist in the pagan epigraphical evidence from the *haidR-rūnō*: 'bright or shining runes' and *gina-rūnaR*: 'magically powerful runes' of the 8th cent. stones of Björketorp and Stentoften (also KJ 96, 97) to the **taitirunąR** (*teitirúnar*), 'joy-runes' and **(a)iuinrunąR** (*ævinrúnar*), 'eternal-runes' or 'life-runes' of the stone of Malt (ca. 800).(Flowers 2003: 5)

1. Technical Terminology

14. Many expressions link runes with a technology of wood-working — which is only to be expected since the earliest inscriptions (as well as the latest) were executed in wood, cf. ON *rúnastafr*, OHG *rūnstab*, OE *rūn stæf* ~ *rūnstæf*: 'rune-stave → runic character;'(124) ON *bókrúnar* (Sdr. 19): 'runes carved on beech wood(?);(125) ON *limrúnar* (Sdr. 11): 'limb-runes,'(126) and the very common ON *rúnakefli*: 'a stick or wand carved with runes.' Two other terms are rather ambiguous, OHG **holtzrūna*:(127) 'wood-rune,' which may be a more generic expression akin to ON *bókrún*, and ON *stinnir stafir* (Háv. 142): 'strong, hard staves' may refer to the hardness of the wood in a symbolic sense in that it was of enduring quality, and thus reflective of the eternal nature of the runes themselves.(128)

The idea that runes were colored red (especially with blood) is expressed in numerous verbal formulas but attributive adjectives and compounds also convey this essential aspect —ON *blóðgar rúnar* ("Sólarljóð" 61): 'bloody runes,' OE *baswe bōcstafas*: 'crimson characters, letters,' ON *dreyrstafir* ("Sólarljóð" 40): 'blood staves.' However, since two of these attestations occur in the medieval "Sólarljóð," it is quite possible that they are later (Christian?) formulations.

In *ES* ch. 72 (verse 48) there is a famous reference to rune magic in which *launstafir*: 'hidden (encoded?) staves' are mentioned. This would seem to be an indication of the use of runic codes or "secret runes" for operative purposes (cf. Genzmer 1952; Olsen 1943) and could be another example of "hiding" or "concealing" as a means to effect operative ends.

Other terms which might be understood in a technical sense are OHG *leodrūna*: 'song-rune, or sorceress with the help of a magical song,'(129) — a clear reference to the use of song in conjunction with runes(130) — and ON *staðlausir stafir* (Háv. 129), literally 'steadless staves → folly, senseless speech.' It is interesting to speculate that this latter term may have originally referred to divinatory terminology and have indicated rune-staves which had no meaningful place in the divinatory reading and hence were rendered meaningless or irrelevant to the question, etc.

2. Beneficial

Certain runic terms indicate benefits or have a generally positive tenor, e.g., ON *líknstafir* (Háv. 8; Sdr. 5): 'body (healing) staves' (cf. ON *líknargaldr*: 'healing spell'), ON *gamanrúnar* (Háv. 120, 130; Sdr. 5): 'joy-bringing-runes → merry talk, familiarity,' and ON *sigrúnar* (Sdr. 6): 'victory-runes.' Also, the compound *auðstafir* (Sdr. 31), which is generally recorded as a poetic paraphrase for "men," obviously had an original concrete meaning 'staves of wealth or treasure' (cf. Egilsson *Lex. Poet.* 1931: 22).(131)

Another group of terms is clearly positive but more general, and perhaps also belonging to the cosmological type, e.g., ON *sannir stafir* (Sdr. 14): 'true staves → truth,' ON *stórir stafir* (Háv. 142): 'powerful, potent staves,' and ON *stinnir stafir* (Hgv. 142): 'strong, hard staves.'

3. Detrimental Terms

In contrast to the positive runic terms there exists a negative terminology which points to things detrimental to human life, health, and harmony. One group refers to interpersonal conflicts, e.g., ON *lastastafir* (Ls. 10, 16, 18): 'staves of reproach taunting, slanderous words,'(132) ON *sakrúnar* (HHII.34): 'runes of insult or strife → strife causing speech' (both of which have overtones of ON *nið*), and OE *beadurūn*: 'conflict rune → secret enmity.'(133) Another more intensive set of terms conveys the idea of ruin or even death and darkness, e.g., ON *feiknstafir* (Grm. 12, Sólarljóð 60, Hervǫrilјóð 11): 'staves of banes, evils → staves of ruinous or traitorous portent' (cf. de Vries 1961a: 115), ON *meinstafir* (Ls. 28): 'injurious staves → baleful words' (cf. De Vries 1961a: 382), ON *bǫlstafir* (Sdr. 30): 'bale-, evil-staves → staves of misfortune, ill-fate,' OE *inwitrūn*: 'malicious, wicked-rune → guileful counsel,' ON *myrkr stafr* (*ES* ch. 72): 'dark stave → deadly, sickness-causing stave,' ON *helstafir* (HHj. 29): 'death-staves → deadly words.'(134) The ON terms *blóðgar rúnar* and *dreyrstafir* may also be understood in an expanded sense as portents of bloodshed, etc. Furthermore, ON *flærðarstafir* (Sdr. 32): 'seductive or deceptive staves → deceptive words' and perhaps the *staðlausir stafir* may indicate psychological deception or confusion.

4. Neutral/Ambiguous Terms

To this broad group of expressions belong terms of apparently cosmological import, those of psychological relevance, and an extensive class of more obviously magical significance. The idea of things ancient being things of great cosmological, religio-magical, or mythic importance is well known in the Germanic world (cf. Bauschatz 1982: 1ff., 117ff.) and it is in this context that the ON *fornir stafir* (Vm. 1; Grm. 35) and *fornar rúnar* (Vsp. 60)(135) may best be understood. The linkage between a time concept and the life and being of man is contained in ON *ævinrúnar*: 'life-long, eternal runes,' and ON *aldrrúnar*: 'life-time runes' (both from Rþ. 43). A general term for the great power of runes is expressed in ON *meginrúnar* (Sdr. 19): 'might-runes' (cf. also *stórir stafir* and *stinnir stafir*). Relevant to the powers of the human psyche itself are ON *hugrúnar* (Sdr. 13): 'mind-runes,' and an expression of the principal manifestation of the mind in ON *málrúnar* (Sdr. 12, GSr. I 23): 'speech-runes.'(136)

Certain other lexical items either appear in clearly operative contexts or betray magical concepts in their etymologies or histories. In the Germanic tradition the connection of the dead and death with operative motifs is a strong one (see sect. 5. above)(137) and it is one firmly rooted in the mythos of the runes (cf. the shamanistic initiatory motif of Háv. 138ff.). In this context, we view the most universal runic compound PGmc. **haljorūnō-*: 'mystery or lore of the realm of death.' As is well known, however, the theme developed into a functional appellative at an early date and eventually became a common fem. PN suffix.(138) This term is attested in the S. and EGmc. dialects, e.g., Go. *haljarūnae* (Jordanes *Getica* XXIV, 121. < **haljarūnos*): 'sorceresses,'(139) OE *hellerūne (pythonissa), hel(h)rūne, helrūna, helrȳnegu*: 'one skilled in the mysteries of the dead, female necromancer, sorceress,'(140) and OHG *hellirūn(a)* which glosses *necromantia*: 'necromancy.'(141) Parallel to these terms is OHG *tōtrūna*: 'necromantic sorceress' (cf. OHG *tōtleod*: 'death-song, incantation') which probably goes back to a similar idea. Belonging to this same field, but apart from the personalized aspect, are ON *helstafir* (HHj. 29): 'death staves.' ON *valrúnar*: 'slaughter, war-runes,' and OE *wælrūn*; 'slaughter-rune, secret of approaching slaughter.'(142)

In Old English, personalized compounds with -*rūn*- even developed into terms for supernatural or demonic beings, e.g., *helrūna*: 'necromancer, monster' and *burgrūne ~ burhrūne* which glosses *furiæ, parcas*: 'furies, fates.' Moreover, an OHG gloss for the magically potent *mandragora* (mandrake) root was *alrūna*, which was apparently already an old appelative for "seeress."(143)

The Sdr. contains three runic compounds with strong operative contexts, i.e., *bjargrúnar* (9): 'help (for women in labor)-runes, or lore,' which is also attested in the Bergen/Bryggen corpus (cf. Liestøl 1963: 41-43),(144) *brimrúnar* (10): '(stormy) sea-runes, or lore' (used to calm the storm), and *ǫlrunar* (7): 'ale-runes' used to avoid betrayal and perhaps to detect poison in drinks (this latter if we view Sdr. 8 as a continuation of 7).(145) All of these are clearly conceived of in a concrete way — to be carved into various objects as a part of the operation (see 16. below). In the same lay but in a different context we find the term *blunnstafir* (Sdr. 2): 'sleep-causing staves' by means of which Óðinn put Sigrdrífa to sleep.(146)

Other terms which indicate a connection with some aspect of operant behavior are OHG *leodrūna* and OE *leodrūne*, which perhaps show an original link between the ideas of song or rhythmic speech and the runes. In addition OE *rūncræft*: 'skill in mysterious lore → skill in explaining mysteries' is interesting when compared to OE *wiccecræft*: 'witchcraft.'(147)

This corpus of evidence leads me to conclude that *$rūnō$- (as well as secondarily *$staƀaz$) originated in the magico-religious field and remained there in some capacity for the duration of the heathen Germanic tradition. It always retained a portion of its originally abstract ("mystery") or collective ("secret lore") meaning, even after it had been transferred to the graphemic runic characters (which might have been minimal signs of expanded bodies of lore). The technical terminology of which *$rūnō$- is a part very often obviously belongs to the operative field of activity; however, it is the nature and function of the operations with runes which must be demonstrated.

Operative Runic Formulas in Written Records

15. Many Old Norse texts — both poetic and prosaic — contain a consistent formula for runic operations which would seem to be archaic and perhaps consequently enduring. It is important to establish this formula as completely as possible according to a set of criteria which indicate the methods and function of magical operations in which runes are used. The time reference for the composition of most of this material spans from the 12th-15th centuries in the case of the saga accounts, back into the 9th-10th centuries in the case of many poetic aphorisms, etc.(148) However, we may be fairly certain that the formulaic actions, and many of the technical terms represented in the texts, indicate much older underlying structures. (This is at least partially corroborated by epigraphical evidence presented in ch. VI).

The use of runes in divinatory operations has been generally supposed by many scholars,(149) but there is only circumstantial or secondary evidence for this. Since this falls somewhat outside the scope of the present study, I will merely present a summary of this evidence. Certain technical runic terminology and contexts(150) seem to indicate the importance of runes in a kind of *passive* communication with an ascriptive numinous reality.(151) For example, the PGmc. terms *rēðan: 'to advise; consult' and *lesan: 'to collect' have been thought to have indicated the interpretative process in runic sortilege.(152)

The most explicit and oldest piece of evidence for the possible use of runes in divinatory practices is given by Tacitus *Germ.* ch. 10 (ca. 98 CE). There we learn that the *pater familiae* or *sacerdos civitatis* would randomly throw a number of slips (*surculi*) of wood from fruit- or nut-bearing trees, marked with certain signs (*notae*), onto a white cloth. After prayers to the gods, and while looking up into the sky, he takes up three slips of wood one at a time and interprets them according to their signs.(153) Somewhat earlier Caesar reports on *matres familiae* among Ariovistus' Germans who used sortilege to determine if they should fight (*DBG* I, 50) and consulting the lots three times (*ter sortibus consultum*) to decide whether to execute a prisoner (*DBG* I, 53).(154) The *notae* of the account by Tacitus may have been runes (especially in light of the new Meldorf brooch find, see VI) — or they may have been non-runic ideographs.(155)

The oldest direct evidence composed in a Germanic dialect is contained in three obscure Eddic passages, two of which occur in the context of mythology surrounding the Norns, i.e., Vsp. 20: [Nornir] *skáru á skíði. . . //lǫg lǫgðu/ lif kuru//ǫrlǫg segja* ('[the Norns] scored on a piece of wood they laid laws, they chose lives, they spoke the 'fates'),(156) and Háv. 111 where the Odinic persona says: . . . *þular stóli á// Urðar brunni at. . .//of rúnar heyrða ek dœma...* ('on the chair of that (cultic speaker,)(157) at the well of Urðr. . . of runes I heard it spoken'). Also, in Háv. 80 it is instructed that: *Þat er þá reynt/er þú at rúnum spyrr//inum reginkunnum*(158) ("It is proven [found] when you inquire of the runes, which are sprung from the 'divine advisors'"). In the Lat. *Lex Frisionum* (XIV, 1, after 850) we read of a simple method of drawing lots from a church altar to decide a murder case. On each of the lots a cross is carved.

Three later historical accounts also contain some information on divination. Alcuin, in his *Vita Willibrordi* ch. 17 (ca. 785-797), reports that some Christian prisoners of the Frisian king Radbōd, who had violated a Frisian sanctuary, were spared execution when, after lots had been cast on three consecutive days, negative results were obtained. Bede (*Hist. Eccl.* V, 10) also gives an account of sortilege used among the continental Saxons to select their war leaders. Various Lat. MSS usually abscribed to Hrabanus Maurus and known by the *name De inventione litterarum* (ca. 800) contain references to runes and divination, cf. Version A *cum quibus* (i.e., *litteras = runstabas?) carmina sua incantationesque ac divinationes significare procurant, qui adhuc pagano ritu involvuntur* ('with these [letters/rune-staves] they signify their songs, incantations, and divinations, for they are still given to pagan rites').(159)

This evidence does not provide us with enough information to conclude much other than that runes were probably used in some capacity in divinatory practices at some point in their history. The ritual formula detailed by Tacitus may have continued in some form, but the only recurring element is embodied in the use of the number *three*.

In order to determine if an actively operant runic formula is present in a text, a set of criteria must be established. 1) Ideally, one would find one or more runic technical terms with a runic direct object and prepositional phrase indicating the thing onto which the runes were carved in the context of parallel or auxiliary ritual actions with a clearly stated magical aim. 2) If two or more actively operative technical terms appear with a runic direct object, the ritual criterion would seem to be satisfied, and the expressed magical purpose less necessary. 3) Minimally, a verb indicating the execution of the runes and at least an understood runic direct object in the context of an expressed purpose must be present.

There are also a number of passages in which the carving of runes is described, but which appear in totally non-magical circumstances and are clear attestations of the profane use of runes in later times, e.g., *Haralds s. haðráða* in the *Morkinskinna* ch. 19, *Flóamanna s.* ch. 24, *Þáttr Þorsteins uxafóts* (*Flb.*, *Olafs s. Tryggvasonar* ch. 203), *Sturlunga s.*, *Guðmundar s.* and *Íslendinga s.* (cf. Kålund 1906-11, I, p. 153 and 480), *Svarfdœla s.* chs. 12; 13; 15, *Gísla s. Súrssonar* chs. 24; 34, *Grettis s. starfsama* ch. 22,(160) *Víglundar s.* ch. 18, and *Ǫrvar-Odds s.* ch. 46. Many other passages mention runes (or "staves") in didactic formulas connected to verbs such as *kunna* (Sdr. 6 *et passim*, Rþ. 45): 'to know,' *kenna* (*Heimsk. Ynglinga s.* ch. 7, *VS* ch. 13, Rþ. 36): 'to teach,' *vita* (Grm. 12) 'to know,' *geta* (Háv. 18): 'to get,' *finna* (Háv. 142): 'to find,' etc. These fall outside our criteria for operative formulas, which are presented in Charts I-III.

The columns of Charts I-III represent the following elements with regard to the operative formulas: 1) the textual location, 2) the direct (runic) object, 3) the verbs directly connected with that object, 4) the substance into which the runes are carved, 5) parallel verbal formulas which might complete or augment the ritual action, 6) any auxiliary ritual actions which might be mentioned, and 7) the stated purpose of the operation.

CHART I

1	2	3	4	5	6	7
Source	Object	Verb	Material Medium	Parallel Actions	Auxiliary Actions	Purpose of Operatiion
Vats. 34	rúnar	reist	á súlu	með ǫllum þeim formála var sagðr	setting of pole	níð-curse
ES 44	rúnar	reist	á (horni)	reið á blóðinu		poison
ES 44 (verse)	rún	ristum	á horni	rjóðum spjǫll í dreyra		detection
ES 57	rúnar	reist	á stǫnginni	segja þær formála		níð-curse
ES 72	rúnarnar	telgði	af (tálkni) ok skóf þæri í eld		burning runes and object (whale-bone) putting runes near a person	neutralizing malevolent effect to heal girl
	rúnar	reist				
Grs. 79	rúnar	reist	á rótinni	rauð í blóð ok kvað yfir galdra	preparation of medium (knife) circumambulations	
Háv. 157	í rúnum	ríst fák				necromancy
Skm. 36	þria stafi	ríst ek		af ríst/a reist		curse/love charm
Sdr. 6	sigrúnar	rísta	á hjalti hjǫrs á vettrimmum á valbǫstum	nefna tysvar Tý		victory
Sdr. 9	bjargrúnar	rísta spenna	á lófa um liðu	biðja dísir duga		to help in birth
Sdr. 11	limrúnar	rísta	á berki á baðmi viðar		limbs bending eastward chosen	healing
Sdr. 7	ǫlrúnar	rísta merkja	á horni á nagli (nauð)			to prevent treachery (detect poison)
Sdr. 10	brimrúnar	rísta leggja	á stafni á sjornar blaði eld í ár			to calm the sea
H-H 32	seiðvillur	reist		með þeim atkvæðum		counter-magical curse
Saxo I,6,4	carminibus	insculptis	ligno			necromancy

CHART II

1	2	3	4	5	6	7
Source	Object	Verb	Material Medium	Parallel Actions	Auxiliary Actions	Purpose of Operatiion
VS 32 GðR. II 22	hverskins stafir	ristnir (róðnir)	í horni	róðnir með blóði		interprsonal communication
Háv. 80	at rúnum	spyrr gorðu fáði				
Háv. 142	stafi	rísta ráða / fá freista / biðja / blóta senda / sóa				
Sdr. 18	rúnar	á váru ristnar af skafnar hverfðar	við inn helga mjǫð			
		sendar	á víða vegu			
Háv. 139	rúnar	nam ek upp		œpandi nam		initiation

CHART III

1	2	3	4	5	6	7
Source	Object	Verb	Material Medium	Parallel Actions	Auxiliary Actions	Purpose of Operatiion
Háv 137	rúnar	tekr				við bǫlvi (therapeutic)
Sdr. 2	blunnstǫfum	bregða				antidote to the svefþorn
Sdr. 13	hugrúnar	reist (réð) (hugði)				to gain wisdom/ wisdom
Sdr. 15-16	(rúnar)	váru ristnar	(24 media)			

—110—

In Chart I we see 15 examples of complete ritual formulas (see 15. below). Chart II contains four complex formulas in mythic contexts, which use present tense paradigms of the runic operation itself in the form of technical verbs. Here it should be pointed out that although the verbs *freista*, *biðja*, *blóta*, *senda*, and *sóa* in Háv. 144 are usually ascribed to the sphere of sacrificial terminology (cf. Düwel 1970b, Liberman 1978: 473-88, Neff 1980), the fact that *biðja* (Sdr. 9) and *senda* (Sdr. 18) also appear in runic contexts lead us to speculate that either 1) the terminologies of runic operations and sacrifices were intertwined or 2) that both sacrifices or runic operations could be conducted toward similar ends or 3) that a sacrifice might have sometimes been an auxiliary action to runic operations — or all of these might be true. The parallel passages from Gðr. II 22 and VS ch. 32 seem to be a unique mixture of magical formulaic action and "profane" purpose — as a simple effort at interpersonal communication. But we do not know what an earlier archetype of this episode might have implied. Another unique formula is that of Háv. 138-139, which represents Óðinn's mythic reception of the runes by means of an initiatory ritual action (of apparent shamanistic character).(161)

As an appendix to these charts the highly suggestive stanzas of Sdr. 15-17 might be added, which although they do not meet our criteria for inclusion as operative formulas, nevertheless demonstrate a magical character through the 24(!) mythic objects onto which it is said the runes are to be carved. This passage would seem to function on a mytho-magical or paradigmatic level.

Runic Ritual

16. As far as the evidence left to us will allow, the basic runic operative ritual(162) may be summarized as: 1) the runic magician 2) carves the runic graphs, 3) colors them (with blood or other dye),(163) 4) speaks an oral formula over the object (which may or may not correspond to the graphic form), and 5) perhaps performs some auxiliary operation in accordance with the purpose of the ritual. This last element may come before, during, or after the performance of elements 1-4. Another definite operative element which may enter into an expanded formula is 6) scraping the runes off their medium in order to destroy them by fire (*ES* ch. 72) or to mix them in a drink (Sdr. 18). Perhaps connected to this last element, but very ambiguous, is whatever is implied in the technical verb *senda* (Háv. 144; Sdr. 18).

Two of the clearest and most complete textual representations of runic operations are offered in *ES* ch. 44:

> *Egill brá þá knifi sínum ok stakk í lófa sér; hann tók við horninu ok reist á rúner ok reið á blóðinu. Hann kvað*:(9)
> *Rístum rún á horni*
> *rjóðumm spjǫll í dreyra*, etc.

('Egill then drew his knife and stabbed the palm of his hand; he took the drinking horn and carved runes on it and rubbed blood on it. He said: We carve a rune on the horn/we redden the spell in blood...')

and in the *Gr. s.* ch. 79:
> *...síðan tók [Þuriðr] kníf sinn ok reist rúnar á rótinni ok rauð í blóði sinu ok kvað yfir galdra. Hon gekk ǫfug andsælis um tréið ok hafði þar yfir mǫrg rǫmm ummæli.*

(...'then [Þuriðr] took her knife and carved runes on the root and reddened them in her blood, and spoke spells over it. She went backwards and widdershins around the wood and spoke very powerful utterances over it.')

(1) In order to perform magic the operator must meet a set of cultural, psychological, *et al.* criteria (see II.1) and most probably be in what is thought to be a special spiritual condition during the action. We have profiles of persons with various magical skills with runes (cf. Egill in *ES*, Þuriðr in *Gr. s.*, Jǫkull in *Vat. s.*, and perhaps Guðrún in *VS*). More important are perhaps the mythic archetypes of the runic magician provided by Óðinn (Háv.) and Skírnir (Skm.) and the initiatory paradigm and instructions of Sigrdrífa (Sdr.). Two semi-historical or historicized figures of apparently numinous, or at least non-human, origin, the dwarf Mǫndull (*G-H s.* ch. 32) and the giantess Harthgrepa (Saxo I, 6, 4) also perform what seems to be a runic type of magic (see Chart I). From the sparse and rather late evidence offered by these sources, we can at least tentatively conclude that the runes and their instrumental use did indeed belong to the sphere of Odinic religion and that the runic tradition held a special place in the scheme of Germanic lore. The method by which runic knowledge was taught is still unclear. It is unfortunate that we have no prosaic, historical evidence in this regard(164) since we are left with only mythic, paradigmatic accounts with no firm linkage between the two.

(2) The act of carving the runes into a material medium is well attested in operative contexts (see Charts I-III), but the carving alone does not seem sufficient to constitute a magical operation as it always occurs in conjunction with other formulaic actions in such instances. The instrument with which the runes are cut is only mentioned twice (*ES* ch. 44 and *Gr. s.*

ch. 79), where the tool is described as a *knífr* ('knife'). The verbs used are ON *rísta*, pret. *reist* (*passim*), *merkja* (Sdr. 7), and perhaps *skera* (Vsp. 20).(165)

(3) In seven instances the act of coloring is at least alluded to. Four times this is expressed through the ON verb *fá*: 'to draw, paint' (Háv. 30, 142, 144, 157), which may have become synonymous with *rísta* in the technical runic terminology at an earlier date (Ebel 1963: 30-35). However, since this verb occurs at least three times in contrast to *rísta* we may be certain that it preserved the meaning "to color" in instrumental runic technology as well. The substance with which the runes were colored is mentioned five times as "blood" (i.e., *ES* ch. 44, *Gr. s.* ch. 79, *VS* ch. 32, Gör. II 22 as *blóð* and *ES* ch. 44 as *dreyr*). The second and third elements seem closely linked, usually as if part of one ritual formulaic unit which seems to prepare the material medium for the fourth element.

(4) Some vocal formula is reported to be spoken over the inscribed (and colored) object in possibly six instances. The clearest attestations are those in *Vat. s.* ch. 34: . . .*með ǫllum þeim formála sem fyrr var sagðr* ('. . .with all those formulas which had been previously spoken'), *ES* ch. 44: *Hann kvað* (+ poetic formula), *ES* ch. 57: *ok segja þær formála* ('. . .and saying those formulas'), and *Gr. s.* ch. 79:. . .*ok kvað yfir galdra* ('. . .and spoke incantations over it'). Two other important attestations of this element are contained in Sdr. 6: *nefna tysvar Tý* ('name, or call Týr twice') and Sdr. 9: *biðja dísir duga* ('ask the *dísir* for aid'). It does not seem at all necessary that the spoken *formálar* represent the graphic runic formula, so the often held assumption that in this stanza Sigurðr is instructed to carve ↑ runes as *sigrúnar* is somewhat conjectural, cf. Düwel (1981a: 164-65). The instruction that, as a part of an operation involving *bjargrúnar* to help women in labor, Sigurðr is to *biðja dísir duga* is another instance of numina in such formulas. Furthermore, it is a link to the obscure reference in Háv. 144 in which *biðja* is mentioned in a possibly runic context. Could it be that this verb represents a technical term for formulaic requests made to numina in not only sacrificial but also runic operations? Also, the arcane runic initiatory stanza of Háv. 139.2-3: *nam ek upp rúnar/œpandi nam* ('I took up the runes/took them calling out') would also indicate the importance of *vocal* activity on a paradigmatic level.(166) In any case, these phrases are clear indications of 1) the speaking of a vocal formula over inscribed forms, 2) the magical nature of the vocal forms (cf. *galdr, formáli*), and 3) the use of numina in such formulas.

(5) Certain auxiliary ritual actions mentioned in the accounts give us some insight into the actions which might have surrounded a runic

operation. In the *níð* examples (*ES* ch. 57 and *Vat. s.* ch. 34) it seems that the actual setting of the *níðstǫng*, with its proper iconographic symbolism, etc., is a part of a complex ritual behavior. A similar impression is given by Þuríðr's careful selection process for the piece of wood to act as a medium for her runic curse (*Gr. s.* ch. 79).(167) Þuríðr is also said to go backwards and counterclockwise (widdershins) around the runic medium. Such circumambulations are mentioned several times in the Germanic magical record (e.g., *Vat s.* chs. 36; 47, *G-H s.* ch. 32, the *Galdrabók* no. 29). The burning of scraped-off runes (*ES* ch. 72, see below) and the apparent importance of placing the runic object itself in close physical proximity to the person(s) to be affected by the formulas (cf. also *ES* ch. 72 and *G-H s.* ch. 28) may also be considered auxiliary ritual actions.(168) This is of course the most difficult element to assess, since it is not directly a part of the actual production of the runic formulas, and has therefore left few traces in the epigraphical record.

(6) Scraping the runes off (ON *skafa af* or *rísta af*) their material medium in order to remove their operative force from the medium is attested three times in both prosaic (*ES* ch. 72) and poetic/paradigmatic (Skm. 36; Sdr. 18) contexts. In two instances, (*ES* ch. 72 and Skm. 36) it is clear that this is done in order to negate the effect entirely (coupled perhaps with the burning of the shavings and the medium). However, in the third attestation the possibility of using this technique to transfer the magical force from one medium to another is presented. Sdr. 18 seems to offer cryptic instructions for an operation in which the runes are carved into a wooden medium and scraped off and mixed into mead — by means of which they were sent out to accomplish some effect:

> *Allar vóro af scafnar,   þær er vóro á ristnar,*
> *oc hverfðar við inn helga mjǫð*
> *oc sendar á víða vega.*

('All [the runes] were scraped off, that had been carved on [the object], and mixed with the holy mead, and sent on wide ways.)

Could the "sending" refer to a method of libation sacrifice — either the pouring out of the rune-mead mixture or otherwise ritually sending it abroad, or to a consumption of the mixture? This latter possibility is perhaps suggested in Sdr. 5 where beer is said to be blended with various elements (including *gamanrúnar*).

This body of evidence would strongly seem to suggest that the runes were at the least a part of the general framework of the established magical thought and practice of the Germanic peoples throughout their pre-Christian tradition (and continued in an underground, fragmented tradition in later times). It also appears more likely than not that the runes themselves were originally thought of as a system of some cosmological and hence operative importance. Recent scholarly judgements to the contrary seem to miss the forest for the trees (see ch. III.3).

Notes for Chapter V

1. Cf. de Vries (1956: I, 172ff.) who discusses at length the animistic as well as dynamistic concepts in the context of Germanic religious outlook.

2. This idea was first explored in a rather universal way by Otto (1936) and later in the Germanic context by Baetke (1942) and Hartmann (1943). Benveniste (1973: 346ff.) provides some insights on the I-E attestations of this dichotomy.

3. Both terms are attested in all older Germanic dialects and seem to have been fundamental to the pre-Christian worldview; however, after the onset of Christian inroads into the indigenous terminology, the conceptual distinction eventually faded. *Wīh- has been totally lost in NE, while it is found only secondarily in NHG (e.g., [ein]weihen: 'to consecrate') and in Scandinavia (e.g., Nor. vie: 'to consecrate').

4. *Wīh- is used to describe something sacred, e.g., ON vé, OHG wīh, OE wīh: 'site for cultic activity, sacred enclosure;' ON vébǫnd: 'ropes used to mark the boundaries of the assembly or court;' OE weoh: 'a (heathen) divine image; idol,' and perhaps in three runic inscriptions (DR 4: Heddeby II, DR 209: Glavendrup, DR 221: Vordingborg) ODan. wē: 'grave mound, sacred enclosure,' as interpreted by Wimmer (1914: 94; 103; 107), cf. also Baetke (1941: 98ff.). These readings are challenged by Moltke-Jacobsen (1941). Baetke (1942: 101) seems to think that the grave-mound and wē were merely räumlich miteinander verbunden.

5. Neff (1980: 5ff.).

6. Cf. Hartmann (1943: passim) and Baetke (1942: passim).

7. That the two terms were understood as an organic whole is perhaps demonstrated in formulaic linkings, e.g., ON vé-heilakt and the EGmc. wīh-hailag on the ring of Pietroassa (KJ 41, ca. 380).

8. That is if it belongs to the same root as gand-; however, it could also reflect the concept of a primal chaotic essence or force, of of a great expansive space, cf. de Vries (1930/31; 1961a: 167-68).

9. South Germanic *bi-ginnan may have a spatial meaning, while the connection between ON gandr and ginn- is rather tenuous, cf. Polomé (1984) and also de Vries (1961a: 155; 167-68).

10. See ch. II, n. 6. That psychic derivatives are to be expected is possibly shown by the OPers. magû: 'member of the priestly class' (< *magho-ti-: 'the mighty one'?).

11. The original sense of *wōð- must have been close to the ON complex, cf. the god-name *Wōðanaz: 'master of inspired numinous activity,' and the I-E cognates, e.g., Lat. vātēs: 'soothsayer,' OIr. fáith: 'seer, prophet,' MWel. gwawd: 'song, poetry.'

12. That this emotive faculty must have been of great importance in the archaic Germanic psychophysical model is evidenced also by the fact that PGmc. *gaist- seems to have belonged to this semantic sphere, cf. ON geisa: 'to rage,' OE gæstan: 'to frighten,' Go. us-gaisjan: 'to frighten,' and most importantly the Go. p.p. usgaisiþs which translates Gk. ἐξέτη in Mark 3:21, cf. Flowers (1983: 124-25).

13. All of these terms seem semantically related, as ON gæfa and gipta, both of which can mean "luck, good fortune," are ultimately derived from PGmc. *giƀan: 'to give (or receive),' and would indicate 'something given or received (from the gods?),' while auja (ON ey) seems to be connected to the concept 'to help' (cf. Krause 1966: 241).

14. Cf. Falk (1926) and de Vries (1956: I, 222ff.). This is also shown by the fact that *hamingja* can be acquired quantitatively and qualitatively and redistributed in a concrete manner, cf. Cleasby-Vigfusson (1957: 236) and Dumézil (1970: 142).

15. Cf. de Vries (1930/31: 51ff.; 1961a: 167), and also Strömbäck (1975: 6ff.), who sees the *gandr* as a substance connected to the magician's soul which can be "sent out."

16. Cf. Lid (1950: 37-58; 59-81) and Bø (1960: 183-85). Ellis Davidson (1973: 31) believes the *gandr* to have been originally associated with the "guardian spirit" concept.

17. Cf. Reichborn-Kjennerud (1924 : 158-91) on the general importance of the names of persons and things in therapeutic magic.

18. Cf. e.g., Storm (1893), Ellis (Davidson) (1943: 137-48) — it would seem that the name, besides being an autonomous power, also acts as a focus for other soul or power conceptions which may be transferred with a name.

19. Examples of this are found in the HHj (prose before stanza 6) and in the *Ála flekks s.* ch. 2, cf. de Vries (1956: I, 181) and also Cleasby-Vigfusson (1957: 445).

20. This power of attraction is behind taboos against naming feared animals, demonic or divine beings, etc., cf. Hegedus (1958: 79ff.).

21. The most famous and explicit reference to this belief in Germanic is found in the Fm. (prose before stanza 2): *Sigurðr dulði nafns síns, fyr því at þat var trúa þera i fornescio, at orð feigs mannz mætti mikit, of hann bǫvaði óvin sinom með nafni* (cf. Neckel-Kuhn 1962: 180). Cf. also Ström (1947: 26ff.), de Vries (1956: I, 298), Simpson (1973: 169).

22. Such general conceptions seem to have been universal among the Germanic peoples; however, their specific manifestations and terminologies sometimes showed wide divergence. For NGmc. attestations, cf. de Vries (1956: I, 209ff.), Strom (1954), Turville-Petre (1964: 221ff.), for the sparse EGmc. evidence, cf. Helm (1937: II, 1, 10-25), in SGmc. the sources are more varied, cf. Helm (1953: II, 2, 44ff.) and Philippson (1929: 51-69).

23. Cf. Mundal (1974) for a complete analysis of the various manifestations of the *fylgja* in Norse literature.

24. In ON tradition, the *valkyrjur* seem to have been part of the Oðinnic mythos and are often attached to certain heroes (cf. Helgi in HHj., HHI, and HHII), cf. Ellis (1943: 66ff.), Ström (1954: 70-79), de Vries (1956: I, 273-74).

25. Cf. e.g., Klare (1933/34: 1ff.), Ellis (1943: 156ff.), Solheim (1958), Ström (1960), Jón Árnason (1954: I, 213ff.; 1955: III, 289ff.).

26. The ON term *draugr* most probably refers to the malevolent or destructive function of these walking dead, and is to be ultimately derived from PIE **dhreugh-*: 'to damage, betray.'

27. This is emphasized by Ellis (1943: 92 *et passim*), but this aspect may have been further accentuated in the literary embellishments and conventions of the Icelandic saga writers.

28. Robberies of *draugar* in their howes are described in several sagas, e.g., *Gr. s.* ch. 18, *Haraðr s. Grímkelssonar* ch. 15, and *Bárðar s. Snæfellsáss* ch. 20, cf. Ellis (1943: 191-94). For a discussion of the evidence — or lack of it — for these practices provided by the runic inscriptions, cf. Düwel (1978). Also, cf. other articles in Jankuhn-Nehlsen-Roth 1978.

29. The most famous examples of this are taken from the *Elder or Poetic Edda* itself, where Óðinn raises seeresses (cf. Vsp., Bdr., Vǫluspá in skamma [= Hdl. 29-44]) to gain cosmological prophecies, and where a certain Svípdagr raises his mother to gain magical skills or spells ('Gróagaldr' or 'Svípdagsmál') and where Freyja awakens Hyndla to make certain genealogical information available to her charge Ottarr (Hdl.). It is possible that to some extent these are mythic reflections of practices in which a living human seeress (*vǫlva*) would be questioned on matters while in a trance-state (cf. Ellis 1943: 166).
165

30. Such uses of corpses by magicians as "sendings" (ON pl. *sendingar*) are known by the technical term *dauðingar* (cf. Solheim 1958: 298).

31. "Mǫndull (a dwarf) went twice widdershins around the slain. He blew and whistled in all the airts and then chanted ancient spells over them and then he said these slain would do no harm." Due to Mǫndull's *fjǫlkynngi*, the wizard, Grímr, is unable to raise the dead men to continue to fight (*G-H s.* ch. 33).

32. Certain episodes of this type emphasize an initiatory theme (e.g., in *Hervarar s. ok Heiðreks* ch. 4 and *Óláfs s. helga* chs. 7-9 [= *Flb.* II, 7-9]) which in some respects correspond to other initiatory journeys into the realm of the dead in Germanic tradition, cf. Ellis (1943: 170ff.).

33. Cf. Birkeli (1938), Ellis (1943: 99ff.), Höfler (1973a: 18-19).

34. Cf. Höfler (1973a) for a survey of this phenomenon. From the vocabulary of Jordanes (*Getica* XIII, 78) it is clear that the *proceres* of the Goths were not ordinary humans but *semideos*, i.e., *ansis* (< *ansuz*).

35. Cf. *Óláfs s. helga* ch. 7 (= *Flb.* II, 7), and a discussion of this and the worship of burial mounds in general by Ellis (1943: 90; 92-96; 100-111).

36. For general treatments of the lesser divinities and their functions in Germanic religion, cf. Grimm (1878: III, 122-160), Jente (1921: 127ff.), Helm (1953: II; 2, 87ff.), Ström (1954), de Vries (1956: I, 241ff.), Turville-Petre (1964: 221ff.), Motz (1973/74).

37. Certain ON dwarf-names, e.g., Gandálfr (Vsp. 12) and Álfr (Vsp. 16) demonstrate an inexorable link between the concepts underlying the *álfr* and the *dvergr*, cf. a general study of dwarf-names by Motz (1973a).

38. Cf. studies by Motz (1981a; 1981b), who shows the often beneficial aspects of the *jǫtnar* in Norse tradition.

39. Not until the Reformation Age do we get examples of the Germanic gods used in "classical" magical invocations, cf. e.g., in the *Galdrabók* no. 43 (N. Lindqvist 1921: 66 and Flowers 2005: 54) following a magical sign we read: *og mæl til þessa hialpe mier. . . yle (?) aller guder þor (o)denn frigg freia Satan Belsebupp og aller þeir og þær sem Walholl biggia. I þijnu megttugaste naffne Odenn.*

40. Cf. Kjær (1914: 219-23), de Vries (1961a: 125), Falk (1924: 9). See also n. 110 and VI.7 and note 17 on *felhan*.

41. Cf. Hampp (1961) and Wipf (1975) for the use of mythic contexts for magical formulas in OHG.

42. Cf. e.g., the reciprocal relationship between men and the gods expressed in the Vedic sacrifice (Gonda 1960).

43. Cf. Eggers (1932) for a typology of magical objects in the Icelandic tradition.

44. This can be irrelevant for our purposes here, if we accept Steblin-Kaminskij's (1973) argument concerning the "syncretic truth" of the saga literature, i.e., that the events

may not be factual but that the world and events portrayed were plausible enough to be accepted by contemporary audiences — and therefore represent an even more important kind of "truth."

45. For comprehensive studies of the magician in Scandinavian literature, see Dillmann (1976), and earlier both Olsen (1935: 177-221; 1935: 5-49) and Ellis Davidson (1973).

46. It has been noticed that in traditional societies (non-Judeo-Christian) "magic" in and of itself carries no moral stigma, and it is more specifically the aims and results of an act (magical or non-magical) which are subject to ethical standards, cf. e.g., Ellis Davidson (1973: 37): "... there is no condemnation of magic as such, and many using it were highly esteemed in the community; it was only condemned and punished when used to injure others or to protect those doing harm." Cf. also Wax-Wax (1962; 1963).

47. Most references are to divinatory acts, cf. Caesar *DBG* I, 50; 53; Tacitus *Germ.* ch. 10, *Hist.* IV, 61.

48. Jordanes *Getica* XXVI, 121. This is supposed to represent events from ca. 200 CE, but it was not composed until 551 CE.

49. Helm (1937: II; 1, 2-31 and 1953: II; 2, 117-166) provides a convenient survey of magical and divinatory aspects of Germanic religion for the post-Roman Age in the East and West (South) Germanic regions.

50. The greatest problem for a historian of these concepts is the ever-present danger that certain features may be literary borrowings or inventions.

51. Cf. the examples given by Ellis Davidson (1973).

52. This folkloristic material is corroborated by runic and primary written evidence which shows that at least semi-learned clerics actually worked quasi-heathen magical operations, cf. Moltke (1938) and the *Galdrabók* (N. Lindqvist 1921).

53. The various Germanic legal codes of the Migration Age (cf. Kiessling 1941) certainly refer to free born persons and often mention the illegal use of magic.

54. Examples of magicians from lower social strata, especially ethnic minorities, are discussed by de Vries (1956: I, 326-27; 331-32), Strömbäck (1935: 198-203).

55. Numerous examples of magicians from royal or landed classes or people from this group who used magicians are available from ON sources, e.g., king Fróði in *Hrólfs s. kraka* ch. lff., Eyvindr (a descendant of Haraldr hárfagri) in *Heimskr. Óláfs s. Tryggvasonar* chs. 62-63, and of course Egill from *ES*.

56. Cf. e.g., Haraldr's burning of 80 sorcerers reported in *Heimskr. Haralds s. hárfagra* ch. 34, or Oláfr's killing of a number of magicians in *Heimskr. Óláfs s. Tryggvasonar* ch. 62-63.

57. See Flowers (1993: 399-400) for a discussion of the relationship between *galdr* and *seiðr*.

58. *En þessi fjǫlkyngi (seiðr), of framðier, fylgir svá mikil ergi, at eigi þótti karlsmǫnnum skammlaust við at fara, ok var gyðjunum kend sú íþrótt.*

59. Cf. Veleda in Tacitus *Germ.* ch. 8, *Hist.* IV, 61; 65, V, 22; 24, who was apparently a figure of supreme religious and hence "civil" authority, cf. also Albrinia ~ Aurinia (< *Albrūna) in Tacitus *Germ.* ch. 8 and Γαννα in Cassius Dio's *Hist. Romanorum* LXVII, 5; 3.

60. Cf. Kiessling (1941: 20ff.). The *Leges Burgundorum* XXXIV mentions as a reason to divorce a woman: ... *maleficium vel sepulchrorum violatricem*...

61. On the role of women in therapeutic magic, cf. Müller (1976: 350ff.).

62. It is a striking statistic that during the witchcraft persecutions in Iceland, of the 125 trials against people for having runes on their person, etc., only nine were women.

63. Cf. Jaide (1937) and Eggers (1932) for a more complete survey of magical behavior in ON sources.

64. For a description of the *útiseta*, cf. de Vries (1956: I, 328-30), Buchholz (1968: 39ff.). This is often necromantic in purpose, and certainly shamanistic in character. Through stillness and prolonged isolation the magician is able to communicate with the realm of the dead.

65. Especially in spontaneous situations, e.g., in times of danger or urgent need, cf. Ellis Davidson (1973).

66. Cf. the *níð*-poetry (Almqvist 1965; 1974, Ellis Davidson 1973: 33ff.). Also, various ON sources indicate the use of *ljóð* or *kvæði* for magical ends (cf. Háv. 140, 146, *et passim*, as well as sagas, e.g., *G-H s.* ch. 33 and *Frostbræðra s.* ch. 10). OE and OHG spells in poetic form (cf. Storms 1948 and Steinmeyer 1963: 365ff.) attest to the same process.

67. Besides some runic evidence for this, there are several references to these types of utterances in the sagas, e.g., the "Irish" spoken in a magical spell (*Vat. s.* ch. 47) or descriptions of the *seiðlæti*: 'sounds of magical chanting' (cf. *Lax. s.* ch. 37). On this whole question, cf. further Olsen (*NIyR* IV, 173), who connects the phrase *mælti írsku* with the idea of *ephesia grammata*.

68. Cf. Heusler (1894; 1926: 55ff.). See also ch. VII of the present work.

69. Other terms, e.g., ON *læknir*; OE *læce*: 'physician', perhaps originally had to do with the use of incantations by Germanic healers (see de Vries 1961a: 371-72). The ON term *seiðr* may or may not belong to this semantic field. If it does, it would have to be a borrowing from some non-I-E language (meaning something like 'sound, noise, etc.'), while if it is indigenous, it belongs to the field of demonstrative action and may come from the idea of "binding," cf. de Vries (1961a: 467-78) on this problematic etymology.

70. Cf. Hauck (1969: 41ff.; 1970a:340) on the representation of this practice in the bracteate tradition. In ON sources we are reminded of the dwarf Mǫndull who whistled and blew into the divisions of heaven (*ættir*) in order to attempt to prevent some men from being raised from the dead (*G-H s.* ch. 33).

71. It is also possible that this is the same root as that which results in *wīh-, and would thus have to be kept distinct from this concept of motion.

72. The act of "consecrating" or "giving" a victim to a god as a curse or magical attack formula is common in Germanic procedures, cf. the formula . . . *Þōr vīgi þig þ(u)rsa drōtin*. . . (DR 419. Canterbury MS Cotton Caligula A XV, see ch. VI.53).

73. For example, *Styrbjarnar þáttr* (= *Flb.* II, chs. 60-61) concerning the victory of king Eiríkr: *[Óðinn] seldi honom reyrsprota í hǫnd ok bað hann skjóta honom yfir lið Styrbjarnar, ok þat skyldi hann mæla: Óðinn á yðr alla!* This passage has been discussed in connection with the Liebenau brooch by Düwel (1972: 140-41).

74. Cf. *Landnámabók* III, 7; 8. In the 7th chapter account, the man who performs the rite is specifically said to be *hamramr*: 'able to change shape; gifted with magical strength.' For a comparative study of the magical hurling of the spear, based on Slavic, Germanic, Roman, and Greek material, cf. Čiževskij (1956), and for a more detailed study of the Germanic tradition, cf. H. Kuhn (1978: 247ff.).

75. Cf. Lid (1921; 1927), Honko (1959: 96), de Vries (1956: I, 296-98).
76. Cf. Hauck (1977: 471ff.) on this theme in the bracteate iconography. In a less therapeutic context, we are reminded of the transfer of the dynamistic *hamingja*-force from Norse kings to their men through hand-to-hand contact (cf. the ON phase: *leggja hamingju við einhvern*: "to give 'luck' to a person."
77. Storms (1948) gives a complete outline of both types of substances used in OE charms.
78. Reichborn-Kjennerud (1924a:133) says of the leek: "*Dens bruk som matvekst lægeurt og som magisk vern har gitt den en anseelse i gammel tid som ingen annen urt. Som trolldomsurt har den hatte en bred plass i nordisk magi.*"
79. Cf. the *Vǫlsa þáttr* verse 4 (= *Flb*. II, ch. 266), see also a discussion of the runic formula **lina : laukaR** in ch. VI. Recent treatments of this unique passage are given by Düwel (1971 : 200ff.) and Steinsland-Vogt (1981: 92-93).
80. Cf. Grimm (1876: II, 996ff.; 1873: III, 348ff.), Cockayne (1864-66 *passim*, esp. 1866: III, 299ff.), Kålund (1907 *passim*), Storms (1948: 78-83 *et passim*).
81. N. Lindqvist (1921). Cf. also Grimm (1876: II, 539; 1878: III, 186ff.), Storms (1948: 83-85 *et passim*). E. Schröder (1893: 264) connects OE *spell*, OHG *spel*, ON *spjall*: 'tale, spell' with PGmc. **spel-*: 'a piece of wood → rune stave,' cf. also de Vries. (1961a: 536).
82. Hdl. 10 tells of the stones of a *hǫrg* ('altar') being transformed into "glass" by the sprinklings with sacrificial blood. Storms (1948: 60-61) reports on practices which involve blood in therapeutic magic.
83. Cf. Reichborn-Kjennerud (1923: 4ff.; 34ff.), who theorizes that due to impurities ale was sometimes poisonous and could cause a condition indicated by the ON word *ǫlþr*. (Háv. 137).
84. On the ritual use of intoxicating drink in Germanic tradition, cf. Cahen (1921), Düwel (1971: 57ff.), Markey (1974), Wiegelmann (1976) and Neff (1980). Concerning the idea that intoxicants were used as a substitute for blood in some rites, cf. A Ström (1966: 334-37).
85. Wiegelmann (1976: 534) notes that the term "ale" may have indeed also referred to various mixtures of grain and honey, and it could have therefore also been a general archaic designation for "mead" as well. "Mead" (ON *mjǫðr*, OE *medu ~ meodu*) is, however, also an archaic I-E term — **medhu-*: 'intoxicant from honey,' cf. Gk. μεθυ: 'wine, an intoxicant.'
86. Krause (1938: 35ff.) produced the first comprehensive study of this topic, while Düwel (1974: 150-53) provides a clear set of criteria for the determination of such ideo- and logographic runes. Olsen (1883: 40ff.) surveys this use of runes in OIce. MSS — which is apparently non-magical in function.
87. Arntz (1935: 238, 1944: 268).
88. For collections of these signs, cf. N. Lindqvist (1921), Kålund (1907: 367-68), Oláfur Davíðsson (1903), and Jón Árnason (1954: I, 432ff.; 1955: III, 466).
89. Hauck (1969: 27ff.) has shown how through a process of re-interpretation, the iconography of certain Roman coin models was transformed into an indigenous amuletic iconography (of probable apotropaic, mystic-initiatory, or shamanistic function.)
90. The discussion of these categories is necessarily conditioned by our topic at hand; for a systematic treatment of "magical objects" in Icelandic literature, cf. H. Eggers (1932).

91. e.g., in the case of the vǫlva, who carries the vǫlr: 'a rounded stick, staff' as a kind of scepter — but it surely had some other magical significance or function, cf. de Vries (1956: I, 319-320; 324).

92. Cf. H. Eggers (1932: 30ff. *et passim*), Falk (1914: 43ff.).

93. Cf. for example, Thrane *RGA* (1973: 268-69).

94. Cf. Cleasby-Vigfusson (1957: 400), and also Moltke (1938a:139). H. Eggers (1932 *passim*) gives numerous examples of the magical properties of certain stones in ON literature.

95. On stone ax amulets, cf. Almgren (1909), Helm (1913: 168; 187ff.), Moltke (1938a:144). Such amulets were also common among the Slavs and were known as *strěly* — which could protect a house from storm, insure good fortune, restore milk to dry cows, etc., cf. Gimbutas (1971: 165).

96. The *Galdrabók* (N. Lindqvist 1921; Flowers 2005) gives instructions on the construction of several amulets from wood inscribed with various *stafir*, cf. nos. 9, 29, 32, 36.

97. Cf. *RGA* I (1973), 268ff. Those objects, which could include various bones, teeth, stones, glass beads, or herbs, might also have been used in various other magical/shamanistic practices.

98. On the Germanic evidence for this type of amulet, cf. Helm (1913: 164ff.). This kind of talisman was also known among the Celts (cf. Pauli 1975 *passim*) and the Scythians (cf. Rice 1957: 145).

99. These skull fragments are the result of the surgical practice of trepenation, which was performed for therapeutic reasons, cf. Helm (1913: 167ff.).

100. H. Eggers (1932 *passim*) reports on rings which make the mute speak, light one's way in the dark, prevent one from losing one's way, warn if one's enemies are near (or banishes them), and which provide riches. The last function is analogous to the mythic accounts of Draupnir (cf. Skm. 21, *ESS. Gylf.* ch. 49).

101. Lidén (1969: 15ff.) reports on the discovery of several gold plaquettes with Vanic images on them. These objects were found mixed in burnt soil around interior post-holes of a structure which must date from ca. 500 CE, which is within the Mære church, Nord-Trøndelag, Norway.

102. In Wulfila's 4th-cent. Go. translation of the Bible, e.g., the phrase υμιν δεδοται γνωναι τα μυστηρια της βασιλειας του θεου is translated by: *izwis atgiban ist kunnan runa þiudangardjos*.

103. The possibility of linguistic borrowing is also present, but the direction of any borrowing is unclear, cf. Marstrander (1928: 176), and Pokorny (1959: 867). It appears that the Finnish *rune*: 'song' is actually a borrowing from Gmc. *runō*: 'row, series,' and not from *rūnō* (Krause 1969: 91-97).

104. There are three possible etymologies for PGmc. *$rūn\bar{o}$-: 1) PIE *$rū$- ~ *reu-: 'to roar, murmur, whisper' (cf. Skt. *ráuti*: 'roars,' Gk. ωρυομαι: 'howl, roar,' Lat. *rumor*: 'noise,' OCS *revǫ*: 'to roar') with a *-n- suffix > *$rū$-n- > PGmc. fem. ō-stem *$rūn\bar{o}$-: 'secret' (cf. Pokorny 1959; Jóhannesson 1951-56: 705; Falk-Torp 1960: 921-25), 2) from a form with an initial PIE labiovelar, *ǵwor-w-on-* a PGmc. fem. *$wrū$-n-$\bar{o}$- could have developed, which could connect it to Gk. ουρανος and Skt. Varuṇa (cf. Dumézil 1939: 24; Polomé 1950: 568-69; 1954: 43, who see in this root the idea of *binding*), and 3) that it is a borrowing from Celtic *$rūn\bar{o}$- (e.g., OIr. *rūn*-: 'mystery') > PGmc. *$rūna$- (cf.

Marstrander 1928: 175-77). The latter seems least likely due to the relative dynamism of the Germanic root, when compared to the semantic stasis of the Celtic one. It is also possible that the word was later borrowed into Celtic from Germanic. Semantically, perhaps *rūnō-* developed from a vocal concept of "magical utterance" to more formal "magical song" and hence to the more general "secret lore" which it expressed (without losing its original vocal significance). At this point, if writing were introduced, it is quite plausible that the graphemes would have been incorporated into this "secret lore" (see ch. IV). Therefore, the Gmc. term *rūnō-* must have had a complex semantic content, which included: 1) secret lore (context), 2) magical song or charm (performance), and 3) character (visible sign, grapheme).

105. Concerning the prefix **gin-*, see sec. 2. of this chapter.

106. Later terms also refer to the coloring of runes, i.e., ON *steina*: 'to stain, paint,' and the loan word *penta*: 'to paint' (cf. Ebel 1963: 37-39).

107. Cf. the use of sacrificial blood to sanctify the altars and holy enclosures in descriptions of Scandinavian sacrifices (cf. Ström 1966: 331-34).

108. This etymological connection is by no means certain (cf. de Vries 1961a: 583; 579-80); however, it is possible that the various Gmc. roots which belong to this field, **taƀ- ~ *tīƀ- ~ *tiuƀ-* originally had something to do with the blood of sacrificial victims — and hence the connection with the color "red."

109. The color red seems important to Germanic magical symbolism, e.g., some magicians are said to wear red pants (cf. *Kormáks s*. ch. 12), cf. de Vries (1956: I, 272-73; 283).

110. The term **felhan* on the Björketorp and Stentoften sts. may also be interpreted as 'to commend, to give over' (cf. Cleasby-Vigfusson 1957: 150), but hardly as Antonsen (1975a: 85ff.) seems to want to see it as a mere commitment of the runic characters to stone. ON parallels are offered in *Skálds*. (ch. I) *Þat þykki mér vera vel fólgit í rúnum*: 'That seemed to me to be well concealed in secrets,' or the phrase *yrkja fólgit*: 'to use obscure phrases' (cf. Cleasby-Vigfusson 1957: 150), see also ch. VI note 17.

111. Earlier etymologies which might have indicated a somewhat ambiguous meaning "taboo," and have connected it with Go. *alhs* (cf. e.g., Bugge *NIæR*: I, 160-67) have largely been rejected (cf. Høst 1980). See VI.34, for a more detailed discussion of the underlying meanings of the formula.

112. For discussions of the *laukaR-* and *laukaR : līna-*formulas, cf. Krause (1934; 1946/47), Lehmann (1955), Düwel (1971 : 204ff.), and Steinsland-Vogt (1981).

113. Cf. Krause (1932: 65-68) for a general discussion of the role of the equine concept and image in rune-magical thought.

114. Due to their inherently formulaic nature, the poetic records may reflect and preserve more archaic usages and linguistic combinations than prose documentation.

115. In the ON terminology, the words *rúnar* and *stafir* seem to be virtually interchangable (see compounds below). This semantic alternation is usually explained on a runo-technical basis, i.e., that the runic characters were originally most often carved on sticks, and therefore the meaning was eventually lent to the material medium itself.

116. This oral or vocal meaning can be inferred from many poetic sources, e.g., Háv. 29, HHII 12, Ls. 10; 16; 18; 28; 29, and the 'Hervǫrðljóð' 11. Also, parallels to vocal concepts (e.g., *ljóð* and *galdr*) are found, cf. Sdr. 5, and the correspondence between ON *líknstafir* and *líknagaldr*.

117. Also OE *(ge)rȳni*: 'religious mystery,' cf. Page (1964: 18ff.).
118. Cf. Page (1964: 18).
119. Cf. Wesche (1940: 45-51) for a discussion of OHG *rūna* and its Lat. glosses.
120. Go. *rūna* or occurs fourteen times in Wulfila's text: it is never used for 'written letter'— which Wulfila translates with *boka*. In addition, *garūni*: 'counsel' (συμβουλιον), appears three times.
121. Cf. Wesche (1940: 46).
122. Cf. de Vries (1961a: 455), Olsen (1935: 199-200), Cleasby-Vigfusson (1957: 505).
123. Cf. Cleasby-Vigfusson (1957: 505), Kuhn (1968b: 64), Fritzner (1896: III, 143), Egilsson (*Lex. Poet.* 1931: 473).
124. See n. 115 above.
125. Cf. also ON *bókstafr* and OHG *buohstab*, which may be later constructions, but it can not be discounted that they too go back to an original meaning 'beech-stave.' Cf. however Liestøl (1963: 41ff.) who reads a Bryggen inscription *ríst ek bótrúnar* and emends Sdr. 9; 19 *bocrvnar* (which is only attested there) to *bótrúnar*: 'bettering, cure-runes.' Krause (1964: 30) also agrees with this emendation.
126. This may refer to the object upon which they were to be carved, a peculiar shape or mode of execution (cf. the later *kvístrúnir*: '[coded] branch-runes') — or it may refer to some more primary arboreal mystery.
127. This form is reconstructed from what appears to be a scribal error *holzmuvvo*, cf. Wesche (1940: 48).
128. See de Vries (1961a: 541; 548) who connects ON *stinnr* with PGmc. **stenþ-*, a dental extention of **sten-*: 'hard, dense.'
129. This word occurs in an 11th cent. Lat. spell against fever in the form *leodrūne*, cf. Wesche (1940: 48).
130. See below in this section for a discussion of various SGmc. and EGmc. compounds in -run(a) as functional designations for a sorceress.
131. This would fit with the common Germanic use of tree/wood metaphors to describe human beings which is ultimately understandable in view of the mythic origins of humanity, cf. Vsp. 17-18 and *Gylfa*. ch. 9.
132. The first element is derived from PGmc. **lahstūz*: 'blame, fault.'
133. Cf. *Bēowulf* 501, Bosworth-Toller (1898: 70).
134. The ON term *hel* refers 1) to the realm of death, 2) to the concept of death itself, and 3) to the goddess of death, Hel (cf. Cleasby-Vigfusson 1957: 253-54).
135. Cf. also the Odinic names Forni: 'the ancient one,' and Forn-Ǫlvir: 'the ancient one consecrated to *alu* (?),' cf. Falk (1924: 9-10), de Vries (1961a: 687).
136. Because of the context of the terms *hugrúnar* and *málrúnar* it is tempting to speculate that they retained some of what could have been their primary meanings, i.e., 'mysteries of the mind' (**hugaz*) and 'mysteries of speech,' respectively. The term *málrunar* may also refer to the (runic?) inlay on spear- and sword-blades (cf. ON *málaspjót* and *málasax*), but cf. Dillmann (1976 II, 176) and Düwel (1981a: 166) who doubt it.
137. The divine mythology would seem to suggest that in the most archaic period, the realm of the dead was conceived of as a source of numinous knowledge directly accessible through rites of a shamanistic character, cf. Buchholz (1968: 31ff. and 52ff.), while in later

times the most often found connection with the realm of the dead could be described as "necromantic," where the dead are called up to impart numinous knowledge. Both seem to be ancient; however, the latter had a more active history in the medieval period — perhaps because of similar practices and beliefs imported from southern cultures.

138. The *rūnō-* theme is found in NGmc. and SGmc. fem. PNs (cf. Förstemann 1900: 1284; Kaufmann 1968: 296-97). Cf. the ON fem. PNs Guðrún, Qlrún, Sigrún, etc.

139. Cf. Helm (1937: II: 1, 22-23; 25-26).

140. Cf. Page (1964: 18ff.), Helm (1953: 11:2, 124ff.).

141. Cf. Helm (1953: II: 2, 124ff.) and Wesche (1940: 48).

142. From the context of these examples it is clear that the prefixes ON *val-* and OE *wæl-* refer to the concepts 'death, dead, slain, slaughter, etc.' (cf. ON *valhǫll, valkýrja*; OE *wælcyrie*, etc.) and hardly to the idea 'Welsh': i.e., 'foreign.' If the term is archaic, it could even indicate 'mysteries of the slain.'

143. The name of a seeress reported in *Germ.* ch. 8, Aurinia ~ Albrinia is generally thought to be derived from Lat. *Albrunia < Gmc. *Albrūna, cf. Much (1967: 119), and also the article on *Alraun* in Kluge-Mitzka (1957: 16), where it is said that the attachment to the mandragora was facilitated by the human appearance of the root.

144. The etymology of the word betrays a primary link with the idea 'to protect (< *berg-an) → to help (by protecting),' and the context given by the Eddic lay makes the meaning clear.

145. See VI.34.

146. Cf. ch. 20 and Sdr. prose following stanza 4 where Óðinn uses the *svefnþorn*: 'sleep-thorn' to effect Sigrdrífa's slumber. The *svefnþorn* may be an herb (cf. Grimm 1876: II, 1007-08; 1878: III, 353) or an actual thorn onto which runes were carved, or they could be parallel abstracted terms as the *svefnþorn* also became a name for a magical sign (:ᛥ:) in later times (cf. Lehmann-Filhes 1898: 288, Jón Árnason 1954: I, 435).

147. Cf. also numerous other compounds in *-cræft* which indicate operative skill, e.g., *āglāc-cræft, bealucræft, dēofol-cræft, uncræft, lybbcræft, drȳcræft* (cf. Philippson 1929: 208-209).

148. On the difficult problems of dating these sources, see Stefán Einarsson (1957: 18ff.; 110ff.) and de Vries (1964; 1967).

149. Cf. e.g., Arntz (1935: 244-50; 1944: 233-48), Altheim-Trautmann (1942: 45ff.), Derolez (1968: 294-98).

150. See 14. above.

151. See II.2 on the concept of an "ascriptive reality" in magical thinking.

152. Cf. Arntz (1944: 293-94), and Kluge-Mitzka (1957: 436). Other terms sometimes connected to runic terminology and clearly within the divinatory sphere are PGmc. *hluta-: 'lot' (cf. OE *hleot ~ hlot*, ON *hlutr*) in ON *hlaut-teinn*: 'lot-twig' (cf. Düwel 1971 : 26ff.), and the highly suggestive OE *wyrdstæf*: 'decree of fate' (cf. Bosworth-Toller 1898: 1288).

153. See IV.3, and note 4, cf. also Much (1967: 129ff.).

154. This account may have influenced a similar one by Alcuin, see below.

155. On the possibility that the *notae* were runes, cf. Arntz (1935: 245ff.; 1944: 236ff.), Much (1967: 189ff.), and on the *notae* more generally, cf. Mentz (1937: 194ff.).

156. On the term *ørlǫg*, cf. Bauschatz (1975: 57ff.).

157. Cf. Polomé (1975: 660-62).

158. On the adj. *reginkuðr ~ reginkunnr*: 'derived or descended from the gods,' cf. Brate (1898: 331ff.). In one case the adj. *regin-kunnigr* refers to a human (Jǫrmunrekkr, Hm. 25), cf. de Vries (1961a: 436-37).

159. Cf. Derolez (1954: 279-59). Version B contains the term *runstabas*. The comment is added that they use this *name quod his res absconditas vicissim scriptitando aperiebant*. So there seems to have been a clear idea that by writing runes one could "reveal hidden things." These references may have been added under the influence of Tacitus' account (*Germ.* ch. 10).

160. Here, the reader of the runes is a woman named Mjǫll, who is also described as being *fjǫlkunnig*: 'knowledgeable in magic.'

161. On Óðinn's self-sacrifice, cf. de Vries (1956: I, 499ff.), Turville-Petre (1964: 42ff.), and on its specifically shamanistic character, cf. Buchholz (1968: 76ff.) and Eliade (19,64: 379ff., *et passim*), and also Fleck (1971) for different initiatory insights. Bugge's view that the 'Rúnaþáttr' is a borrowing from Christian tradition (1889: 291ff.) has largely been rejected.

162. Cf. also Dillmann (1976: II, 247ff.).

163. We know from archeological data that certain dyes or paints were used in the epigraphical tradition to color the runes and the adjacent iconographic details, cf. Jansson (1963: 158ff.).

164. The only prosaic references to this process are the *VS* ch. 13, where it is said that Reginn taught Sigurðr *rúnar*, and the obscure allusion to Egill and Einarr Helgason discussing poetry, etc. (*ES* ch. 78).

165. In the older epigraphical tradition, the Eggjum st. (KJ 101) provides an interesting contrast where it is said that . . . *ni saxe stæinn skorinn*. . . : '. . . the stone (is) not cut by an (iron) knife. . .' Cf. also the idea that many younger rune-stones were inscribed by means of pick-hammers (Nielsen-Moltke 1980).

166. The antecedent of the present participle *œpandi* (< *œpa*: 'to call, or shout out') is grammatically ambiguous, however, from the context it is evident that it refers to the Odinic persona. In this regard it is interesting to note that an apparent byname of a later *rúnameistari* was perhaps a *nomen agentis* developed from this verb, i.e., Öpir, see Thompson (1972: 16).

167. Cf. also the injunction to select limbs bending to the *east (lúta austr limar)* for the healing *limrúnar* (Sdr. 11).

168. Another attestation of this would seem to be the carving of *seiðvillur*: 'spells to counteract sorcery' under the *seið*-platform upon which the *seiðmenn* were situated (*G-H s.* ch. 28).

Chapter VI

Corpus of Older Operative Formulas

1. Knowledge of the formulaic elements in the runic corpus, and their role in operative communication, or magic, has, until now, been limited by the lack of a systematic collection of these elements, and by the absence of a scientific framework — social and religious-historical — in which to place them. In this chapter, I arrange the epigraphical evidence systematically, together with commentary, in order to facilitate a better understanding of the possible magical significance or non-significance of these inscriptions.
In the older runic corpus there exists a group of *formulaic elements*, which are often considered to have a "magical" function of some kind. These elements are sometimes the total content of the inscription, or they may seem to act as *units* within the context of a more elaborate inscription. Because of the repeated use of certain types of phrases, words, or sequences,(1) these elements have often come to be regarded in a special "magical" category.

Essentially, I have identified four major runic magical formulaics: 1) the rune-master formula, 2) word-formulas, 3) rune-formulas [of which there are two kinds, a) sequential, and b) non-sequential], and 4) explicit elaborated formulas in which a magical motive is more or less clearly stated. We must concentrate on analyzing the runic corpus according to this typology, which may occasionally necessitate repeated discussion of certain complexes, and in some instances inscriptions will not be treated comprehensively (for discussions of these elements in their complete contexts, see Krause 1966). As a general practice, the readings presented by Krause are used as bases for interpretation, but important variants are noted, and in some cases improvements suggested.

RUNE-MASTER FORMULAS

2. The rune-master, or rune-carver, formulas(2) offer a variety of complex problems.(3) In chapter four we attempted to explore some of those questions from a socio-anthropological viewpoint, but here we wish to concentrate on the formulaic aspects of the epigraphical evidence itself. It seems imperative to follow Dillmann (1981: 28-31) in his effort to distinguish clearly between the functions of a rune-master, who has the ability to both conceive and execute an inscription, and a rune-carver (or runographer), who may in fact be illiterate,(4) and who would then only have the ability to actually carve the runes in accordance with a rune-master's model. This distinction is probably more pertinent to the study of the younger fuþark, where the rune-master and runographer are juxtaposed in the signature.(5) However, when we turn to the older corpus we are faced with a more ambiguous situation. The ratio of inscriptions before ca. 700 CE in which the rune-master/runographer is directly mentioned is only about 35 out of 250, and of them only about ten are unambiguous.

Rune-Master Formulas: Criteria

3. In order to be considered an unambiguous rune-master / runographer formula, the inscription must contain at least a proper name (or appellative) antecedent to a technical verb which indicates that person executed the inscription. The most ambiguous forms are those which appear to consist of a single proper name (usually masculine). These have usually been interpreted as the name of the rune-master,(6) but objectively we can never be sure if, when faced with an ambiguous proper name on a brooch, for example, we are dealing with the name of the rune-master, the runographer, the donor, the receiver, the craftsman who made the object — or even a divine or animal name.(7)

We can be reasonably certain that during the older period, most of the unambiguously signed inscriptions actually represent the name of a rune-master and not merely that of a runographer. This is due to a combination of the fact that the older inscriptions are technically quite simple, and that it seems unlikely that the tasks of conception and execution would have been necessarily fulfilled by separate individuals. The bracteates may form an exception to this rule, but the "signatures" on them usually seem to identify the rune-masters and not the bracteate-masters(8) (cf. e.g., IK 11, 70, 128, 156, 184, 189, 241, 1-2, 340).

Rune-Master Formulas: Types

4. In general, we have three major types of rune-master formulas. Two explicit formulas are classified according to the person of the verb:

  1) first-person
  2) third-person
      and there is an ambiguous type:
  3) isolated PN

First-Person Formula

5. The most conspicuous rune-master signature in the older period is the "*ek*-formula." This formulaic phrase is classically introduced by the first-person pronoun (PNor. *ek*) followed by a variety of elements which perhaps should be archetypically portrayed: *ek* + N.N. + technical verb + object (i.e., 'I, N.N. carved, colored, etc., the runes'). In fact, it seems impossible to determine if there was chronologically any archetypal form from which the others were derived. Moreover, the formula appears to have been stereotyped to such an extent that it could be represented in contracted or expanded forms so that in the corpus we encounter essentially four types:(9)

  I. ek + N.N. (+ byname) + verb + object

  II. ek + N.N. (+ byname) + verb

  III. ek + { byname / N.N. } (+ byname)

  IV. ek + { byname / N.N. } + *hait-* + byname

There are a number of variations within these types, however, the chief criterion for classification within this category would seem to be the presence of the first-person pronoun, or the first-person form of the verb. The typological distinctions within this class are determined by additional syntactic elements. Although all of the formulas clearly belong to one or the other type, virtually none conform in every feature — and in each case important questions surrounding the actual reading of the inscription must be considered.

I."I, N.N. color the runes"

6. Type I is generally characterized by ek plus a PN and/or byname (often functional(10) rather than personal), and/or an antecedent first-person verbal form which has as its object a substantive in the accusative. However, the essential elements of this formula are: 1) a first-person verbal form which indicates the execution of runic characters, or their consecration, or the preparation of the material medium which bears the inscription, and 2) an object which either relates to the runic characters themselves or to the material medium upon which they are portrayed.(11) A total of 17 inscriptions would seem to belong to type I, which can be further subdivided into three classes:

A) *rūna* as object (9 inscriptions)
B) objects other than *rūna* (4 inscriptions)
C) miscellaneous verbs and objects (4 inscriptions)

Corpus of I.A.

7. One group within this class contains a combination of a runo-technical term (i.e., **faihju* or **writu*) and an object restricted to the term *rūnaR* resp. *rūna*.

KJ 63: Einang st. (E. Nor. 350-400) is broken off at the beginning, but we can at least be fairly certain that the initial runes of what remains represents the end of a proper name — *-daga[s]tiR*. The fragment appears: . . .**dagaxtiRrunofaihido** which is read by E. Moltke (1938, 111ff.) as: -*daga[s]tiR rūnō faihidō*: '(I) . . . dagast, colored the rune.'(12)

KJ 70: Järsberg st. (W.Swe., 500-550) consists of two rune-master formulas, one of which could be read: A. **ekerilaR** / B. **runoRwaritu** — *ek erilaR / rūnōR waritu*: 'I, the rune-master/carve the runes,' (but see also 15b.). The *svarabhakti* vowel in *waritu* may be compared to that in **harabanaR** — *HrabanaR*: 'Raven' in the same inscription.(13)

KJ 67: Noleby st. (C.Swe., ca. 600) is an elaborate and problematic inscription which certainly contains a first-person formula: **runofahiraginakudo**— *rūnō fāhi ragina-ku(n)dō*. . . 'A rune I color, one derived from the divine advisors. . .' Krause (1966: 149, 151) reads *fāhi* as an apocopated form from early PNor. **fāhju* (< **faihju*), while Antonsen (1975, 55-56) reads *rūnō fahi ragina-ku(n)dō tōj-eka*: 'I prepare the suitable divine rune.' He assumes that *fahi* is a fem. acc. sg. y-stem adjective with the meaning 'suitable,' antecedent to *rūnō*. . . *ragina-ku(n)dō* which together is the object of the first-pers. sg. verb with enclitic pronoun *tōj-eka*: 'I prepare.'

KJ 17a: Eikeland clasp (SW Nor. ca. 600) consists entirely of a runemaster formula, with the addition of a possibly temporal expression: **ekwiRwiwiowrituirunoRasni** — which may be read: *ek WīR Wīwio writu ī rūnōR ą̄ s(i)n(n)i*:(14) 'I, Wi, for Wiwia, carve in the runes at this time' (cf. Krause 1966: 47-48).

IK 156: Sievern-A is damaged, and appears to have an error in the formation of its runes, nevertheless it is read by both Krause (1966: 270-72) and Antonsen (1975a:65) as: (R-L) ṛwri[t]u— *r[ūnōR] writu:* '(I) carve the runes.' This would be an atypical rune-master formula in which only the first-person verb with an abbreviated runic object appears. But it is of course runologically ambiguous.

7. Another group of formulas also contains the restricted runic object form, but in combination with first-person verbal forms with more apparent magical significance.

IK 128: Nebenstedt I-B probably bears an abbreviated form of the object (cf. IK 156: Sievern-A, KJ 64: Barmen[?] and possibly IK 386: Wapno-C), and is read by Düwel (1977: 89ff.) as: **glïaugiRu ïurn R**(15) — *Glï augiR wïu r(ū)n(ō)R l(aukaR)*: "(I), GïaugiR ('the gleaming-eyed one') consecrate the runes, leek (= increase, fertility)!"(16) The runic sequence **uïu** is generally understood as *wīju* (< **wīhu*): 'I consecrate' (cf. KJ 27: Kragehul and possibly IK 312, 1: Overhornbæk II-A).

In the two closely related curse formulas on the stones of Stentoften (KJ 96) and Björketorp (KJ 97), there seems to be a specialized use of the verb **felhan*, which apparently has an original sense of 'to hide, conceal, bury.'(17) The magical function of such a concept is discussed in VII.6. The relevant portion of KJ 96: Stentoften st. (ca. 650, S. Swe.) according to Krause (1966: 210; 216) reads:

(V) **hideRrunonofelAhekAhederAginoronoR—**

(V) *h(a)ideR-runo* **no** [= *ronu*](18) *felaheka hedera ginor(ū)nōR:*

(V)'A row of bright runes I-hide here, magically charged runes.'

KJ 97: Björketorp st. (ca. 675, S. Swe.) is based upon the same curse formula, and is perhaps somewhat later than Stentoften.(19) The corresponding portion is read by Krause (1966, 217-17) as:

B.(I)**hAidRrunoronu/** (II) **fAlAhAkhAiderAg** (III)**inArunAR**. . . —

B.(I) *haidR-rūnō ronu* (II) *fal^ah^ak haid^era* (III) *g]ina-rūnaR*. . .(20) '(I) A row of bright runes/ (II) I-hid here/ (III) magically charged runes. . .'

Both Björketorp and Stentoften present a complex runic object, which consists of 1) 'a row of bright runes' (fem. acc. sg. *ronu*: 'sequence,' cf. Krause 1969: 96-97; 1971: 119 *et passim*) and 2) 'magically charged runes' (fem. acc. pl. *gina-rūnaR*).(21) This formula acts as a charge for the following more explicit magical curse of the inscription (see sect. 50).

KJ 72: Tune st. (ca. 400, SE. Nor.) represents a tenuous example within a third group in which we find the runic object antecedent to a first-person verbal form with a less exclusively runotechnical sense — *wurkjan*: 'to make, shape.'(22) The pertinent section of this inscription appears:

A. (I) **ekwiwaR**. . . (II)/. . . **worahto**: r. . ./ which may be read *ek WiwaR*. . .*worahto r(ūnōR)*: 'I, WiwaR ('the consecrator,' 'the one who is consecrated,' or the kite-hawk?) . . . made the runes' (cf. Krause 1966: 163-64 and see sect. 31.). The main problem here is that the r-rune may not be clearly seen on the stone which is broken off at that point.(23)

Corpus of I.B.

8. This class of first-person formulas contains a variety of objects for more or less runo-technical verbs. The first group has a technical verb of some kind which seems to indicate the carving or coloring function.

IK 241, 1-2: Äskatorp-F and Väsby-F which are apparently stamped from the same die, pose several problems in their readings (personal examination: 6.1.1982). The actual runes on both bracteates may be read:

    1   5   10 15 20   25
    uuigaReeṛilaRfihiduụụilald

The complex r. 18-21 is quite confused, with the appearance of r. 19 as virtually two vertical parallel lines and the branch of r. 20 as more an extension from the bottom of r. 21. In any case, the first 18 runes may be interpreted as: *Wi(n)gaR e(k) erilaR f[ā]hid[ō]*. . 'Wi(n)gaR ('the consecrator'?). I, the rune-master colored. . .' Runes 19-25, which represent the object of *f[ā]hidō*, can be interpreted (cf. Krause 1966: 264) as parallel to IK 212, 1: Overhornbæk II-A **uilald** — *wilald*: 'art-work.' This could refer to either the bracteate itself or to the "spiritual art-work" represented by the runes. However, Noreen (1927: 151ff.) and Moltke (1941: 540-41) reject this reconstruction.

The curious sword grip of Rasquert (or Raskwerd) presents a unique inscription in the Frisian corpus. It has been read by Buma (1966: 86ff.) as: **ekumæõlkloka**— OFris. *ek Umae õ(i)k loka*: 'I, Umw carve you.' Buma's interpretation suffers from both an over-imaginative approach to the actual reading of the faint runic shapes, and from his understanding of *loka* as 'carve,' which is conjectural (cf. Düwel-Tempel 1968: 379ff.).

IK 112, 1: Overhornbæk II-A presents an example of a non-runic object combined with what appears to be the technical term **wīhu* (cf. Ebel 1963, 79-81 and IK 128: Nebenstedt I-B, see sect. 7.). The runes of Overhornbæk II-A appear in two lines, the first of which may be read:

```
    1    5       10   15      20    25
    ⑄ uþaþiṭ⌒ ihuilaldṭ⁴ ụiụụ ◊ ṭw |
```

Much of this inscription remains obscure with only isolated runic sequences capable of any interpretation. Krause (1966: 265-66) reads "runes" 1-4 as possibly [*A*]*uþa* (a masc. PN) and r. 5-7 as *þit*: 'this,' while r. 11-16 form the only clear complex [*w*]*ilald*: 'art-work' (cf. Moltke 1941: 308-10). Among the following runes we would expect to find the verbal antecedent to *wilald*. After what is perhaps an ideographic or ornamental two-character sequence ᚽ⁴, Krause understands runes 19-21 as *wiu*: 'I consecrate,' however, Olsen (1907: 19ff.) sees in the sequence r. 17-21 the PNor. form *tauju*: 'I prepare'(24) (cf. KJ 67: Noleby, KJ 43: Gallehus, KJ 30: Garbølle, and IK 189: Trollhättan), the possible magical significance of which is discussed in sect. 50. In the final analysis, all except the complex **uilald** remains tenuous.

Corpus of I.C.

9. The miscellaneous third class presents a wide range of formulaic possibilities. One of the most famous runic inscriptions, KJ 43: Gallehus gold (drinking?) horn (ca. 400, S. Jutland), bore a paradoxical text which read: **ekhlewagastiR: holtijaR : horna tawido:** *ek HléwagastiR HóltijaR / hórna táwido*: 'I, Hlewagast Holt (i.e., man of the grove), (or, descendant of Holt), made the horn.'(25) This inscription seems paradoxical because the *ek*-formula, which is otherwise indicative of a rune-master formula, is juxtaposed to an apparently extraordinary craftsman's signature. Elements which tempt one to consider this something other than a craftsman's signature are: 1) the *ek*-formula, 2) the apparent alliterative verse form in which it is composed,(26) 3) the possible interpretation of *holtijaR* as 'a man

of the wood or grove,' (cf. the possible sacral significance of the grove in Germanic religion), and 4) the apparent cultic function of both Gallehus horns themselves (cf. Krause 1966; 102). The master-formula may refer to the symbolic forms on the horn, which are enigmatic, yet suggestive of cultic meaning. In any event, Gallehus forms a unique first-person master-formula in which the object is concrete and the verb non-runo-technical (cf. also the third-person formula on K.30: Garbølle, box).

The other three inscriptions in this class all have more or less abstract objects. KJ 74: Reistad (450-500, S. Nor.) reads: (I) **iuþingaR** (II) **ekwakraR: un(n)nam** (III) **wraita**— *IuþingaR ek WakraR: un(d)-nam wraita*: 'Iuþing (rests here). I, Wakr undertook the carving' (i.e., Wakr executed the inscription). We may understand the first-pers. pret.-pres. *un(d)-nam* as meaning either 'I undertook' (cf. Krause 1971: 159) or as 'I have learned' (cf. Marstrander 1930, 245-50). In each case the verb would act as an indirect, perhaps more highly stylized, mode of expressing the fact that Wakr carved the runes, and has knowledge of them. The neut. acc. sg. *wraita*: 'the carving,' could, if we accept Marstrander's interpretation, refer to *runic writing in general* and not be limited to the inscription at hand — although it would seem to have a crucial function in the effectiveness of the present inscription.(27)

KJ 67: Noleby st. (ca. 600, C. Swe.), which has already been partially discussed (sect. 7), contains perhaps a further first-person formula: (I)/. . .**tōjḙka** (II) **unaþ[o]u**. . . This is read by Krause (1966: 150-51) as: (I). . .*tōj-eka* (II) *unaþ[o]u*: '. . .I prepare satisfaction (in the grave). . .' Grammatically, most investigators would tend to agree with this reading (cf. v. Friesen 1933: 30-31; Nordén 1934: 99ff.; Klingenberg 1973: 126-27), however, much remains unexplained as to the runography, phonology, and semantics of this 11-rune complex. The use of the rune shape ᛃ **j** seems quite early, and the reading of the following characters (bind-rune?) ᛖᚲ **ek** must remain conjectural. Also, the apparently mistaken interpolation of an o-rune in what probably should have read *unaþu* (cf. ON *unaðr*: 'happiness, luck') — which is interpreted as 'satisfaction' by Krause, 'rest' by von Friesen and as simply 'happiness' by Klingenberg (who proposes an ingenious solution to the runological problem, 1973: 127-29) — remains phonologically inexplicable.

IK 189: Trollhättan-A consists entirely of a first-person verbal form antecedent to an abstract magico-legal term.(28) The inscription reads: **tawol aþodu**— *tawō laþōdu*: 'I perform a summons/invocation.' The first-pers. sg. pres. *tawō* (< **tawōn*): 'to prepare; perform' is perhaps a secondary formation from PGmc. *taujan: 'to do, make' (cf. KJ 30; 43),(29) while laþōdu may be understood as an acc. sg. u-stem (< *laþoduR): 'summons, invocation' (cf. ON lǫðuðr 'invitation, invitor,' Krause 1971: 40-41, 47; Antonsen 1975a: 63) and to be the semantic equivalent of laþu (sect. 40.).

II. 'I, N.N., colored.'

10. The second type is principally distinguished by the presence of 1) a rune-master name, 2) a runo-technical verb, and 3) the lack of any object. The runemaster names are never titular (erilaR, gudija, etc.) and may or may not be functional bynames. Five of the six inscriptions in this type employ a form of faihidō: 'I colored → carved,' (see V.16.) while the remaining one seems to have a form of *writan.

Corpus of II

KJ 73: Rö st. (ca. 400, W. Swe.) bears a complex text, the rune-master portion of which may be broken off at the beginning, but which reads: . . . ṣtainawarijaRfahido — Krause (1966: 170) reconstructs this sequence as: [ek] StainawarijaR fāhidō: '[I], Stainawari ('defender of stones'), colored (the runes).' Indeed, the first-person pronoun may have stood at the beginning on this formula because: 1) there would have been space for it before the stone was broken, and 2) it would have corresponded both spatially and formulaically with **ekhraRaRsatido[s]tain[a]** — ek HraRaR satidō staina: 'I, Hrar, set the stone' in the first line of the inscription. It is difficult to determine if StainawarijaR could have been an official/functional byname, with the meaning 'the one who is defender of the (grave) stones' — perhaps a kind of magico-religious function — or if it is merely a personal name with no further significance.(30)

IK 11: Åsum-C must be read (personal examination 6.1 1982)(31) (R-L) **eh̄eikakaRfahi** — ehē. ik AkaR fāhi: 'To the horse. I Ak color.' The formula-word ehē (< *ehwaR) is discussed in 39. The alternate ik form for ek is explicable either through South Germanic influence, or as merely a regular development of PIE *e (cf. also the variant forms erilaR ~ irilaR).(32) Fāhi has been treated under Noleby (sect. 7). The name AkaR would appear to be more a functional designation (< *PIE *ag-: 'to go, drive,' cf. ON aka: 'to move, lead') with the meaning 'leader.'(33)

IK 340: Sønderby (Femø)-C probably does not, as Krause speculates (1966: 268-69), bear an inscription related to Åsum-C. It seems more reasonable to assume that this inscription, which can be read: (R-L)

ekfakaRf — *ek FakaR f(āhidō)*: 'I, Fak, colored,' represents an independent text. The regular form of the first-person pronoun is followed by what appears to be a normal (non-functional or titular) masc. o-stem PN (cf. OHG Faco, Facco, Faho < PGmc. **fahaz:* 'horse').(34) It is not clear the extent to which such a name, related to ON *fákr*: 'horse,' could have had a magico-religious meaning. The final f-rune must most probably be understood as an abbreviated form of *fāhidō* (or *fāhi*?), and while it could be interpreted as an ideographic rune = **fehu*: 'cattle, mobile wealth' (with the magical function: 'prosperity'), as does Marstrander (1929: 35) — it seems doubtful in this case due to the evidence of parallel inscriptions.

KJ 60: Vetteland st. (after 650, SW Nor.) is an informative, yet fragmentary, inscription (sect. 52.), the legibility of which is sometimes difficult (personal examination: 5.26.1982). The final line of the text may be read: (III) . . . **daRfaihido** which clearly seems to be the remains of a masc. nom. PN -*daR*, plus the 1-pers. pret. *faihidō*: 'I colored, carved' (cf. Bugge *NIæR*, I: 442-43; Krause 1966: 138). The inclusion of the *ek-*formula may by no means be excluded on spatial grounds. As on the Rö st. (KJ 73), the rune-master formula possibly stands in juxtaposition to a "stone-setter's" formula.

KJ 164, 1 (Op. 53): Weingarten s-fibula (6th-century, Württemberg) contains what appears to be a female rune-master formula (sect. 31), which may be read (cf. Opitz 1977, 49; 199-201): (I) **alirguþ : ik** (II) **feha : writ la**, *Alirgu(n)þ : ik Feha : writ. . .*'Alirgunþ. I, Feha, carved. . .' The two runic complexes, concluded with double-pointed word dividers, would seem to be otherwise unknown fem. nom. PN: Alirgunþ, which could be an ordinary compound name (< **alisa-:* 'alder,' and -*gunþ:* 'battle'), and *Feha*, which is not only otherwise unattested, but which also offers no easy etymological solution (cf. Arntz-Jänichen 1957: 126ff.; Krause 1966: 306; Opitz 1977: 200). Typologically, we could expect a rune-master byname to follow the first-person pronoun, however, the reading of r. I: 8-9 is not certain. The form of the verb seems certain to be either a formulaic abbreviation (<**writan*) followed by a word divider, or a first-person form with an illegible final rune. In any case the subject of the verb is clearly Feha. Alirguþ could be Feha's "profane" name, or it could refer to someone else, e.g., the owner or giver of the fibula. The doubtful final two runes could be read as ideographs: *l(aukaR)* and **a(nsuR)*, but whether or not these may be considered the objects of *writ*, remains an open question.

The more recently found ivory ring of Pforzen (ca. 600) also shows a female-rune-master formula: **ņe:aodliþ:urait:runa:** — fem. PN -*odlinþ wrait runa*: '-odlind carved the rune'(Düwel 1997c: 19).

Another more recent find, the Nydam ax-handle (300-350) presents three names or titles in the nominative, all of which could refer to the same person. These substantives are *WagagastiR* ('flame-guest' = 'smith'?), *SikijaR* ('inhabitant of wetlands') and *AiþalataR* ('oath-speaker'). With difficulty a first-person verb form *wihgu*, 'I dedicate,' can be read, preceded by the operative formula **alu**. (Cf. McKinnell 2004: 94-95)

III. 'I, the rune-master.'

11. With the third type of first-person forms, we find that the more terse the formula is, the more functional the designations of the rune-master become. The formula is characterized by the presence of the first-person pronoun, followed by a functional designation of the rune-master. These designations seem to fall into one of four classes:

    A. socio-functional (titular) byname
    B. descriptive cognomen
    C. combination of A and B
    D. ambiguous, miscellaneous.

The decision to consider certain terms as "socio-functional" was largely made on historical grounds. Both *erilaR ~ irilaR* (KJ 16, 56, 69, 71, 27, 29, 70, 128?) and *gudija* (KJ 65) later evolved into clearly defined social functions, or official titles (cf. ON *jarl* ← *erilaR*, and *goði* ← *gud-ōn*.(35) However, it is not certain whether these terms bore much of this official quality in the age of the older runic inscriptions. One has only to compare OE *eorl*: 'warrior,' to see that *erilaR* must have had quite a broad semantic field. On the other hand it can not be doubted that *erilaR*, whether it was originally an ethnic or functional designation, must have taken on the special, virtually titular, meaning of 'rune-master' in the North Germanic territory from between ca. 450 and 600, however, the actual etymology of *erilaR* ← **er-il-az* remains obscure (cf. de Vries 1961a: 104; Krause 1966: 44; Andersen 1948; 97ff., Musset 1965: 149-50, Antonsen 1975a:36; also afler 1971: 143 and Elgqvist 1952).

Descriptive, or characterizing bynames cover a wide range from pure adjectival descriptions, which are not commonly found outside this type, to the same kind of functional bynames found in all the other types. These seem to be appelatives assumed by the rune-masters as special sacral names which somehow describe their unique functions or some magical aspects of their characters.

Corpus of III.A.

12. KJ 16: Bratsberg bow fibula (ca. 500, S. Nor.) is read: e͡kerilaR— *ek erilaR*: 'I, the rune-master.' Except for the extraordinary use of bind-runes (V. 10.), this inscription is a simple form of the classic rune-master formula.

KJ 71: By st. (550-600, SE Nor.) is a complex inscription, which also contains a third-person rune-master formula. This seems, however, to be preceded by a simple first-person formula: e͡kirilaR— *ek irilaR*: 'I, the rune-master.' The representation of *erilaR* as *irilaR* occurs in two other inscriptions (KJ 56 and 69) and seems to be a regular allophone (cf. Krause 1971: 63).(36) The final three runes of an apparent auxiliary inscription to KJ 55: Valsfjord are read by Marstrander (1951: 20) as: **eaR**— *e(ril)aR*: 'rune-master,' which must remain doubtful on purely runological grounds (cf. also Bugge *NIæR*, I: 350-52).

Corpus of III B

13. KJ 12: Gårdlösa clasp (ca. 200, Skåne) was found in a woman's grave and is read by Krause (1966: 35) as: **ekunwodiR** — *ek unwōdiR*: 'I, the one free from rage.' The final runic character appears: ᛣ and for typological reasons is interpreted by Krause (1966: 35) as a special simplified bind-rune ᛁ + ᛦ. Runologically, this is of course problematical, but Antonsen's reading (1975: 31): *unwōdz* poses phonological problems (e.g., lack of thematic vowel), although it might seem runologically less speculative. The root *wōd-* would seem to designate some detrimental aspect by which the rune-master remains untouched in the performance of his work (cf. also Marstrander 1952: 110-14). Since **wōð-* is the root of the divine name **Wōðanaz* > ON Óðinn, the apparent god of the rune-masters in later days, this formula presents an interesting question in the history of Germanic religion. What was **wōð-* and why would the rune-master wish to be free of it in this context? **Wōð-* has been generally interpreted as 'inspired mental activity, fury' (cf. Polomé 1969: 268-69). Normally this would seem to be a fundamental element in the rune-master's work, but in this case the master wishes to indicate that he is without **wōð-*. This is perhaps to insure that the power of **wōð-* may not function in the proximity of the wearer of the clasp which he has filled with the essence of **unwōð-* (V. 2).

KJ 64: Barmen st. (400-450, W. Nor.) was found with another rune-less *bauta*-stone, which together perhaps formed part of a stone-setting (no grave was found in the area). Its runes may be read: ękþirbijąRrų. It seems certain that the inscription is complete and that no further runes stood after the u. The whole is interpreted by Krause (1966: 145-46) as: *ek þirbijaR rū(nōR)*: 'I, the one who weakens: (carved the) ru(nes).' This reading is far from being free of controversy. Olsen (1936: 18ff.) sees an old patronymic in *-ija-* in *þirbijaR*: 'son of ÞirbaR,' while Antonsen (1975a: 48), with rather weak historical semantic evidence, interprets this complex as a *yo-*stem adj. = 'one who makes strong(!).' More convincing are Krause and Marstrander (1938: 367-69) who see a rune-master epithet in the *nomen agentis þirbijaR* (<.*þirƀijaR*): 'one who weakens → (*þirƀaR*).' (See note 116.) This would be a description of the rune-master's task in this inscription to make impotent any persons or entities which would disturb the stone (formation). As to the meaning of r. 11-12, most scholars see the word *rūnō(R)* in abbreviated form — which seems generally correct — yet it does not follow that the complex represents the object of an unexpressed verb. Another interpretation could be that here the cryptic form **ru** has the collective force of 'magical invocation' (cf. Andersen 1964: 107ff.), so that the sense of the inscription could be: 'I, the one who makes all weak. Ru(ne) (= magically potent invocation)!'

KJ 53: Kårstad st.-cliff (ca. 450, W. Nor.) was carved into a rock-face within the context of Bronze and Iron Age picto- and ideographs. Its runes can be read: (R-L)(I) **ekaljamarkiR** (R-L) (II) **baijxR** (cf. Krause 1966: 118). Line I may be interpreted without too many objections as: *ek aljamarkiR*: 'I, the stranger (= one from another land).' While line II presents more runological difficulties, it seems most reasonably to be understood with Krogmann (1962: 157-58) as a derivative of PGmc. *baij-az*: 'warrior.'(37) Therefore, the *ek*-formula would present the rune-master as a 'foreigner' (perhaps a 'guest,' retainer, see IV), it is also possible that this may have been a stereotyped designation and not a description of the rune-master's personal history. The added appellative further defines his social role (retainer?), but it hardly seems to be a formal title of any kind.

KJ 55: Valsfjord st.-cliff (ca. 400, M. Nor.) is usually (Bugge *NIæR*, I: 344-49; Krause 1966: 123-25) read as: **ekhagustaldaRþewaRgodagas**— *ek hagustaldaR þewaR Gōdagas*: "I, 'the young warrior' (am) the retainer of Godag." Structurally and semantically, Valsfjord and Kårstad seem to have much in common. Again we are met with an *ek*-formula which identifies the rune-master as an outsider — here perhaps an intra-clanic one. The term probably originally indicated a son or young man who was only in possession of a small enclosure outside the chieftain's stronghold (*hagustaldaR* = a compound from **haga-*: 'enclosure,' and **staldaR*: 'possession, dwelling').(38) The term *þewaR* (Go. *þius*: 'servant,' OE *þēow*: 'servant,'

ON -*þér* in PN compounds: servant [of], etc.), in this context would clearly indicate a retainer in the retinue of Godag. The possibilities for the deeper meaning behind these words seem to be two: 1) if *hagustaldaR* still contained its apparent original sense at this time (which seems probable), then it could contrast with *þewaR*, i.e., 'I (who am an) errant warrior (am now) the retainer of Godag,' or 2) it may be a more simple *ek*-formula which merely contains a double, but semantically similar, designation for the rune-master.

Corpus of III.C.

14. KJ 65: Nordhuglo st. (ca. 400-450, W. Nor.), which may originally have been attached to a grave mound, reads in its entirety: (R-L) **ekgudijaungandiRih**— *ek gudija ungandiR* ih. . .: 'I, the priest, (who am) immune from magic.' The term *gudija* could have meant an official priest of some kind by this time (cf. Go. *gudja* Ulf. tr. 'ιερευς: 'priest').(39) *UngandiR* may easily be compared to the similar construction *unwōd-* in KJ 12 Gårdlløsa. The root *gand-* probably had already assumed a culto-magical significance even if it is derived from an original meaning 'staff, stick' (see V. 3). Therefore, Antonsen's interpretation (1975: 47) of *ungandiR* as a masc. PN: 'the unbeatable one' must be rejected. In this context *ungandiR* would probably mean 'one who is protected from detrimental magic' → 'one who can perform effective magic' (cf. the idea that failed magic is caused by foreign counter-magic). The final two runes may be 1) ideographic magical runes $\bar{\imath}(sa)$, $h(agla)$ = 'ice, hail!' (Krause 1966: 147), which could represent the destructive or apotropaic forces invoked by the rune-master in the context of grave-magic, this if the inscription is complete, or 2) the remains of a formula: $\bar{\imath}$ $H(uglu)$: 'in Huglo' (cf. Olsen *NIæR*, II: 620-21).

KJ 56: Veblungsnes st.-cliff (ca. 550, M. Nor.) is another rock inscription (cf. KJ 55 Valsfjord and KJ 53 Kårstad) in an inaccessible place along an inlet from the Romsdalsfjord. Its runes are read by Krause (1966: 126-27) as: **ekirilaRwiwila**| — *ek irilaR Wīwila*: 'I, the rune-master, Wiwila [and marker].' The first rune ᚾ represents a bind-rune which is also found on two other occasions in this same formula (cf. KJ 71: By and KJ 16: Bratsberg). The final "rune" is read as a terminal marker (*Schlusszeichen*) by Krause (cf. Bugge *NIæR*, I: 320-21),(40) however, I see no compelling reason not to interpret this as a logographic rune = $\bar{\imath}(sa)$: 'ice!,' which would give the inscription its specific, perhaps apotropaic, magical purpose. This must remain speculative in any case.

KJ 69 Rosseland st. (ca. 450, SW Nor.), the archeological data for which is ambiguous (cf. Krause 1966: 154ff.), apparently also contains a name other than that of the rune-master. It reads in its entirety: (R-L) **ekwagigaRirilaRagilamudon** — *ek WagigaR irilaR Agilamu(n)dōn*. *WagigaR* is an otherwise unattested ambiguous rune-master name (sect. 31.),(41) which may or may not be interpreted as a characterizing epithet. Krause (1966: 155) sees in it just such a name = *"der stürmisch Dahinfahrende"* (< **wag-*: 'to move'). Although both Krause and Marstrander (1951: 15-16) outline a wide range of possibilities for the interpretation of this name, it is clear that it is in apposition to *irilaR*. The name fem. PN *Agilamundō* is here in either the gen. or dat. If it is gen. it could yield either 1) 'I, *WagigaR* the runemaster of Agilamundo' or (cf. Marstrander 1951: 12ff.) 2) 'I, *Wagigar*, the rune-master, (son) of Agilamundo' (favored by Krause), or if the name is in fact a dat.: 3) I, *WagigaR*, the rune-master, (carved the runes) for Agilamundo.' The second possibility would suppose a matronymic, which is not entirely unexpected in North Germanic, while the third possibility would place the stone in the original context of a grave (which the shape of the stone suggests).

Corpus of III.D.

15. IK 341: Sønder Rind-B presents a unique inscription which seems to contain the first-person pronoun appended to the normal word for 'friend': **u̯iniRik̯**. R.1 is an inverted **u** ꓩ) , while r. 7 is reversed: > :. The graphic representation **ik** is also found on IK 11: Åsum-C. So the runes could be interpreted: *winiR ik*: 'A friend I (am).' For runological and typological reasons this must remain a pure conjecture, however. Krause (1966: 272) interprets its sense as '(As) a friend I (wrote this).' Such a formula might indicate the benevolent nature of the rune-master's power toward the wearer → protection by that power, or it could be interpreted as an invocation of friendship and goodwill for the wearer within her society. This is a common aim of spells found in the Icelandic *Galdrabók* (cf. N. Lindqvist 1921).

KJ 39: Nedre Hov (300-350, E. Nor.) is a fragmentary inscription on a tanning knife (?) found in a cremation burial mound, which consists of 6-3 unrecognizable runes on one side, while the other bears the fragment: **ekad.** . . — *ek Ád* . . . -or *ek And*-, which is probably best interpreted as a rune-master formula of the type: *ek* + rune-master name. Anything beyond this is conjectural.

IV. 'I, the rune-master am called the crafty one'

15b. The fourth type of first-person formulas seems to be a distinctive extension of the third type, in which an [emphatic] mode of linking two appelatives of varying kinds is provided by means of the verb *haitan: 'to be called,' (typically with an enclitic first-person pronoun -eka). Here the emphasis continues to be on the identification of the first-person pronoun (or verb form) with the name(s). There is rare mention of actual rune-carving (see KJ 70), and this or any other verbal activity always seem to be appended to the central theme of rune-master identification (see KJ 70; KJ 27; IK 98).

Corpus of IV

KJ 29: Lindholm bone amulet (ca. 500, Skåne), in addition to its complex rune formula (see 48.), contains a rune-master formula which may be read: (R-L) **ekerilaRsawilagaRhateka**— *ek erilaR sā wīlagaR ha(i)t-eka*: 'I, the eril (= rune-master) am called the crafty one' (cf. Krause 1966: 69-72; but also Marstrander 1952: 99-108). This piece is definitely an amuletic in function, and has been carved in a cresent-like shape, with an apparently fish-like or serpentine iconography. It was found isolated in a bog, which if it was deposited there in ancient times as a part of the ritual connected with its creation is suggestive of its its purpose. It is most likely a curse formula.

KJ 27: Kragehul ash spear-shaft (500-550. Fyn) is executed with multistroke runes similar to those on the Lindholm amulet. Besides a complex and runologically problematic formula (see 15.), it contains a relatively clear *haitan*-formula, which is rendered by (Krause 1966: 65-67) as: **ekerilaRasugisalasmuhahaite** — *ek erilaR A(n)sugīslas múha (~ Muha) haite*: 'I the eril (= rune-master), am called the retainer (or son) of Asgisi.' The archeological position of the spear shaft would most certainly indicate that the weapon had been sacrificed in a bog, as the spear was broken and was found with a deposit of other objects, which were doubtless the booty of sacrificed weapons after a battle.

KJ 70: Järsberg st. (500-550, cent. Swe.) is probably an example of a stone (perhaps together with a configuration of other stones) used to sanctify or set apart a ritual or legislative site (cf. Düwel 1978) as no grave was found in its vicinity. The non-linear inscription poses significant problems for the reading (cf. Moltke 1981b), but the final sense of the whole is clear (see also sect. 6 above). If Olsen's (*NIæR*: III, 223-24) reading (which is generally followed by Krause 1966: 156-58) is correct,(42) the actual rune-master/carver formula is preceded by the formula: I **ubarhite : harabanaR** II **hait**— *Ubar h(a)iti, HrabanaR hait[e]*: 'Ubar, I am called; (the) Raven, I am called.' While *HrabanaR* may or may not have been a common PN, the appellative *Ubar* (if complete) would be a characterizing byname: 'the malicious one' (cf. ON *úfr*: 'rough, hostile'), see sect. 31.

IK 98: Sjælland II-C also contains a clear *hait-eka*-formula which may be read: (R-L) **hariuhahaitika : farauisa** — *Hari-uha haitika fārawīsa*: 'Hariuha, I am called, who knows dangerous things' (see sect. 50 for a reading of the whole inscription).

IK 41, 2: Sklonager I-A may also contain an atypical *hait-eka* formula, but it can only conjecturally be reconstructed from I. **Araxx** II **tikaxxxxxx** — as **Ara. . . (hai)tika. . .*: a PN + the formulaic *hait-eka*.

Survey of Viking Age and Medieval Material

16. Although there are many examples of rune-master formulas on Viking Age rune-stones, the use of the first-person formula seems to have yielded in time to the third-person construction (sect. 19.). However, there are some examples of the *ek*-formula, of which I give a representative outline here. The examples do not pretend to be comprehensive (nor do any of the Viking and Middle Age treatments presented in this study), but are rather an attempt to show the continuation and modification of a tradition faced with socio-cultic changes. These are essentially three types of first-person rune-master (or runographer) formulas in the later tradition: A) archaic rune-master formulas, B) various Christian formulas, and C) atypical rune-master formulas.

Type A

17. In the age of transition between the older and younger traditions, we find the complex Gørlev st. (DR 239, ca. 800, Zealand) which contains the formula: iaksatarunarit — ODan. *iak satta rūnar rētt*: 'I set the runes rightly,' i.e., the rune-master set the runes of the whole inscription within the magical rules of effectiveness (cf. Moltke 1929: 184-85).

Later in Uppland, there appears to be an example of an enclitic first-person pronoun (cf. KJ 29 Lindholm, KJ 59: Ellestad, KJ 96: Stentoften, KJ 97: Björketorp, KJ 77 Myklebostad, and IK 98: Sjælland II-C) in an archaic classic rune-master formula: U.654 Varpsund st.: **al(x)ikraistik runar** — OSwe. *Al(r)IkR ræist-ek rūnaR*: 'I, Alrik, carved the runes.' The enclitic pronoun is also appended to a proper name on Ög. 165 Skgnninge st.: **xxþurkilxkristxstinxþaxnsi:aufti:tus** — OSwe. *Þorkœll-k rēst stēn þænsi* *øfti Tosta*: 'I-Þorkell, erected this stone after (= in memory of) Tosti.' There is a more complex rhythmic rune-master formula on the Tose I st. (*NIyR* no. 13, I: 31-35, 1050-1100, SE Nor.): **runar : ek : rist : aŭk.raþ : na : sta.ue** — ONorw. *rūnar ek ríst ok ráðna stafi*: "runes I carved and 'read' (i.e., interpreted) the staves" (cf. D. Rygh *NIyR*, I: 31-35).(43) Öland 28: Gårdby churchyard st. provides another example of the importance of the concept of *ráða*: /x **riti** x **iakþu raþa + k(a)n** — OSwe. *risti iak þý ráða kann*: 'I carved (so that) you can read (them). The perfect tense of the verb appears in the rune-master formula on *NIyR* no. 121, I: 116-119 Ål church I (13th cent. SE Nor.):(44) **:nuhæfiekristit: alra** — ONorw. *nú hefi ek ristit allra*: 'Now I have carved all of them (= runes?).' Finally, we may mention another stone from Östergötland (66) in the Bjälbo churchyard to which an *ek*-formula has been appended: **:in ik : anti** — OSwe. *en iak ændi*: 'but I executed it (i.e., the inscription).' In all of these examples it is clear that the first-person pronoun has been generally removed from its initial place of emphasis to less emphasized positions in the formulas.

An interesting example of the use of the first-person formula during the post-medieval period is provided by the famous spell no. 46 of the *Galdrabók* (cf. N. Lindqvist 1921: 72ff.) which begins: *Rist æg þ(ier) Otte ausse*. . . 'I carve (or write) you eight *áss*(-runes). . .' (see sects. 48 and 53).

Type B

18. An inscription which can not be classified as a first-person rune-master formula, but which is nevertheless highly suggestive for our purposes here, is the crucifix of Lunder church (*NIyR* no. 108, II: 102-07). The runes are carved onto the leg and arm of the figure of Jesus, and read: (A) **ekhæitijesusnaþarenum** (B) **ekþolde harþandauþ** (C) **to:mas** — ONor. *ek heiti Iesus Nazarenum. ek þolða harðan dauþ. Tomas*: 'I am called Jesus of Nazareth, I suffered a painful death. Tomas.' The figure dates from the middle of the 13th-century. Here the *ek*-formula is again found in an emphasized position, and it refers to a divine being. It would be tempting to see in this formula evidence for the sacral nature of the rune-master expressed in the older formulas, however, due to the lack of apparent continuity and the fact that Christian Revelation-formulas(45) may be at the source of these later formulas, this must remain conjectural.

Two other church inscriptions from Norway belong to the *credo* genre of epigraphy. They are interesting for their emphasis on the *ego*. The Kaupanger church inscription II (*NIyR* no. 388, IV: 199), with an initial *ek*, simply says: **ektruiaguþ** — ONor. *ek trúi á guð*: 'I believe in god,' while (*NIyR* no. 445, IV: 272) Udven church III, which separated the *ek* with word dividers, reads: **tilguðrsvil.ek** — ONor. *til guð[r]s vil.ek*: 'I want (to go) to god.'

Type C

19. The nominative first-person pronoun is rare in the younger inscriptions, but there are examples of it in what might be considered rune-master formulas but these do not conform to previous types. For instance, there is the apparently magical DR 263 Skabersjö clasp (10th cent., Skåne), which reads in part (see 49.): . . **iakasuþuilaunat** — ODan. *iak Ásu því lønnæt*: . . .I have repayed Ase with it (i.e., the clasp or the magical formula?).' This follows a sequence of 16 **R**-runes. We can only guess that the *iak* mentioned here is indeed the rune-master who is reimbursing the woman Ase for some loss she incurred. Quite different, but just as puzzling is Trondheim VII (*NIyR* no. 467, V: 34), which is a wooden knife handle upon which is carved: **ik.fan.knifb** — ONor. *ek fann knif* **b**: 'I found the knife **b**.' The meaning of the inscription is obscure, as is that of the final rune (which may be "pointed" and thus be read **p**, however, it is clear that the first-person pronoun is both emphasized and that the *ek* is to be best understood as the rune-master.

Third-Person Formulas
N. N. carved (the runes)

20. The third-person rune-master, or rune-carver, formula, which thoroughly dominates in the tradition of the Viking Age, is relatively rare in the older period. Although less direct, the third-person form is just as clearly a rune-master formula when combined with runo-technical verbs and runic or runo-magical (e.g., *laþōþ*) objects. Those formulas fall into two main types, which are also chronologically distinguished.

      I. N.N. + verb (before 400)   - 2 inscriptions
      II. N.N. + verb + object (after 450) - 7 inscriptions

Because of the rarity of type I, it is rather tenuous to classify it as a "type." However, type II may be tentatively further divided into three classes based upon the type of grammatical object involved: A) with a "runic" grammatical object (i.e., *rūnōR* or *staba*), B) with a runo-magical object (i.e., one which in some way refers to the runic formula, C) non-runic object.

Corpus of I.

21. KJ 13a Nøvling brooch (ca. 200, N. Jutland) originates from a woman's grave, and is given by Krause (1966: 37-39) as: **bidawarijaRtalgidai** — *BidawarijaR talgidē*: 'Bidawari: (the one who defends that which is desired of him?) cut (the runes into the brooch).' It seems that the carver of the inscription mistakenly cut ᚠ for ᛗ. The term **talgijan* seems to have originally been a technical one for working in wood (cf. MHG *zol*: 'a block of wood' and ON *telgja*: 'to carve or shape wood,' Dutch *telg*: 'twig, branch'). Krause suggests that this term could have been transfered to working in metal as well (perhaps under influence from early runo-technical language?). Thus the inscription would be a direct runemaster document. However, Moltke (1963: 39-40) understands this as an example of a rune-carver working from a model cut into wood (hence the technical term for wood carving) by a rune-master. Moltke would then translate: 'Bidawari cut (the runes into wood).' If this rune-carver was analphabetic, then this reading would explain the error of **ai** carved for **e**. The name *BidawarijaR* may or may not be a functional rune-master name (cf. *StainawarijaR* in KJ 73: Rö, and see sect. 31 in this chapter).

KJ 30: Garbølle (Stenmagle) yew-box (ca. 400, Zealand) was a single bog-find, and is read by Krause (1966: 72-73) as: **hagiradaRitawide** : — *HagiradaR ī tawide*: 'Hagirad made (the runes) in (the box).'(46) In this reading, the adverbial preposition is dependent upon the verb. This is a well documented construction in the Old Norse literary runo-technical language (*á reist* Skm. 36:6; *váro í horni*/. . .*stafir* Gŏr. II 22: 1-2; *á horni*. . .*rísta* Sd. 7:4; *rístum rún í horni* Egill *lausavisur* 3, SKJ I: 43 — cf. Krause 1961: 264). The third-pers. sg. verb *tawidē* (< **taujan*) is elsewhere attested in the older corpus in first-person constructions (cf. KJ 43: Gallehus and KJ 67: Noleby). The compound name from **hag-i-*: 'skillful' and **rād-az*: 'advice, counsel; advisor' would mean 'giver of skillful council' (cf. ON adj. *hagrāðr*: 'giving correct or wise advice'). This could easily be a functional rune-master name — cf. the Óðinsheiti *Hagyrkr* or *Hagvirkir*: 'worker of skillful works' (Falk 1924: 15), the dwarf- (and special runic!) name *Hagall*: 'the skillful one,' (cf. HHII, prose following 1; 2: 2) and semantically PGmc **ragin-* > ON *regin*: 'divine advisors → gods' is also suggestive. On the other hand, the first element is later found in ordinary personal names in Old High German (Förstemann 1900: 716-17; Kaufmann 1968: 162). The vertical final-marker has parallels in KJ 29: Lindholm and perhaps in KJ 56: Veblungsnes.

A more recent find is the Udby (South Jutland) rosette fibula (3rd cent.) which is easily read by Stoklund as: **talgida:omal**. the first-part of the insciption is levoverse, while the latter part is rectoverse. It can be read: *Loma talgida*: 'Loma (masc.-PN) cut (the runes).'(Stoklund 1990: 4)

Corpus of II.A.

22. KJ 98: Istaby st. (ca. 625, S. Swe.) is a *bauta*-stone which was originally positioned above ground over a burial chamber (v. Friesen 1916: 28). In its entirety it is rendered by Krause (1966: 218-20) and by Marstrander (1951: 156-57) as: A.(I) **AfatRhAriwulafa** (II) **haþuwulafRhAeruwulafiR** B. **warAitrunAR þAiAR** — A.(I) *af(a)tR Hariwul(a)fa* (II) *Haþuwul(a)fR Haeruwul(a)fiR* B. *w(a)rait rūnaR þaiaR*. 'After (= in memory of) Hariwulf — Haþuwulf, the descendant of Haeruwulf, carved these runes.'

Here we have a simple third-person rune-master formula in the context of a memorial inscription. It is noteworthy that the information we receive about the rune-master and his work far outweighs that which is given about the deceased. This naturally leads to the conclusion that if the rune-master formula is not the reason for the inscription it is certainly an essential element.

Op. 16: Freilaubersheim bow fibula (ca. 575, Rhine-Hessen), was found in a woman's grave in a row-cemetary, and its rune-master formula is read by both Krause (1966: 283-84) and Arntz (1939: 215-31) as: **boso : wraetruna** — *Bōso wraet rūna*: 'Boso carved the rune.' The remainder of the inscription is apparently a greeting from the person who perhaps donated the fibula, which reads: **þk : daþina : goḷīda**: — Franconian *þ(i)k Daþina golida*: 'Daþina greeted you.' The OHG name Bōso (or Buoso) is a common one in Germanic (OE Bōsa, ON Bósi).(47) The object of the third-pers. pret. verb is the singular 'rune' (*rūna*): 'the secret lore, or writing,' for which we have North Germanic parallels in K.63: Einang and K.67: Noleby. The evidence of wear on the runes indicates that the fibula was used for some time after the runes were carved and before it was buried with its owner, so it would not be an example of a funeral inscription, as with KJ 8: Beuchte (cf. Düwel 1976).

The more recently found (1979) loom fragment from Neudingen (6th cent., SW Germany — cf. Opitz 1981: 26-27; 29-31) contains a clear example of a rune-master formula parallel to that of Freilaubersheim, with a fem. nom. PN in the rune-master position. This would be the second example of an apparent female rune-master formula (see sect. 32.) after Op. 53 (KJ 164.I): Weingarten I (see sect. 10.). The wooden object was found in a woman's grave (nr. 168) in the Alemannic grave field of

Neudingen/Baar. Opitz reads the third-person construction as: /. . .bliþguþ:uraitruna — . . . Bliþgu(n)þ : wrait rūna, which is to be translated: '. . .Bliþgunþ carved the rune.' As with Freilaubersheim, the rune-master formula is juxtaposed to an apparent dedicatory formula, which is more difficult, but which is read by Opitz as: Ibi.imuba:hamale — Alem. l(iu)bi Imuba : Hamale, which may be understood as either 1) 'Imuba (F-PN) (wishes) joy for Humal (Masc.-PN),' or as 2) 'Joy for Imuba from Hamal.' Of course the reconstruction of Ibi to l(iu)bi (an abstract with i-umlaut adj. OHG leob 'beloved,' cf. Op.15: Engers; Op. 49: Weimar A, bow fibula; Op. 51: Weimar C, buckle; Op. 52: Weimar D, amber bead) remains conjectural, but based upon the typological evidence of the South Germanic inscriptions, it seems most probable.

Opitz gives no evidence as to the freshness of the inscription, it is, however, possible that it represents a kind of funeral inscription in which Hamal had carved by Bliþgunþ effectively to wish Imuba a joyous existence after death.

KJ 95: Gummarp st. (ca. 600, S. Swe.) has been lost since the great fire of Copenhagen in 1728 and we are dependent upon drawings made by Jon Skonvig and Peder Syv (cf. Moltke 1956: 143 and 1958: 94-98). This drawing may be transcribed as: (I). . .hAþuwolAfA (II) sAte (III) . . .stAbAþria (IV) fff. If we assume the inscription is complete, except for the nominative marker R after r. (I) 10, then it may be read (with Krause 1966: 206-08) as: (I) Haþuwolfa[R] (II) sat(t)e (III) staba þria (IV) f(ehu) f(ehu) f(ehu): 'Haþuwolf set three staves: (3 x wealth).'(48) However, v. Friesen (1916: 21-27) would reconstruct the inscription on the model of a memorial stone (cf. KJ 98: Istaby), and read it: (I) [aftR] Haþuwol(a)fa (II) [N.N.] sat(t)e (III) staba þria (IV) fff: 'After Haþuwolf, [N.N.] set three staves fff.(49) Krause's interpretation is more attractive because it requires less conjecture, but for our purposes here it is worth noting that both interpretations contain a third-pers. sg. rune-master formula. The construction 'to set staves' is clearly equivalent in runo-technical terms to the formula 'to carve runes.'(50) On the Gørlev st. we saw this verbal term, while in two other examples the staves and the stone are parallel in the construction (cf. Sö 56: Fyrby: . . .setu:stain:auk:stafa:marga: '. . . set the stone and mighty staves,' and Vs. 1: Stora Ryttern: . . .seti:stff:auk: sena:þasi. . .: '. . .set the staves and this stone. . .').

If Gummarp is not a memorial stone, then it is most probably a purely magical inscription which is intended to invoke the powers of the three *fehu staves explicitly expressed in the formula. The relatively small size,

—148—

63 cm high, of this stone is comparable to that of KJ 102: Roes (75 x 55 cm), which also seems to be of a primarily magical character. Gummarp must also be understood within the context of the other contemporary Bleking stones (KJ 95-98).

IK 184: Tjurkö I-C contains a sometimes non-runo-technical third-pers. sg. verb *wurkjan*, in a rhythmic formula. The inscription is read by Krause (1966: 272-74) and by Moltke-Jacobsen (1942: 547-49) as: (R-L) **wurterunoRanwalhakurne··heldaRkunimudiu···** — *wúrtē rūnōR / an wálha-kúrnē– HeldaR Kunimu(n)diu*: 'Held worked the runes on welsh grain for Kunimund.' The syntax of the formula is apparently conditioned by the effort to shape a poetic text. Here the runes are said to have been "worked" on the object (cf. the use of the preposition in KJ 30: Garbølle 19.). Otherwise in the older period *wurkjan* has *rūnō ~ rūnōR* as its object in perhaps only KJ 72: Tune st. and that is open to question. In most cases it seems ambiguous as to whether the "working" or "making" refers to the runes or to the object upon which they are executed. By the Viking Age, however, the term came to mean "to compose," as well (cf. Ebel 1963: 53-55). The phrase *an walha-kurnē*: "on the grain of the 'Welsh'" is perhaps a kenning for 'gold' (= the bracteate). "Welsh" is here a general term for "foreign" or "southern" as opposed to northern (cf. ON *valskr*: 'foreign, esp. French,' OHG *wal(a)hisc*, OE *wealhisc*: foreign, esp. British or 'Welsh'). Both of the personal names recorded on this bracteate would seem to be ordinary and non-functional (sect. 31.). If the masc. *KunimunduR is indeed purely personal, it would perhaps represent a rare example of a bracteate inscription at least originally composed for a specific person (cf. also IK 26: Börringe-C, IK 161: Skodburg-B).(51) Formally, this bracteate would seem to be an amulet with a runic inscription which specifically dedicates its effects (which based on the kenning would most likely be to bring prosperity) to *KunimunduR.

Corpus of II.B.

23. Another bracteate inscription, IK 70: Halskov-C, preserves a third-person rune-master formula in conjunction with what appears to be a scrambled 22-rune sequence, or *ephesion grammaton* (46-48.). The first 17 runes of the inscription are: (R-L) **nxeturfahidelaþoþ. . .**, which may be read: *NxetuR fahidē laþoþ:* 'NxetuR wrote ('colored') the summons.' The third-pers. sg. pret. *fahidē* is the only part of this reading which is absolutely certain (Jacobsen-Moltke 1942: 531-32). However, for typological reasons we would expect this *verbal terminus technicus* to be preceded by a PN and to be followed by a grammatical runic object. The

sequence **nxetur** has not yet been explained, but seems to be a u-stem masc. PN (cf. SigaduR KJ 47 Svarteborg medallion and *haukōþuR* KJ 66: Vånga st.). Runes 13-17, **laþoþ**, are interpreted as a younger apocopated form of *laþōþu* (cf. IK 189: Trollhättan-A — see sect. 40.) by Krause (1966: 267 and 1971: 41;90).(52) The *laþoþ* or *laþo* probably refers to the following runic formula, and the whole represents a rune-master formula juxtaposed to a magical or encoded sequence of runes.

An Old English inscription on a bone plate (.9" x 3.5") of unknown provenance in Darbyshire, which dates from the 8th-century, bears the runes: **godgecadāræhaddaþiþiswrat**. Page (1999: 163-64) points out all of the ambiguities surrounding the interpretation of these staves, and the possibilities of the magical function of its syntactic formula are discussed in sect. 51 below. In any event, the final 13 runes clearly present a third-pers. sg. pret. formula, which may be read either 1). . .*Hadda þē þis wrat*, or 2) . *Hadda þy þis wrat*. These would render the alternate translations of 1) . . .Hadda who carved/wrote this,' or 2) '. . .Hadda because (he) carved/wrote this.' Another ambiguity is that we can not be sure whether *wrat* refers to the carving of the runes into the bone plate, or to the writing of a book to which the plate might have been attached (cf. Bately and Evison 1961: 301ff.).

Corpus of II.C.

24.   KJ 71: By st. (550-600, SE Nor.), which appears to have originally lain upon or in a grave mound (cf. Bugge *NIæR*:   I, 90; 115-16), bears a complex inscription with a nominal first-person rune-master formula — *ek erilaR* (sects. 11.-12.) and an indecipherable concluding runic sequence of 6 staves, as well as a central third-pers. sg. formula. The third-person construction is given by Krause (1966: 159-61) as: /. . .**hroRaRhroReRortebataRinau[x]talaifu**. . ./ . . .*HroRaR HrōReR ortē þat aRina ūt Ąlaifu* . . .: 'Hror descendent of Hror worked out this slab for Alaif. . .' The interpretation of this as a rune-master formula is far from certain since neither the verb *ortē* . . . *ūt*, nor the neut. acc. sg. object *aRina* (< **azina-*): 'stone slab'(53) are specifically runo-technical terms. It could well be that Hror is the one who dressed the stone (its shape suggests such work was done on it) so that it would be suitable for its function upon or inside the mound. We are faced with a problem similar to that of the Gallehus horn (KJ 43) when we try to determine the role of Hror in relation to the role of rune-master. Is Hror 1) a rune-master identical to *erilaR* and thus the conceiver and executor of the runes, 2) a rune-carver, different from the *erilaR*, or 3) the stone-mason who only shaped the stone — and

whose work is commemorated by the rune-master/carver? There does not seem to be any way to decide absolutely which of these possibilities is correct. If we *understand ortē þat aRina ūt* as a simple reference to the stone-mason's work, then the third possibility would seem most likely — and would certainly raise some interesting questions as to the importance of these masons in the religious history of the period. On the other hand, if the verb and object are interpreted as a reference to the intellectual task of composing (and/or executing) the runes, then the direct juxtaposition of the first and third-person formulas would indicate a complex rune-master formula (perhaps in a historical transition stage between the two forms). Bugge (*NIæR*; I, 107-09), followed by Krause (1966: 161), interprets **alaifu** — *Alaifu* as an ordinary fem. PN (ON Álof). Krause reads it as a dat. sg. with the meaning 'for Alaif.'

The final six runes, which read a. **dR** b. **rmþi**, have been tentatively interpreted by Bugge I: 110-12) as: *d(ohtu)R r(ūnōR) m(arhidē) þ(aR) ë(haR)*: '. . .(for A. his) daughter, Eh marked these runes,' and by Noreen (1927: 376) as: *D(ag)r r(ūnar) m(erk)þe*: 'Dag marked the runes.' These interpretations are, of course, highly conjectural.

Survey of Viking and Middle Age Material

25. In the younger tradition, the use of the third-person formula becomes more common and the verbal terminology becomes much more complex with the idea of *carving* the runes expressed by not only *ríta* or *rísta/rista* but also with *marka*: 'to mark,' *skera*: 'to cut,' *skrifa*: 'to write' (after ca. 1200), *gera*: 'to make,' and *hǫggva*: 'to hew,' and the idea of coloring them expressed not only by **faihjan* > *fá*, but also by the more rare forms *rjóða*: 'to redden,' *steina*: 'to stain,' and *penta*: 'to paint' (cf. Ebel 1963 for the use and frequency of these various verbal forms). Other fundamental developments in the younger tradition are the absolute increase of the frequency of runic monuments (from the approximately 250 monuments before 750 CE to the over 5,000 known to have been executed after that time), and the proliferation of the memorial stones common in Denmark (especially between 950 and 1150 when 146 of 178 stones known in the early 20th-century fall — cf. Wimmer 1914, 40-48) and in Sweden (a total of ca. 2500 stones which only begin to become common after the middle of the 11th-century. This relatively high level of rune-stone production represents a kind of industry which might have caused a technological and social revolution in certain aspects of the runic tradition. Of these features, the most relevant for our work here is the proliferation of the runographers' signatures.(54) Formally, they bear a close resemblance to

the older rune-master/ rune-carver formulas, however, we can not know the nature of their functional relationship for certain.

The third-person rune-master or runographer formulas may be classified as either: 1) without predicate object: 'N.N. carved' or 2) with predicate object: 'N.N. carved the runes.' In the second type there is an increased tendency to use verbs which can have as their objects *both* the runes and the thing (usually *stæin*) upon which the runes are carved. More complex formulas also develop from this with multiple verbs and/or objects. However, since these find no parallel in the older tradition, we will leave them to be discussed elsewhere. For similar reasons, the common contract formula, of the type: N.N. *létt raisa stæin*: 'N.N. had the stone erected' must also remain outside our treatment here.

Because of the vastness of the formulaic third-person material in the younger traditions, a more statistical approach is needed in order to present both its numerical magnitude as opposed to the older traditions, and at the same time to try and demonstrate some of its variations and its relative distribution. The figures presented here have mostly been drawn from Ebel (1963).

In the Viking and Middle Ages, the concept of "carving" is attested in runographer formulas over 250 times, and that of 'hewing,' or 'making' around 70 times. The idea of 'coloring' becomes generally rarer, with a total of only 17 occurrences in this period, with the reflex of **faihjan, fá*, only represented as late as the Viking period (to about 1050).

1) 'N.N. carved/colored.'

The forms without predicate objects have a little over 100 attestations, with the occurrence of words which convey the idea of 'carving' represented in 95 cases and "coloring" in around 9 instances. The usual term for "carving" is either the weak verb *rista* (61 occurrences) or its strong counterpart *rísta* (15 occurrences), while *marka*: 'to mark' was sometimes used in Viking Age Sweden (8 times) and *skara* 'to score'(55) was rarely employed (3 attestations) after 1150 in Denmark and on Gotland. After 1200 the terminology of bookhand entered into the runo-technical vocabulary. The term *skrifa*: 'to write,' as with pen and ink, is found in 7 inscriptions (6 from Sweden, 1 from Norway). These were most surely made by priests who transferred the technical terminology from one writing technique to the other (cf. Ebel 1963: 28-30). The strong form *rísta* without a predicate object is only common in medieval Norway (10 attestations), while the weak form is almost exclusively represented in Viking Age Sweden (56 attestations, of which 50 are in Uppland).

Approximately 70 inscriptions use the ambiguous terms *gera*: 'to make, do,' or *hǫggva*: 'to hew, cut' in objectless formulas.

The largest number (ca. 53) of these occur in Sweden during the Viking and early medieval period, of which 45 use *hǫggva* and only 8 *gera*. Around 15 of these attestations of *hǫggva* are used in conjunction with a preposition at: "for," or efter: "after" in memorial formulas.

Only about 9 possible inscriptions of the type 'N.N. colored' are known. Of these 6 use *fá*, and are distributed throughout the Scandinavian region. The remaining 3 from the early medieval period use the term *steina*: 'to stain, color,' which is usually appended to a formula for 'to carve.' A model objectless formula of this type appears on Sö 347 Gersta: **esbern . risti . auk . ulfr . stainti—** OSwe. *Æsbjærn risti, ok UlfR stændi*: 'Asbjurn carved and Ulf stained (the runes).'

Although these objectless forms may represent a kind of lapidary brevity, it is nevertheless interesting that formulas of the type found in the older period, which omit the predicate object (in both first and third-person forms), should find such close formal correspondence in the later period when the inscriptions themselves were becoming ever longer and more syntactic. It seems quite possible that this omission of object represented a special type of formula, the full significance of which we can now only speculate upon.

2) 'N.N. carved/colored the runes'

Formulations which include the runic grammatical object (usually *rúnar*) remain more common, with a total of just over 200 attestations. Of these, the vast majority convey the formula 'N.N. carved the runes' with the *rista/rísta* verbal form — and again these are mostly found in 11th-century Sweden with just over 90 occurrences. The term *marka* is again found with the object *rúnar* in 4 inscriptions from the same period. However, a good number (ca. 30) with the strong form *rísta* are found in Norway — of these 20 are from the medieval period and 5 from the Viking Age. In addition, 6 other Viking period Norwegian formulas of this type are known from the British Isles. *Gera* is only rarely used in connection with *rúnar* (three attestations from the Viking and Middle Ages), however, *hǫggva* is the antecedent to a runic predicate over 30 times in Swedish Viking Age formulas.

The idea "to color runes" certainly remained a strong concept and indeed seems to have been normal in actual practice in the Viking Age and after (cf. Jansson 1962: 147-55, and see VII. 11), however, the epigraphical evidence for this practice remains meager. To the nine inscriptions without predicate objects, we can only add a possible eight with a runic predicate.

Of these five are with *fá* and come from the Viking Age — but this time concentrated exclusively in Sweden. The remaining three examples use three different verbs. We again find an attestation of *steina* on Öl. 43: Gärdslösa church (11th cent.): /. . .**tuar risti: runaR**. . .**stain[di]**. This may be reconstructed as ([*Od*]*dvarr*?) *risti rūnaR— stæin[di]*: 'Oddvar(?) carved the runes (and) stained (them).' It is possible that both *stæindi* and *risti* should have *rūnaR* as their object.(56) A term which probably originally had a magico-cultic significance is *rjóða*: 'to redden' (Ebel 1963: 36-37), but it is only possibly attested in one inscription. Sö 206: Överselö church which reads in part: . . .**runum ru[x]niR**. . ./. This has been reconstructed by Brate-Wessén (1924: 182-83) as: *rúnum ruðniR*: 'reddened with runes' (see V.15.). Here, *ruðniR* would be the plural form of either an adjective or participle. Finally, there is a now lost medieval inscription from Kjos church (*NIyR* 69: I, 202-04) which might have contained the word *penta*: 'to paint,' as a runo-technical term.

The problems surrounding the younger rune-carver signatures may, for reasons outlined above, be considered quite different from those of formally similar elements in the older tradition. What seems most important to keep in mind for our present purpose is that: 1) there seems to have been a formal continuity which could suggest a strong institutional framework (see ch. IV) and 2) despite the apparent irrelevance of the signature to the main portion of most memorial inscriptions it seems to have been an important — even essential — element in the overall formulation (sometimes even added outside the serpentine bands). The second point would suggest that the nature and function of these "signatures" was more than that of a simple craftsman's signature.

Appendix: Personified Object — 'N.N. made me.'

26. In the older tradition only one inscription is possibly of this type — KJ 14: Etelhem clasp (ca. 500, Gotland). It is read by Bugge (*NIæR*: I, 148ff.), and accepted in Krause (1966: 39-40) as: **mkmrlawrta[s]**— *m(i)k M(ē)r(i)la w(o)rta*[x]: 'Merila made me.' The last **a**-rune is followed by what appears to be another isolated Ƿform, however, this may also represent a non-runic end-marker. Because this formula is unique in the older period, it is not discussed in detail here (cf. Ploss 1958 for the development of inscriptions of this type and their place in Germanic epigraphical tradition). This could be a formulaic influence from either Latin or Greek — which is interesting for the possible documentation of intellectual exchange between the northern and southern regions during the 5th-century.

The formula perhaps appeared as an anomalous southern import and fell quickly into disuse because it did not fill a need in the runo-technical formulaic language. However, it was later re-imported in the medieval period (only 3 inscriptions of the type N.N. *gerði mik* are known from the Viking Age). In the Scandinavian Middle Ages we find a total of 56 inscriptions with the predicate object *mik*, of these 14 are of the purely runo-technical type, i.e., 'N.N. carved me,' while 42 are of the more ambiguous 'N.N. made me' type. Furthermore, it is noteworthy that the greatest concentration of the *mik* inscriptions is found in Norway with between 26 and 28 of the total.

In the Anglo-Saxon tradition the formula entered at a much earlier time, cf. the 8th-century partially runic stone of Alnmouth, which contains the formula *MYREDaH.MEH.wO[RHTE]*— *Myredah meh worhte*: 'Myredah made me,' and the 9th-century (again only partially runic) Lancashire ring, which reads æ*DRED MECAHEAnREDMECagROF*: 'Ædred owns me, Eanred engraved me.' The now lost, and undated, but apparently purely runic, brooch of Northumbria (cf. Stephens I, 386-87) also contained a similar formula, which supposedly could be translated: 'Gudrid made me (and) Ælchfrith owns me.'

For this material, the most important question from our viewpoint is: how did those who carved the inscriptions consider the animate quality of a) the runes themselves, which appear to speak in the 'N.N. carved me' forms, or of b) the object upon which the runes are carved? These may represent archaic beliefs epigraphically expressed for the first time in these inscriptions — or they may be merely formulaic craftsman's signatures transferred from Latin tradition.

Ambiguous Restricted Proper Names

27. Besides those formulas which give us good reason to believe that certain proper names or adjectival bynames indicate the rune-master or runographer, there are approximately 80 inscriptions which contain proper names either:

I) in total isolation (ca. 35), or

II) within the context of runic or rune-like formulas (ca. 40), which give no indication of the role played by the person(57) mentioned in the production of the inscription. Krause (1966) generally assumes that when an isolated masc. PN appears on a loose object it may be interpreted as that of the rune-master — and therefore a radically reduced rune-master formula. This is an assumption which must be re-examined in the context of archeological and other runic data (cf. Dillmann 1981, and see sect. 32).

Special problems which must be taken into account when reading these usually terse documents are the archeological context (upon what type of object does it appear?, was it connected to a grave?, was the grave that of a man or woman?), dating, and linguistic-geographical placement (North or South Germanic?). As far as the nature of the name itself is concerned, it is important to consider whether it is a well-attested mundane personal name, or a characterizing rune-master byname (sect. 31). Also, in this regard it must be mentioned that the *nomen agentis* spear names are not discussed here, because they doubtlessly refer to the object and not to the carver (see sect. 41).

Because of difficulties which involve the classification of isolated proper names without further runic context, they must be analyzed according to the type of object upon which they occur, the archeological context of the object and the technique used to execute the inscription. The objects may be either 1) *manufactured* for a specific utilitarian or ornamental purpose, and in this case the runes may be a) carved or b) minted (i.e., on bracteates),(58) or 2) *natural* with minimal human alteration (*bauta*-stones, etc.).

I. Isolated Proper Names
Manufactured Objects

28. In the older period, at least 23 inscriptions of this type occur on manufactured objects. The *) indicates that the interpretation is problematical on runological or phonological grounds.

1) Carved Runes
Found on North Germanic Brooches and Clasps.

*Meldorf, brooch.(59) **hiwi** — *Hiwi* acc./dat. fem. PN(?). (ca. 50, S. Jutland) [fem. grave?].

KJ 10: Himlingøje II. **w̨iduhudaR** — *Widuhu(n)daR* nom. masc. PN (ca. 200. Sjælland) [fem. grave].

*KJ 11: Væløse **alugod ᛉ** — *Alugod* voc. masc. PN(?). (ca. 200, Sjælland) [fem. grave].(60)

*KJ 13: Næsbjerg. **w̨araflusa** — *Waraflusa* nom. masc. PN(?) (ca. 200, S. Jutland) [masc. ~ fem. grave].(61)

KJ 9: Himlingøje I. **hariso**— *Hariso* nom. fem. PN (ca. 350, Sjælland) [fem. grave].

South Germanic Brooches.

*KJ 139: Liebenau. **rauzwi**— *Rauz-wi(h)* nom. masc. PN (350-400, N. Germany) [masc. grave].(62)

Op. 13: Donzdorf. **eho**— *Eho* nom. masc. PN (500-20, SW Germany) [fem.].(63)

Op. 7: Bopfingen. **mauo**— *Mauo* nom. masc. PN (500-600, SW Germany) [fem. grave].

KJ 143: Engers. **leub**— *Leub* nom. masc. PN (ca. 600, W. Germany) [fem. grave].

KJ 141: Friedberg. **þuruþhild**— *Þuruþhild* nom. fem. PN (ca. 600, W. Germany) [fem. grave].

*KJ 152: Nordendorf II. **birl[x]ioel[x]**— [?] (ca. 600, SW Germany) [masc. ~ fem. grave].(64)

KJ 155A: Dischingen A. **winka**— *Winka* nom. fem. PN (600- 700, SW Germany) [masc. ~ fem. grave].

KJ 164II: Weingarten II. **dado**— *Dado* nom. masc. PN (ca. 700, SW Germany) [fem. grave].(65)

North Germanic Utilitarian Objects

KJ 26: Vimose, comb. **harja**—*Harja* nom. masc. PN (ca. 250, Fyn) [bog find].

Flleseje (Slemminge), tanning knife (?). **witrŋ ~ witro**
        1) *Witring* voc. masc. PN.
        2) *Witr-ing(waR)* nom. masc. PN.
        3) *Witrō* nom. fem. PN (ca. 500, Lolland)[bog find].(66)

KJ 49: Førde, fishing weight. **aluko**— *Alukō* nom. fem. PN (ca. 550, W.Nor.) [loose find].(67)

South Germanic Utilitarian Object

KJ 161: Gammertingen box. **ado a[x]o** — *Ado A[d]o* nom. masc. PN x 2. (500-600, SW Germany) [fem. grave].

North or East Germanic Martial Objects

KJ 23: Vimose, scabbard fitting. (R-L) **awŋs**— *Awings* E. Gmc. masc. PN (ca. 400, Fyn) [bog find].

Illerup, shield fitting. **swarta** — *Swarta* nom. masc. PN (ca. 200, N. Jutland) [bog find].(68)

Miscellaneous Carved Runic Objects

KJ 45: Køng, statue. /[x]xxŋo . . .*ingō* NGmc. nom. fem. PN (ca. 500, Fyn) [loose find].

KJ 42: Strårup, ring or diadem. **leþro** — *Leþrō* NGmc. nom. fem. PN, or SGmc. nom. masc. PN (ca. 400, Jutland) [masc. ~ fem. grave].

2) Minted Runes
(bracteates)

IK 131: Norway-A. **anoaṇa̠** — *Anoana* nom. masc. PN -*an*-stem. (Nor.).
IK 367: Körlin-C **waiga**— *Waiga* nom. masc. PN -an stem. (E.Pommerania?).
IK 386: Wapno-C. (R-L) **sabar** — *Sabar-* (EGmc.?) nom. masc. (PN?). (Poland).(69)
IK 51,2: Killerup-B. . . .**undR** . . .*undR* frag. of a nom. masc. PN(?). (Fyn).

Natural Objects
(stones)

29. These stone objects may have had any one of three functions: 1) a *bauta*-stone, which would have stood above ground on a grave mound as a marker, 2) a barrow-stone, which would have been buried *within* the mound itself, or 3) a sacral stone, which was not attached to a grave, but rather seems to have acted as a marker of sacred space (often with other stones in certain configurations) for ritual and/or juridical purposes, cf. Düwel (1978). When we are lucky, we can determine the nature of the stone from the archeological reports, but quite often such reports are lacking or incomplete and we must rely on typological criteria, which principally depend on the size and shape of the stone. Smaller and/or flatter stones would tend to be placed in the barrow-stone category, while longer and/or taller ones, which seem to have been dressed to stand upright, would be more likely candidates for *bauta*-stones (cf. Olsen 1916: 227ff.; Krause 1935: 9-20, but also Bæksted 1951). With most of these inscriptions which consist exclusively of a single PN, it is virtually impossible to determine whether the name of the dead or that of the rune-master is recorded. If there appears to have been no grave in the vicinity, and a 'sacred enclosure' is

suspected, then a rune-master name would be the best interpretation, while for typological (and socio-cultic) reasons a female name would most likely indicate the name of the deceased. Otherwise, this question remains open (see sects. 28-31). A question mark in brackets in the following descriptions indicates that there is no reliable archeological report on its original position.

1) *Bauta*-Stones
(probably attached to graves)

KJ 66: Vånga. (R-L) **haukoþuR** — *HaukoþuR* nom. masc. PN (ca. 500, Vg.) [?].
KJ 87: Skärkind. **skiþaleubaR** — *Ski(n)þa-LeubaR*. double nom. masc. PN (ca. 450, 8g.) [?].
KJ 90: Sunde. (R-L) **widugastiR** — *WidugastiR* nom. masc. PN (ca. 500, WNor.) [fem. grave].
KJ 93: Bratsberg. **þaliR** — *ÞaliR ~ WaliR*. nom. masc. PN (450-550, NW Nor.) [masc. grave].(70)
KJ 94: Tveito. **tAitR** — *TaitR*. nom. masc. PN.(71)

2) *Bauta*-Stones
(probably not attached to graves)

KJ 88: Møgedal. (R-L) **laiþigaR**— *LaiþigaR*. nom. masc. PN (500-50, SW Nor.) [free-standing stone].(72)
KJ 92: Eidsvgg. **HaraRaR**— *H[a]raRaR*. nom. masc. PN (450-500, W. Nor.) [stone circle].(73)
KJ 91: Tørvika A. (R-L) **ladawarijaR**— *La(n)dawarijaR*. nom. masc. PN (400-50, SW Nor.) [masc.? grave].(74)
KJ 89: Tanem. **mairlŋu**— *Ma[i]rlingu*. nom. fem. PN (ca. 500, M Nor.) [fem. grave?].(75)

II. Proper Names in Elaborated Context

30. As opposed to strictly isolated, or restricted personal names, a more formulaic analytical approach may also be taken toward the names found in an elaborated runic or symbolic context. Here, the contextual elements of the inscription are classified according to the same formulaic categories upon which this chapter is constructed. The basic dichotomy is between: 1) the non-syntactic auxiliary elements, which may consist of non-declined lexical elements (formula-words [*alu, laukaR*, etc.] or other personal

names) or apparently ideographic runic signs or other non-lexical signs —
or — a combination of these words and signs, and 2) those elements which
involve the grammatical person in a syntactic context (in which a verb must
be either stated or implicit).

Manufactured Objects.

Well over 40 inscriptions of this type occur on manufactured objects,
and of these just over 30 are carved — mainly into brooches of various
kinds.

A. Carved Inscriptions with Lexical Elements

North Germanic

*KJ 48: Fosse fitting. ḳa[l]a alu— *Kala alu.* nom. masc. PN + subst. (500-50, S. Nor.) [crem. grave].(76)

South Germanic

A group of South Germanic inscriptions bear pairs of groups of private
names. It has been assumed by Arntz (1939, 468-69) and Krause (1966,
277ff.) that such formulas represent abbreviated forms (some of which
include the word *leub* in 'wish formulas'). These could be completed in a
variety of ways, e.g., "Giver (wishes [love for]) Receiver," "Giver (gives
this brooch to) Receiver," etc. These "givers" and "receivers" may be
individuals or pairs.(77) The magical nature, and more specifically the runo-
magical nature of these inscriptions is, however, doubtful.

Op. 20: Griesheim, brooch. **kolo agilaþruþ** — *Kolo Agilaþruþ* nom.
masc. PN + nom. fem. PN (7th cent. W. Germany) [fem. grave].

KJ 140: Soest, brooch. **rada daþa [atano]** in runic cross.(78)

Rāda Daþa At(t)ano(?) fem. PN x 2 + nom. masc. PN (550-600, N. Germ.)
[fem. grave].(79)

There are also two brooch inscriptions which may hold forms of
Germanic divine names in the context of personal names.

*KJ 151 I: Nordendorf I. a. **logaþore** b. **wodan** c. **wigiþonar** d.
awaleubwini[x] — *Logaþorē Wōdan Wigiþonar Awa Leubwini*[x] nom.
masc. divine name x 3 + nom. fem. PN + nom. masc. PN(80) (600-50, SW
Germany) [masc. or fem. grave].

*KJ 160: Balingen. (R-L) aṣuẓdnloamiluk — *asuz D(a)n(i)lo Amilu(n)k* divine name < **ansuz* + nom. masc. PN(81) + nom. masc. patronymic. (600-50, S. Germany) [masc. or fem. grave].

The last three inscriptions of this group with word-formulas contain Christian formulaic elements.

KJ 166: Bezenye brooches. A. **godahid unja** B. **ḳarsiboda segun**(82) — A. *Godahi(l)d (w)unja* B. *(i)k Arsiboda segun*.(83) nom. fem. PN + subst./(pers. pron.?) + nom. fem. PN + subst. 'Godahild (wishes) joy./(I) Arsiboda (wish[es]) blessing.' (530-600, W. Hungary) [fem. grave].

KJ 142: Bad Ems, brooch. a. **madali**[x] b. **ubada** — *Madali u(m)bada*: 'Madali (gives or wishes) consolation' (cf. Krause 1937: 213-15 and Arntz 1939: 200). — nom. masc. PN + subst. (before 600, W. Germany)[grave find].

Op.27: Kirchheim, brooch. **badah**[x]**ali**— *bada H*[x]*ali*: 'consolation (is wished by) *H-ali*.' Subst. + (nom. masc. PN?). (500-600, SW Germany) [fem. grave]. This form would be virtually identical to that of Bad Ems. The runes are followed by what might be an ideograph: 卐

The word *(umbi-)bada* would seem to be a Christian formulation with the approximate meaning 'consolation (after death?),' but cf. Opitz (1977: 131) who also suggests a connection with a doubtful PIE **bhe-/bho-*: 'to warm, roast, quicken(?)' > PGmc. *baþa*: 'bath' — with the subsequent Christian idea of "rebirth." Typologically, these inscriptions could correspond to pre-Christian formulas on KJ 8: Beuchte.

With (Non-Lexical) Ideographic Elements
North Germanic

*KJ 21: Torsberg, shield. (R-L) **aisgRh**(84)— *Ais(i)g(a)R h.* nom. masc. PN + ideographic h [= *h(agla)*: 'hail'] — cf. Krause (1966: 56). (ca. 200, S. Jutland) [bog find].

KJ 11: Værløse, brooch. **alugod** ᛟ — *Alugod*(85) voc. masc. PN + ideographic sign. (ca. 200, Sjælland) [fem. grave].

*KJ 7: Aquincum, brooch. a. **fuþarkgw** b. **jlain:kŋia**— *fuþarkgw* (first 8 runes in sequence) + jl + *ain-k(unni)ngia*. A ten-rune sequential formula + nom. masc. prop. adj. (= 'the lone friend'). (ca. 530, Hungary) [hoard find].

KJ 28: Kragehul, knife shaft. (R-L) 1. . .**uma bera** 2. . . . **aau**. (500-50, Fyn) [bog find]. Only the sequence **bera** can be interpreted with any certainty as a NGmc. masc. PN **Bera**: 'bear.' Line 2. is probably an ideographic sequence (Krause 1966: 69), while r. 1-3 in line 1. remain obscure. It could represent a word related to OE *huma*: 'shaft of the weaving comb' and thus be a runic designation of the function of the object (cf. KJ 18, 26, 27[?], 43, 50) — cf. Gutenbrunner (1936/37: 169-70). Marstrander (1951: 24) suggests the remnants of the first element of a compound name, while Krause (1966: 68) mentions an OE herb name *uma* and also considers the possibility of the remainder of a verb form in -*numa*: 'one who has learned something' as a further designation of the runemaster.

South Germanic

KJ 8: Beuchte, brooch. a. **fuþarzj** b. **buirso** — fuþar z j *Būriso* (Krause 1966: 26-29). First 5 runes in sequence + z j + nom. masc. PN (550-600, N. Germany) [fem. grave].(86)

Thames, sax. **fuþorcgwhnijzpxstbeŋdlmœaæyea beagnoþ** — (imperfect OE fuþorc-sequence) + nom. masc. PN (*Beagnoþ*). (8th-9th cent., S. England) [river find].

*KJ 153: Heilbronn, fitting. (R-L) **lkarwi** — lk + *Arwi*: 1k(87) + nom. masc. PN (600-700, SW Germany) [masc. grave].

KJ 167: Szabadbattyán, buckle. **marŋ sd** — *Mar(i)ng-(s)* ḍ. nom. masc. PN + d or sd.(88) (400-450, Hungary) [?].

KJ 162: Wurmlingen, spear-head. ⩜ **:idorih** — [x]: *Dorih*. rune-like ideograph or ornament + nom. masc. PN (600-50, SW Germany) [m. grave].(89)

*KJ 158: Steindorf, sax. **whusibald**xxx — w *Husibald*xxx: (ideographic w-rune?) + nom. masc. PN + [?]. (600-50, S. Germany)[masc. Grave].(90)

3) With Syntactic Formulas

Both of the North Germanic inscriptions in this category are on objects of a martial character.

*KJ 20: Torsberg, scabbard fitting. (ca. 200, S. Jutland) [bog find]. Which reads: 1. **owlþuþewaR** 2. **niwajemariR**. Two interpretations seem possible here:

1. *o(þala) W(u)lþuþewaR* (or *W[o]lþuþewaR*)

2. a) *ni wajemariR* or b) *ni waje mariR*:

'(Hereditary property ᚨ) [of?] *Wulþuþew* (= 'the servant of Ullr') a) the not badly famed,' - or - b) 'do not spare, *Mær* (= sword-name)!'(91)

Not only is there perhaps a syntactic formula present in the second part, but there is also a possible use of an ideographic o-rune, so that the whole formula would appear: [ideograph + nom. masc. PN + negative + adj.], or simply: [nom. masc. PN + negative + adj.]. The name in line 1. may be that of the rune-master, of the owner, or of the sword itself.

KJ 22: Vimose, scabbard fitting. (250-300, Fyn) [bog find], is again an extremely difficult inscription which appears: 1. **mariha iala** 2. **makija**, and which can be read: *Mari aih* (h-metathesis?) *Al(l)a makija*: 'Alla owns *Mær* (= 'the famous one' [sword-name]) as sword' (cf. Marstrander 1929c: 228ff., and Krause 1937: 181-82 and 1966: 58).(92) In this reading, Alla would be the owner of the sword mentioned, but he might also be the rune-master and/or priest (cf. Krause 1937: 182 and Moltke 1932: 83-96).

B. Minted Inscriptions

Of the nine inscriptions with restricted proper names, all but two also contain what could be considered a word-formula, or these could be reconstructed (e.g., *laþu, alu, laukaR, auja*), see 32-40.

1) With Single Word-Formula

IK 163: Skonager III-C. **niwilia** (R-L) **lþu** — *Niu[j]ila l[a]þu*. nom. masc. PM + nom. substantive.

IK 43: Darum V-C. **niujil alu** — *Niujil(a) alu*. nom. masc. PN(?) + nom. substantive.

IK 42: Darum I-A. (R-L) **frohila laþu** — *Frohila laþu*. nom. masc. PN + nom. substantive.

2) With Two Word-Formulas

IK 26: Börringe-C. **tanulu:al laukaR** — *Tanulu al(u) laukaR*. nom. fem. PN + nom. substantive + nom. substantive.

3) With Another PN

IK 76: Hitsum-A. (R-L) **foRo glola** — *FoRo Glola*. NGmc. nom. fem. PN + nom. masc. PN or SGmc. nom. masc. PN + nom. fem. PN.(93)

4) With Another PN and Runic Formula

IK 161: Skodborg-B:
(R-L) **aujaalawinaujaalawinaujaalawinjalawid**— *auja Alawin auja Alawin auja Alawin j(era) Alawid!* subst. + voc. masc. PN x 3 +

ideographic rune + voc. masc. PN.(94) The *auja-* formula represented here can be compared structurally with that of the use of *alu* on the comb of Setre (KJ 40), which perhaps contains a two-fold *alu* Nanna! (see discussion of **alu** below).

5) With *Ephesia Grammata* or Unexplained Single Ideographic Runes

IK 58: Fyn I-C. **houaR laþuaaduaaaliia alu** — *HouaR laþu aadaaaliia alu.* nom. masc. PN (?) + *ephesion grammaton* + nom. subst. (?).(95)

KJ 47: Svarteborg medallion. (R-L) **ssigaduR** — *s SigaduR.* ideographic rune (?) + nom. masc. PM., which could also be read: *S(i)siga(n)duR* (cf. Düwel in: Düwel-Müller-Hauck 1975: 152-56).

Natural Objects

In the North Germanic tradition, there are some inscriptions which might fit into this category; however, each is unique.

1) With Lexical Elements

KJ 86: Berga, *bauta*-st. (R-L) **saligastiR fino** — *SaligastiR Fin(n)o.* nom. masc. PN + nom. fem. PN (ca. 500, Sö) [burial mound complex in vicinity?].(96)

KJ 85: Skåäng, *bauta*-st. **harija ✳ leugaR** 7 — *Harija ✳ LeugaR* 7 nom. masc. PN x 2 (ca. 500, Sö) [?].(97)

2) With Ideographic Elements(98)

*KJ 54: Himmelstalund, rock-carving. (R-L) **braido** — *Braido* (?) nom. fem. PN [+ Bronze Age pictograph] (400-550, Ost.) [carved in the context of pre-existing Bronze Age rock-carving].(99)

3) With Syntactic Formulas

Two of the three formulas included here(100) (Opedal and Roes) are discussed in greater detail in sects. 51-52. In these three inscriptions it is possible that the rune-master has used his name connected to more elaborate linguistic forms other than the classic rune-master formulas.

KJ 58: Årstad, *bauta*-st.(?). A. **hiwigaR** B. **saralu** C. **unwinaR** — A. *HiwigaR.* B. *sar alu.* C. *UngwinaR.* nom. masc. PN + adv. + nom. substantive + gen. masc. PN i-stem (< **UngwiniR*). "Hiwig. Here (is) 'magic' (see 34). Ungwin's (grave).(101) (ca. 550, SW Nor.) [half buried with line C underground in a masc. cremation burial mound].(102)

*KJ 76: Opedal, barrow-st. (?). May contain an oblique first-person rune-master formula, and the whole could be translated: 'Burial. Bora, my sister, dear to me Wag.'(103)

KJ 102: Roes, talismanic or barrow (?) st. bears what is probably a third-person verbal formula which refers to an arcane magical practice (sect. 51). The formula is translated by Olsen and Krause as: 'Udd drove this horse (out).'(104) A pictograph of a horse appears on the stone.

Typology of Rune-Master/Carver Names

31. In order to summarize the onomastic data contained in the foregoing inscriptions and to interpret their collective meaning more effectively, a general classification of the names and other appellatives which possibly refer to the rune-carver or rune-master is necessary.(105) Two types of inscriptions are considered: I) those which either formulaically (with the *ek*-formula) or grammatically (with verb [and object]) indicate a rune-carver function and II) those which occur in ambiguous grammatical contexts or in isolation. We make the attempt to decide whether an appellative(106) is either a) functional (i.e., not the person's given name but one assumed for operative purposes, a cultic name, etc.) or b) common (i.e., one which could just as easily be the person's natural or given name). This latter category is generally determined by comparing the name with other known onomastic data from the area. However, since much of the epigraphical evidence is so early, it is often difficult to be certain as to which category a name belongs. What might have been a functional cultic name in ca. 200 CE might have become a common given name by 800-1000.

I. Rune-Master/Carver Contexts
a) Functional

A number of PNs would appear to belong to this category, i.e., *A(n)sugislaR* (KJ 27): 'sprout of god (?),' or 'hostage of the god' (cf. de Vries 1961a: 168), *A(n)sula* (KJ 24): 'the little god (<*ansuz*),' *FakaR* (IK 340): '(gelded) horse (?)' (cf. the *Óðinsheiti*: *Jálkr* Grm. 49: 'a gelding'), *Glī-augiR* (IK 128): 'the gleaming eyed one,'(107) **Ha(u)kopuR* (KJ 67): 'the one having the essence of a hawk,'(108) **WagaR*(109) (KJ 76) 'one who vigorously moves forth,' a) *WīgaR* or b) *Wi(n)gaR* (IK 241,1,2): a) 'the sanctified' or b) the sanctifier, '(110) *WīR* (KJ 17a): '[< PNord. *WīwaR* <

*wīh-wō-(?)] the sanctifier,'(111) *WīwaR* (KJ 72): 'the sanctifier (?),' *Wīwila* (KJ 56): 'the little sanctifier(?).'(112)

What appear to be *functional* bynames are: *aljamarkiR* (KJ 53): 'the one from another territory or frontier, stranger,'(113) *fārawīsa* (IK 98): 'the one knowing dangerous things' (cf. Høst 1960: 542; Krause 1966: 262, but cf. also Antonsen 1975a: 65-66 who reads *fara-wīsa*: 'travel-wise'), *hagustaldaR* (KJ 55; 75): 'owner of, or heir to a small enclosed piece of land → (errant) warrior,'(114) *hrōR*(115) (KJ 71): 'the swift, agile one,' *þirbijaR* (KJ 64): 'the one who weakens [nomen agentis <*þirbijan*: 'to make slack, weak](116) *ūbaR* (KJ 70): 'the malicious one,'(117) *ungandiR* (KJ 65): 'the one unaffected by (malevolent) magic,'(118) *unwōd[iR]* (KJ 12): 'the one unaffected by magical rage,'(119) *wagigaR* (KJ 69): 'the one who moves vigorously forth,'(120) **waraflusa* (KJ 13): 'the one who guards (himself) against idle speech,' (cf. Krause 1966: 37), (*sā*) *wīlagaR* (KJ 29): 'the crafty, deceitful one.'(121) It is interesting to note that all of this type of appellative occur in rune-master formulaic contexts (see sects. 2-22.).

Another type of byname, which appears to be an 'official' or institutional designation, is also attested only within clear rune-master formulas. *ErilaR* (in the form: *erilaR* in KJ 16, 27, 29, 70, and IK 241, 1-2; and in the form: *irilaR*(122) in KJ 56, 69, and 71) seems to act as the primary title for the rune-master regardless of its ultimate etymology.(123) The term *gudija* (KJ 65): 'priest' (cf. ON *goði*: '[heathen] priest; priest-chieftain' PNord. **godan-*)(124) is a further indication of the religious significance of these formulas, while *þewaR* (KJ 55): 'retainer, thegn; servant' re-establishes the essential social context of the rune-master within the retinue.(125)

b) Common

A number of names appear in more or less explicit rune-master formulas which are best understood as non-functional, common names, i.e., *Eanred* (Lancashire, cf. Okasha no. 66), *Eoh* (Kirkheaton, M. p.86), *Hadda* (Derbyshire, M. p. 40), *HaþuwolafaR* (KJ 95; 98), *Hariūha* (IK 98): 'the young warrior?' (<**hari-(j)unha*, cf. Krause 1966: 262), *HlewagastiR* (KJ 43), *SigimaraR* (KJ 59). Other names with questions as to their functional significance are: *HagiradaR* (KJ 30): 'giver of skillful counsel,' which could reflect an Odinic aspect (cf. the *Óðinsheiti*: *Hagyrkr ~ Hagvirkr*),(126) *HeldaR* (IK 184): 'the fighter(?)(127) *HrabanaR* (KJ 70): 'raven' (which could also have an Odinic aspect), *HraRaR ~ HrōRaR* (KJ 73; 92) 'the alert, lively one(?),' *StainawarijaR* (KJ 73): 'defender of the stone,'(128) and *WakraR* (KJ 74): 'the wakeful one.'(129) A few names are also runologically questionable, i.e., *AkaR* (IK 11): 'leader(?)' (or misrepresentation of *FakaR* in IK 340?), *-dagastiR* (KJ 63, probably the remains of a common name ending in *-gastiR*: '-guest'), *N-etur* (IK 70) n[x]etur, OFris. (Rasquert, cf. Buma 1966),(130) *UddR* (KJ 102) which could represent the common ON name *Oddr* — but which is conjecturally reconstructed by Olsen *NIæR*: III, 164-69 from a complex bind-rune structure:

II. Ambiguous contexts
a) Functional

To this group belong PNs which may indicate some typically functional aspect, but due to the lack of objective contextual evidence the connection must remain more or less conjectural,(131) i.e., **A(n)sugaR* or *A(n)sugasdiR* (KJ 77): 'the one belonging to the gods' or 'the guest of the gods' respectively,(132) *Glōla* (IK 76): 'the little glowing one,'(133) the name *HaukobuR* (see under I above) also appears in an isolated context (KJ 66), *LeugaR* (KJ 85): 'the bright one' (< PGmc. **leuga-*: 'shining, white'),(134) **Niujila* (IK 43; 163): 'the little new one' (<*niuja-*: 'new'),(135) *Rauz-wī(h)* (KJ 139): 'the reed (= spear)-sanctified one,'(136) *Sisi-ga(n)duR* (KJ 47): 'magic-magician' (cf. Düwel 1975: 151-57), *Waiga* (IK 367): 'powerful, or ecstatic one,'(137) *WidugastiR* (KJ 90): 'the guest in the forest' — which is tempting to conceive of as an initiatory name for a rune-master,(138) and related to which might be **Widuhu(n)daR* (KJ 10): 'hound of the forest (= wolf?)' as a rune-master designation (found in a woman's grave), and the rather difficult **Wulu-þewaR* (KJ 20): 'servant, or retainer of **WulþuR* (> ON *Ullr*).'(139)

b) Common

A number of appellatives also seem to be simply common given PNs, and their ambiguous contexts leave much room for interpretation. Archeological evidence is our only aid in determining if we are possibly dealing with a rune-master inscription. Masc. PNs found in connection with definite or suspected fem. graves are: SGmc. *Burisō (< **buriso** KJ 8), cf. Förstemann (1900: 351) and Krause 1966: 28), *Harisō* (KJ 9) if SGmc., *God(agaR)* (KJ 11),(140) *BidawarijaR* (KJ 13a): 'the one who defends that which is desired of him' (Krause 1966: 38) or 'defender of the oath' (Antonsen 1975: 30-31).(141) Another group perhaps connected to graves of unknown gender is: (EGmc.?) *Idda* (KJ 6), cf. Förstemann (1900: 943), Förstemann-Kaufmann (1968: 213), *Lepro* (KJ 42), if it is SGmc. and therefore a masc. form, cf. Förstemann (1900: 999[?]), *SigaduR* (KJ 47) < PGmc. *Sigi-hapuz*: 'victorious in battle,' cf. Krause (1966: 107). While on several *bauta*-stones, which may or may not have been in the vicinity of graves, appear the names: *Harija* (KJ 85), *SaligastiR* (KJ 86): 'hall-guest,' *Skinpa-LeubaR* (KJ 87): 'fur-*Leub*' (cf. Förstemann 1900: 1018ff.),(142) and *LandawarijaR* (KJ 91): 'defender of the land.' Several also occur on loose finds for which there is little archeological context: *Alla* (KJ 22), cf. OE, Go. *Alla* and OHG *Allo*, an EGmc. patronymic *Awings* (KJ 23), cf. OHG *Awo* (Förstemann 1900: 217), *Harja* (KJ 26), *Bera* (KJ 28): 'the bear-like one,' *Alawin-* and *Alawid-* (IK 161), *Sabar* (IK 386), which, if it is an abbreviation, could belong to a group of PNs with the prefix *Sab(a)-*, cf. Förstemann (1900: 1285-86), and the OE *Beagnōp* (Thames, M. p.127-29).

There are also a few bynames which do not seem to be functional, but which belong to this category, e.g., *Taitr* (KJ 94): 'the happy one' (cf. ON *Teitr*), *HīwigaR* or *HiwigaR* (KJ 58), which would mean 'the home-loving one' in the case of the former and 'the downy one' in the latter, *Swarta* (Illerup, shield buckle, cf. Düwel 1981a: 138-39; 1981b: 81) 'the black (haired?) one,' also *Sabar* (IK 386) may be a masc. nom. sg. adj. 'intelligent, the intelligent one,' cf. Krause (1966: 275-76). But even here, these bynames may have had some operative function. The fact that we read of **taiti-runąR**: 'joy-runes,' on the Malt stone (ca. 800 CE) perhaps provides some context for the term in the runological milieu.

It is useful to note the predominance of magico-religious concepts and associations which occur especially in the rune-master formulas. There are also quite a number of such functional names in more ambiguous contexts. In general, it seems that this system of possible rune-master names conveys three levels of purpose by the rune-master; 1) to identify himself with his work or with the location (i.e., with all types of self-designations), 2) to establish his authority in various realms of activity (with various official titles and religio-magical bynames), and 3) to somehow alter or transform his identity (with adjectival, functional, bynames), see VII.2.

Female Rune-Masters

32. For the older period, it has been generally assumed that runic practice was an exclusively masculine province (see ch. IV). However, a preponderance of certain new South Germanic evidence indicates that women too were rune-carvers.

The s-fibula of Weingarten I (KJ 164 I, Op. 53, see 10), found in 1955, contains what is probably best interpreted as a first-person *ek-* rune-master formula. But because of runological problems with the form of the personal pronoun and the verbal conjugation, and onomastic difficulties with the form **feha**, the fem. identity of the carver remained in some doubt. In 1979, the discovery of the Neudingen loom fragment (cf. Opitz 1981: 26-27; 29-31, see 20) with its clearly legible third-person formula *Bliþgund wrait rūna*: 'Bliþgund carved the rune' provided corroborating evidence which lends added significance to the Weingarten inscription, and opens up the possibility that further South Germanic inscriptions may have been executed by women.

Because our only verifiable evidence for this phenomenon exists in the unique cultural context of 6th- to 7th-century Alemannia, at most only South Germanic material may be considered as a possible field for other fem. rune-master formulas. Any inscription which contains a nom. fem. PN would theoretically provide a possible example of a fem. rune-master (eleven sure SGmc. examples); however, on typological grounds at least six of these (KJ 140, 147A; B, 148, 151, Op. 20) are made doubtful, as they seem to belong to the dedicatory formula type.143 Two of these are the fairly certain formulas of Weingarten I and Neudingen, while of the remaining three, two (KJ 141 and 155A) contain an isolated fem. PN, and the third (KJ 166, AZ 27; 28, Op. 5; 6, Langobardic, ca. 550) bears a possible *ek* + fem. PN formula in a clearly Christian context. Another group which might be considered as the work of fem. rune-masters is represented by inscriptions with a nom. masc. PN found in women's graves (e.g., KJ 143, 149, 156, 161, 164 II; Op. 7, 13). Of course, these could just as easily be masc. rune-master formulas or the name of the donator of the object. However, they are obviously not owners' marks. On the other hand, two of them (KJ 149, 156) seem to be dedicatory formulas of some kind,(144) while (Op. 13) Donzdorf is clearly a maker's mark (cf. Düwel-Roth 1977). Some of the remaining four inscriptions may then represent a heretofore unidentified type in which the fem. rune-carver scratches the name of her beloved on her brooch or other possessions. This may constitute lovers' frivolity — or it could have an operative significance as a mode of attracting and/or holding a desired lover, etc.

Against this latter interpretation is the basic conclusion reached in IV.22. that the presence of fem. "rune-masters" in the culture is perhaps an indication of the breakdown in the traditional pre-Christian society which supported the operative activities of a restricted group of rune-masters. This is not to say that an "underground," non-establishment and operant runic tradition could not have developed. Such a development is in fact suggested by the Neudingen inscription.

WORD-FORMULAS

33. Words which act as concrete (or abstract) lexemic symbols, or word-formulas, seem to have an instrumental function in the older runic tradition.(145) Furthermore, these appear to be analogical extensions of the use of symbolic substances and/or mythic constructs in the magical lore of the Germanic peoples (see V.9). Each of these word-formulas must be examined in their 1) isolated and 2) complex runological contexts before any conclusions as to their formulaic function may be reached.

alu

34. The runic complex **alu**(146) represents PGmc. *alu- ~ *aluþ-: 'ale, intoxicating drink'(147) (see V.9.), however, its etymology beyond this remains problematic. Polomé (1954: 45ff.) connects it with Hitt. terms for sorcery, i.e., *alwanzaḫḫ-*: 'to enchant,' *alwanzena*: 'enchanted,' *alwanzatar*: 'enchantment' (< *alwanza-),(148) and to Gk. αλυω: 'I am ecstatic, outside myself,' and to Latvian *aluot*: 'to wander about.' From this, a general semantic development for Gmc. *alu- could be supposed in which an originally religio-magical sense of '(magical) ecstasy' was transferred on the one hand to a cultic drink used to induce this state (*alu(þ)-> ON ǫl OE *ealu*), and on the other hand to magical (apotropaic?) benefits derived from its power (*alu(h)-, cf. Go. *alhs*, OE *ealh*: 'temple' [i.e., 'a protected, sanctified place'],(149) and OE *ealgian*: 'to defend'). Conant's (1973) conjecture that **alu** represents a nom. acc. pl. *allu > ON ǫll (i.e., all [the gods?] as an invocation formula must be doubted on typological grounds. See VII.3 for a further discussion of the instrumental significance of this word formula.

A. Corpus of Isolated *alu*-formulas
1. Definite

KJ 57. Elgeshem st. (400-500, S. Nor.) was found inside a grave-mound and is most probably either a barrow-st., or perhaps originally a *bauta*-st. It is clearly read:(150) (R-L) **alu**.

KJ 46. Körlin gold finger ring (500-550, E. Pomerania) is now lost and little is known of the circumstances of its discovery beyond the fact that it was found together with three bracteates and two coins (cf. Krause 1966: 105-06). It bears two inscriptions, one of which is: (R-L) **alu**, and the other is apparently a combination bind-rune/code-rune representation of the same complex (see sect. 2 below).

Five bracteates also have isolated alu inscriptions which may be easily read, i.e., IK 24: (R-L) **alu**, IK 44: (R-L) **alu**, IK 78: **alu**, IK 97: (R-L) **alu** — all of which are C-type, and IK 74: **alu** — which is a B-type.

There is also the more recently found so-called *Kleinbrakteat* of Hüfingen I (550-750), discovered in a woman's grave with the formula (R-L) **alu**. Imitations of Roman capitals also appear on the piece (Düwel 1997c: 18).

2. Reconstructed

KJ 19: Nydam arrow shafts (3rd-5th cent. N. Schleswig) came from a bog find (probably part of a sacrifice of war booty) and one of these, which is positively runic, has what appears to be a scrambled **alu** inscription:(151) (R-L) **lua** reconst. **alu**. Other runic or rune-like signs on these arrow shafts include ᛏ R,   l, X g, *et al.* It is uncertain whether these inscriptions were made by the warriors using them, or by their conquerors, who sacrificed them.

KJ 46: Körlin (see above) also bears the curious form: ᛡ which is perhaps to be interpreted as a bind-rune **âl** and a further runic code designation (see IV. 11) 1:2 (first *ætt*: second rune) = **u**, so that the figure may be reconstructed: **alu** (cf. Krause 1966: 106). Marstrander (1952: 203-07) reads this figure as 2:1 = h(*agala*), and compares it to KJ 52 (see below).

Related to the possible Körlin bind-rune is the ceramic stamp on the three cremation urns of Spong Hill which appear ᛡ ᛏ ᛡ and which have been convincingly interpreted as a series of three bind runes: **âa ll ûu** — *alu alu* (C. M. Hills 1974; Düwel 2008: 82).

The Horvnes bone comb (6th cent.) has a fragmentary inscription: **aallu///** which is best interpreted as the *alu*-formula repeated twice: *alu alu*. (Knirk 2004: 18) Here the runes have been analyzed into identical pairs, either intended to "conceal" the formula, or to intensify it.

A recently discovered arrow from Nydam (Nr. 4919) from about 200CE bears the runes (R-L) **lua**, which is likely to be a scrambbled **alu**-formula (Stoklund 1995: 4).

Beyond these, there are three bracteates with inscriptions which may represent botched attempts at **alu**-formulas, i.e., the C-type IK 199: **tlu**, the A-type IK 331: (R-L) **tau** (in both of which a ᛏ-form would have to have been wrongly executed for a ᚠ and ᚱ form respectively), and the B-type IK 61: **aʲ**.

B. Corpus of Contextual *alu*-formulas
1. legible, in syntactic contexts

KJ 101: Eggjum st. (ca. 700, W. Nor., see 50.) has the longest of the older inscriptions, the formulaic conclusion to which seems to be:

Alumisurki
alu missyrki
'*alu* to the wrong-doer!'(152)

Missyrki would then be a masc. dat. sg. of a *nomen agentis* *missyrkiR*, and the formula would form a suitable close to the entire complex inscription, the purpose of which is at least partially to prevent grave robbery.(153)

KJ 40: Setre bone comb (600-650, SW Nor.) bears the *alu*-formula once or twice, depending on the reading of the runic complex B. **AluṇaAlu naṇA** one favors. This could be a vocative formula: *Alu Na(nna)! Alu Nan(n)a!* (cf. Olsen-Shetelig 1933: 45ff.), or partly an *ephesion grammaton Ahu* (= 'water') *naalunanA* (cf. Jacobsen-Brøndal 1935: 58ff.). Jacobsen reads the configuration ᚺᛜ as **ahu**— *ahu*: 'water,' which, although r. 2 of the complex is ambiguous, is regarded as unlikely by Krause (1966: 89).

KJ 52: Kinneve barrow-st. (550-600, Vg. Sweden) is a small (7.5 x 4.5 cm) talc tablet which was probably originally a barrow-stone (cf. Krause 1966: 114-15) with the inscription: (R-L). . .**siRaluh**. When considered as complete, this may be read *siR alu h(agala)*: 'Be thou protection (i.e., *alu*) [for the grave]! Hail [= ruin]!'(154) However, if it is fragmentary, the most accepted reading *is (æ)siR alu h(agala)*: "Gods, 'protection,' hail" (cf. Marstrander 1952: 203-07).

KJ 58: Årstad st. (ca. 550, SW Nor.) was found connected to a grave mound, and its size and shape (121 x 78 x 13 cm) would indicate that it was probably a *bauta*-stone. It may be read: A. **hiwigaR** B. **saRalu** C. **uŋwinaR**: *HiwigaR saR alu UngwinaR*: "Hiwig. Here (is) 'protection' (i.e., *alu*). (This is) Ungwin's (grave)."(155)

—172—

KJ 29: Lindholm amulet (ca. 500, Skåne), the rune-master formula of which is discussed in sect. 15 above, also contains an extensive non-sequential rune formula (see 48 below) concluded by the word-formula *alu* — 'I, the eril am called the crafty one. **aaaaaaaaRRRnnn[x]bmuttt:alu**: (see Olsen *NIæR* III, 237ff., Marstrander 1939: 292ff., Krause 1966: 69-72, Flowers 2006: 72ff.).

The difficult inscription of the Nydam ax-handle (300-350) presents us with three masculine names or titles and the sequence (R-L): **alu:wihgu**. This sequence can be translated tentitively as '**alu**: I dedicate...' But it is unclear as to whether the runes are the implied object of the dedication (cf. McKinnell 2004: 94-95).

2. Legible, in Non-Syntactic Contexts

KJ 11: Værløse clasp (ca. 200, Sjælland), which was found in a woman's grave (see 30. and n. 140 above) may be read: **alugod + ᛄ** — *alu Gōd(agaR* masc. PN.(156)

KJ 48: Fosse clasp (500-550, S. Nor.) is now lost, but was found in a cremation grave and bore an inscription which could be reconstructed: **ka[l]a alu** — **Kala alu*. Kala would represent a masc. nom. PN (cf. ON *Kali*).

In addition there are four bracteates in this category: IK 43 Darum V-C bears the *alu* formula preceded by what is probably to be reconstructed as a masc. nom. PN **Niujila*. Two others have *alu* within the context of other word-formulas, i.e., IK 149: Skåne I-B **laþulaukaR.gakaRalu** — *laþu laukaR *ga(u)kaR alu* and IK 166: Skrydstrup-B **laukaR alu**: *laukaR alu* (see discussions of these other word-formulas below). The bracteate inscription IK 135: Ølst-C **hag alu** has generally been read: *hag(ala) alu* as an abbreviated rune-name 'hail (= ruin)' plus *alu* (cf. Krause 1966: 258-59), where the rune name might easily be understood as a word-formula.

IK 105 Lellinge-B **salusalu** has sometimes been read s-*alu* s-*alu* (Krause 1966: 257), but it seems far more likely that we are dealing with a double word-formula *salu-salu* (see below).

3. Reconstructed and in Syntactic Context

Only one inscription, the runologically problematic KJ 59 Ellestad st. (ca. 800, Ög. Sweden), may belong to this category. A syntactic legal formula: 'I, Sigimar, absolved from guilt, set up this stone.'(157) To this, a cryptographic representation of an *alu*-formula based on the younger fuþąrk *aett* arrangement (see Fig. IV) has been reconstructed (cf. Krause 1966: 134-35). This is, however, far from certain.

4. Reconstructed and in Non-Syntactic Context

All of these inscriptions are found on bracteates and therefore we can not be sure as to whether the formulas were intentional, or merely the result of imperfect transference of a formula from a medium executed by a runemaster to that crafted by the bracteate master. One group of these contains at least some element other than *alu*, which is either legible or which can also be reconstructed,(158) i.e.,: IK 13: Allesø-B: (R-L) **lauR⌖oþa Rlut: eaþl** has been reconstructed: *lau(ka)R oþa(la)R (a)lu f(waR): e(hwaR) laþ(u)*, IK 26: Börringe-C **ṭanulu al laukaR** : *Tanulu al(u) laukaR*, IK 58: Fyn I-C **houaR laþuaaḍuaaaliiạ alḷ** — *HouaR* (= 'the high one') *laþu* [*ephesion grammaton*] *al*[*u*], and IK 300: Meglemose III-C (R-L)A. **hoR** B. **tlþḳṃhi** C. (L-R) **alḷ** : *Hō(ua)R* [*ephesion grammaton*] *al*[*u*].(159)

A second group within this category occurs in highly conjectural contexts in which no other elements are clearly recognizable, i.e., IK 129: Nebenstedt II-B and Darum IV-B: (R-L) **lïiaþRmtl** (L-R) **iro⌖teal**: [*ephesion grammaton*] *al*[*u*],(160) and IK 289: Kjellers Mose-C (R-L) **iixx xxxall** [?] *al*[*u*].(161)

Appendix on *medu*

34b. A gold bracteate found near Undley, Lakenheath, West Suffolk in June of 1981 bears a levoverse inscription:

ᚠᚳᛗᚨ·ᚷᚳ ᚷᚨ·ᚷ·ᚷ ᚷ

This can be transcribed either a) [x] **gā gō gā · maga · medu**, or b)/ [x] **gǣ gō gǣ · mǣgǣ · medu**.(162) The distinctive o-rune clearly shows that this is an Anglo-Saxon or Frisian inscription. Regardless of how r. 1-8 are to be interpreted, r. 9-12 seem to represent OE *medu*: 'mead.' If this is so, it would be an important piece of evidence for the use of the names of (magico-religious) intoxicating drinks as word-formulas, and would parallel Gmc. *alu-.

ota

35. This runic word-formula appears on four C-type gold bracteates (Fjärestad-C [IK 55], Tjurkö II-C [IK 185] and two more recent finds from

Gadegård, Bornholm). On these bracteates the form **ota** appears in isolation. From Hüfingen in South Germanic territory also come a pair of small gold pendants which imitate Roman coins. Alongside imitations of Roman capitals there also appears the formula **ota**. It is most likely that *ota* reflects the word *ōtta*, which renders Old Norse *ótti*: 'fear, dread' < PGmc. **ōhtan*, 'terror.' (Düwel 2008: 54, 59) The apotropaic function of the formula clearly works by frightening off adversaries or malificent influences in a manner similar to the way the medieval magical sign called the *ægishjálmr*: 'helm (covering) of terror, awe' (cf. Rm. 14ff.; Fm. 17, 44, etc. and also later magical associations in the *Galdrabók*, N. Lindqvist 1921 and Flowers 2005, where it is identified with the sign ※).

auja

36. This relatively rare word-formula occurs in two, perhaps three, runic inscriptions and is generally thought to be a neut. substantive, and to mean 'luck, good fortune, well being.'(163) The etymology of *auja* is uncertain, but Marstrander (1929a: 120-22) connects it to Skt. *ávati*: 'filled with divine power, he helps,' and OIr. *con-ói*: 'protected.' Betz (1979: 243) derives it from PIE **aw-yo-*: 'help.' In ON it is reflected in *ey* (only in the *Landnámabók*): 'luck, well being' (cf. de Vries 1961a: 19; 106) and in the ON PN prefix *Ey-* (cf. *Ey-vindr*, *Ey-steinn*, etc.). Elsewhere in Gmc., it is reflected in Go. *awi-liups*: 'expression of thanks.'

Two bracteate inscriptions contain the formula in divergent contexts:

IK 98: Sjælland II-C may be read: (R-L) **hariuhahaitika farauisa : gibuauja · : · t̄t̄t̄** — *Hariaha haitika, firawisa. gibu auja.* [*tiwaR* x 3 (?)]: 'Hariuha, I am called, one who knows dangerous things. I give good fortune. . .(164) The formula *gibu auja* is especially interesting because it occurs in a syntactic pattern which calls for an acc. (cf. Krause 1971: 117). However, since the neut. (*i*)*ja-* stem does not demonstrate a distinctive inflection, *auja* remains uninflected — which is typical of these word-formulas.

IK 161: Skodberg-B is generally interpreted:
(R-L) **aujaalawinaujaalawinaujaalawinjalawid**— *auja Alawin! auja Alawin! auja Alawin! j(ēra) Alawid!*: 'Hail Alawin! Hail Alawin! Hail Alawin! A good harvest! Alawid!'(165) It seems clear that this inscription is an invocation of *auja* ('good fortune') and of *jēra* ('good harvest') for Alawin made by (the rune-master?) Alawid.

A more recently found Alemannic inscription, the Oetting brooch (550-600, which was found in a woman's grave placed over the right eye of the corpse) is read by Betz (1979: 241-45) as: **awijabrg** — *Awija b(i)rg*: 'Awija (= divine [fem.] helper) protect (the wearer of this brooch)!' Although there are runological problems with this text, it would form an interesting parallel to possibly *alu*-prefixed names, e.g., *Aluka* (KJ 49) and *Alugod-* (KJ 11).

laukaR

37. The meaning of the term *laukaR* is uncontested as 'leek'(166) (ON *laukr*, OE *lēac*, OHG *louh* < *laukaz*: any one of a number of plants of the genus *allium*). This type of herb is widely thought to have therapeutic powers (see V.9.), and because of its quick, straight growth of leaf, it is seen to symbolize fertility, increase, and growth. As such it is not an unexpected concrete word-symbol for the rune-masters to use.(167)

As a word-formula, *laukaR* is attested in perhaps as many as eighteen inscriptions, all but one of which are on bracteates. It appears in isolation some seven to eight times, and in various runic contexts in six to eleven inscriptions. The reason for these numerical variations is that the formula has been conjecturally reconstructed for several bracteate texts, six of which seem doubtful. The criterion used here for the reconstruction of probable *laukaR*-formulas is that at least four of the six runes of the word must appear in correct sequence; less than that and the form may only be designated possible.

A. Corpus of Isolated *laukaR*- Formulas

A perfect form in isolation only appears once, i.e., on IK 8: Års II-C **laukaR**, while it can be reconstructed with high probability on five other bracteates: IK 229: (R-L) **lkaR**, IK 267: (R-L) **xlkaR**, IK 298: **lakR**, IK 301: (R-L) **lkaR**, IK 330: (R-L) **lkaR**, and possibly on one other IK.II.129: **xluR**. The runic form ᛚ (l) seems to have been a fairly regular variation in the bracteate corpus.

B. Corpus of *laukaR*-Formulas in Runic Contexts

Clear forms of *laukaR* juxtaposed to other word-formulas occur in four inscriptions, three of which are on minted bracteates. The engraved runic text in which the term appears is the famous KJ 37 Fløksand tanning knife (ca. 350, SW Norway) **linalaukaRf**(168) — *līna laukaR f(ehu)*: 'flax, leek, livestock' as symbols of fertility, increase, and prosperity.(169) The three

—176—

bracteate inscriptions can be read: IK 26: **tanulu alu laukaR**—*Tanulu alu laukaR* (*Tanulu* = fem. PN?), IK 149: **labulaukaR · gakaRalu**, which is read by Krause (1966: 256-57): *labu laukaR ga(u)kaR alu* (*gaukaR* = 'cuckoo bird,' a Germanic symbol of spring, renewal, and hence fertility [?]), and IK 166: **laukaR** (R-L) **alu** — *laukaR alu*.

One bracteate inscription, IK 13: Allesø-B may also contain a defective *laukaR*-formula which is rendered: (R-L) **lauR ⚡ oþa Rlut:eaþl**,(170) where r. 1-4 may be(reconstructed *lau(ka)R*. (For a reading of r. 5-15, see 33. above.)

C. Doubtful *laukaR* Inscriptions

The six forms which do not fulfill our criterion for being considered as a *laukaR* formula, but which have on occasion been mentioned as possibilities are: IK 101: (R-L) **foslau** — **fos** — *lau(kaR)*,(171) IK 147: **lRolu**, IK 309: **lRllþe**, IK 244: **ligilhRx** - or - **ldlhRx**, and IK 357: **[l]khiRx**. These may be botched attempts to copy the *laukaR*-formula. This group often demonstrates internal formal affinities, but they are too defective to be considered as formulaic representatives of this type.

D. *LaukaR* Ideographs

Finally, because this word-formula is so prominent in the runic record, there has been a tendency to read isolated l-runes logographically as l(*aukaR*).(172) There are seven inscriptions in this category, three of which are South Germanic and hence doubtful. KJ 7: Aquincum bow fibula (ca. 530, Hungary, perhaps Langobardic), contains a clear **fuþark**-formula (see 44.) along with an obscure series **jlain:knia** tentatively read by Krause (1966: 23-25) as *j(ēra)! l(aukaR) ain-kunningja*: 'a good harvest! Increase! The intimate friend (wishes this for the owner of the brooch).' The other two are: KJ 153 Heilbronn-Böckingen belt-fitting (7th cent., Württemberg, Alemannic) (R-L)**larwi** — *l(auk) Arwi*(173) (here *Arwi* could be the runemaster or the giver of the belt), and Op. 9: Billach disk fibula (600-650, Switzerland, Alemannic), which has what might be two reversed l-runes outside the ductus of a reconstructed syntactic formula (see sect. 52). In the north, we find a single l-rune type sign carved on one of the Nydam arrow shafts (cf. Krause 1966: 51), and an isolated l-rune following the runemaster formula of IK 128 Nebenstedt I-B (see 7), which may have a logographic interpretation (Düwel 1977). Also, there are two repetitive l-rune formulas. One of these is on a bracteate IK 24 Fyn II-C: (R-L) **nę** ··

tblllI, while the other is KJ 38: Gjersvik bone tanning knife (ca. 450, SW Nor.): (R-L) **dxxopilllllllllll**. The ten l-runes of Gjersvik have with some justification been identified with the *līna-laukaR* formula of the typologically parallel tanning knife of Fløksand.

līna

37b. Because of the close juxtaposition of the word *līna* and *laukaR* on the tanning knife of Fløksand (KJ 37) and the mentioning of these two substances, flax and leek, in the fourth verse of the *Vǫlsa þáttr* with magical connotations, the term *līna* has sometimes been seen as one of the runic word-formulas, akin to *laukaR* as an herbal substance. The sequence of runes **liin** is sometimes found in bracteate inscriptions, which has led some interpreters to conclude that this is a corruption of the rare word-formula **līn(a)**.

salu

38. This word-formula is attested perhaps only twice in the runic corpus, i.e., IK 105: Lellinge-B: (R-L) **salusalu** — *salu salu*(174) and the runologically uncertain IK 101: Faxe-A: (R-L) **foslau**. Although both have been suspected of concealing *alu*-formulas, it is likely that we are dealing with *salu* in IK 105 and that a reading of **f-o** *salu is most probable for IK 101, with the **f**- and **o**-runes acting as logographic representations of the **fuþark** (see sect. 44).(175) But what does the complex **salu** mean? Grienberger (1906: 138ff.) interpreted it as a substantive *salu*: "*traditio*, a giving over, delivery" (cf. ON *sala*, OE *salu ~ sala*), which could be understood in a metaphorical sense or religious sense as a sacrifice or gift (of benefit) given by a god, etc. A more recent etymology by Lundby (1982) equates it with ON *sǫl*: 'the samphire' (see V.9). This would then place *salu* is the same category as *laukaR* as a concrete symbol-word that represents a therapeutic herb.

ehwa-

39. As a word-formula, some form of this runologically difficult complex may appear in up to 14 exclusively bracteate inscriptions. But nowhere is it absolutely clear. The archetypal form of the runic complex, according to Krause (1932: 62-65; 1966: 242-44), might have been ᛗᚺᛖᚹᛗ **ehwe** — *ehwe*: 'to the horse' (masc. dat. sg. < *ehwaR); in some cases with an additional ideographic M-rune before the whole complex.(176) The use of equine iconography or symbolism in Germanic magical practice is

widespread,(177) cf. the use of a horse's head on the *níðstǫng* made by Egill (*ES* ch. 57), the importance of the equine image in the *hólmganga* ritual (*Kormáks s.* ch. 10), as well as the central role of the horse in Germanic shamanistic practices(178) and fertility cults.(179) Pictographic representations of horses juxtaposed to runic inscriptions (cf. Eggjum st. KJ 101 and Roes st. KJ 102) or of horse and rider (cf. Mjöbro st. KJ 99 and all C-type bracteates) appear common and are probably a part of the iconography of the Odinic cult (cf. later Gotlandic pictographic stones, S. Lindqvist 1941-42). Another possibly related equine formula is contained in the Kylver st. inscription (KJ 1) **sueus** (see sect. 48).

A. *ehw*-Formulas in Isolation

All of the isolated forms must be to some extent reconstructed. The least problematic is IK 352: Skåne V-C ᛗᚾᚠᛁ᛬ **ehwu̯**, where the final **u̯** may have been intended as a ᛗ form. The same may be true of IK 233; 365, 1-3, 5-7, all of which basically have the basic ᛗᛗᛋ ᛁᛁ **eēlil**, which could have degenerated from a model ᛗᚾᛦᛗ **ehw̄e**. While IK 57, 1 and IK 365, 4, which show a common form: ᛗᛁ↑ᛁᛁ **eltil**, perhaps had a prefixed ideographic e-rune and developed from an archetypical form: ᛗᛗᛦᛗ **e.ehe** (cf. the form in IK 11). This may also simply represent a further degeneration from **ehwe**. An interesting variant is provided by IK 39, which is read by Krause (1966: 245) as **ïlwl** but based upon personal examination of the piece (02.06.1982) a reading ᛊᛁᛁᛁ **ïlwi** appears more likely. This could have developed from a form ᛊᚾᛁ **ïh̄wi ~ ehwe(?)**.(180)

B. *ehw*-Formulas in Runic Contexts

There are only two inscriptions which seem to belong to this category. The first is the fairly legible IK 11: Åsum-C: (R-L) **eh̄eikakaRfahi** — *ehe (e)k AkaR fāhi*: '(Consecrated) to the horse! I, Ak color (the runes).' (See 10.) While the other is the problematic IK 182: Szatmar: **tu̯aleltl** — **lni** in which r. 5-8 may represent a form similar to that of IK 57 *et al*. The rest of the inscription is unclear (see sect. 34 on r. 1-3). Cf. also the Kylver palindrome (sect. 48).

laþu

40. This abstract word-formula seems to be a fem. nom. sg. ō-stem *laþu* (PGmc. **laþō-*): 'invitation, summons → an invocation (to numinous powers)',(181) cf. ON *lǫð*: 'a bidding, invitation.' There is also an extended *nomina actionis* form *laþōþu ~*laþ-oþu* with the same meaning.(182) *Laþu*

does not belong to the concrete symbol-word category, but rather to a more abstract class better understood as part of the magico-religious terminology.(183) From an operative point of view, this could be a graphic symbolic representation of the vocal formulas spoken over runic forms and/or a performative declaration of the purpose of the amuletic medium as a whole to summon (divine) help.

A. *Laþu*-Formulas in Isolation

IK 83: (R-L) **laþu** — *laþu* is clearly legible, while on IK 264: **laþa** the a-rune is somewhat flattened (personal examination 06.01.1982) but **laþa** seems the most correct reading. This form is probably Gotlandic or Gothic (cf. Krause 1971: 150). A degenerated form of this formula may be present on the Anglo-Saxon silver bracteate of Welbeck Hill (Lincolnshire) [= IK 388]ᚾᛇᛇ (R-L) **læw** (in OE runes) which Page (1999: 180-81) believes to be a distant copy of a *laþu* bracteate text from Scandinavia.

B. *Laþu*-Formulas in Runic Contexts

Most of these are legible, i.e., IK 42: (R-L) **frohila laþu** — *Frohila laþu* [masc. PN + laþu], IK 58: **houaR laþuaaduaaaliia alu** — *HōuaR laþu* [*ephesion grammaton*] *alu*, IK 149: **laþulaukaR ·gakaRalu** — *laþu laukaR ga(u)kaR alu* (see various word-formulas), and two elaborated forms,(184) IK 70: **nxeturfahidelaþoþ   mhlsiiaeiaugrsþnbkeiaR** — *Nxetur* (PN?) *fahide   laþoþ* [+ *ephesion grammaton*]: 'Nxetur colored (wrote) the invocation, summons . . .' (see 9), along with IK 189: **tawol aþodu**— *tawō laþōdu*: '(I) prepare an invocation, summons.'

There are also two runologically problematic texts, i.e., IK 13: Allesø-B (sect. 37.), r. 13-15 of which read . . .**aþl** (interpreted by Krause as a possible scrambling of a *laþu*-formula [1966: 250]), and IK 163: **niuwila** (R-L) **lþu**(185) — **Niujila l(a)þu*.

Nomen Agentis Spear Names

41. Runic inscriptions occur on eight known spear heads. Five of these appear definitely to be *nomen agentis* names for the weapons themselves, an additional one may be reconstructed as such, while two seem to be something other than this type. The use of a spear in operative acts is well known (see V.8), and if the general interpretation of these appellatives is correct,(186) these magico-poetic names could easily be understood as operative formulas. An instrumental communicative process could perhaps

go on between a weapon so endowed with a magical 'personality' and its owner(s); and between it and the (protective) weapons of the enemy.(187) Furthermore, it may be possible that such magical weapons were intended to act against the protective numina of an enemy. These spears would certainly not be employed in normal combat, and were probably either held as royal talismans or used as magical spears to dedicate the enemy to the gods, etc.

The inscriptions which belong with some certainty to this group are: KJ 31: Øvre-Stabu (ca. 150, E. Nor.), found in a man's cremation grave and read **raunijaR** — *RaunijaR*: 'the tester, the one who tests (the enemy, etc.),' (cf. ON *reynir*: 'a trier, examiner'); KJ 32: Dahmsdorf (ca. 250, Brandenburg), which was also found in a cremation grave and which bears various auxiliary ideographic signs (swastika, triskelion, tamgas, etc.),(188) reads (R-L) **ranja** — *Rannja*: 'the assailer' (< *rannjan*: 'to run (causitive);'(189) KJ 33: Kovel (ca. 250, E. Poland), a loose find which may be read (R-L) **tilarids** — EGmc. *Tilarids*: 'target-rider, the rider toward the target.'(190)

There are three more recently found (1979-80) spear heads from Illerup bog (Skanderborg, Den., both ca. 200) and Vimose (Fyn, Den., ca. 200) all with identical inscriptions. Illerup I is stamped and ca. 1 cm in length, while II is etched as is the object from Vimose. This formula has most recently been interpreted as **wagnijo** — *Wagnijō*: 'the running, moving; wayfarer.' The grammatically feminine form of this formula marks it as unique.(191)

Another spear head inscription, which may be reconstructed as a *nomen agentis* name, is KJ 34: Moos (ca. 300, Gotland), found in a cremation grave. It would at first appear to read (R-L) **sioag**, which is nonsensical.(192) However, Krause (1966: 80-81) reads the inscription (L-R) **gaois**, which is justifiable since only the a-rune is reversed, and reconstructs an EGmc. *nomen agentis* *gauīs ~ *gaujis* (< *gaujan: 'to bark, roar,' cf. ON *geyja*: 'to bark'): 'the barker, roarer.'

There are two runologically problematic spear heads which definitely do not belong to this category. KJ 35: Rozwadów (ca. 250, S. Poland, EGmc.) is archeologically part of the same tradition as KJ 31-34, and may be partially read . . .**krlus**, which remains without a convincing interpretation.(193) KJ 162 Wurmlingen (600-650, SW Germany, Alemannic), found in a man's row grave, bears the inscription **dorih**(194) — *Dorih* (masc. PN < **Dor-(r)īh* < **Þor-rīh-*: 'powerful in courage?'). The PN may be that of the maker, owner, or of the rune-master. Because this inscription is typologically isolated, little more can be said as to its function.

Unique and Ambiguous Word-Formulas

42. Essentially three kinds of runic complexes fall into this category: 1) lexemes which might typologically belong to the word-formulas, 2) rune names in extended forms, and 3) pronounceable runic sequences which might represent otherwise unknown words.

We have already discussed two of these, OE *medu* (sect. 35.) and *līna* (sect. 37, and note 169) in their proper contexts. Two others which might belong to this group are: Fælleseje (Slemminge) moose horn tanning knife (?), (ca. 500, Lolland) **witrŋ** — *witring*: 'proclamation → inscription'(195) and IK 149: Skåne I-B (see sects. 34 and 37) with the runic complex **gakaR** which has been reconstructed as *ga(u)kaR*(196) 'cuckoo (bird).' We would therefore have an abstract symbol word typologically akin to *laþu* and a concrete symbol word similar in type to *ehw-* (since it represents a living being of symbolic value).

Rune names may appear in abbreviated forms on two bracteates, IK 13: Allesø-B (see sect. 37.) with the runic sequence **oþa   R** which Krause reconstructs as *oþa(la)R*: 'hereditary property,'(197) and IK 135: Ølst-C: (R-L) **hag alu**. This latter six-rune sequence has been interpreted as an abbreviation of *hag(ala)*:'hail,' plus *alu* (see 34.).(198)

There are a number of runic complexes, especially on bracteates, which might accurately represent otherwise unattested words, or which might be degenerated forms of such words. The form **ota** (see IK 55, 152, 185) might represent a word *ōtta* (cf. ON *ótti* <*ohtan-*): 'fear, dread,' see Düwel (2008: 54), while **liia** (cf. IK 58, 129, 2) may be a degeneration of *līna*. Those may, however, be *ephesia grammata*.

Word-formulas of the type outlined here seem to be a special feature of the older tradition as we find few repeatedly used cryptic lexemes in the younger corpus. (The *-istil*-formulas may constitute a major exception to this when we read them as scrambled word-formulas.) On the other hand, rune formulas appear to have proliferated in the years following the onset of the Viking Age.

RUNE-FORMULAS

43. The expression "rune-formula" is intended to encompass all those complexes, series, or sequences of runic characters which convey no apparent linguistic meaning, and are thus devoid of semantic content as far as natural language is concerned. A relatively large number (ca. 52) of these sequences occur on bracteates, and with these we can rarely be sure that we are not merely dealing with forms hopelessly scrambled by analphabetic

bracteate-masters.(199) However, where intentional *ephesia grammata* seem present, it is interesting to note the comparison between what appear to be reflections of a graphic school (characterized by unpronounceable but often repetitive or otherwise clearly intentional formulas, cf. e.g., KJ 29) and an oral school (distinguished by pronounceable sequences, cf. e.g., IK 377: 1). The tendency to ascribe anything that we do not understand to "magic" must be avoided, but at the same time it should be realized that the genre of "alphabet magic" is a common one in operative behavior (cf. Dieterich 1901; Dornseiff 1922; Jacobsen-Moltke 1942: 773-74). There are essentially two main classes of rune-formulas: I) sequential (which to one degree or another is governed by the **fuþark** order) and II) non-sequential (which may be random, repetitive, etc.). The inscriptions occur in two types: 1) those in isolation, as exclusive runic material on the medium, and 2) those in various runic contexts. The two important sub-categories are a) those which are pronounceable, and b) those which are not.(200) This gives us some insight into whether those were representations of verbal formulas, or whether they were purely graphic.

I. Sequential Formulas
Isolated **fuþark** Inscriptions

44. In the older period only two inscriptions consist of unelaborated **fuþark**-formulas, i.e., the Grumpan-C bracteate (IK 260) which may be transcribed **fuþarkgw** ⋯⋯ **hnijïp[Rs]** ⋯⋯ **tbemlŋod** ⋯⋯ and the more ambiguous, and probably non-magical marble pillar of Breza (KJ 5, ca. 550, near Sarajevo, Bosnia) transcribed: **fuþarkgwhnijïpzsteml**. . . . We can assume that the latter part of the row was broken off; however, it should be noted that the **b**-rune was also left out.(201)

Contextual fuþark Inscriptions

Several more **fuþark**-formulas occur in some type of runic context. Most of these are non-syntactical runic compositions. For example, in Scandinavia we find the complete **fuþark** series on KJ 1: Kylver st. (400-450, Gotland):

A. **fuþarkgwhnipïRstbemlndo** 🙰 B. **sueus**,

and on a bracteate: Vadstena-C (IK 377, 1):

luwatuwa · fuþarkgw:hnijïpRstbemlŋod:.

(See sect. 48 on the formulas **sueus** and **luwatuwa**.) On the Continent, apparently intentionally incomplete fuþarks occur on three brooches. Two

—183—

of these, KJ 8: Beuchte (550-600, N. Germany) and KJ 7: Aquincum (ca. 530, Hungary), are more than likely operative in character.(202) Beuchte reads: A. **fuþarzj** B. **buirso** (> *Būriso*), with r. A. 1-5 forming an abbreviated fuþark, plus an apparent two-rune formula **zj** and a PN Būriso appended to it. (See sect. 31.) Aquincum can be read: A. **fuþarkgw** B. **jlain:kŋia**, and is clearly an example of the fuþark represented by the first older *ætt*,(203) while Krause reads B. as *j(ēra)*! *l(aukaz)*!(204) *ain-kunningia*: 'A good year, and increase! The close friend (wishes this for the owner of the brooch),' (1966: 24-25). The third inscription from the continent, KJ 6: Charnay brooch (550-600, N. France), is probably non-magical. It contains an abbreviated inscription of r. 1-20 and a syntactic phrase which Krause (1966: 22) read as *unþfinþai Iddan Liano*: 'May Liano find (out) Idda,' (i.e., decipher the name with the aid of the provided **fuþark**).(205)

Survey of Viking Age and Medieval fuþark-Formulas

45. The relative number of **fuþark** inscriptions drops off rather dramatically throughout the Viking Age (from ca. 800-1100 CE). However, with the Scandinavian Middle Ages (after ca. 1100) the relative number increases just as dramatically.(206) In the Viking Age, the **fuþark** appears mainly in stone inscriptions (which otherwise also dominate the material typology of the period); while in the post-Viking Age various material types are found, e.g., bone, metal, wood, bricks, as well as stone. In this section, typical representatives will be discussed.(207)

Viking Age Fuþarks

The most famous of the younger **fuþark** inscriptions is the Gørlev st. (DR 239, see Fig. III, ca. 800-850) which occurs in the context of runemaster as an *-istil*-formula,(208) and a syntactic formula:

A. 1) þiauþui : risþi : stin : þansi : aft : uþinkaur :
2) fuþarkhniastbmIR : niut ual kums
B. 1) þmkiiissstttiiillliaksatarunarit
2) kuniarmuntRkrubxxxxxx

ODan. *Þjauðvi ræsþi sten þansi aft Óðinkaur.* **fuþarkhniastbmIR.** *Niút vel kumls.* **þmkiiissstttiiilll** *iak sata rúna(r) rétt. Gunni ArmundR. . .*: Þjodvi raised this stone after Odinkarr. [fuþark. . .] Enjoy well the monument.(209) [*þistil · mistil · kistil*] I set the rune(s) correctly. Gunni Armund. . .'(210)

The wooden sticks of Narssaq (Greenland, ca. 1000)(211) and Heddeby I (800-900)(212) also contain **fuþąrk** inscriptions in runic contexts, as does Maeshowe V (M. p.99).(213) Abbreviated fuþąrks appear on the Heddeby bowl (DR 417): **fuþx** and on the Kamien st. (ca. 1040, Pomerania): A. **fuþ** B. **kur**.(214)

Medieval fuþorks

In later times it becomes common to find fuþork inscriptions in the archeological context of churches. These are often on bricks, which were inscribed before they were fired.(215) From the Norwegian stave church at Eidsborg, Telemark (after 1250, *NIyR* II: 260-61) comes a wall-plank with a formula which partially reads: . . .**lllllliiiiifuþorkḥ**, which is a suggestive parallel to the *-istil-* inscriptions.(216)

Outside church environments, sequential fuþork formulas continue to occur well into the modern age in all previously established contexts. From the early Middle Ages (all from the 12th cent.), there are two ribs from Schleswig bearing fuþorks. Schleswig V has a complete fuþork with each rune divided from the next one by various numbers of points: **·f·u·þ:o:r:k:h:n:i:as:t:b:m:l:y**,(217) while Schleswig VII contains a fuþork with an additional inverted **gr**.(218) Although the fuþork order must have been well established in the medieval period, eventually an alphabetic order for the runes began to be attested in epigraphy, cf. e.g., Øster Marie st. (DR 396, ca. 1400): **abþef | ighikl | mnoPR stu X** and in modern age Iceland (17th-18th cent.) we find a combination of a runic alphabet and the *sator*-formula (cf. Bæksted 1942: 206), which would indicate that the sequential formulation had not lost its operative function.

II. Non-Sequential Formulas
A. Isolated
1. Pronounceable Formulas

46. When pronounceable *ephesia grammata* occur outside a sequential or syntactic runic context, it is difficult to determine whether we are simply faced with a chance occurence, or with an intentional vocal form. In the older corpus, there are 15 such inscriptions, all but one of which occur on bracteates. The main phonetic criteria for such complexes are the lack of irregular consonant clusters, and the regular interspersion of vowels. In lengthy complexes this would tend to defy the odds of an absolutely random choice of runic shapes by illiterate bracteate-masters.

The longest multisyllabic formulas of this type are found on IK 95: **sndiluuulRḷḷisiusahsi** and IK 162: **ildaituha** (R-L) **liRaiwui**. Quadrasyllabic or bisyllabic forms are apparent on IK 105: **salusalu**(219) and IK 131: **anoaṅa**,(220) while another form may be present on IK 101: **foslau**.(221) Less likely bisyllabics are found on IK 39: **ïlwi** and IK 91: (R-L) **gui**. The monosyllabic examples are: IK 61: (R-L) **lu**; IK 331: (R-L) **tau**; Welbeck Hill: **law ~ laþ**;(222) and IK 94, 1-2: **lït**. Two more seem to fall into special categories because of their repetitive continuant, i.e., IK 373: **tu llḷḷ** or vocalic, i.e., IK 158: **fua uu**, qualities. The one non-bracteate inscription, the Illerup spear shaft plane(223) **afi(l)aiki**. . . may or may not belong to this category.

2. Unpronounceable Formulas

This is by far the largest group of rune-formulas with just over twenty representatives — all but one of which are found on bracteates. It seems clear that where no reconstruction is possible, we are probably dealing with scribal *ephesia grammata*. These complexes appear: IK 75: **luRþl te oḍ**, IK 129: **lïïaþRmtl irRo⚡teal**,(224) IK.I.142: **a(w)iri uRi ahs[x]ia**, IK 147: **lRoḷu**, IK 148: . . .**(u)laliþhimRuiihxhslhuihdaeRuumihhhiR**, IK 182: **tualeltl lni**, IK 197: **xṣḳlaŋḳṇṇilwwṇėḳḳṇniïuxuxx**, IK 199: **tḷu**, IK 214: **tg**, IK 309: **lRllþe**, IK 237: (R-L) **tþad lxita**, IK 244: **ldḷhR(i)**, IK 249: (R-L) **nę ·.· tblll**, IK 255: **lalgwu**, IK 267: (R-L) **ṣḷkaR**, IK 295: **?Deuixoxxjụgṣ/iþalnRbṣxxC**, IK 299: **aualhR oa sejṣḳuḷ**, IK 339: (R-L) **alwehhuuuþwạuuuaewdaluuu?**,(225) IK 251: **xnþxskoglauilatklallll-txnþxuxlugl**, IK 353: (R-L) **lþdụlu   uldaul**, IK 357: **khiRḷ**, IK 358: **xuḳu[i ~ u]**, IK 375: **xhxktnlaahluiiefk**. A problematic inscribed complex is found on (KJ 36) Frøslev wand, which was found in a grave mound: **(x)RiliR**: — possibly a palindrome for **liR**? This reading supposes that the word is to be dated to the 4th-5th cent., however, if it is dated in the younger period, the palindrome could be read **lim — lim**: 'limb.'

Appendix on Old English Amuletic Rings

47. There is an interesting group of four amuletic rings,(226) all of which bear genetically related formulas in Anglo-Saxon runes. The four formulas appear:

1) Bramham Moor (= Electrum ring, National Museum, Copenhagen):
   ærycriufel ycriuriþon glæstæpontol.
2) Kingmoor (Cumberland, gold ring, British Museum):
   A. tærycriufltcriuriþonglæstæpon   B. tol.
3) England D (unknown province, bronze ring, British Museum):
   This is probably a modern copy of Kingmoor
   A. +ærcriufltcriuriþonglæstæpon B. tol
4) England C (unknown provenance, agate ring, British Museum):
   ✳✳ ery.ri.uf.dol.yrï.uri.þol.wles.te.pote.nol.

From a runological standpoint, 1-3 are almost identical, while the agate ring (4) shows some variations, e.g., r. 3 and 11 have the shape ᛗ (from ᛚ in the other forms), and r. 19-20 appear ᛁᛣ, where we expect ᛏ. ᛪ. There is also an alternation between the vocalic runes ᚠ [æ] and ᛗ [e].

Harder (1931, 1936) attempted to read some semantic sense into these formulas,(227) but this seems unlikely. Dickins (1935) recognized a reflection of magical *ephesia grammata* found in Old English charms in various portions of these formulas, especially in the initial complex **ærcriu** which is also found as **ærcrio** or **aer crio** in charms for stanching blood (cf. Cockayne 1865: II, 54, 112; III, 78). The variations in these formulas seem typical of scribal errors, and it appears that these are in fact epigraphical representations of manuscript forms. It is interesting that the runes were chosen for the transfer into epigraphy. It can be supposed that the runes did serve to intensify the operative effect of these clearly amuletic objects (cf. Page 1999: 112-13).

B. Contextual Non-Sequential Formulas
1. Pronounceable Formulas

48. Because these formulas occur for the most part in runic contexts which demonstrate a relatively high rate of competency, we can be more certain that we are dealing with intentional forms. Nine pronounceable formulas, three on bracteates and six on inscribed media, render forms in three types of formulaic contexts, a) sequential (**fuþark**. . .), b) non-syntactic lexemes (symbol-words), and c) syntactic formulas.

The Kylver st. (KJ 1, ca. 400-450, Gotland) was probably part of a grave chamber.(228) Outside the ductus of its complete **fuþark**-formula and tree-like sign, it bears a runic complex: **sueus** which is pronounceable as an *ephesion grammaton*, but which has generally been interpreted as a palindrome for Gotlandic *eus*: 'horse,' discussed elsewhere. The famous

Vadstena and Motala C-bracteates (IK 377, 1-2) contain one of the most certain of this type of formula in the ductus of a complete (R-L) **fuþark** sequence. The complex is most generally read: **luwatuwa**,(229) which has no apparent semantic content, but formally seems to belong to a repetitive vocal formula as could also be represented in IK 105 and IK 131. Conversely the sequence has also been read as **tuwatuwa**, and the repeated word **tuwa**, related to a word for "sacrifice," or to one meaning "raw wool."(See McKinnell 2004, 102)

Two inscriptions clearly contain PN's in connection with apparent *ephesia grammata*. The Kragehul knife hilt (KJ 28, 500-550, Fyn): (R-L) A. . . .**uma·bera** B. . . .**aau** perhaps bears a rune-master inscription . . .**uma**(230) *Bera* (see sect. 31.), plus **aau**, although this may be a mistake for **alu**. Fyn I-C (IK 58) probably contains a rune-master name, *HōuaR*: 'the high one' (see sect. 31), and in a separate sequence *laþu* **aaduaaliia**. While the complex **gakaR** on IK 149 has been fairly convincingly reconstructed as a symbolic word-formula *ga(u)kaR*: 'cuckoo' (see sect. 42), formally it must also be included in this category as it is embedded within a group of otherwise objection-free word-formulas, i.e., *laþu, laukaR*, and *alu*.

The possibly continuant formula (R-L) ||||||||||| is found on (KJ 38) Gjersvik tanning knife (ca. 450, SW Nor.). This complex, which has generally been interpreted as a logographic formula *laukaR* x ten, or *līnalaukaR* x five.(231) This complex is preceded by a heavily damaged sequence **dxxfioþi** which may itself be an *ephesion grammaton*.(232)

Three pronounceable rune formulas occur in the context of syntactic inscriptions. The Noleby st. (KJ 67, ca. 600, C. Swe.) contains compound syntactic formulas (see sect. 50.) in which the runic sequence :**suhurah:susi** ᛗ is embedded, while the now lost Gummarp st. (KJ 95, ca. 600, Blekinge, Swe.) bears a simple rune-master formula followed by what is most probably three logographic f-runes (see VII.9.). In South Germanic territory we also find (KJ 164,1) Weingarten I s-brooch (6th cent., SW Germany) with a female rune-master formula to which seems to be appended the two-rune formula **la**. These might be interpreted as logographs for *l(aukaR)* and **a(nsuR)*, but given the cultural context of this inscription, such a reading seems unlikely.(233)

2. Unpronounceable Formulas

Of the eight inscriptions with formulas belonging to this category, three of which are on bracteates, only three are obvious attempts to represent *ephesia grammata*. All but one of these contain an appellative of some kind. The South Germanic brooches of Beuchte (KJ 8) and Aquincum (KJ 7) both contain abbreviated **fuþark**-formulas and apparent appellatives, into which are imbedded two-rune sequences: Beuchte **Rj** and Aquincum **jl** (see 48). There are other inscriptions with runologically problematic PNs and/or word-formulas. The Krogsta st. (KJ 100, ca. 550, Uppland, Swe.): A.(R-L) **mwsieijx** B.sïainaR is probably an *ephesion grammaton* and a (PN?) S[t]ainaR.(234) In what seems to be a defective copy of a formula with a genetic relationship to (IK 58) Fyn I-C, the runologically difficult (IK 300) Maglemose III-C appears to be an attempt to represent the PN HōuaR with **hoR**, and the *alu*-formula with **alḷ**, between which is inserted the complex **tḷpḳmhi**. The (IK 13) Allesø-B bracteate has been discussed above (sect. 33) as a possible example of degenerated word-formulas, however, since no word-formula appears there in a complete form, this must at least be considered as an *ephesion grammaton*.

Three random runic sequences also occur in the context of syntactic rune-master formulas. A bracteate, (IK 70) Halskov-C, contains a 22-rune series, appended to a fairly clear rune-master formula Nxetur (PN?) *fahide laþoþ*: 'N. colored (→wrote) the invocation,' which can be read **mhlsiiaeiaugrsþnbkeiaR**. It is certainly feasible that this complex is a representation of the *laþoþ* on some level — but as it stands we can only interpret it as an apparently graphically determined *ephesion grammaton*. The (KJ 71) By st. (550-600, SE Nor.), after a runologically difficult master formula, translated by Krause (1966: 160-61) as 'I, the rune- master — HrōR son of HrōR, worked this slab for Olof. . .'(235) there follows an apparently non-semantic complex **dRrmþï**.(236) Of all these formulas, the most famous and most certainly operative, is the inscription B (A is a rune-master formula, see sect. 15b) on the Lindholm "amulet" (KJ 29, ca 500 Skåne). Line A. reads: **aaaaaaaaRRRnnn[x]bmuttt:alu:**.(237) It is possible that this compound inscription serves an apotropaic function — but its mode is that of aggressive magic — more akin to a curse. This aggressive aspect is apparent on two fronts: 1) the functional byname *sā wīlagaR*: 'the crafty one,' and 2) the conspicuous formulaic relationship between this sequence and those of the (17th cent.) *Galdrabók* no. 46: *Skriff desser staffer a kalffskind huit med blod þinum. . . og mæl, Rist æg þ(ier) Otte ausse Naudir Nije þossa ōretten. . .*: 'Write these staves on calf-skin with your own blood. . .and say: I write to you eight *áss*-runes, nine *nauð*-runes, thirteen *þurs*-runes. . .'(238) and a *kvennagaldur*(239) recorded by Jón Árnason (1954: I, 435): *Risti ég þér ása átta, nauðir níu. . .* Krause (1966:

70-71) reads the runes of the formula in an ideographic sense, i.e., eight *ansuR*-runes as an invocation to Óðinn, three *algiR*-runes as apotropaic signs, (four?) *nauðiR*-runes as distress (caused or prevented?), etc.

Survey of Viking Age and Medieval Rune-Formulas

49. During the Viking Age itself (after ca. 800), random sequences of runes are relatively rare. This may in part be due to an increased standardization demonstrated in the orthography of the rune-masters, which may in fact be a reflection of a renewed formalization of the social fabric which supported these "word-smiths." (See IV.17.) For the Middle Ages (after ca. 1150), after the social transformations brought on by the advent of Christianity, runological skills seem to degenerate (thereby perhaps causing a rise in the number of unintentional random sequences). Also, foreign complexes transcribed into runes from the Latin alphabet are introduced.

Viking Age formulas of this type fall into two different categories: 1) intentional *ephesia grammata* which may be, a) repetitive, or b) random, and 2) the -istil-formulas.

The weaving temple of Lund (DR 311) may contain an *ephesion grammaton* with **aallatti** after a syntactic love/curse formula (see 53),(240) while a clearly repetitive formula is borne by Skabersjö clasp (DR 263) **RRRRRRRRRRRRRRRR** (i.e., R x 16) — a numerical repetition which also reflects its position in the younger fuþąrk. In the Viking Age, the most conspicuous sequence was the -istil-formula.(241) This unique formula type is clearly attested in seven locations, with several more examples which seem to reflect this sequence to some degree.(242) There appears to have been two formulaic traditions. One represented by the Lomen inscriptions and the *Bosa s.* (verse 9):

r.a.þ.k.m.u.:iiiiii:ssssss:tttttt:iiiiii:llllll

and one by the Borgund,(243) Ledberg, and Gørlev inscriptions:

þmkiiissstttiiilll

In each case, the runes prefixed to the repetitive -istil sequence are to be combined with it to form lexemic word-formulas, e.g., **þistil**: 'thistle,' **mistil**: 'mistletoe,' **kistil**: 'a little box,' etc. But some forms which result seem to be nonsensical, e.g., **aistil, vistil**. However, in the case of words such as **þistil** — *þistill* and **mistil** — *mistill*, it is easy to see a parallel to the herb-name word-formulas (*laukaR, salu*[?] of the older period. The function of these words would seem to be apotropaic based upon symbolic analogs to their stinging or poisonous characters.

Medieval

In the Middle Ages formulas of this type occur in three categories: 1) apparently degenerated forms, 2) intentional *ephesia grammata*, which again may be a) repetitive, or b) random in nature, and 3) various formulaic complexes transcribed from southern traditions.

To the degenerate category(244) clearly belong inscriptions such as DR 267 Lilla Isie comb . . .**uhob (i)uknioiti(i)**, others which occur in otherwise legible contexts are more likely to be intentional, e.g., (DR Till. 3) Æbelholt bone A. **amóræmm:et**. . . **þhækko:star:dx**. . . B. **agoæuro:uos:. . .x! sanrorōn·gasdaeraṅg**. . . — A. *amorem* (+ *ephesion grammaton*) B. *ago auro vos* ('with gold, I urge you') . . . (+ *ephesion grammaton*).(245) A most curious group of inscriptions of this general type is represented by a number of Upplandic rune-stones which seem to be completely nonsensical. These are examined in detail by Thompson (1972), who believes them to have been executed by analphabetic or incompetent rune-carvers.(246)

Repetitive *ephesia grammata* are relatively common in the medieval runic record, e.g., (DR 247) Roskilde stave which bears a multiple repetition of the two-rune formula **uþ**,(247) or (DR 416) the so-called Absalon's ring, which contains a PN + a five fold repetition of a single rune: 1) **þorkæiryyyyy** — "Þorger (+ y x 5). Another group within this category repeats in a random fashion larger runic complexes, e.g., (DR 170) Jerslev amulet-st. A. **mlblmb** B. **mbl**, which is an obvious attempt to represent three permutations of a three-rune complex, or (DR 57) Vedslet amulet st. A. **þmkrhli** B. **iklmrþh** C. *A*xh**þa**, lines A. and B. of which are recordings of the same non-semantic rune-formula.(248) More random in composition are formulas such as those found on other clearly amuletic objects, e.g., (DR 43) Vejle stone ax(249) **lyfætyio+** or the more recently found lead-plate of Västannor (Dalarna) A. **mkulxxsasimx** B. **nusaaon**. . ., cf. Gustavson-Brink (1979: 228ff.).

Certain magical formulas from Mediterranean traditions became popular in the Scandinavian Middle Ages (and beyond). The most conspicuous examples are *agla* — which is actually an anagram for the Hebrew *a*(*ttah*) *g*(*ibbor*) *l*(*eolam*) *a*(*donai*): 'thou art strong in eternity, o lord!,'(250) and the widely known *sator* magic square formula.(251) It is unlikely that these formulas were understood in their original meanings by medieval Scandinavian magicians. These appear to be set sequences transmitted more or less intact. The **agla**-formula occurs several times in the runic corpus,(252) e.g., on (DR 203) Revinge amulet ring:(253) **aroþa aglagala laga** — *arota* (< Gk. αρετη: virtue?) + *agla* in three permutations, while the *sator*-square has been found in at least seven inscriptions; two from Gotland (nos. 143 and 149), two from the Bryggen in Bergen, one from Iceland — and the most recently found fragmentary inscription on the Närke bowl:(254)

<blockquote>
sator
aræpo
tænæt
</blockquote>

Operative Syntactic Formulas

50. Syntactic formulas are those which show an elaborated morphological code, which might minimally include an oblique substantive as the object of a verb (explicit or implied), or active verbs of operative function with explicit or implied objects that are to be affected. The operant formulas fall into several types: 1) performatives (direct linguistic operative acts, cf. Austin 1962), 2) imperatives (direct commands given, usually to animate beings), 3) juridics (operative use of legalistic formulas) and 4) analogies (operative use of analogical situations, often in mythic/epic form), 5) supplications (prayers). Examples from the latter type are primarily Christian formulas (cf. Hampp 1961: 110-140).

There are relatively few older inscriptions which fit into this general category (23 will be discussed here). Certain criteria have been applied to determine the possible degree to which a given inscription has an operative force, i.e., unambiguously operant inscriptions are those which are both runologically clear (or at least relatively so) and contain some overt indication of the operant aim of the inscription; ambiguously operant inscriptions are those which are either runologically problematic or which have only implied aims; while speculatively operant inscriptions are dependent upon doubtful or speculative reconstructions and interpretations. In the following discussions, each inscription is treated as a whole in order to preserve the fundamental context of each formula, however, these syntactic inscriptions may contain more than one formulaic type. (See ch. VII.) Although readings presented by Krause (1966) are used as bases for interpretation, important variants are noted and certain improvements suggested.

1) Unambiguously Operant Inscriptions

Although grave-magic (directed against either the *draugaR/ *dauðingaR or potential grave robbers) has been cited as a motive for runic inscriptions (cf. Düwel 1981b), the only overt reference to this motive in the older epigraphic record(255) is found on the complex KJ 67: Noleby st. (ca. 600, C. Swe.), which was found in a stone fence, but which was probably originally a barrow-st. (cf. Krause 1966: 148ff.). The reading given by Krause (following Brate 1898: 328ff.) is:

I.   runofahiraginakudotojéka
II. unaþou:suhurah:susixhwatin
III. hakuþo

I. *rūnō fāhi ragina-ku(n)do tōj-eka* II. *unaþ[o]u*:**suhurah:susix** *hwatin* (?) III. *Ha(u)koþu*: 'A rune (= 'secret knowledge') I color, one stemming from the advisors (= 'divine powers'). I prepare satisfaction (in the grave) **suhurah susix** May they (i.e., the staves of the rune-formula?) make the hawk-like one sharp (i.e., the rune-master with a gaze sharp as a hawk?)!'

There seems to be general agreement on the complex **unaþou** as *unaþu* acc. sg. of a u-stem ('satisfaction'), cf. ON *unað*: 'delight, happiness.'(256) So that at least one explicitly stated magical aim of the inscription would be to cause the dead to be content with the grave and not to venture forth as a *dauðingaR*. The complex **suhurah:susix** is probably best interpreted as an *ephesion grammaton*.(257) As a pronounceable rune formula (*Zaubergemurmel*), **suhura-h**... is compared to Norw. *surra, sūra* and Swe. *surra*: 'to sing a lullaby' (with emphatic *-h-*) by de Vries (1961a: 560).(258)

The most famous magical formulas in the older tradition are the two almost identical juridical "curses" found on the Blekinge stones of Stentoften (KJ 76) and Björketorp (KJ 97). The Stentoften st. (ca. 650) in its entirety may be read:

I.   niuhAborumR
II. niuhagestumR
III. hAþuwolAfRgAfj
IV. hArwolAfRmAgiusnuhle
V.   hideRrunonofelAhekAhederAginoronoR
VI. herAmAlAsARArAgeuwelAdudsAþAtbAriutiþ

I. *niuha-būrumR* II. *niuha-gestumR* III. *HaþuwolfR gaf j(āra)* IV. *HariwolfR magiu's nū hlē* V. *h(a)idR rūnō* [*ronu*](259) *felheka hedra ginor*[*ū*]*noR* VI. *hermala(u)sR argeu wēlad(a)ud sā þat briutiþ*: "To the new farmers, (and) to the new foreigners, Haþuwolf gave good harvest. Hariwolf is now protection for his (son retainer?). A row of bright runes I hide here, magically charged runes — restlessly because of 'perversity' a deceitful death (has) the one (who) breaks this (monument or stone arrangement)."(260) Runologically, the main problem is with IV. r. 16-21, which have been read as an *ephesion grammaton* (cf. DR 357; Antonsen 1975a: 85-87), but as a third-pers. pres. subj. < **snuhwan*, cf. ON *snugga*: 'to look (out after),' i.e., may Hariwolf look out after his son,' by Jacobsen (1935: 23-24), while Marstrander (1952: 151) mentions a possible variant: *Herjólfr megi nú snui áre*: 'Herjolf turned the year (i.e., made good harvest) for his son.'(261)

The Björketorp st. (ca. 675) consists entirely of a curse-formula which may be read:
A. **uþArAbAsbA**
B. I. **hAidRrunoronu**
   II. **fAlAhAkhAiderAg**
   III. **inArunARArAgeu**
   IV. **hAerAmAlAusR**
   V. **utiARwelAdAude**
   VI. **sARþAtbArutR**

A. *ūparba-spā*! B.I. *haidR-rūno ronu* II. *falhk hedra*. III. *g*]*ina-rūnaR. ærgeu* IV. *hearma-lausR*, V. *ūti æR wēla-daude*, VI. *sāR þat brȳtR*: "Prophecy of destruction! The row of bright runes I hid here, magically charged runes. Because of 'perversity,' restlessly, out there is (given) to a deceitful death, the one (who) breaks this (monument or stone arrangement).'(262) The complex **uþArAbAsbA** has also been interpreted as a first-pers. sg. pres. 'I prophesy destruction,' (cf. DR 360, Jacobsen 1935: 36-38, Marstrander 1952: 123).

Apparently, the Björketorp inscription has but one function, i.e., the prevention, by means of a magico-juridical curse,(263) of the destruction of the site. The formula relates the crime after it has stipulated the sentence — to be carried out by means of the efficiency of the formula itself (and of the will of the rune-master). The Stentoften formula has a compound function. In addition to its juridical curse formula, it contains a performative formula with an apparently complex motive of providing prosperity and protection (i.e., *jāra* and *hlē*).

The longest and most difficult of all the older inscriptions is the Eggjum st. (KJ 101, ca. 700, W. Nor.). It is beset with a number of runological and interpretative problems. In their essential linguistic features, the readings of Olsen (*NIæR*: III, 77-197), Jacobsen (1931: 80ff.), Nordén (1934: 105ff.), Høst (1960: 489ff.), Krause (1966: 227-35), and N. Å. Nielsen (1968: 53ff.) are largely in agreement. Krause (1966) gives the reading:

I. nissolusotuknisAksestAinskorinnixxxxmạRnAkdạnisnịþ
rịŋRniwiltiRmạnRlAgixx

II. hinwArbnAseumạRmAdeþAimkAibAibormoþAhunihuwẠRobkạm
hArișạhiạlạtgotnAfiskRoRfxxnAuimsuwịmạdefoklịfxạxx
xxxgAlạnde

III. Alumisurki

This would appear in normalized early ONorw.:
I. a) *Ni's sōlo sott ok ni saxe stæinn skorinn*
b) *Ni l(æggi) mannR næðan, is niþ rinnR*
c) *ni vīltiR mænnR læggi a(b).*
II. a) *Hin(n) varp *nāsēo mannR māðe þæim kæipa ī bormoþa hūni.*
b) *HuæR ob kam *hæri-oss(?) hī ā land gotna?*
c) *FiskR ōR f[ir]na-*vim suim[m]ande, fogl ī f[i]an[da lio] galande.*
III. *Alu missyrki!*

According to Krause, this would be translated: "(Ia) The stone is not touched by the sun and (is) not scored by an (iron) knife. (b) No man may lay (it) bare, when the waning moon runs (across the heavens). (c) Misguided men (or sorcerers?) may not lay (the stone) [aside?]. (IIa) Here (the) man (= the rune-magician) sprinkled this (stone) with the sea-of-the-corpse (= blood), with it (i.e., with the blood) he rubbed the thole of the well drilled boat(?). (b) As who (i.e., in what shape) is the lord-god (= *WōðanaR) (or: who is as a warrior) come hither onto the land of warriors (or: of horses?)? (c) A fish swimming out of the (terrible) stream, a bird screaming [into the enemy band?]. III. 'Protection' [against] the wrong-doer!"

This complex formula has generally been interpreted as having to do with some type of "grave magic."(264) But against whom is this magic directed? The pivotal line of the inscription is III, which is rather glossed over by Krause (1966: 231-34).(265) Olsen (*NIæR*: III, 180-81 *passim*) reads this line together with the cryptic *Ormari* and the final **is** of II as: [Ormari] is... Axxxmisurkx, and reconstructs: *Ormari es a[linn] *misyrk[i]*: 'for Ormarr an avenger (i.e., a wolf) is born (or reared).' Jacobsen (1931: 80ff.) interprets this line as **sA tu misurki** — *sā dō mis(s)yrki*: 'he died because of a misdeed,' while Høst would read the line as a fem. rune-master inscription (see sect. 32.): a. . .**u is urki** — (fem. ō-stem PN) *is yrki*: 'This is N.N.'s work.'(266) Krause's reading seems to make the best sense in the context of the whole inscription.

It is somewhat more likely that the formula is directed against potential grave robbers — perhaps even sorcerers (*vīltiR mænnR?*) who would use the body as a *sendingr ~ dauðingr*, etc.(267) — because of the direct reference to intervention from the outside (I.b-c),(268) than against the possible *draugr* from within the grave.(269) Reier (1952) presents a radically different interpretation in which he sees the whole inscription as a reference to a permanent site for the performance of Odinic human sacrifice.

Only one bracteate inscription qualifies in this unambiguous category, i.e., the (IK 98) Sjælland II-C formula:

hariuhahaitika : farauisa : gibuauja ᚠ [=ttt?]

This is easily read as: *Hariūha haitika fāra-wīsa, gibu auja*: 'Hariuha I am called, who knows dangerous things,(270) I give good luck!' It is the explicitly performative formula *gibu auja* (see also sect. 36.) which is of interest here. It seems most likely that it is *Hariūha* who is the giver of *auja* — by means of the performative act itself.

The Strand brooch (ca. 700, C. Nor.) may be a unique example in the older period(271) of a type of formula more common in the Viking Age in which an explicit operative seems to be directed against the walking dead. Krause (1966: 48-49), in agreement with Nordén (1937: 159), reads this formula as: **siklisnahli** — *siglis nā-hlē*: 'the jewel is protection against the dead (i.e., the walking dead).'(272) Olsen (in von Friesen 1933: 85, and in *NIyR*: V, 1-20), however, favors the reconstructed reading: *sigli's n[Auþ]A hlé*: "the jewel is protection against 'distress'."(273) In either case it is clearly an operative formula.

Outside Scandinavia, another unique formula is found on the Frisian yew stave of Westeremden B (AZ 38, ca. 800), which clearly seems to fall into the category of an operative epic/mythic analogy. The runes of this unquestionably genuine(274) Frisian inscription are sometimes problematic, but were read by Arntz (1939: 389ff.) as: Ia) **ophamugist[a] ṇ damluþ** b)

[i]wimcœstaþukn II. iwiosust dukale — *Ophāmu gistanda Ámluþ. Íwim œest āh þukn: Íwi ōs-ust dūkale*: 'Against Opham, Amluth took up position. The surf submitted to the yew: The surf submits to the yew.'(275) The way the runes are executed would suggest that (I) was carved carefully by an accomplished rune-master, while (II) was cut with some haste and/or lack of ability. The inscription itself would suggest further that (II) was not carved until out on the stormy sea — the calming of which seems to be the motive of the line. This would then be the functional equivalent of the ON *brimrúnar* (see V.13).

2) Ambiguously Operant Inscriptions

On runological or interpretative grounds, somewhat less certainly operative are nine other syntactic inscriptions. Most of those must be relegated to this sub-group because their motives remain obscure; they are damaged, or their runes are in some way ambiguous, etc.

The most obviously damaged of these formulas is (KJ 27) Kragehul spear shaft (500-550, Fyn) which is broken into five fragments. Of these, parts 1-2 belong directly together, as do parts 4-5, with a medial, isolated fragment 4. These fragments are most usually read:(276)

ekerilaRasugisalasmuhahaitegagagaginugahe. . .lija. . haglawijubig. . .

These runes are interpreted by Krause (1966: 67) as: *ek erilaR A(n)sugīslas mūha* (or *Mūha*) *haite*. g̃a g̃a g̃a . (= *gibu auja* -or- *gebu ansuR*), *ginu-* g̃a *he[lma-tā]lija* (or *[ta]lija[tō]*) *hagla wī(g)ju bi g[aiRa]*. . 'I, the rune-master, am called Asgisl's retainer (or: son Mūha). I give good luck (or: gift to the god?), magically working (sign) g̃a. Helmet destroying(?) hail (= ruin). I consecrate to the spear. . .' The latter part of the formula is what interests us most here, but it is unfortunately the most damaged. The reconstruction, although it seems sensible, is nevertheless conjectural on Krause's part. Marstrander (1952: 26-31) is only willing to reconstruct fragments 4-5 as *hagala wiju*: '. . .I consecrate hail. . .,' while Antonsen (1975a:35-36) is even less willing to speculate on the meaning of these segments. There does, however, seem to be a general consensus that the bind rune ⋇ is to be read g̃a and to have the meaning *gibu auja* (see Sjælland II-C above)(277) or *gebu-ansuR*. If Krause is correct, this would be an example of the spear-hurling ritual formula discussed in V.8 — with the intention of destroying the protective weapons (in this case the helmets?) of the enemy.

Runologically clear, but rather obscure as to interpretation, is the whetstone of Strøm (KJ 50; ca. 600, N. Nor.) which is to be read:

A. wateħalihinohorǹa
B. ħaħaskaþiħaþuligi
— and transcribed in the form of a work-song (see VII.5):
A. wātē hál(l)i híno hórna!
B. hāha skáþi! haþu líg(g)i!(278)

Krause interprets the verb forms wātē, skaþi, and liggi as third-pers. sg. opt. and would translate the inscription: 'May the horn wet this stone! Scathe the hay! May the (second) crop lie!'

Antonsen (1975b) rightly criticizes this interpretation and sees the verb forms as second-pers. sg. imperatives and translates: 'Wet this stone horn! Scathe, scathe! Lie, that which is mown down!'(279) The unique operative force of this versified formula is made clear by Antonsen's interpretation (1975b: 129): 'The whole point of the worksong is an admonition to the horn to wet the whetstone to permit it to sharpen the blade properly so that the scythe will cut the hay or grain clean and the latter will lie. . .' Therefore we would have an example of operative communication between human volition and the substance of the stone, a process in which the carving of runes was obviously an important means — probably as a reinforcement of a vocally performed formula.(280)

The stone of Kalleby (or Tanum) (KJ 61; ca. 400, Bohuslän) poses significant problems in interpretation. If it is complete, the runes may be read: (R-L) þrawijan·haitinaRwas. The first complex (r. 1-8) is read by several scholars as a gen. sg. of a -(i)jan- stem masc. PN: *þrawija-,(281) which would tend to relegate this inscription to the "memorial" category (see VII, note 11). However, others have read it as a verb þrawijan: 'to long or yearn (for)' (cf. ON þreyja, OE þrowjan),(282) which would place the inscription in a clearly operative category as a "documentation" (i.e., objectification) of a performative act. The formula could be read: þrawijan haitinaR was: 'he (a dead man) was ordered to yearn (for the grave).' The operative function of such an inscription would then perhaps be to hold the dead in the grave (cf. Noleby, KJ 67), and as an apotropaic device to protect the community of the living from malevolent dauðingar (see Krause 1966: 140).

Runologically questionable is (KJ 62): Tørvika B st. (450-500, SW. Nor.), which was found as part of a burial chamber wall of a cremation grave.(283) The runic shapes are mostly either anomalous forms or bear what appear to be extraneous branches, etc. Høst (1954) attempts a reading, with which Krause (1966: 141-42) cautiously agrees: (R-L) **heþrodweñgk** — *heþrō dwen*! [*g(ebo) k(aunaR)*]: 'dwindle hence!...' The term *dwen* is interpreted as a second-pers. sg. imp. (cf. ON *dvína*: 'to dwindle, cease'). Høst reads the form *dweno* (i.e., ON *dvína*),(284) but r. 9 seems to be clearly **g** and not **o**, and therefore we are left with two runes which would appear to be ideographic. A conjectural syntactic reconstruction of this formula might be *g(ibu) k(aunan)*: "I give 'putrification'(285) (to the dead)" in order to destroy possible *dauðingar*, or *g(ibu) k(ēna)*: 'I give the torch, fire' (i.e., of cremation).(286) In either case, the imperative formula would be directed against the dead.

Two inscriptions that are mainly third-person formulas are the stones of Gummarp (KJ 95) and Roes (KJ 102), both of which require a certain interpretation of symbolic elements in order to clarify their operative force. The Gummarp st. (see sect. 21 for a full discussion of its formula) contains three **f**-runes, which when interpreted logographically, yield *fehu*: 'wealth.' From this we can suppose that this is an operative formula for the acquisition of wealth and prosperity — probably for the whole community in the context of other Blekinge stones.

The Roes st. (ca. 750, Gotland) is more difficult. This small stone (75 x 55 x 8 cm) was found under the roots of a hazel bush, and on its face, juxtaposed to the runic formula, is the image of a horse. The text is runologically difficult, but the most convincing interpretation is offered by Olsen (*NIærR*: III, 164ff.) and accepted by Krause (1966: 235-36): **iuþin:udRrAk** — *jū þin UddR*(287) *rak*: 'Odd drove this horse' (i.e., the one pictographically represented). Most interpretations refer to the horse (Gotlandic *jū*),(288) which is apparently virtually a semantic element in the whole formula. The image of the horse is common in Germanic curses (cf. the use of the horse in *nīð*-formulas), and it seems to be conceived of as an agent by which magical or divine power is projected.(289) Therefore, we may conjecture that the operative function of this stone is that of a curse, and it may have worked in a way similar to that of the *níðstǫng* (cf. *ES* ch. 57; *Vats. s.* ch. 34). It is also interesting to note that Egill's "cursing pole" was of hazel wood, and this stone was found under a hazel bush.(290)

The Frisian Britsum inscription (AZ 9, ca. 600) is a runologically difficult yew-stave, the shape and material of which would already make us suspect that it is an amulet of some kind.(291) Although the dialect of the text is Old Frisian, runographically it appears to be non-Anglo-Frisian (see Miedema 1974: 108ff.). Its runes may be read:

I. þinīaberetdud
II ...n:bįrįdmi
III. liu

Arntz (1939: 161ff.) interprets the text as: *þin ī ā ber! et dūd [bere]n! birid mī Liu*: 'Always carry this yew! In it power is contained! Liu (PN?) carries me.'(292) An alternate interpretation is given by Miedema (1974: 114): 'Always carry this yew (amulet) in the retinue. Liu (PN). -n (PN) carries me.'(293) The former reading makes the operative nature of the stave more obvious, however, neither reading makes the motive explicit. Typological evidence, coupled with the evidence of either reading, would seem to suggest that this was a general protective amulet (used by a warrior).

Appendix on Christian Formulas

51. Before we leave this group of ambiguous formulas, we might consider two apparently Christian inscriptions that also fulfill our criteria. The bone plate of Derbyshire (M. p. 40, 8th cent.) is of unknown function (Page 1999: 163). The runes can be fairly well read and interpreted as: **godgecadæræhadda(ŋ)þiþiswrat** — *God gecaþ aræ Hadda(n) þi þis wrat*, which according to Page may be translated five different ways: 1) "God will preserve the honor of Hadda who incised this," 2) "God preserves his minister Hadda who incised this," 3) "God saves by his mercy Hadda who wrote this," 4) "God increases (*gecaþ* < *ge-ecan*) the possessions of Hadda who wrote this" and 5) "God will preserve the honor of Hadda because (*þi*: *þy*) he wrote this." The demonstrative pronoun *þis* may refer to the inscription itself, or to a document or book to which the plate might have been attached (see Bately-Evison 1961). Each interpretation above could be considered an operative formula which indicates the source of numinous power (*god*), the performative action (*wrītan*), and the desired result or motive. Due to the obvious theological context of the Derbyshire bone, we might have expected a supplicative formula with a subjunctive verb as we find on the Whitby bone comb (M. p.134, ca. 9th cent.) the bilingual text of which may be read: **d[æ]usmæus godaluwalu dohelpæcyn...** — *Dæus mæus. God aluwaldo helpiæ Cyn-*: 'My god. May god almighty help Cyn- (PN with *Cyn*-theme?), see Page (1999: 164-65). This would be classified as a supplicative prayer formula that petitions for the good will and blessing of the deity.

3) Speculatively Operant Inscriptions

52. Two of the most famous inscriptions which must be placed in this category are the stones of Vetteland (KJ 60) and Opedal (KJ 76), both of which were probably originally directly or indirectly connected to graves. Vetteland (ca. 350, SW. Nor.) is only fragmentary and was restored to its present state and read by Marstrander (1946):

I. ...flagdafaikinaRist
II. ...magoRminasstaina
III. ...darfaihido

I. . . *flagda-faikinaR ist.* II. . . .*magōR mīnas staina.* III. . . .*daR faihido.* This is reconstructed and translated: '[This place] is menaced by fiends. [I, N.N., set] my son's stone. [I,] N.N.-*daR* colored (carved) (the runes).'(294) Besides the performative force of lines II and III, an important explicitly operative formula may be contained in line I., which Krause (1966: 137; 1971: 172-73) reads as a root form *flagda-* [cf. ON *flagð*, pl. *flǫgð*: '(female) monster, giant(ess)'] — probably at this time more generally 'fiend,' prefixed to a masc. nom. sg. of a past participle of an otherwise unattested verb **faikan*: 'to menace, terrorize' (cf. ON adj. *feikn*: 'terrible').(295) Antonsen (1975a: 38) less convincingly interprets this complex as '. . .is subject to deceitful attack (i.e., *flegda*: 'attack;' *faikinaz* masc. nom. sg. adj. 'deceitful'). With the former reading, it is fairly easy to see the past participle in apposition to a masc. nom. sg. noun (e.g., **stadiR*: 'place') so that the whole may be interpreted as a curse formula of apotropaic function, i.e., an invocation to dangerous fiends to protect the burial complex from would-be grave robbers or necromantic sorcerers.

The Opedal st. (ca. 450, SW Nor.) is a complete text, but is runologically problematic, and has invited a number of divergent interpretations.(296) The runes may be read: (R-L) A. **liubumeR** | **wage** | B. **birgŋguboroswestarminu**. Irregularities in the ductus of the runes (see Krause 1966: plate 36), have allowed several scholars to read the text in the order B.-A., e.g., von Friesen (1904) initially read: *Birg Inguborō, swestar mīnu liubu mēR Wagē!*: 'Help, Ingubora — my dear sister — me, Wag!,' which he revised to: *birgingu Borō swestar mīnu liubu mēR Wagē*: 'A burial. Bora, my sister, (is) dear to me, to Wag' (1924). However, von Friesen seems to have ultimately agreed with Marstrander (1929b: 158-96) in 1933, when he translated the whole: '(This is a) burial. My dear sister,

Bor(g)a. May she preserve me.' This is interpreted to be a wish that the dead sister will do no evil to her living brother because he buried her according to correct custom. This interpretation is dependent upon reading the complex **wage** as a subj. *wagjē* (cf. ON *vægi* < *vægja*: 'to spare, preserve'). On purely runological grounds, Antonsen's (1972; 1975a: 40) reading seems preferable in some regards: *liubu*(297) *mez* (:) *Wage*(:) *Birgnaggu Boro swestar minu*: 'Dear to me — to Wag — (and to) Birgnggu is Boro, my sister.' With the readings of *birg* as an imperative, or *wagē* as a subj. verb (either of which would leave room for an operative interpretation indicating some kind of active interaction between the worlds of the living and dead) in serious doubt — we are left to deal with the significance of *liubu*. This is not likely to be an expression of sentimental affection between siblings. It is more probable that on some level *liubu* indicates a desire for congenial relations between the dead and living.(298)

A syntactic formula totally dependent upon a speculative reconstruction by Olsen (*NIæR*: II, 640ff.) is perhaps borne by the Gjersvik bone tanning knife (KJ 38, ca. 450, SW. Nor.), which was found in a cremation grave. Its levoverse inscription reads: **dxxfioþillllllllll**, reconstructed by Olsen as *d[ís]fioþ i(RwiR)* (= ON *dís fjar yðr*) + ten l-runes (see sect. 37). This would be a clear curse formula similar in mode to the *níðstǫng*-curse recounted in the *ES* ch. 57, where it is described how Egill directs the *landvættir* against Eirikr and Gunnhildr. Another speculatively reconstructed formula is on the South Germanic disk brooch of Balach (KJ 165; Op. 9, 600-650, Kanton Zürich, Switzerland), discovered in a woman's row grave. The runes can be read fairly easily: I. **frifridil** II. **du** III. **ftmįk**. To each side of this complex are two levoverse l-runes, and at the end of line III there is a peculiar comb-like form. Complex I is generally interpreted as a masc. PN (OHG *Frīdel*, see Förstemann 1900: 524ff.), with a reduplicated familiarizing prefix (see Krause 1966: 307), as the giver of the brooch. Complexes II and III may be reconstructed as *du f(a)t(o) mik!*: 'take, or embrace thou me (i.e., the giver Fridel)!' (But see also VII.5.). Such an interpretation coupled with the perhaps erotic elements represented by the l-runes, would be sufficient to classify this as an example of love magic. Opitz (1977: 13-14; 195-97), who follows Klingenberg (1976), takes this idea much further into the realm of speculation with a crypto-erotic interpretation for which there is little sure evidence.

Two South Germanic inscriptions which may contain the word-formula *auja* are the Alemannic Oetting brooch (Betz 1979: 550-600, SW Germany) and the Frisian brooch plate of Hantum (AZ 20). Betz reads the Oetting runes as: **awijabrg** and reconstructs the text *Aw[i]ja b(i)rg!*: '(Divine)

Helper (fem.), protect (the wearer of this brooch)!' Although this reading is suspect, the fact that the brooch was placed over the right eye of the female corpse makes us think that it had some magical function.(299) The Hantum bone plate bears a formula aha:k ~ æhe:k, for which Arntz (1939: 256) gives an alternate reading auja'k: 'I (have) luck,' but for which the more likely readings are either *Æhæ (i)k*: 'I (am called) Æhæ' (see Miedema 1974: 114) or *āch ā (i)k*: 'I own (this) forever' (see Kapteyn 1933: 199ff.).

Survey of Viking Age and Medieval Syntactic Formulas

53. In the younger periods, formulas of the unambiguously magical type become relatively more frequent. It should also be noted that these inscriptions become more complex, and in many instances more formulaic or standardized at least with regard to limited elements. Although the personal power of the rune-master must have remained important (of the inscriptions discussed below, six contain direct references to the rune-master/carver), there is a remarkable increase in the use of non-human numina (especially of a malevolent sort) in the formulas.

The younger syntactic formulas may be discussed in six roughly defined categories that can be easily compared to the corpus of older inscriptions: 1) juridical cursing or apotropaic(300) formulas found on many stones, 2) 'grave-magic' seemingly directed against *aptrgǫngumenn*, 3) general counter-demonic formulas (usually for healing purposes), 4) complex formulas that employ mythic or epic elements, 5) a miscellaneous directly performative group, and 6) later Christian prayer formulas with elements of Mediterranean magic.

As many as eight younger inscriptions contain formulas that seem to be continuations of the type found on the stones of Stentoften, Björketorp, and perhaps even Eggjum. They all appear to be directed against malevolent humans who would disturb the object upon which the inscription is carved. The first six of the following formulas are appended to typical memorial inscriptions, which would indicate that at least in some instances such formulas were directed against grave robbers.(301) The probable significance of certain words used to describe the potential malefactor seems to indicate the possibility that the "robbery" could have had a magical motive (cf. the use of corpses as *sendingar/dauðingar*, etc. (See V.5.)

Glemminge st. (DR 338, ca. 1000, Sjælland): uirþi:at:rata:huas:ub briuti — ODan. *werþi at (rata?) hwa's upp briuti*: 'He shall become a (*rati?*),(302) whoever breaks (this stone or grave).' Here the juridical force is clear — if one disturbs the stone or its environs, he will become a *rati*, or will be known as one by his society.

Sønder-Vinge st. II (DR 83, 11th cent., N. Jutland): ... **sarþi:auk | siþr[a~i]ti : saR:mạnR: | ias · auþi:mini:þui | | xuþị: bịxxti. . .** — ODan. *særþi ok sēþ. rati saR mannr aes øþi minni þwi . . . b[r]iuti*: '. . . performed witchcraft and sorcery.(303) A *rati* (is) the man who would lay waste to this monument (or) break (it).' Whereas the Glemminge st. contains the verbal formula *verða at*: 'to turn into' (cf. also Glavendrup, Tryggevælde, and Saleby below), Sønder-Vinge II (along with Skern II) contains a sort of nominal imperative. The relationship between the problematic complexes **sarþi** and **siþ** and the subject of the following formula is uncertain.

Skern st. II (DR 81, 10th cent., N. Jutland): **siþi:sa: mạnr:is |:þusi :kubl : ub : biruti** — ODan. *Sēþi sā mannr æs þøsi kumbl upp briuti*: "A 'sorcerer' (is) the man who breaks up this monument (or stone-setting).'

Glavendrup st. (DR 209, ca. 900, Fyn): **at·rita·sa·uarþi·is ·stain·þansi· ailti·iþa ·aft·anan·traki** — ODan. *at (rita?) sā werþi, æs stēn þansi (ailti?) æþa øft ạnnạn draugi*: 'Into a *rati* he will turn, whoever (*ailti*) the stone, or removes it for another (person).' The exact meaning of the runic sequence **ailti** is also uncertain,(304) but it is clear that it is a third-pers. sg. pres. subj. and that it represents some destructive or detrimental act with respect to the will of the rune-master.

Tryggevælde st. (DR 230, ca. 900, Sjælland), on the backside of the stone is the formula: A. **sauaþi · at · rita · isailtistain · þansi** B. **iþahiþantraki** — ODan. *sā werþi at rita æs (ailti?) stēn þænsi æþa hæþan dragi*: 'He will turn into a *rita*, whoever (*ailti*) this stone, or drags it away.'

Saleby st. (Vg. 67, 1000-1050): **uarþiat + rata + aũk | | atarkRi + kunu + saR + iashaukuit | | krus + h[uas] + uf + briuti** — OSwe. *Werþi at (rata?) auk at argRi kunu, saR es haggwi (krus?), hwa's of briuti*!: '(He) will turn into a *rati* and into a perverse woman, whoever carves a cross(?) (into this monument) (or) whoever breaks (it) down!' This interpretation, which generally follows that of Jacobsen (1935: 52), is far from certain (see also Lindqvist 1940: 126-27; N.Å. Nielsen 1968: 18-19). If this is correct; however, we would have a parallel between *rati* and *argri kona*, which would bring us close to a *nīð*-type formula.

The curse formula on the Sparlösa st. (Vg. 119, ca. 800) is more ambiguous. Typologically, the Sparlösa st. seems more similar to the Stentoften or Eggjum formulas with perhaps cryptic allusions to ritual performances.(305) On the other hand, its curse — or protective formula — is not dissimilar to the other juridics. N. Å. Nielsen (1968: 103ff.) reads line III.B. as [sa s] į ukriþ sarsk snui binti — OSwe. *Sā sīi ugriþ, sær(þ)sk, 's snui bendi*: 'He who alters the character (i.e., corrupts the writing), may be an outcast, perversely immoral.'

The *operative* nature of these formulas is not commonly agreed upon. Some scholars would have us believe that the texts were intended to be read as "warnings" by potential malefactors (see e.g., N. Å. Nielsen 1968: 47-48, and Antonsen 1980b: 133ff.). This view is unsatisfactory on several grounds, e.g.: 1) it implies a general literacy rate for which there is no evidence for the 7th-11th-century,(306) 2) it ignores the contextual and typological evidence on the stones themselves which indicates a magico-operative function for the formulas, and 3) it neglects the similarities between this type of formula and the well known magical function of *nīð*-compositions.

Younger inscriptions that appear to be directed against the walking dead (or perhaps the use of the dead bodies by living magicians?) would be supporting evidence for the interpretations of the older stones of Tørvika B, Kalleby, etc. The Gørlev st. (DR 239, ca. 800, Sjælland) contains the formula: **niu ual kums** — ODan. *niút wel kumbls!*: 'enjoy (or: use) well the grave (or: monument)!'(307) This occurs in the complex text of a memorial formula, a complete **fuþąrk**-formula, and a rune-master formula. The Norre-Nærå st. (DR 211, ca. 800, Fyn) bears a simpler text: A. **niąut:kumls** B. **þurmutR** — ODan. *niút kumbls, ÞormundR*: 'Enjoy (or: use) the grave (or: monument), Thormund!' This formula has generally been interpreted to function as an injunction to the dead to be satisfied in the grave and not to wander abroad (see Sierke 1939: 52-53). The Ulfsunda bronze amulet (see Nordén 1943: 146-54, ca. 800) was found in a grave and is only 0.95 x 1.65 cm in size. Nordén thinks it to be directed against the walking dead, but such an interpretation is totally dependent upon taking it to have been carved and placed in the grave especially for this purpose. Nordén reads the text: A. **uxsxxurakRutimisfulkiR** B. **fakiskaþiua** — OSwe. *v[e]s[at]-tu órvakr úti, misfylgir! fangi skaði vá!*: 'Be thou not too lively outside (the grave), walking dead (*gengangere*)! May the evil-doer get misfortune!' This interpretation is, however, questionable since the term **misfylgir* is not attested elsewhere and it could be understood as a less precise designation for a maleficent entity from which a living person could have sought protection through the runic amulet. We are faced with a similar situation with the Högstena bronze amulet (see Jungner 1936: 278-304; Svärdström 1967: 12-21, 1100-1150), which is read by Svirdström as: A. **kal anda uiþr kankla uiþr riþąnda uiþ** B. **uiþr rinanda uiþr sxxianda uiþ** C. **r siknxxa uiþr fxrąnda uiþr fliuh** D. **ąnda sxx alt** fuxxna uk um duxa — OSwe. *Gal anda viðr gangla viðr, riðanda við(r), viðr rinnanda, viðr sitianda, viðr signanda, viðr faranda, viðr fliughanda. Skal alt fyrna ok um døia*: 'I chant against the spirit (of the dead), against the walking (-dead), against the riding ones, against the sitting ones, against the ones falling down, against the traveling ones, (and) against the flying ones. All shall decay and die away.' Again we must decide whether this formula is directed against a *draugr* (as a curse to hold him in the grave) or against all manner of malevolent sendings (see Sierke 1939: 95-96).

Besides the Högstena amulet, several other formulas mention non-human entities in operant attempts to manipulate them. Another use of the present participial forming a designation for such a being is found on the Hemdrup stave (see Moltke 1985: 350 *et passim*, 9th cent., N. Jutland), which reads: **uanþikiba · fiukati · asaauaubi** — ODan. *wan þik æta Fiuga(n)di, Asa!* (+ *ephesion grammaton*): 'The Rushing-one (a fever devil?) will never be able to destroy you, Ase. . .' The Canterbury charm (DR 419, M. p.33-34, 1050-1150), which is a unique example of a runic formula reproduced in a manuscript (MS Cotton Caligula A XV, 119v-120v), reads:

A. **kurilsarþuarafarþunufuntinistuþurigiþik**
B.**þursatrutiniurilsarþarauiþraþrauari**

ODan. *Gyril sårpværa, far þunú, fundin es-tu. Þorwígi þik þ[u]rsa dróttin! Gyril sårpværa. Wiþr aðraværi*: 'Gyril, causer of pain, fare now (forth), you have been found! Þórr consecrate you, lord of the thurses. Gyril, causer of pain. Against blood poisoning.' At least partially similar to the Canterbury charm is the Sigtuna copper amulet I (see Nordén 1943: 171-72; Moltke 1934: 436; Sierke 1939: 93-94, ca. 1100, Uppland, Swe.),(307) which may be read:

A. **þur + sarriþu + þursatrutinfliuþunufuntinis B.1. afþiRþriaRþrarulf + 2. afþiRniunöþiRulfriii 3. isiRþisisiRaukisuniRulfrniutlu A.2. fia** — OSwe. *þurs sarriþu, þursa dróttin, fly þu nú! Fundin es (þu)! (H)af þér þrear þrar, úlf! (H)af þér niú nöþer, úlfr!* ||| *isir þisisir auki es uner, úlfr! Niut lyfia*: 'Thurs of wound-fever, lord of the thurses! Flee (you) now! (You) are found! Receive you three sufferings, wolf! Receive you nine miseries (or bonds?), wolf! ||| the ice(-runes), these ice(-runes) may increase, so that you will be content, wolf! Make use of the amulet!' A copper amulet from Sundre (see Gustavson-Brink 1981: 186-91, 9th cent., Gotland) bears a simpler formula that can only be partially read as: A. **þunurburus** B. **xxxhatrnxx** — OSwe. *Þunur-þurus, . . . hatr n[im]!*: Þunur-þurus (a demonic name), take hate!'

A unique medium is provided by the skull plate of Ribe (see Moltke 1976: 120-21 *et passim*; Kabell 1978, 750-800, S. Jutland), which was certainly the result of a cranial trepanation. The arrangement of the inscription clearly indicates that the hole was bored before the runes were carved, which would seem to suggest either that: 1) the plate had already been used as an amulet without runes, or 2) the hole was bored as part of the original surgical operation. The reading by Kabell would favor the latter possibility. He reads: A. **ulfurAukuþinAukH** (= ⱨ) **utiuRHiAlbburisuiþR** B. **þAiM** (=ᛖ)**AuiArkiAuktuirkuniG**(=ᛪ)**hole] buur** — Odan. *UlfuR auk Óðinn auk HoddjōR! Hjálp borr es wiðR þeim á werki; auk dvergkunning bý or!*: 'Ulf and Odin and Hodd! The drill is help against the one at work; drive the dwarf-king(308) from his abode!'

As far as the use of epic or mythic material in younger inscriptions is concerned, two examples that have unambiguously operant motives are the Heddeby stave II and the Kvinneby copper amulet. Kvinneby (see Nilsson 1976: 236-45, 1050-1100, Öland, Swe.) bears a complex formula that contains imperative and performative elements, as well as an analogical formula in a mythic framework. Its runic text proper, which is preceded by five as yet undeciphered *galdrastafr*-like forms that appear to be bind-runes, is read by Nilsson as:

I. ᚼᛁᚦᛚᚴ**tiRþiRbirk** II. **bufimiRfultihu**
III. **risþeRuisinbral** IV. **tilufranbufaþorketih**
V. **ansmiRþemhamrisamhuR** VI. **hafikamflufraniluit**
VII. **feRekiafbufakuþiRu** VIII. **untiRhanumaukyfiRhan** IX. **um**

— OSwe. *Tir þeR ber-k, Bofi meR fullty! HvaR es þeR vissi? En ber alt ī illu fran Bofa. Þórr gœti hans meR þœim hamri sam uR hafi kam, flo fran illu. Vit ferr œigi of Bofa. Gud eRu undiR hanum ok yfiR hanum*: 'Glory to thee bear I, Bove. Help me! Who is wiser than thee? And bear all in (the form of) evil from Bove. May Þórr protect him with that hammer which came from the sea (and which) fled from evil. Wit fares not from Bove. The gods are under him and over him.' It is certain that this amulet has an apotropaic function, but one that appears directed toward the psychic rather than physical well-being of Bove. The protective power of Þórr's hammer is invoked in a prayer-like formula (with the subj. form of *gœta*: 'to guard, protect'), as well as the power of the gods in general, who are placed above and below Bove.(309)

The Heddeby stave represents an inept attempt to copy a model by a carver of little runic knowledge (see Kabell 1977: 67). Moltke (1976: 304-

05) will venture no comprehensive interpretation, but sees it as an example of a runic missive. Indeed, the first portion of the inscription would seem to relate a narrative about a sword fight between men named Úlfr or Oddulfr and Auðrikr or Aurikr. However, Kabell's reading of the runic sequence: **:kafiþu:at: ualR·ạkiu: likR:** which follows this narrative would tend to suggest that the stave itself had some magical-therapeutic function. He interprets this complex as *gefi þo-at vǫlR e(n)gju-ligR*: 'May the wand (ON *vǫlr*) give away (i.e., alleviate) the affliction (ON *engja*).' This reading is, however, highly conjectural.

There are also several examples of a rather disparate group of performative formulas. The most direct of these would be the Viborg clasp (DR 100b, 900-925, N. Jutland), which may be read: **lukisliua** — ODan. *lok æs læwa*, translated in DR as *'slut er (det) med ulykker(?).'*(310) This may have been a general amulet, or one intended to act against some specific affliction. A famous inscription is found on the Lund weaving temple (DR 311, 10th cent., Skåne), the runes of which may be read: **skuaraR:iki·mar:afa   mạn:mñ·krat·aallatti**   —   ODan. *S(i)gwaraR I(n)gimar afa man m(i)n grad + ephesion grammaton(?)*: 'Sigvor's Ingimar will get my sorrow.' Although this interpretation is hardly clear in all respects, it is generally supposed to mean that the carver is an unhappy suitor of Sigvor, a maid presently attached to Ingimar. By means of the inscription, the carver attempts to transfer his "love-sickness" to Ingimar — and thereby indirectly win Sigvor.(311) Amatory magic in the form of a curse was apparently not uncommon in this period (cf. Skm. 25ff.). Often thought to be similar in motive to the Lund inscription is the weaving comb of Trondheim I (*NIyR* no. 461, V, 26-29, N. Nor.). Its runes were rather conjecturally read by Bugge (1902) as:

unakmæyiu[ẹḳvịḷ]atreoælensfilæsthafþe —

ONorw. *un(n)ak mæyju ek vit-at rẹa Ællends fúlla víf ækkja ha(g)aoi*: 'I loved the maid. I do not want to torment the foul(312) Erlend's wife — as a widow she would be suitable (for me).'(313)

Two other remarkable but somewhat ambiguous inscriptions may be given as examples of this strictly performative group. The yew-stave of Schleswig (see Moltke 1985: 483-486, 1050-1100, S. Jutland), composed in almost perfect *ljóðaháttr*, may be read:

    A. **runaR·iak·risti·a·r(i)kiata·tresua**
    B. **reþ ·saR·riki·mogR·asiR· a·artakum**
    C. **hulaR·auk·bulaR·meli·þeR**
    D. **ars·sum·magi**

— ODan. *rūnaR iak risti* // *ā rīkjanda trē swā reþ saR rīki mǫgR* // *asiR ā ārdagum* // *hullaR ok bullaR* // *mæli þæR ars sum magi*: "Runes I carved on 'ruling'(?) wood, thus the mighty lord reads (them): (the) Æsir (i.e., the pagan gods) in days of yore, the 'hullers' and 'bullers'(?), (will) declare: for you, your ass is like your stomach."(314)

The complexes **r(i)kiata**, and **hulaR** and **bulaR** are problematic. If **r(i)kiata** is a present participle *rīkjanda* (cf. ON *rīkja*: 'to rule, reign'), it may refer to the operative power of the stave, while *HullaR* and *BullaR* may be *heiti* for the pagan gods. Although Moltke (1985: 386) would like to interpret this text as a sort of rude bar-room missive in runes; based on internal evidence, it seems more likely that the stave represents some *nīð*-like operative formula. From a magical-formulaic viewpoint it is interesting to note that the carver appears to place the operative curse-formula in the mouths of the gods — although the beginning of the text is an archaic rune-master formula. This provides a clear paradigm of the communicative theory of operative acts. Another remarkable formula is found on the Sigtuna copper amulet II (see Nordén 1943: 154-70, 11th cent., Uppland, Swe.), which Nordén reads: A.I. **ik·ak·uk·ris·dū iueg onþR tuṅglnum II. sifgeuinum III. oyr þät aṅge·äiþþät skin B.I. xek·þ·sig þrio x nauþR niu II. uiur nank(?)**(315) — OSwe. **ik.ak.uk:** *Ris du ī vägh under tung(o)nom sifgefnom! ör þat, ange! öþ þat skin! ek sigh þ(urs) þrio nauþer niu. viur nan'k: 'ik.ak.uk.* Raise yourself up and away under the benevolent stars those benevolent ones ! Madden this, mist! Annihilate this, light!(316) I call three thurs(-runes), and nine need(-runes)! In the capacity of a priest (*viur* < *vé-vǫrðr*), I perform the conjuration.' If this interpretation is anywhere near correct, Sigtuna II would be an example of an archaic performative formula of considerable complexity. Although Nordén wants to see this inscription as an anti-*dauðingaR* formula, the archeological record is inconclusive (cf. Nordén 1943: 154). From a formulaic viewpoint, Sigtuna II appears to be a combination of a pronounceable *ephesion grammaton* (**ik-ak-uk**), imperatives (A.I.-III.) and rune-master formulas (B).(317)

In contrast to this still vibrantly archaic, traditional form of runic formulas — there exists a whole medieval tradition of magical runic formulas that usually seem to be mere transpositions of ecclesiastical Mediterranean forms into runes. Explicit syntactical examples of this tradition are characterized by *prayer* (i.e., supplicative) formulas that entreat animistic entities to perform the will of the supplicant. These generally fall outside the historical and typological scope of this study; however, any survey of a number of them would show the essential difference between the traditional Germanic and Christian types. An example that perhaps also demonstrates characteristics of slightly more archaic formulas is the Odense lead plate amulet (DR 204, 13th-14th cent., Fyn), which can be read: A. + (u)nguensine: pr(i)nsin(e) sal:kotolon B. anakristi: anapisti (k)ardxxr:nardiar C. :ipodiar:kristus uinkit kristus reg D. net:kristus imperat·kristus abomni E. malome asam: lipert: kru*x* kristi F. sit: super me·asam·hik:et ubikueo G. tkhorda· + inkhorda tkhordai H. + agla + sanguis kristi signet me +. Lines A-B and the first seven runes of C, as well as line G, consist of forms obviously inspired by Greek formulas, which here serve as pronounceable *ephesia grammata*.(318) The rest of the inscription is in Latin, and may be translated: 'Christ is triumphant, Christ reigns, Christ bids, Christ free me, Aase, from all evil; the Cross of Christ be over me, Aase, here and everywhere. . . *agla* blood of Christ bless me.' This clearly demonstrates an apotropaic motive, and Moltke (1936: 120-21) goes even further when he says that "its purpose was to remove a sickness from a living person and transfer it to the dead one." Be that as it may, from a purely operative formulaic viewpoint there are certain similarities with lines G.I of the Kvinneby amulet, as well as with an even later apotropaic formula found in the *Galdrabók* (see n. 21).

Notes for Chapter VI

1. Although in runology that which is not easily understood has often been ascribed to "magic," many problematic runic sequences do seem to be intentional formulas, most probably of emotive-instrumental function (see ch.VII.4).

2. A rune-*master* is one who can conceive and execute an inscription, while a rune-*carver* may only be able to execute it. Sierke (1939: 107-09) provides a convenient survey of these formulas, which is generally followed here.

3. See also ch. IV. Some questions surrounding the rune-master inscriptions have been recently explored by Dillmann (1981).

4. With regard to the possible illiteracy or lack of knowledge on the part of the rune-carver, cf. Moltke (1976: 71), Thompson (1975: 77), and Musset (1965: 223).

5. Cf. Thompson (1975), Jansson (1969: 486-505), and Brate (1925).

6. This especially in NGmc. territory, cf. Krause (1966 *passim*), but in South Germanic areas this is far less certain, cf. Arntz (1939).

7. Cf. Dillmann (1981: 30), and on the possibility of divine names, cf. Müller in: Düwel-Müller-Hauck (1975: 159ff.).

8. Cf. Hauck (1972). This is most probably due to a procedure whereby the bracteate-master (or "amulet-master") actually copied the runic text from a model provided in wood, etc., by a rune-master.

9. Cf. Andersen (1961: 107ff.), Sierke (1939: 107ff.) for comprehensive classifications.

10. See sect. 31 on functional names and bynames of the rune-masters.

11. For an analysis of these types of runo-technical verbs and objects, see Ebel (1963).

12. See VII.2-3, for a discussion of the use of the singular *rūnō* in the epigraphical corpus.

13. Cf. the reading of Järsberg by Moltke (1981b: 86), which would throw doubt on the syntax of this formula as read by Olsen (*NIæR*: III, 223-24) and Krause (1966: 156-58) and place it within expanded type IV. See note 42 below.

14. The runological problems with this inscription are contained in its final runes. Liestøl (1965: 157) refers to it as *uforstålege slutten*. Antonsen's (1975a: 58-59) reading is unreliable, cf. Høst (1977b: 154).

15. The reading of r. 1-14 had already been established by Bugge I, 125-27) and Krause (1966: 269-70); however, rather arbitrarily, Antonsen (1975a: 62) adopts the older reading of Henning (1889: 130) of r. 13 as g and does not interpret the resulting sequence **uæurgz** (as read by him).

16. See sect. 37 for a more detailed analysis of the religious-historical significance of the term *laukaR*.

17. PGmc. **felhan* < PIE **pel-* 'to cover,' carries the basic meaning of concealment. Cf. also the *Óðinsheiti*: *Fjǫlnir*: 'the concealer' (see V.5, note 40), and de Vries (1961a: 125). (See also V.13.)

18. The runic sequence **runono** may reflect a collapse of *rūnō-rōnu*: 'a sequence of runes' (as in the Björketorp version), or an error for the gen. pl. of *rūnōR-rūnō*, cf. Krause (1971: 165); Antonsen (1975a: 86).

—211—

19. On the relative dating of Stentoften and Björketorp, cf. Krause (1966: 217).
20. Cf. Krause (1971: 140-41).
21. On the etymology of *gin(n)-, see V.2.
22. *Wurkjan more often appears in third-person formulas with the medium upon which the runes are executed as the grammatical object, cf. Ebel (1963: 53-55).
23. Linguistically, the most logical completion of the line seems to be r(ūnōR) (cf. Stephens 1866: I, 249), however, Antonsen (1975: 44-45) ignores the rune and supplies the sense "inscription."
24. Marstrander's (1929a: 124) etymology which connects *taujan to the word-formula auja, with the meaning 'to fill with luck,' is not convincing. The word itself seems to be a nonspecialized term for 'to do,' or 'to prepare,' cf. Go. taujan: 'to do,' OE togean: 'to make,' OHG zouwen: 'to prepare,' ON týja: 'to do, work,' cf. de Vries (1961a: 583-84), Cleasby-Vigfusson (1957: 647).
25. For a comprehensive bibliography on the Gallehus inscription, cf. Jacobsen-Moltke (1942: 24-28; 587), Andersen (1961: 89ff.), and Krause (1966: 97-103). A more recent and controversial study is forwarded by Klingenberg (1973), which is critically reviewed by Düwel (1979).
26. On the verse form of the Gallehus formula, see Lehmann (1956: 28ff.).
27. Antonsen (1975a: 52-53) proposes a radically different reading in which he sees an R-rune following the m-rune in line II (where Krause [1966: 171] recognizes only bedeutungslose Schrammen). The resulting form unnamR is interpreted as a masc. nom. sg. adj.: 'the untakable' (i.e., 'the unconquerable'), in agreement with WakraR. The following wraita is understood as a first-pers. sg. pret., and therefore Antonsen would translate the rune-master formula: 'I, Wakr, the untakable, wrote (this).' But this is an atypical byname (see sect. 31), and is therefore somewhat doubtful.
28. For a discussion of the relationship between magical and legal terminology and formulas, see VII.5.
29. IK 331 Selvik-A reads (R-L) tau. This may be interpreted as a scrambling of the formula-word alu with an erroneous t for l, see 34, and cf. Krause (1966: 240, note 2) and Bugge I, 267-68). However, this may also represent a unique, purely verbal, rune-master formula: first-pers. sg. pres. tau (< *tauju): 'I make, do' (cf. Krause 1971: 74; 122 and Olsen NIæR: III, 241).
30. Cf. Krause (1966: 169) and Antonsen (1975a: 44), who interpret the name as defender of the stone [monuments? fortifications?] .
31. Antonsen's (1975: 78) reading of r. 3 as u may not be supported, nor his interpretation of fahi as an adjective: 'suitable' (See sect. 7).
32. Krause (1971: 63; 87; 120) explains the i as either: 1) a runographic error, 2) WGmc. influence, or 3) development from an originally unstressed position in the sentence.
33. Cf. Antonsen (1975a: 78).
34. Cf. Förstemann (1900: 493).
35. On the etymology of goði, see note 39 below, and on the various derivations of jarl, see note 123.
36. Antonsen (1975a: 51; 58; 110) wants to read all these forms as erilaR, however, his readings have not found general support (cf. e.g., Høst 1977).
37. Cf. also Antonsen (1975a: 52) and Krause (1966: 119). The speculations by Olsen (1929: 31ff.) that baij(a)R represents a personal or ethnic name, and that by Marstrander

(1951: 20) that these six runes (which he reads **baijaR**) should be understood as *magiske runer* (i.e., an *ephesion grammaton*) must be doubted.

38. Cf. Krause (1966: 124), Antonsen (1975a: 46) and de Vries (1944: 98ff. and 1961a: 214). The meaning 'errant warrior' is suggested by the socio-economic position of a son with little inherited property. He could be expected to seek his fortune in the service of a foreign lord.

39. According to Krause (1971: 94), the form **gudija** may represent a special runographical tradition in which the *-ij-* combination is used after short syllables, where we would expect the simple *-j-* spelling, cf. Go. *gudja*: 'priest,' ON *goði*: '(heathen) priest' < PGmc. **gud-jōn* < *PIE *ghut-yōn*: 'the one who deals with the god(s).' On the other hand, Antonsen (1975a: 47) sees *gudija* as an agent suffixed form < PGmc. **gudijōn*: 'one who pours out libations or calls (to the god[s]).' This latter etymology is not completely satisfactory on phonological grounds. The PIE root **ghu-tō-* may either indicate 'the invoked one' or 'the one to which libations are poured' > PGmc. **gud-am*: 'god,' cf. Go. *guþ*, ON *goð* OE/OS *god*, OHG *got*, cf. Antonsen (1975: 47), de Vries (1961a: 181; 1961b: 214ff.).

40. Marstrander's reading (1951: 19-20), also taken up by Antonsen (1975a: 58), of the final sign as an **n**-rune seems unlikely. Such a reading would make *Wīwilan* a masc. gen. sg. and the inscription would have to be translated: 'I, the rune-master of Wiwila.'

41. *Wag-* is the pret.-stem of PGmc. **wigan*: 'to go, move,' with the adj. suffix (see sect. 31.). *Wag-* is a common theme in Gmc. PNs, cf. OHG *Wago*, OE *Waga*. Cf. also KJ 76: Opedal st.: *Wagē* masc. dat. sg. (< **WagaR*): 'the one who moves forth.'

42. Moltke (1981b: 86), based on spatial typology, reads the formula: **ekerilaR ubaRh(a)ite:hárabanaR háit(e) runoR waritu** — *'Jeg erilen kaldes den stridbare (egentlig den, der rejser sig mod noget fjendtligt), men jeg hedder Ravn, jeg skriver runer.'*

43. Cf. Háv. 142 and see V.15.

44. This, together with a massive amount of Nor. medieval inscriptions, was found inside a stave-church, cf. Olsen *NIyR*, *passim*.

45. Cf. Feist (1922).

46. In this inscription, r. 9 is understood as a multi-pointed word divider by Bæksted (1947: 204), Marstrander (1952: 83-85), and by Moltke (most recently 1985: 88) — which would cause it to be read *HagiradaR : tawide : 'HagiradaR made (the box).'* However, Krause's comparisons of photographs made before and after conservation of the piece lead him to the conclusion that the sign was indeed an **i**-rune (cf. Krause 1961: 262-66, Düwel 1968: 17-18).

47. Arntz (1939: 224-25) forwards two etymologies for Bōso: 1) < **bosa-*: 'ineptas; nugas,' cf. OCS *basnb* : 'incantation,' and therefore 'conjurer, one who knows magical formulas' (cf. Henning 1889: 82-83), and 2) PIE **bis-/bas-*: 'light,' and thus a more regular PN. Arntz favors the latter, although the derivation from PIE seems gratuitous.

48. Here the three staves are understood as representations of the ideographic content of their name, PGmc. **fehu*: 'livestock, mobile property,' cf. the OE Rune Poem: *feoh*: 'wealth;' and the Norwegian and Icelandic Rune Poems — *fé*: 'wealth, gold,' cf. Flowers (2002).

49. Cf. also Jacobsen-Moltke (1942: 405-407), Marstrander (1952: 153-55), and I. Lindqvist (1923: 65-76).

50. Cf. Ebel (1963: 68-69).

51. Cf. Müller in: Düwel-Müller-Hauck (1975: 159-163) on the problem of PNs on bracteates.

52. Antonsen (1975: 79) only interprets a fem. acc. sg. a-stem *laþō*: 'summons.'

53. Noreen (1923: 375-76) interprets *aRina* as 'elevation,' referring to the grave mound itself. Also, cf. Klingenberg (1973: 179-82) for an alternate interpretation of the original function of the slab as a hearth-stone used in the process of brewing cultic drinks.

54. Cf. Brate (1925) for lists of Swedish rune-carvers (also studies by Thompson 1972; 1975). On Danish material, cf. Jacobsen-Moltke (1942: 645), and for Norwegian material Olsen (*NIyR*: II, 623ff.). Cf. also Jansson (1969: 496-503).

55. This is the form used on the Eggjum st. (KJ 101), see 50.

56. The odd gap between **runaR** and **stain** conceivably could have been filled with another PN which was only stained and not carved into the stone, see Jansson 1963: 154).

57. Some of these PN forms could in fact be otherwise unknown divine names, cf. Müller in: Düwel-Müller-Hauck (1975: 159-63).

58. Here we will not take into account the Anglo-Frisian runic coins (cf. Page 1999: 117-29) due to their obviously non-magical character.

59. Cf. Düwel-Gebühr (1981).

60. This classification would be suggested by a reading given by Krause (1966: 34), however, Marstrander's interpretation (1951: 48; 57; 1952: 79ff.) *alu God(agaR)*, with an ideographic reading of the **d**-rune, would place it in the second type (see 28.).

61. This reading according to Krause (1961: 255-62): *waraflusa*: 'the one who protects (himself) against idle speech, or gossip,' but also cf. Marstrander (1952: 85-98): **sinwaraw**— *Sinwara w(unju)*: 'Sinwara ('always alert'), and Moltke (1963:38): **warafnisa**— *warafnisa*: 'he who protects himself from silly laughter.'

62. Düwel (1972: 134-41) suggests this is a PN (with early disappearance of the strong nominal flexion in WGmc., pp. 139-40), but also sees it as most probably the name of the owner of the brooch (p. 140). However, the question of who actually carved the name is not clear.

63. Cf. Düwel-Roth (1977: 409-413) for various interpretations of this inscription (pp. 411-12). On the basis of both archeological and runological criteria Düwel and Roth determine that Donzdorf is a Jutlandic piece with a maker's formula (which is SGmc.) inscribed in Jutland and later imported into Alemannic territory.

64. This inscription is almost impossible to interpret. Wimmer (1894: 78-80) read it as a double name *Berl(i)nio Erling*, for other interpretations, cf. Arntz (1939: 305-307) and Krause (1966: 294-95).

65. Brooch II was found together with a matched brooch I (see 32.), however, there is no indication that one inscription belongs to the other.

66. These three readings are suggested by Moltke (1976: 77-78; 81-82), while Krause (1966: 89) forwards the possibility that it is a word-formula *witring*: '*Kundgabe* → inscription' (sect. 42).

67. *Alukō* would seem to contain the root *alu*, and could be interpreted as a familiar personification of the concept. However, the name is known in more mundane contexts in the masc. OHG form *Aluco* (9th cent.) and in the OE form *Aluca* (also 9th cent.), cf. Krause (1966: 109-10), Förstemann (1900: 87), and Kaufmann (1968: 31; 432-33).

68. On the reading of the inscription, cf. Ilkjær-Lønstrup (1981: 49-56), Düwel (1981a: 138ff.; 1981b: 81; 1983: 125).

69. *Sabar* is possibly a nom. masc. adj. form < PIE **sap*-: 'to taste, perceive,' or an abbreviated form of a compound name, the second element of which begins with **r**-: e.g., *Saba-r(ich)*, cf. Förstemann (1900: 1285ff., 1287).

70. The stone is now lost and we are dependent upon drawings. For this reason, the first rune may be read **w**, however *þaliR* seems more probable, cf. Bugge I, 363-66) and Krause (1966: 201-02).

71. Although this stone was found with the inscription face down on a grave mound, there is the possibility that it was moved from another mound and placed in that position. The size and shape of the stone (1.07 m [rune-side x 70 cm x 60 cm) would possibly indicate that it was originally a barrow-st. (cf. Bugge (*NIæR*: I, 431-35) and Krause (1966: 202-03).

72. This was originally a large stone (3.04 m x 1.2 m x 0.35 m) which was found lying face down most probably on or near its original location in a vicinity where no grave of any kind was found (cf. Olsen *NIæR*: II, 711-13). Krause interprets this as a memorial stone — although it could have also been a sacral stone (as Järsberg, Björketorp, et al.).

73. The stone was originally located in an upright position in the middle of a circle (ca. 4.50 m in diameter) of tightly placed stones. It must have stood about 2 m. high. In the eastern quarter of the circle a layer of ash was found which may have been a cremation burial, but it may have served other purposes (cf. Bugge *NIæR*: I, 449-51).

74. The stones of Tørvika A and B were found as a part of a stone grave chamber, which had been plundered. Tørvika A has obviously been cut down from a larger stone (the final **R**-rune is split off). This has led to speculation that it was originally part of another mound — perhaps an upright *bauta*-st., cf. Bugge (*NIæR*: I, 278-83), and Krause (1966: 199-200).

75. It appears that the Tanem st. was originally buried inside the smaller of two closely connected mounds, however, the archeological reports are confused (cf. Bugge *NIæR*: I, 367-69). The mound was probably that of a woman, and the name on the stone is also fem. *Mārilingu*: 'descendant of *Mārila* (Krause 1966: 197; Antonsen 1975: 69). This would therefore seem to be an example of the name of the dead carved into a stone then placed inside the grave (cf. KJ 81 and 83).

76. If the Værløse brooch (KJ 11) is read as *alu God(agaR)*ᛟ, then it too would belong to this class, but it seems more likely that it belongs grouped with the type PN + ideographic sign.

77. Cf. also Opitz (1977: 165ff.) for other interpretations.

78. A similar runic cross is found on the sword of Schretzheim (Op. 40), cf. Kingenberg-Koch (1974). On Soest it may be interpreted as an encoded kind of magical meaning.

79. At least five other SGmc. inscriptions present virtual lists of PNs, both masc. and fem., for which various formulas are reconstructed, cf. the Weimar finds (Op. 49, 50, 51) and the Schretzheim locket (Op. 38).

80. Cf. Düwel (1981b: 79; 1982) would read what has generally been interpreted as a divine triad as a syntactic formula in which *logaþore* is understood as a masc. nom. pl.: 'schemers.' He reads the three-word complex: 'schemers they are, namely Wodan and Wigithonar.'

81. *Danilo* may be either a private masc. PN, or according to Opitz (1977: 112ff.) it may be a reflection of Daniel in Christian mythology — and thus be classified as a second 'divine' or mythic name, cf. also Op. 22 Hailfingen.

82. It appears possible that the forms **unja** and **segun** were added by a later carver.

83. This could be an obscure and somewhat doubtful *ek*-formula, which could further corroborate a fem. rune-master tradition.

84. See Düwel (1981a: 136-37) for a review of the various interpretations of this difficult runic sequence.

85. Vocative forms of masc. PNs can also be found on IK 161: Skodborg-B.

86. Work by Düwel (1976; 1981b: 77-78) has shown that this inscription was actually cut shortly before its burial, which strongly suggests that the inscription had some function connected with the funeral ritual.

87. Krause (1966: 295-96) suggests a possible reconstruction of *l(au)k*: 'leek' for the questionable first two characters. He also admits the possibility of an *ik*-construction. Similarly, Opitz (1977: 25-26) only reads a k before the PN and suggests an *ik*-formula.

88. The complex **marŋ sd** may be interpreted as SGmc. *Maring* + **sd** = *s(egun) d(eda)*: 'Maring made the blessing,' or as EGmc. *Marings* + **d**. The peculiar formation of the final **d**-rune ᛞ makes it possible that we are dealing with an otherwise unknown ideograph. A similar formula may be present in KJ 166 Bezenye and KJ 157 Schretzheim locket, cf. Krause (1934: 1-4), Arntz (1939: 357-59), and Opitz (1977: 42-43; 101-111), who sees the final sign as part of a 'Dag-motif.'

89. It is certain that the initial sign can not be read as a graphemic rune because similar signs occur elsewhere on the piece in an apparently ideographic or ornamental role, however, its position in the ductus of the runes suggests parallels with KJ 11: Værløse, KJ 85 Skåäng (cf. Düwel 1981a: 157-58).

90. Due to the poor legibility of many of its runes, the Steindorf sax inscription has been read a number of ways. Krause (1937: 232-33) chooses not to interpret the signs before or after *Husibald*, while Arntz on two occasions reads significance into them (1936: 132; 1939: 353-55). In the latter contribution, Arntz read the *w(īhu) Husibald l(a)ba*: 'I, Husibald consecrate (the sax) with an invocation.'

91. Cf. Grienberger (1900: 289-91) for the reading of line 2. Also, cf. Marstrander (1929c: 222ff.) for a reading of 2b., and further Krause (1937: 178-80), Jacobsen-Moltke (1942: 19-21), Marstrander (1952: 10-17) and Krause (1966: 53-55). The initial two runes in line a. may be read as a metathesis of *owlþu-* for *wolþu-* (cf. Marstrander 1952: 11-12).

92. Cf. also Noreen (1923: 393) and Marstrander (1952: 37- 44).

93. See Düwel (1970a: 284-87) on the linguistic anomalies of this inscription. He favors a NGmc. reading in which *FōRō* is a fem. nom. PN and the diminutive nom. masc. *glōla* < *glow-ula: 'the little glowing one' is a designation of the rune-master, cf. *Glī-augiR* on IK 128: Nebenstedt-B.

94. Cf. Salberger (1959: 18ff.) on the reading of r. 32 as *j(ĕra)*. Bæksted (1943: 21ff.) on the other hand reads the rune as an error for another *auja*, which seems less likely. On the meaning of *auja*, see 36, and cf. IK 98 Sjælland II-C with its formula *gibu auja*. (See sect. 50) For a possible parallel for the voc. forms, cf. KJ 11 Værlrøse — *Alugod*-(?).

95. *Ho(ua)R* has been reconstructed based on analogy with **houaR** — *HouaR* on IK 58: Fyn I-C, but the fact that this inscription consists entirely of ambiguous forms makes its inclusion here tenuous.

96. Stephens (1866: I, 176): 'At some little distance north-west are several burial mounds and *bauta*-stones...together with a stone-setting.'

97. Skåäng also bears an 11th cent. inscription (cf. Brate S. 32), and could have been moved from the location it originally had in the 5th cent., so archeological data concerning its older situation are impossible to determine. The two signs after the names are perhaps personal marks of identification (cf. Krause 1966: 192).

98. KJ 100: Krogsta st. may also belong to this category if one interprets the sequence s[t]ainaR as a nom. masc. PN — which seems possible (cf. OSwe. *Stæinn*, Brate 1925: 117 and Salberger 1978: 134-39).

99. Himmelstalund can only be included here on tenuous grounds. It does seem that the runes (or rune-like signs) were intentionally inscribed into the ductus of the boat- or sled-like pictograph, however, because the two complexes were not originally juxtaposed and because the reading of the runic sequence itself is so doubtful, this must remain conjectural.

100. KJ 99: Möjbro might also be included here. Although most interpret the PN *FrawaradaR* in the first line of the inscription as a reference to the memorialized dead, the interpretations of the second line are conjectural enough that some doubt may remain as to this reading.

101. An interesting alternate interpretation would be: "Higwig (lies) here. Here is the 'magic' of Ungwin." This seems grammatically plausible, however, the spatial arrangement of the lines (A and B grouped with C some distance below) speaks against it, as do the numerous stones with only the gen. form of a PN which have been interpreted as 'PN's (grave).' Also, cf. Antonsen (1975a: 34-35 and the review by Høst 1977: 151-52).

102. Cf. Bugge (*NIæR*: I, 228).

103. Cf. v. Friesen (1924a: 124-26) and Krause (1966: 176-77).

104. Cf. Olsen (*NIæR*: III, 164-69), Krause (1966: 235-36), but cf. also Marstrander (1952: 168-80).

105. The South Germanic inscriptions will not be systematically discussed here because for the most part they do not seem to contain functional rune-master onomastic material (cf. Krause 1966: 277-311, Arntz 1939 and Opitz 1977).

106. If elements are so ambiguous or illegible that it may not be determined if we are dealing with a PN or appellative (e.g., KJ 11, 13, 14, 35, 39, 45, 52, 54, 60, 93, 100) they will be left out of consideration.

107. On *Glï-augiR* and *glōla* (see note 93), cf. Düwel (in: Hauck 1970: 284ff.), Krause (1966: 269-70).

108. Actually **hakuþo** but reconstructed from the nearby (KJ 66) Vånga st. (see under II below).

109. Reconstructed from the apparently masc. dat. sg. *Wagē*. Possibly an otherwise unattested common PN.

110. Cf. Krause (1966: 264).

111. These forms could be attestations of the loss of medial *-*h*- in NGmc., with a *nomen agentis* *-*wō*-suffix, which is well attested in EGmc., cf. Go. *wil-wa*: 'robber,' *bid-ag-wa*: 'beggar' (Krause 1968: 163; 1971: 66-67). The a-stem declension of the form *WīwaR* remains problematic. It perhaps represents a secondary, artificial construction, or it could etymologically belong to the Gmc. stem *wī-*: 'to hunt,' cf. OHG *wīo* and ODutch *wīwōn*: 'the hunter → kite hawk' (cf. Kluge-Mitzka 1957: 849). If this latter possibility is

—217—

correct, **WīwaR** and **Wīwila** would mean 'the kite hawk' and 'the little kite hawk' respectively, which are not typologically unexpected functional rune-master names, cf. KJ 66 and 67.

112. The whole *wīh- complex seems fundamental to the runic lexicon. It may appear in appellatives, e.g., the possible agent form *wīh-wō-(?) (> **WīwaR**?) and as a verb *wīhjan (> first-pers. sg. wīju: 'I consecrate'), cf. KJ 27.

113. This term probably indicates that the rune-master was a foreigner in a *gastiR* relationship with a local chieftain, which would fit with the supposed wandering of the *erilaR*/rune-masters (see IV).

114. Perhaps as a PN on KJ 75: Kjølevik st., see note 38.

115. Perhaps also a PN.

116. The form *þirbijaR* is difficult (see sect. 13, and VII.2), but it is most attractive to derive it from a root *þirb-: 'un-leavened,' cf. OE *ðeorf* and OHG *derp*: 'unleavened.' Therefore the original meaning of the agent-suffixed form could have been 'the one who makes as unleavened bread, lifeless, weak,' cf. Marstrander (1938: 361), but cf. also Antonsen (1975a: 48).

117. This type of name is what we might expect in an Odinic context, cf. *Óðinsheiti* such as *Bǫlverkr*: 'worker of evil,' and the use of the adj. *illúðigr*: 'evil-boding' to describe Óðinn, cf. Falk (1924, *passim*), and Turville-Petre (1964: 50ff.).

118. *UngandiR* < *un-gand-iz*: 'unaffected by *gand*-.' (See V.3. on the ambiguous nature of *gandr*, and see VI.2.)

119. *UnwōdiR* < *un-wōðiz*: 'unaffected by *wōð*- (= magical rage, fury)'. This is analogous to the ON PN *Úmóðr* (cf. OHG *Unmuot*) which may go back to a similar concept, cf. Flowers (1983) on the relationship between *mōð*- and *wōð*-. Also, cf. Marstrander (1952: 112) on the whole complex of names in *un-* in Gmc.

120. On *wagigaR*, see note 41 above.

121. The form *wīl-ag-aR* is an adj. with *-ag- suffix (cf. *wag-ig-aR*). On the root *wīl- ~ wēl-, cf. ON *vél*: 'artifice, craft, trick,' and the *Óðinsheiti*: *Vílir*: 'the crafty.'

122. The development of *e → i* is a regular one (cf. Krause 1971: 63) so the form *irilaR* is hardly unexpected. However, the form in *i*- is in fact rather limited — found only in Norway during the 5th-6th cents. The older form in *e*- was either conserved or archaized (probably because of its special socio-cultic function).

123. The relationship between ON *jarl*, OE *eorl*; the runic forms **erilaR** ~ **irilaR**; and the ethnic name (*H*)*eruli* (reported in Classical sources) is difficult to determine. Cf. a review of early scholarship by Jacobsen-Moltke (1942: 646), and an exhaustive treatment by Elgqvist (1952). It is possible that *(h)e-* in *(H)erulus* would be a regular representation of Gmc. *erilaz* as represented by Latin speakers (cf. v. Friesen 1924a), or an *ablaut* form (Noreen 1903: 398), but the *-i-* remains an unresolved problem in the relationship between ON *jarl* and PGmc. *erilaz*. It seems most likely that they are derived from the same etymon PIE *er-*: 'to set in motion, to rise up,' cf. de Vries (1961a: 290; 295) and Antonsen (1975a: 36).

124. This word is ultimately derived from PGmc. *ghu-tō-, see note 39 above. De Vries (1961b: 214) also connects this word to Old Gaulish *gutuater*: 'priest' (i.e., 'father of the voice').

125. Cf. KJ 20 where *-þewaR* may have some religious significance based on an analogical relationship between the follower of a god and the retainer of a lord.

126. *Hag-* is relatively rare as an appellative theme in NGmc. (Krause 1966: 73), cf. e.g., the name of the tutelary dwarf *Hagall* in HHII (but in SGmc. cf, Förstemann 1900: 716ff.).

127. Perhaps an otherwise lost masc. form of the well-attested fem. **hild-* (ON *-hildr*, etc.), cf. Krause (1966: 273).

128. This if the "stone" had some kind of religious significance (e.g., a stone-arrangement type temple, or if it refers to the stone itself), cf. also KJ 13a and 91 for the theme **-warijaz*.

129. Otherwise well attested as a PN theme, cf. Krause (1966: 171) and Förstemann (1900: 1487ff.).

130. The reading of this whole inscription is conjectural.

131. A number of apparent PNs in such contexts may refer to numinous beings of unknown historical position, e.g., *Alukō* (KJ 49) fem. PN with the suffix *-ō* indicating a personified endearment added to the root *alu-*, *Tanulu* (IK 26) fem. PN [< **tanjan*: 'to stir up, incite'?], *Frohila* (IK 42): 'the little lord,' and *HouaR* (IK 58 and 300): 'the high one (?),' cf. the ON *Óðinsheiti* : *Hárr*.

132. This is runologically conjectural, with the runic complex in question reading **asugsdiR**.

133. Cf. Düwel (in: Hauck 1970: 284ff.), cf. also *Glï-augiR* under I above.

134. Alternatively, *LeugaR* may be connected to PIE **leugh-* 'ceremonially binding,' cf. Krause (1966: 192), but in either case it could represent a sort of priestly function.

135. Cf. Krause (1966: 240; 255).

136. Cf. Düwel (1972) who sees this name as possibly understandable in light of the Víkarr episode in *Gautreks s*. ch. 7.

137. The PGmc. root **waig-* is sometimes found as a second component in compound names, cf. ON *Gullveig* (Vsp. 21ff.), but rarely alone, cf. Bavarian *Weiko* (Förstemann 1900: 1496; Kaufmann 1968: 377-78). Here it should probably be connected to ON *veig*: 'a strong intoxicating drink; strength' (cf. Turville-Petre 1964: 158-59; Krause 1966: 274-75; de Vries 1961a: 651).

138. The name is not otherwise attested in NGmc., and since it was found connected to a woman's grave (Krause 1966: 198), it could not be a memorial. The compound is, however, found in SGmc., cf. Förstemann (1900: 1568).

139. See section 29 and note 91 above.

140. Runologically questionable, see section 34 below, and note 76.

141. The common second PN theme *-warijaR* (cf. Förstemann 1900: 1532) is attested three times in the corpus (KJ 13a, 73, and 91).

142. A common Gmc. PN theme (PGmc. **leuƀa-*: 'dear, beloved,' cf. Kaufmann (1968: 229-31).

143. Cf. Arntz (1938; 1939: 468-69, *et passim*).

144. KJ 156 St. Schretzheim fibula is interpreted by Opitz (1977: 80-81) as a possible dedication to Wodan in the form of the *viator indefessus* (masc. dat. sg. *si(n)þwagadin*), while KJ 149 Weimar amber bead contains PNs in the context of the substantives *þiuþ*: 'friendliness' and **leobida* (see Opitz 1977: 90-91).

145. For general discussions of these word-formulas, cf. Jacobsen-Moltke (1942: 1046) and Krause (1966: 239ff.).

146. For a recent review of scholarship concerning this complex, see Høst (1980), cf. also Jacobsen-Moltke (1942: 629-30).

147. Earlier views that **alu** was a "magical formula" (= *ephesion grammaton*), cf. e.g., Marstrander (1929a: 78; 87; 1952: 82-83), have been abandoned and general identity with ON *ǫl*, OE *ealu*, etc., largely accepted, cf. Krause (1932: 69ff.; 1966: 239), Polomé (1954; 1996), and Høst (1980).

148. This has recently been objected to by Neu (1974: 77ff., and note 138) on the grounds that the Hitt. form is not clearly attested in the texts.

149. Cf. the semantic parallels with Gmc. *wīh-* (see V.2).

150. Cf. Bugge (*NIæR* I, 159-67), Krause (1966: 129-30) and Bæksted (1951: 77).

151. Cf. Wimmer (1887: 57, and note 5), Marstrander (1929a: 137; 1952: 19), Krause (1966: 50-52).

152. See sect. 50 below. For general bibliography, cf. Olsen (*NIæR*: III, 77ff.), Jacobsen (1931), Krause (1966: 227-35).

153. It seems most likely that the stone was originally part of a grave chamber, see Krause (1966: 227ff.) and Düwel (1979a) but cf. also the less likely solution offered by Meissner (1934) which would make the stone part of a sacrificial ritual site. Cf. also Reier (1952).

154. Cf. Jungner (1924: 232ff.). But Polomé (1954: 49ff.) sees the possibility of reading *sīR aluh*: 'be thou protection,' with the preservation of an *-h-* suffix, cf. Go. *alhs*, OE *ealh*.

155. Cf. Krause (1966: 130-32).

156. This reading is favored by both Krause (1966: 34) and Marstrander (1952: 79-83). But Krause also mentions the possibility of a voc. PN *Alugod!* (with **alu-* theme), cf. also KJ 49: *Alukō* (fem. PN?), and Marstrander also suggests a less likely *alu g(ibu) o(þala) d(agaR)*: '**g**, **o**, and **d** are protection.'

157. As read by Krause (1966: 132-36), cf. also Marstrander (1952: 226-32).

158. Cf. the reconstructions suggested by Krause (1966).

159. In IK 58 and 300 it appears that the bracteate-master was unable to distinguish between ᚺ **u** and ᚨ ~ ᚠ ~ ᚢ **l**. On the masc. PN *HōuaR*, see sect. 30 above.

160. The reading of the whole complex is highly conjectural, see the sections on *laukaR-līna* and *oþalaR* below.

161. Cf. Jacobsen-Moltke (1942: bracteate no. 17).

162. From a preliminary reading provided by R. I. Page and corroborated by photographic evidence. The probable date of the inscription (450-550) would make transcription (a) more likely, cf. West (1983).

163. Cf. Jacobsen-Moltke (1942: 634), de Vries (1961a: 19), Krause (1966: 241).

164. For the general reading, see Krause (1966: 252) and Jacobsen-Moltke (1942: bracteate no. 61), where they translate: '*Jeg Hariuha kaldes den ulykkesvise* (or — *Jeg kaldes Hariuha den ulykkesvise), jeg giver lykke.*' For the rune-master formula, see section 15b.

165. This reading given by Krause (1966: 241-42), but cf. also Antonsen (1975a: 76-75): 'Luck, Alawin. . .,' etc., and Jacobsen-Moltke (1942: bracteate no. 8): '(*Lykke for*?) Alvin. . .' etc.

166. But cf. Olsen (*NIæR*: II, 650ff., and 668, note 3), who thinks of it as a bearer of the purifying and protective powers of water.

167. On the general importance of this word-formula, see Krause (1934: 5-17; 1946/47: 60-63), Jacobsen-Moltke (1942: 681), and W. Lehmann (1955).

168. The final ᚨ form is thought by Krause (1966: 86) to have been added later, while at one time Olsen (*NIæR*: II, 650-52) read it as an abbreviation of *alu* — which seems unlikely since if it were a logograph it would more regularly represent the rune name **a(n)suR*.

169. On the combination of *līna* and *laukaR*, cf. Schnippel (1929: 65-68), Sierke (1939: 97), W. Lehmann (1955), Krause (1966: 85), Düwel (1971: 204ff.), and Steinsland-Vogt (1981). (See also *līna* below.)

170. Cf. Krause (1966: 250).

171. Mentioned by Krause (1934: 6).

172. Krause (1946/47), based on evidence from *runica manuscripta*, speculated that the original name (or an alternate) of the l-rune was in fact **laukaz*: 'leek' as opposed to the more usually reconstructed **laguz*: 'water.' If this is to any degree true, the logographic readings of ᛚ become more plausible.

173. On a possible parallel to *Arwi*, cf. Schönfeld (1911: 31) *Arva-*.

174. Reading first given by Grienberger (1906: 138ff.).

175. Krause (1966: 258) seems to favor this possibility for the Faxe bracteate, cf. Grienberger (1908: 382ff.).

176. For variant interpretations which also connect the complex to **ehwaR*: 'horse,' cf. Marstrander (1929a: 77), and who sees it as a voc. form, Schlottig (1938: 74-77), who posits a dual form.

177. Cf. Krause (1932: 65-68).

178. On the importance of the horse in Germanic shamanism, cf. Eliade (1964: 380, *et passim*), and Ellis Davidson (1973: 38).

179. On the connection of the horse to fertility cults, cf. Ström (1954: 22ff.), Düwel (1971: 145ff.).

180. Cf. the conjectural decipherment of the tree-like sign at the end of the Kylver fuþark by Klingenberg (1973: 279) ewe or ewe: 'to the horse' or 'to the yew(?).'

181. For studies of the word, cf. Grienberger (1908: 400ff.), Olsen (1930: 165-76), Krause (1934: 8; 1966: 253; 1971: 150 *et passim*), Jacobsen-Moltke (1942: 681), Antonsen (1975a; 61).

182. Cf. Krause (1971: 40-41; 109 *et passim*).

183. The verbal form **laþan* (ON *laða*, Go. *laþōn*: 'to invite, summon') could be understood as a parallel to ON *biðja* in the runic terminology, see V.16.

184. These are both generally interpreted as acc. objects of the verbal forms which precede them (cf. Krause 1971: 149; 168, and Antonsen 1975: 63; 79).

185. The upper part of the l-rune is almost obliterated and the lower part of the branch of the u-rune is flattened so that this form must be considered conjectural.

186. Cf. von Friesen (1924a: 128), Marstrander (1929a: 218ff.), Krause (1937: 19-23; 1966: 74ff.), Düwel (1981a: 146ff. and 1981b).

187. Cf. Düwel (1981a).

188. The tamgas are apparently owner's marks and perhaps even magical signs of Sarmatian origin which were borrowed into Germanic tradition, cf. Sulimirski (1970: 151-54, *et passim*).

189. Cf. Krause (1966: 76-77), Arntz (1939: 1-19).

190. Three slightly differing interpretations seem possible: 1) 'the rider hence (into the enemy),' 2) 'the capable rider,' and 3) 'the target rider' (with **tila-** interpreted as an adverb or preposition, an adjective, or a noun), see Düwel (1981a: 144-45).

191. See Düwel (2008: 27) and McKinnell (2004: 43-44).

192. Read as such by Marstrander (1929b: 234) and Jansson (1963: 10).

193. Arntz (1939: 426ff.) reconstructs this as an EGmc. rune-master formula [i]k (e)ruls.

194. As read by Düwel (1981a: 157ff.) based on personal examinations (cf. also Arntz 1939: 94). Krause had read an initial **i**-rune (1966: 304-05).

195. This reading given by Krause (1966: 89). However, Moltke (1976: 77-79; 81-82) gives three other possibilities: 1) *Witring!* (voc. masc. PN), 2) **Witr-ing(w)aR* (masc. PN, owner of the knife), or 3) *Witrō* (fem. PN).

196. Cf. Krause (1937: 35; 1966: 256-57) who interprets the cuckoo as a symbol for the spring and hence of fertility. The fact that it would rhyme with *laukaR* also makes this reconstruction very attractive.

197. Single ideo- or logographic o-runes may appear on KJ 20, 25, 41, and on IK 13, 75, 129.

198. Cf. Krause (1937: 484; 1966: 258-59), and Marstrander (1952: 206). Less likely are interpretations which involve a PN. The **h**-rune may appear as a logograph on KJ 21, 52, or 65.

199. Numerous examples in the bracteate corpus of botched attempts to imitate Roman capitals indicate the level of alphabetic incompetence among some bracteate-masters.

200. Most degenerate forms obviously owe their shape to repeated inaccurate copying, and may only secondarily be ascribed to this category. The bracteate-master may distribute inaccurately inscribed items, but from the receiver's viewpoint it may not lessen the operative function of the amulet. Moltke (1976a: 80) sees such inscriptions as *svindel beregnet på at stikke godtroende kunder blår i øjnene*.

201. Breza is generally held to be graffiti of non-magical intent. Among the inscriptions from other fragments there was also found a Latin ABC. On runological grounds it may be guessed that this row was carved by a Langobard (cf. Krause 1966: 20).

202. On the Beuchte brooch, cf. Düwel (1976; 1981b: 77-78) who sees it as an example of heathen grave magic, and concerning Aquincum, cf. Krause (1966: 23-26).

203. The *ætt* system is discussed in IV.11, and its operative-formulaic implications are briefly explored in VII.6.

204. On the ideographic or logographic use of runes, cf. Düwel (1974).

205. The meaning of *unpfinþai* is too ambiguous for any overt magical intent to be ascribed to it, e.g., as an example of love-magic used by Idda to attract and/or keep Liano. It is more an example of interpersonal communication. Cf. also interpretations by Marstrander (1937: 496) and the discussion by Arntz (1939: 173-92).

206. All statistics with regard to the younger **fuþark** are subject to change because of the regularity of new finds, especially in the Heddeby/Schleswig, Sigtuna and Lund sites.

207. There is no unified collection of younger fuþark inscriptions, cf. Sierke (1939: 109-114) for a convenient survey. Otherwise they must be culled from the various editions of the younger inscriptions, see bibliography.

208. See section 49 on the -*istil*-formulas.

209. On the interpretation of *kuml*, cf. Thamdrup (1981: 7-12).

210. The Gørlev st. is discussed in detail by Moltke (1929/30: 172-85; 1936/37: 252-62), cf. also Sierke (1939: 53-54).
211. Cf. Moltke (1961: 401-10).
212. Cf. Moltke (1976: 302, *et passim*).
213. Cf. Wimmer (1874: 193ff.), Sierke (1939: 111).
214. Cf. Eggers (1968: 8ff.) who interprets inscription B as a byname derived from the verb *kura*: 'to sit or lie still' —or— 'to hide, conceal.'
215. Cf. Moltke (1976: *passim*).
216. See sect. 49. It also suggests a five-fold repetition of the syllable: *li*.
217. Cf. Moltke (1976: 383-85).
218. Cf. Moltke (.1976: 384-86). Schleswig III may also contain a sequential formula. It reads A. **fuþarsb** B. (R-L) **fuikb**, however, this is probably best explained as an erotic-magical inscription: *fuð ars*: 'cunt (and) ass,' plus an *ephesion grammaton* (cf. Moltke 1976: 383; 385).
219. Reconstructed otherwise in sect. 38 above.
220. Perhaps also an unattested PN, see sect. 31 above.
221. Reconstructed otherwise in sect. 38 above.
222. Generally reconstructed as a *laþu* inscription, cf. Page (1999: 180-81) and see sect. 40 above.
223. Cf. Ilkjær-Lønstrup (1981: 53), Düwel (1983: 125).
224. See section 34 above for reconstructed elements.
225. Doubtful reading with possible admixture of Roman capitals.
226. For a general bibliography of studies concerning these rings, cf. Marquardt (1961). The most important studies are those by Harder (1936) and Dickins (1935), cf. also Page (1999: 35, 112-13).
227. The most notable examples of these are by Harder (1931; 1936). He eventually reconstructs the runic text as **ærür iufel uri-uriþon glæs-tæpon tol** '*Bevor Übel . . . des Bogenringes des Glanzbandes Zoll.*' This speculative interpretation is rightly criticized by Dickins (1935).
228. There is some confusion in the archeological reports as to the exact original position of the slab, cf. Jansson-Wessén (1962: I, no. 88), Marstrander (1929a: 67ff.), Krause (1966: 12). However, it seems certain that the stone belonged to some part of the chamber, and typological criteria suggest that Bæksted's (1951: 78) or Antonsen's (1980b: 135-36) speculations that it was carved for another (perhaps didactic) purpose and only later found its way to the grave seem doubtful.
229. This reading is best from a runological viewpoint, cf. Bugge (*NIæR*, 5), Grienberger (1924: 275), and Krause (1966: 14-15), however, on a typological basis, the reading **tuwatuwa** is also possible, cf. Marstrander (1929a: 77-78), and Krause (1937: 433).
230. This difficult complex has been read as a complete word *uma* (< **uhman-*) by Gutenbrunner (1936/37: 169-70) meaning 'upper most part, end, grip,' and may refer to the object itself or be an *Óðinsheiti*. Krause (1966: 68-69) also sees a possibility that it refers to an herb-name, but he thinks it most likely that the complex is incomplete and must be reconstructed with a -[n]*uma* suffix which indicates one is learned in the prefixed concept, e.g., ON *fullnumi*: 'having learned fully, become an adept in a thing.'

231. Cf. Olsen (NIæR: II, 640ff.), who connects this with the līna-laukaR formula on the tanning knife of Fløksand (KJ 37). Krause (1946/47: 62) identifies the l-rune with laukaR: 'leek' (see 37), whereas I. Lindqvist (1923: 75) more conventionally links the complex with the concept *lagu: 'water.'

232. For Olsen's speculative reconstruction, see section 52 below.

233. Opitz (1977: 200-201) sees the complex as a defective object of the verb writ.

234. Because of the apparent mistake of ᛊ for ᛏ we can not be sure how accurate part A. of the inscription might be, cf. Krause (1966: 225-27), Wessén-Jansson (U.1125). Marstrander (1952: 270-76) speculates that inscription A. is an encoded PN of some kind, and that the ᛊ in B. is in fact a hahal-rune form 1:1 (= t) with the usual reordering of the ættir (see Fig. IV). Archeologically, this stone appears to have been a fixture of a gravefield stone arrangement, but does not seem to have been attached to any particular mound.

235. Cf. also Bugge I, 89ff.; II, 529ff.), Grienberger (1906: 115), Noreen (1923: 375ff.), Antonsen (1975a: 80-81).

236. This complex has been speculatively reconstructed by Noreen (1923: 375-76) as D(aga)R r(ūnōR) m(arki)þi: 'Dag marked the runes.'

237. On this reading, cf. Krause (1966: 69-72), and also Grienberger (1900: 291-93), Jacobsen-Moltke (1942: 315-17; 593; 609), Marstrander (1952: 28; 99-108), but also Antonsen (1975a: 37) who reads the complex **sawilagaR** as a masc. PN: 'the sunny, bright one.'

238. Cf. N. Lindqvist (1921: 72-73) and Flowers (2005: 55).

239. This formula is certainly for the winning of a woman's love, however, in Germanic tradition this often took the form of a curse, cf. Skírnir's threats to Gerðr in order to win her love for Freyr, e.g., Skm. 36: *"Þurs ríst ec þer / oc þría stafi. . ."*

240. This is perhaps related to the rune formula ailti found on the Glavendrup st. (DR 209), cf. Andersen (1946: 171).

241. On the -istil- inscriptions, cf. Sierke (1939: 53-56), Olsen in: von Friesen (1933: 108), Moltke (1936/37: 255-56).

242. DR 239 Gørlev, NIyR 75, 132, 167, 364, 365, and Og. 181, while the less certain ones are NIyR 366, 367, 167, 137.

243. In the Borgund inscriptions (XVII, XVIII), cf. Olsen (NIyR IV, 174-77) the word formulas are actually spelled out, e.g., Borgund XVII, divided the words read: *tistil mistil ok in þiriþi þistil*: "'tistil,' mistletoe, and the third- (the plant) thistle."

244. For a survey of such inscriptions in Danish territory, cf. Jacobsen-Moltke (1942: 1049-51).

245. Moltke (1976: 394) reads the final three legible runes **ang**. . . as perhaps the remains of Lat. *angelus*.

246. It is interesting to note that Thompson (1972: 528) remarks on the tendency for the ordering of the runes in these inscriptions to be governed or influenced by the fuþark sequence, which leads us to believe either: 1) the order was known to some extent even by analphabetics, or 2) the non-sensical inscriptions were not as randomly composed as they might first appear.

247. Cf. Moltke (1938a: 135; 1976: 393-94).

248. It is no doubt significant that the first three runes of line A. are **þmk**, cf. *þistill mistill kistill* formulas above.

249. The object itself (which measures 16.5 x 6.5 cm) probably dates from ca. 2000 BCE, however, the inscription dates from the 11th cent.

250. On the *agla* formula, cf. Jacobsen-Moltke (1942: 1046), Moltke (1938a: 112).

251. On the origins and history of this formula, cf. Fuchs (1951), who sees it as an encoded form of a *pre*-Christian version of the *pater noster*-formula, and Moeller (1973) and the bibliography there.

252. Some other notable attestations of the runic *agla*-formula are Borgund I (cf. Rygh *NIyR*: IV, 140-42), and the Saleby bell, cf. v. Friesen (1933: 232-33).

253. The ring itself is of Sassanid-Persian origin (3rd-7th cent.) with a Pahlavi inscription, cf. Moltke (1938a: 125; 128; 1976: 392).

254. Cf. Gustavson-Brink (1979: 233ff.).

255. See below on ambiguous references to this motive. More explicit, typologically similar evidence from the Viking Age corpus would suggest this motive was present in an earlier period.

256. Cf. Brate (1898), v. Friesen (1933: 30-31), and Krause (1966: 148-51). Antonsen (1975a: 55-56) will not venture an interpretation of this complex, while Marstrander (1952: 207-215), by means of an *ætt*-reordering, wants to see an unattested fem. PN in the form of a doubtful runic code.

257. Various unconvincing attempts have been made to interpret this complex, e.g., v. Friesen (1933: 30-31) reads the rest of the inscription as **su hur(R) ah su sihni [u]itin hakuþo** and interprets it: 'this formula (cf. ON *hurr* PNor. **hurruR*) and this image (i.e., the image of the carving) indicates that this is a grave (that must not be harmed).' Marstrander (1952: 214), by switching the runic values of the second and third *ætt* of the **fuþark**, tries to read the complex as **datur at dude** — *dóttur at d(a)uðe*. While Klingenberg (1973: 172) would read **suhurah** in reverse, i.e., **haru-hus** and interpret either *haru-hūs*: 'house of sack-linen (= initiatory tent),' or *hāru-hūs*: 'house of the grey-one (= *Wōðanaz).'

258. This could also be connected to Nor. *surre*: 'to be confused,' and have the function of confusing would-be grave violators, etc.

259. Reconstructed on the basis of the Björketorp formula.

260. Cf. Krause (1966: 210-17). For variant readings, cf. I. Lindqvist (1923), Jacobsen (1935: 15ff.), DR 357, Marstrander (1952: 121ff.), Antonsen (1975a: 85-87).

261. Much less likely (on runological as well as typological grounds) is Marstrander's reading (1952: 118-27; 151): (n)ú *snýk hāðe*: 'I speak forth the incantation which will bring misfortune,' which he wants to see as parallel to **uþArAbAsbA** in the Björketorp formula.

262. Cf. Krause (1966: 214-17), and also Lindqvist (1923: 158ff.), Jacobsen (1935: 24ff.), DR 360, Marstrander (1952: 123ff.), and Antonsen (1975a: 87-88).

263. Antonsen's view (1980c: 133ff.) that in these formulas there *is* "*ikke det mindste spor av magiske elementer; den har en rent juridisk karakter og 'værner' mindesmærket, idet den forkynder at eventuelle ødelaeggere skal stå udenfor samfundets normale beskyttelspligt*," seems unfounded on several grounds. His theory is predicated on the idea that potential desecrators could *read* the inscription — which was probably not the case (although the presence of the runes might have acted as a visible deterrent). Also, the question arises: By what power or authority would this juridical sentence be carried out? Magical formulas from many cultures follow "juridical" formalities.

264. Cf. Olsen (*NIærR*: III, 77ff., 268ff.), Nordén (1934a; 1934b; 1936), Høst (1960: 489-554), and Krause (1966: 234).

265. Krause's reading of III was generally accepted by N. Å. Nielsen (1968) and Düwel (1983: 36), but cf. alternatives discussed by Düwel (2008: 41).

266. The interpretation *walwu is wirki*: 'this is the vǫlva's work' (cf. Høst 1960: 530-31) is unlikely on typological grounds. Cf. also Kiil's (1964: 29-30) reading **f alumisurki** —*falu misyrki*: "they (i.e., the 'fish' and 'bird') buried the wrong-doer."

267. See V.7. This is especially likely if we are to interpret *viltiR mænnR* (Krause: '*irregeführte Männer*') with Jacobsen (1931) or Reier (1952) as 'sorcerers.'

268. Cf. Düwel (1979: 235-36).

269. Cf. Nordén (1936: 241-48; 255ff.).

270. Antonsen (1975a: 65-66) interprets *fara-wīsa* as 'the travel-wise.' In DR bracteate no. 61, this complex is translated '*den ulykksvise*.'

271. Olsen (*NIyR*: V, 1-20) considers this inscription as part of the younger corpus.

272. This interpretation was given by Olsen as an alternate reading (cf. Olsen-Shetelig 1933: 69-72).

273. On typological grounds, this reconstruction has some merit, both because of the evidence for ideographic use of the **n**-rune (*nauð*) and because an amuletic brooch would be less likely to have reference to a specific malevolence to be protected against.

274. Cf. Miedema (1974: 116), also Düwel-Tempel (1971: 384).

275. Kapteyn (1933: 160-226) and Miedema (1974: 116) prefer the translation: 'In Opham Amluþ defended himself. Before the yew(-amulet) the surf had to bow. Before this yew(-amulet) the surf now bows.'

276. Cf. Krause (1937: 481-84; 1966: 64-68), DR 196, Marstrander (1952: 26-31), Antonsen (1975a: 35-36).

277. Antonsen (1975a) reads *auja gebu*: 'I give protection.'

278. This reading is given by Krause (1966: 112); however, that of Antonsen (1975a: 54-55; 1975b) does not differ runologically in any substantial degree.

279. The form *haþu* is interpreted by Antonsen (1975b: 129) as a reflex of PIE **kot-w-m*: 'that which is cut down,' cf. ON *hǫð*: 'war, slaughter,' and the divine name Hǫðr, also the compound theme in OE *heaþu-*: 'battle.'

280. Kiil's (1953: 80ff.) interpretation of the inscription as one against the walking dead must be rejected on linguistic and typological grounds.

281. For example, most recently by Marstrander (1952: 196-203), and Antonsen (1975a: 42-43).

282. Cf. e.g., v. Friesen (1924: 129-35), Nordén (1934b: 103; 1940: 321ff.), and Krause (1966: 139-40).

283. Bæksted (1951: 83) maintains that both Tørvika A and B (KJ 91 and 62) were *bauta*-stones only later used in the construction of the burial chamber.

284. Høst's (1954) interpretation reads: *heðra dvína k(aun)*: 'dwindle hence *kaun*' (with *kaun* referring either to the dead, or to an "evil spirit" which causes disease, etc.).

285. This based on the meaning of the rune name **kaunaz*: 'sore, swelling, disease, etc.' Cf. also Nordén's interpretation (1937: 150; 1941: 54) of **kaunaz*: '*Beschwörung gegen Feinden und Wiedergänger*.'

286. Based on the alternate rune name **kēnaz*: 'torch, fire,' cf. OE rune name *cēn*: 'torch.' Since this was definitely a cremation grave, this interpretation seems plausible.

287. On the reading of this bind-rune, see sect. 31 above.

288. Cf. e.g., Bugge (1900) *iu þin udR r[ai]d*: 'Odd rode this horse in,' Nordén (1937) *iuþin udR rak*: 'Odd avenged himself on this horse.' Marstrander (1952: 173), however, gives a radically variant reading: *[h]iu þin D(agr) umb ā(r) f(ehu)*: 'Dag hewed this for good harvest (and) wealth.'

289. See VII.10, and cf. also Krause (1932: 65-68) on the horse-image in rune magic. Equine iconography seems to dominate in the runic tradition when we include all the C-type bracteates (with the horse/rider complex), the bracteate word-formula **ehw*-(see sect. 39), the three pictographic stones (KJ 99: Möjbro, KJ 101: Eggjum, and Roes), and the apparent equine interpretation of the palindrome on KJ 1: Kylver st. The direct link between the horse and the numinous is indicated in *Germ*. ch. 10, where we read — *sacerdotes enim ministros deurum, illos* (i.e., *equos*) *conscios putant*: '... they regard the priests as the servants of the gods, but the horses as their confidants.'

290. See tree lore in V.9. On the hazel, cf. Marzell (1930/3.1: 1527-42). The particular bush under which the Roes st. was found certainly was not there in 750, but this kind of bush may have been perennially common to the locality.

291. This artifact is consistently referred to as an "amulet," cf. e.g., Arntz (1939: 154-67), Buma (1951: 306ff.), and Miedema (1974: 114). Cf. also Elliott (1957).

292. In the reading of **dud** as 'power' or 'virtue,' Arntz follows Bugge (1908) who reads the text I. *þīn ī ā ber et dūd* LID///. . .-*n birid nī̆*: 'Always carry this yew, power lies in it. . .-*n* (PN) carries me.'

293. Miedema generally follows the reading of Buma (1951: 306-16), where **dud** is read as OFris. *dūð*: 'retinue, host of battle.'

294. Cf. Krause (1966: 136-39).

295. The two ON terms *feikn* and *flagð* are juxtaposed in a medieval Norwegian inscription, cf. Olsen (*NIyR*: II, no. 170).

296. Cf. v. Friesen (1924a: 124ff., 1933: 24), Marstrander (1952: 224ff.), and Antonsen (1972; 1975a: 40).

297. Antonsen unjustifiably reads this complex as **leubu**, cf. Høst (1977: 152).

298. Cf. Marstrander (1952: 224).

299. It is not certain whether the inscription was carved as part of a funeral rite, or whether its placement was purely secondary to its original function.

300. The "controversy" over whether these are curse-(*forbandelse*) or protective-(*verne*) formulas (cf. Jacobsen 1935; N. Å. Nielsen 1968; Antonsen 1980c) seems misplaced at one level, since it seems that their function or *motive* is apotropaic while their mode is a juridical "curse," see ch. VII.

301. There is no evidence that the Björketorp and Stentoften sts. were in any way connected to graves.

302. The meaning of the complex **rata ~ rita** is uncertain. It is most likely a weak masc. noun in the oblique case (dat.) as the object of *at*. Cf. Andersen (1968: 175ff.).

303. On the meaning of **sarþi** and **siþ**, cf. N. Å. Nielsen (1968: 19ff.).

304. Cf. Andersen (1946: 71-87; 1968: 175ff.).

305. Cf. e.g., N. Å. Nielsen (1969).

306. This aspect could be partially accounted for if it were made more explicit that the warnings were directed at rune-master/sorcerers who might commit acts of desecration in the performance of some rites of *seiðr*, cf. N. Å. Nielsen (1968: 48ff.). This does not seem

very likely or logical given that runic knowledge appears to have been fairly exclusive within the social elite in pre-Christian times. Such acts of desecration of the rune-master's craft would probably come from persons outside that social context, and therefore they would not be literate in runes.

307. For a comparison of the two formulas, cf. Høst (1952).

308. The term *dvergkunning* is interpreted by Kabell (1978: 44) to have the expanded meaning: 'mightiest causes of sickness,' i.e., that a *dvergr* is the cause of the disease.

309. Similar placement of protective forces may be found in medieval runic inscriptions (cf. Odense lead plate, DR 204), as well as in later written formulas (cf. *Galdrabók* no. 21, N. Lindqvist 1921 and Flowers 2005).

310. Here *lok* is interpreted as a neut. nom. pl. (cf. ON *lok*: 'end, conclusion') and *læwa* as a neut. gen. pl. (cf. ON *læva* ← nom. *læ*: 'bane, plague, evil, etc.'). Nordén read this inscription on several occasions (1937: 157-60; 1943: 186) and concluded that it was directed against the walking dead. The piece was found inside the top of a grave mound. Moltke (1976: 295-96) tries to get away from any magical interpretation with the reading **lukis liua**: 'Leve's ~ Live's (masc. gen. sg. PN) clasp(?).' But here he goes further into the realm of philological conjecture than before.

311. Cf. Olsen (1908), Krause (1935: 33; 1943: 45ff.) and Sierke (1939: 100). Moltke (1976: 296) supposes the carver to have been a rejected woman. This is not impossible, but it seems unlikely from a sociological viewpoint.

312. On the adj. *fúla*, cf. Gering (1917: 63).

313. Cf. also the more cautious reading by Liestøl (*NIyR*: V, 28-29), who reconstructs r. 10-14 as **mikil**, and interprets the first part of the inscription as: 'I loved the proud maid...' He leaves the rest without a comprehensive interpretation.

314. Cf. also Moltke (1976b: 76-88) and Düwel (1958: 138). See also spell 46 in the *Galdrabók* (Flowers 2005, pp. 55-56).

315. In this complex the runes **iur nank** are executed in Hälsinga runes. (See Fig. III.)

316. The interpretation of this line (A.III.) is highly conjectural. Nordén (1943: 163-64) translates and interprets it *Gör detta (ristade) galenskapsfyllt, (sejd) anga! Förinta detta (ristade), sken!* The mist (or odor?) and light are invoked against the object of the formula, i.e., the walking dead(?).

317. The particular rune-master formula type in which the runes themselves, or the rune names, are invoked is not attested in the period. However, it seems to have been a well-established tradition with roots sufficiently deep that it was still employed in early modern times, cf. e.g., the formula: *...og mæl : rist æg þ(ier) Otte ausse Naudir Nije þossa öretten...*: '...and say: I carve (or write) you eight *áss*(-runes), nine *nauð*(-runes), thirteen *þurs*(-runes)...' (*Galdrabók* no. 46, N. Lindqvist 1921 and Flowers 2005) — recorded in Denmark sometime after 1650!

318. Several examples are also found in the Greenlandic corpus (cf. Moltke 1936). Note also the magical formula *agla*, see sect. 49.

Chapter VII

Magical Formulaic Analyses

1. Great uncertainty has characterized the study of runes and magic in the past. Runological studies also appear subject to pendular swings in attitude between the position that runes *are* magic to the idea that there is nothing "magical" about them (see ch. III). While I do not pretend to be able to settle this question with the present study, I do propose to give it certain *foci*, i.e., concentration on the possible characteristics of the runemasters (see ch. IV) and on the semiotics of the runic inscriptions themselves (see ch. II). On a systematic level, we know almost nothing concerning the numerical lore that may or may not have conditioned runic operations, or about the ideographic use of runes for operative purposes. These areas have caused the most controversial forays into rune-magical speculation. That complex of data identified as the "runic system" makes such speculation tempting, and even provides a tenable framework for some of this guesswork. In this study; however, they are generally left in the background.

The two assumptions which underlie the present work are: 1) the possibly operative force of runic inscriptions is most interpretable at *a linguistic-formulaic* level,(1) and 2) all the inscriptions represent attempts at *communication* of some kind. It seems most timely at this juncture in the study of runes and magic to investigate the older runic corpus from this semiotic perspective.

In ch. II I presented a generalized semiotic theory of operative or magical acts. In the context of the runic tradition it seems clear that in many cases the rune-carver/master (I) encodes a formula on a lexical and on a graphic (runic) level, and (II) executes or performs this message in a more or less complex manner (i.e., carving, coloring, speaking, and perhaps performing auxiliary actions, see ch. V) in a given medium as the direct object of his action — all of which is received by an empathetic "decoder" of the indirect object (receiver). The message is virtually "read" by this receiver, and reciprocal action, in accordance with the complex nature of the encoded form, is expected. The runic corpus itself gives us evidence for the nature of the encoding phase of this process, which is the composition of the total message in an *effective form*. This form would perhaps have to be composed several levels, e.g.: 1) graphic, 2) lexical, and 3) syntactic (or prosodic).(2) Evidence for the elements of the execution phase are circumstantial and sometimes indirect. Yet we do know from the fact that the inscriptions were carved, that runes were *cut*; the archaic verb form **faihjan* indicates the early practice of coloring the runes, and the possible etymology of the word "rune" (see V. note 104) may point to an original vocal performance as an integral part of the process.

The idea that effective communication can only take place between empathetic systems is crucial. It points up the necessity for a (perceived) similarity between 1) the communication source-encoder (rune-master) and 2) the message itself, and the complex or entity with which communication is being attempted. This seems fundamental to the understanding of the functional nature of the rune-master (as a magical persona) and of his message (as an often complex, multileveled formula).

In ch. VI, I was able to identify four major types of formulaic elements in various inscriptions: 1) rune-master formulas *ek*+PN/byname (+verb + object), 2) substantive word-formulas *alu, laukaR*, etc., 3) rune-formulas, which may be a) sequential **fuþark**... , or nonsequential permutations, e.g., l·u·w·a·t·u·w·a, and 4) syntactic formulas of more or less explicitly operative intent.

These formulaic elements must now be analyzed on several levels in order to determine their operative features. Each type of element must to some extent be approached on its own terms, but the basic levels of this analysis are: 1) the phonic/lexical or vocabulary (i.e., the basic linguistic units of the formulaic element), 2) the compositional or formulaic or the composition (i.e., how these units are arranged). From this basis, two other levels are deduced: 3) the operative *mode* (i.e., *how* the formula is "magical") and 4) the operative *motive* (i.e., *why* the formula was executed). In addition, there will generally be included a comparative typology of the media of the inscriptions (e.g., stones, bracteates, brooches, etc.) and the formulaic elements.

Rune-Master Formulas

2. These formulas, discussed exhaustively in ch. VI.2-32, are perhaps the most complex with which to deal, because of their significant variations within a tightly formulaic structure. Viewed as a whole, rune-master/carver formulas occur in seven possible types:

Ia. [*ek*+PN (+byname) + verb + object.]
Ib. [first-person verbal form (+object).]
II. [*ek*+PN (+byname) + verb.]

III. [*ek*+ $\begin{Bmatrix} \text{byname} \\ \text{PN} \end{Bmatrix}$ (+byname).]

IV. [*ek*+ $\begin{Bmatrix} \text{byname} \\ \text{PN} \end{Bmatrix}$ + *hait-* + $\begin{Bmatrix} \text{byname} \\ \text{PN} \end{Bmatrix}$.]

V. [PN + verb] (third-pers.)
VI. [PN + verb + object.] (third-pers.)
VII. [PN]

We can be fairly certain that the first-person formulas (I-IV), and the third-person formulas (V-VI) with runo-technical verbs represent rune-master/carver inscriptions, while the isolated PN remains ambiguous.

Vocabulary

Lexemes to considered in these formulas for their possibly magical or operative functions are essentially: 1) the first-person pronoun *ek*, 2) the various names and bynames, 3) the runo-techncial verbs, and 4) the objects of those verbs.

1) The first-person pronoun seems to be a pivotal elements in the most typical rune-master formulas,(3) which is doubly reinforced in type-IV formulas with the verb **haitan*, usually with the enclitic pronoun: *hait-eka* (see VI.15b). With this pronoun, the rune-master brings himself to the center of the matter.

2) The myriad of appellatives used in these formulas is treated in ch. VI.31. From the analyses presented there, and elsewhere in ch. VI, it is clear that there are several kinds of appellatives employed: i.e., a) originally fucntional PNs, which may reveal something of the rune-master's more or less permanent function or position in society, b) functional bynames, which appear to be more temporary, or occasional, names employed by the runemaster for specific operations, c) "official" or institutional designations, which act to set the rune-master apart in an exclusive group, and to characterize that group, and d) the common PNs from which we can gain

little information except that it is an identification of the rune-master/carver.

3) Runo-technical verbs (*writan: 'to carve,' *talgijan: 'to carve' [in wood], *faihian: 'to color') and more ambiguous verbs (*taujan: 'to fashion', *tawōn: 'to prepare', *wurkjan: 'to make, shape', *und-neman: 'to undertake, to learn', *felhan: 'to hide, conceal', *wīhjan: 'to consecrate') which are used in runic contexts, all point to the importance of the actual performance of this phase of the communicative runic process. While the runo-technical verbs indicate certain concrete actions performed in order to effect the physical inscription, the more ambiguous ones may give us some glimpses into the magical thought-processes — i.e., that the conception of the formula was important,(4) that it was perhaps a complex process, with sacral implications, and that the concept of concealment was sometimes crucial, see section 6.

4) Objects of these verbs can give us insight into the perceived nature of the "magical channel," or the formula, with which the rune-master believed he was working. The most common of these is the word *rūnōR*: 'runes' itself (see ch. VI.6). The fact that it sometimes occurs in the (collective?) singular *rūnō*: 'rune' is indicative of the archaic conception of the whole (vocalized?) formula as a "secret," or "mystery" which can be thought to have the operative function of communication with a hidden reality. Other words which occur in this context (*wīlald*: 'art-work,' *wraita*: 'carving,' *horna*: 'horn,' etc.) indicate certain technical aspects, while others (*laþōdu ~ laþoþ*: 'summons, invocation,' *unaþu*(?): 'happiness, luck, satisfaction') point more in the direction of the "intellectual" work of the formulaic construction, or of its purpose (see VI.8-9).

Composition

On the strictly semantic level, the ways in which these words might be arranged do not seem fundamental. The formulas are common enough, and so thoroughly stereotyped according to formulaic rules, and they are readily understandable in elliptic forms.

The basic unit of the classic rune-master formula is [ek + appellative]. In this nominal sentence, we may supply the verb "to be," i.e., "I *am* the (rune-master)." Extended type-IV formulas provide us with the verb *haitan, which usually supplements the nominal phrase, and which further emphasizes the social position of the rune-master — others know him by these names. This unit establishes a substantial link between the *ek*-pronoun and the appellative subject of the formula. The link between the carver (designated by *ek*) and the appellative is especially interesting when we find apparently functional PNs, or clearly functional bynames or "official" designations. In these instances, the rune-master, by his complex act of executing the formula, effects a connection between himself and this function. His act is sometimes extended and made more explicit with the addition of the verbal and objective forms (but these are implicit in types III and IV as well): "I, the rune-master — carved the runes."

It should be noted that the third-person formula appears to be functionally parallel to that of the first-person. The first-person form may be more indicative of the kind of magical thought at work, but both forms coexist and thrive in the period. From a purely linguistic point of view, the carver/master has removed himself to some extent from direct action in the process. On one level this may be a stylistic variation. But the curious fact that with the first-person forms, the verbs are often found in the *present* tense, and that in the third-person forms they are exclusively preterit, would also indicate that this removal is more profound. It appears that this distancing of the process in time and in person may have some operative significance as a way of placing the formula in a 'pastness' mode — which may in turn be considered to lend it effective, "causal" force.(5) What *has been* in the past affects events and conditions in the "non-past." This is perhaps a principle fundamental to the occasional use of preterit forms in such formulas.

On the prosodic level, the rune-master formulas often seem to show efforts at a rhythmic performance, and alliterative composition, e.g.,:

KJ 70:	ék érilaR / rūnō wrítu
KJ 17a:	ek WīR Wīwio / wrítu ī rūnōR
KJ 74:	ek WákraR ún(d)am wráita
KJ 65:	ek gúdija ungándiR...
KJ 29:	ék érilaR / sā wīlagaR háiteka
KJ 96/97:	háidR-rūnō rónu / félheka hédra gínno-rūnōR
IK 184:	wúrtē rūnōR an wálha-kúrnē

This may be some indication of the rhythmic character of the performed vocal formulas — but it would be too conjectural to go beyond this at this time, cf. I. Lindqvist (1923). The operative function of this elementary versification would perhaps be an effort to render the message in a form more empathetic to the essence of that "other reality" toward which the communication was perhaps directed.

Mode

Rune-master formulas seem to be magical in a rather unique way. But if we are allowed to assume that the mythology of the rune-masters was closely allied to that of *Wōðanaz (see IV.16), and that this mythology was at all similar to the later mythology of Óðinn — certain possible analogies emerge. One is immediately struck by the similarities between the number of functional and titular rune-master names and bynames, and the many *heiti* of Óðinn. Where these appellatives have a mythic function as *Óðinsheiti*, they may have an analogously magical function as rune-master names.

The *mode* of this magic is transformative. The rune-master first actually turns himself into a semi-divine being through a complex process which consists of: 1) the very act of carving the runes in which he participates in one of his patron god's principal activities, and 2) a basic formula: e.g., [*ek* → *erilaR*], which is perhaps reinforced by the extension of the formula: e.g., *writu runoR*:

```
transform ─────────────────> act
ek → erilaR                  writu rūnōR
```

This is then a graphically reinforced verbal, "performative," rite (see II.1.). It is conceivable that, by means of such formulas, the rune-master is able to assume a sort of "magical persona" analogous to that of *Wōðanaz, and apparently in a fashion similar to that employed by Óðinn in mythology. The rune-master does not invoke the god but acts in the role of a god. He participates in the function of a god in a ritualized sense — or at least he is employing an operative technique which is considered to be the gift of the god.(6) It is important to realize that apparently cultic, initiatory, or magico-religious names and bynames could indicate that the *ego* of the formula may not have been conceived of as the "normal" *ego* or identity of the man, but rather as the transformed ritual *ego* — or persona. This ritually transformed *ego* would then be the *authority* governing the magical operation, see Hampp (1961: 121ff.).

Motives

Even after this transformational mode has been tentatively accepted — we are still left with the problem of *why* these formulas would have been executed in the first place. There seem to be three classes of motivation for such formulas, which can be grouped according to content. For purposes of this analysis, we can divide the formulaic corpus into three groups in two classes. Class I consists of rune-master formulas in simple contexts, which includes those appended to memorial or other formulas. Within this class, there are those which a) give no concrete indication of an operative motivation (i.e., the names and/or bynames are neutral), and those which b) indicate some special function by means of the names/bynames. Class II consists of rune-master formulas in complex contexts, i.e., those integrated into other formulaic elements.

Group Ia) would be those simplest in form: 'I, the rune-master (carve the runes),'(7) but most difficult to interpret as to motive. It seems most reasonable to conclude that these formulas were intended to imbue the medium (physical object or its vicinity) with the non-specific magical force of the rune-master — which could be apotropaic in function or motive. On the other hand, it is also conceivable that these formulas were sometimes used in a more "religious" way, and that they represent the traces of a rite of transformation of some kind. This type of names (see VI. 31) generally emphasizes some innate magico-religious quality of the rune-master.

Group Ib) gives us more to analyze as far as a specific operative intent is concerned — but each interpretation is dependent on sometimes problematic readings of the obscure rune-master names and bynames. Examples of this group would include the seven inscriptions which contain bynames which appear to emphasize rune-master qualities easily converted to an active sense:

KJ 12: Gardlösa silver clasp from ca. 200 (Skåne), found in a woman's grave, bears the formula: **ekunwod[iR]**: 'I, the one free from (magical) rage' (see IV.31). By assuming the characteristic of *unwōð-* and carving this formula into the clasp, the rune-master is able to transfer to the clasp that quality (of himself) by contagion. If this inscription was made to be worn by the living owner of the clasp, this could easily be interpreted as an apotropaic formula intended to prevent the magical *$wōðaz$ of a malicious magician from affecting the wearer. On the other hand, if it was carved as part of a funeral rite (cf. Düwel 1981b: 77-78 on Beuchte) it could be interpreted as a method of preventing the walking dead, or of the use of the corpse by a magician. (See V.5) In all cases, it is the prevention of the activity of the *$wōðaz$ which is central.

KJ 65: Nordhuglo *bauta*-stone from ca. 425 (W. Nor.), found in the vicinity of grave mounds, bears the perhaps incomplete formula: (R-L) **ekgudijaungandiRih. . .** — *ek gudija ungandiR ih*: 'I, the priest (am) immune from (malicious) magic' (see V.3). Here, by the same process at work on Gardlösa, the rune-master/priest seems to be protecting the graves in the vicinity from the practice of a kind of *gandr* by magicians, which could involve the use of corpses, etc.

KJ 13 Næsbjerg clasp from ca. 200 (S. Jutland), discovered in a grave, perhaps bears an obscure and problematic functional rune-master byname **waraflusa*: 'he who is on guard against idle speech or nonsense,' cf. Krasue (1966: 37). Since it appears that decorative motifs were carved on the clasp after the runic forms, we can safely assume that the runes were not a funeral inscription. Krause (1966: 37) interprets this as a self-designation of the rune-master who "*damit vermutlich ausdrücken wollte, dass er nicht unbesonnen einherspricht, sondern seine magisch wirkenden Worte vorsichtig wählt.*" This would place the Næsbjerg formula in the less dynamic, more general group of bynames (since we expect that this would be characteristic of all rune-masters). However, if we interpret *-flusa* as being some kind of malicious (magical) speech of others (cf. OHG *flōsari*: 'liar,' *giflōs*: 'deceitful speech'), then a conjecturally operative meaning: 'he who (magically) guards against deceitful speech' could be suggested. In this latter case this would then be an apotropaic amulet against the malicious intent of others.

Two inscriptions found in completely non-funeral, and impersonal, environments are the stones of Barmen (400-450, W. Nor., KJ 64) and Järsberg (500-550, C. Swe., KJ 70), both of which may have originally belonged to stone circles or settings and therefore belong to a group of inscriptions which sanctify localities(8) (see Düwel 1978: 233ff.). The Barmen st. bears the formula **ekþirbijaRru**, the most accepted reading of which seems to be *ek þirbijaR rū(nō)*: 'I, the one who weakens, (carved) the rune(s).'(9) If we take this interpretation as most likely, this could be understood as a curse, or apotropaic formula, which threatens to make anyone 'weak,' or 'powerless' who tries to disturb the stone or its environs. The fact that the apparently cognate ON nouns *þjarfr*: 'a vile person,' and *þirfingr*: "an 'unleavened,' common person" are used as insulting epithets allows this reading to be tenuously classified among the *nīð*-formulas, cf. Krause (1966: 145).

Antonsen's interpretation as 'the one who makes strong' (1975: 48) would make this a more general, less dynamic rune-master byname (see VI.31). The Järsberg st. (see sect. 15b.), whether we accept Moltke's reading (1981) or that of Olsen (*NIæR* III, 223ff.), bears one, or perhaps two, threatening rune-master bynames. *HrabanaR*: 'raven' (cf. ON PN *Hrafn*, OE PN *Hrefn*, and OHG PN *Hraban*), may have already been a common given name — but it could also be conceived of as a bird of

*Wōðanaz and as an initiatory or operative name of some kind. The byname *ūbaR*: 'the malicious one,' however, clearly points to the threatening function (cf. KJ 29, IK 98) of the rune-master — which implies that his malificent power will be released if the stone is disturbed (cf. the function of KJ 96/97, and see also VI.5). In the cases of both Barmen and Järsberg, the runic inscription may also have a more general sanctifying function.

The Lindholm amulet (KJ 29) and the Sjælland II-C bracteate (IK 98) also contain menacing rune-master bynames. But because they provide additional operative context, they are treated in the second group.

Formulas in group II are characterized by a juxtaposition of a rune-master formula, which is the source of at least part of the "magical authority," to a more explicitly operative formula, which may contain additional instrumental force. Often such inscriptions give clearer indications of the magical motive. This group contains a number of formulas which might be considered as curses. The Stentoften (KJ 96) and Björketorp (KJ 97) stones bear legalistic curse formulas (see sect. 5), the chief authority for which seems to be the personal power of the rune-master and his runic formula — *haidR-rūnō rōnu falhk hedra, ginna-rūnaR*. The rune-master formula on the Vetteland st. (KJ 60) appears to work in conjunction with an invocation to malicious entities (*flagða-faikinaR*) as protection for the grave mound (see 5.). A complex formula is borne by the Lindholm amulet (KJ 29) which consists of three elements: 1) a functional/titular rune-master formula, 2) a non-sequential rune formula, and 3) the word-formula *alu*. The only keys to the magical function of this inscription are contained in the meaning of the rune-master designation *wīlagaR*: the crafty, deceitful one,' and in the fact that the rune-formula corresponds in some detail to one found in the *Galdrabók* (N. Lindqvist 1921, no. 46) the function of which is a curse. On runological as well as more general grounds, the Roes st. (KJ 102) can only tentatively belong to this group. The interpretation of the stone as a curse formula is dependent upon the correspondence of the horse, both in the word (*jū*) and in the pictographic representation, with the practice of using equine imagery in Germanic curses. (See VI, note 289.)

There are also several formulas which appear to have the effect of attracting beneficial influences. Two of these could be interpreted as examples of the operative function of logographic runes, i.e., KJ 95 Gummarp st., which has three f-runes (*fehu* 'prosperity') appended to a rune-master formula, and the Nebenstedt I-B bracteate (IK.1.128), which has a single l-rune (*laukaR*[?] 'increase') in an analogous position.(10) The logographs would then function as motives for the operation, i.e., the attraction of prosperity and increase (or fertility) respectively. Another, the Tjurkö I-C bracteate (IK 184), may work on an equally cryptic basis by means of a kenning for gold *walha-kurn*: "'Welsh' grain." None of these give any further indication of their operative force in the rune-master names. On the other hand, the Sjælland II-C bracteate (IK 98) provides an interesting parallel between parts of a compound formula in which the rune-master is identified by the ominous term *firawisa*: 'one who knows dangerous things,' and continues to declare *gibu auja*: 'I give good fortune.' This could represent a combination of an apotropaic personal formula and a performative beneficial formula. (See sect. 5.)

The most certain single example of "grave magic" (i.e., magical formulas used to hold the dead in their graves)(11) is provided by the text of KJ 67: Noleby st. (ca. 600, C. Swe.).(12) The authority used in this formula is clearly the *ego* of the rune-master — but it also seems combined with that of the runes and of the gods on another level. (See sect. 5.) This authority is contained in the verbal formulas *rūnō fāhi*: 'I color the rune' and *tōj-eka *unaþu* ← **unaþou**: 'I prepare satisfaction (in the grave?),' as well as by the probable addition of the (functional) rune-master name *Ha(u)koþu* (acc.): 'the hawk-like one.'

In this group there is also a pair of formulas which seem sacrificial or cultic in character. The Åsum-C bracteate (IK 11) with the inscription — *ehē. ek AkaR fāhi*: '(Sanctified?) to the horse. I, AkaR colored (the runes),' is ambiguous as to operative intent, but we can assume that it is not a curse formula. Runologically problematic, the spear shaft of Kragehul (KJ 27) contains a complex formula (sect. 5), part of which would seem to 'consecrate' (i.e., dedicate) an enemy of their weapons to the spear — thereby foredooming them. (See V.9; VI.51.)

Two bracteate inscriptions, (IK 70) Halskov-C and (IK 189) Trollhättan-A, could just as easily belong to group I. They are suggestive without giving us any further concrete information as to the operative motive of the formula. Trollhättan-A uses a first-person verbal formula: *tawō laþōdu*: 'I prepare the invocation,' and Halskov-C employs a third-person rune-master formula: *Nixetur fahide laþoþ*: 'N. colored the invocation.' The word-formula *laþōdu ~ laþoþ* would only indicate that some force (animistic or dynamistic?) was called into the medium through the authority of the rune-master. (See sect. 3 on *laþu-*.)

When we look at how the typology of runic media (objects upon which runes are carved) might correlate to possible magical motives of the rune-master inscriptions, we see that bracteates are used exclusively for beneficient (if sometimes ambiguously so) purposes, while maleficent formulas tend to be found on stones. Ultimately, however, stone and organic media also may be used for virtually any type of runic formula.

Word-Formulas

3. These symbolic lexemes, discussed at length in VI.33-42, appear in what seems at first glance to be a confused mass of permutations of other word-formulas, PNs, and rune-formulas. However, some distinct formulaic patterns emerge when the corpus is examined as a whole. The five basic formulas which emerge are:

I. word-formula. [in isolation].
II. word-formula + word-formula (+ word-formula + word-formula).
III. PN + word-formula (+ word formula). [in various orders]
IV. PN + word-formula + word-formula.
V. PN (+ word-formula) + rune-formula + word-formula.

There are also a few instances of word-formulas in elaborated syntactic contexts. It must be noted that the vast majority of these formulas appear on bracteates with sometimes confused forms. We will therefore only discuss in detail those forms which seem to be intentional. (See the criteria outlined in ch. VI.)

To be considered a word-formula, a lexeme must: 1) seem to have some extraordinary symbolic content based on its a) etymology and/or b) on its contextual use in the runic/non-runic Germanic vocabulary, and/or 2) be a recurring formulaic element in the runic tradition itself. The catalog of these terms appears to be divisible between concrete symbols, i.e., those which ultimately refer to physical substances, and abstract symbols, i.e., those which refer to non-physical concepts or processes. Concrete terms would include *alu*: 'ale,'(13) *laukaR*: 'leek,' *līna*: 'flax,' *salu*: 'the samphire,'(14) **ehwaR*: 'horse,' and perhaps *gaukaR*: 'cuckoo,' while the abstract group would contain *laþu*: 'invocation, summons,' *auja*: 'luck,' **oþalaR*: 'hereditary property,' *witring*: 'declaration,' and perhaps *ota*: 'terror.' In all cases, however, they must be considered *symbolic*, or analogous to the concept which they represent in the cultural frame of reference to which they belong. The only word-formulas that provide enough context for deeper analysis are *alu, laukaR*(-līna), *salu, *ehwaR, laþu,* and *auja*. The *nomen agentis* spear names constitute another kind of typologically determined word-formula (cf. VI.41).

Composition

In formula types I-V above, all the word-formulas appear in a *restricted code*,(15) i.e., they are not syntactically connected to any other element in the formula. This seems to have been the way in which the word-formulas were most usually employed, and there are examples of this type from the corpus for each of these symbolic words. *Alu*, *laþu*, *auja*, and perhaps **ehw-*, however, also appear in *elaborated* code, i.e., they are syntactically connected to some other element(s) in the formula. There are certain significant patterns with regard to the restricted codes. *LaukaR* never appears with a PN (unless *alu* is also present), while *alu* and *laþ-* often appear juxtaposed to PNs. It is noteworthy that *alu* seems most usually to appear in terminal position. Also, the runologically problematic **ehwaR* formula (on bracteates) is almost always in isolation.

The elaborated codes, which are limited in number and diverse, fall into three tentative classes in which word-formulas are either in 1) the nom. (in nominal phrases) — all with *alu*, i.e., *sīR alu(h)*: "be thou *alu*, or 'protection'(?)" (KJ 52), *sāR alu*: 'here (is) *alu*' (KJ 58), *alu missyrki*: '*alu* to the wrong-doer' (KJ 101), 2) the acc. (as the direct object of a verb) — either *laþ-* or *auja*, i.e., *tawō laþōdu*: 'I prepare the invocation' (IK 189), *N. fahide laþoþ*: 'N. colored the invocation' (IK 70), *gibu auja*: 'I give good luck' (IK 98), or the dat. (in a single dedicatory [?] formula) — *ehē*: 'to the horse' (IK 11).

Mode

The mode of word-formula operations is quite simple. It basically consists of a concept embodied in a word, which is apparently loaded with sacred/magical significance,(16) transferred in a ritualized way to a medium of communication (i.e., the runes on a given object). The special personality of the rune-master still seems to be the pivotal factor in the process. Concrete word-symbols stand for the substances themselves, which become the object of linguistic as well as physical manipulations. Word-symbols that stand for animate symbolic beings (i.e., **ehw-* and **gaukaR*[?] are similarly manipulated in a slightly more metaphorical way (analogous to pictographs, etc.). The verbal or abstract concept word-symbols actually constitute a performative process — or the secondary record of such a performance. In an explicit, but terse, fashion, they actually express the motive of the operative communication. In each case, the medium is transformed by the runic inscription into a channel for the communication of the rune-master's will. In turn, it often seems to function as the channel for the expression of the returned communication — in the form of beneficence, protection, etc.

Motives

The possible magical motives of the execution of word-formula inscriptions span a broad spectrum. Since the genre seems to be primarily a bracteate tradition, we can assume that the motive is one beneficial to the potential wearer of the amuletic object. Most problematic of the word-formulas is the most widely attested form *alu* — which appears not only on bracteates but also stones (barrow- and *bauta*-stones), and other organic and inorganic media (ring, clasp, comb, arrow, bone amulet). Its etymology (see V.34) remains problematic; however, the analyses presented in this work may provide some indication of its original meaning through a classification of its function within the runic tradition.

On bracteates, *alu* appears only in restricted-code formulas, in isolation, or in the context of PNs (rune-master names?), *ephesia grammata* and other word-formulas. As all elements in these compositions seem to have their own peculiar importance, there is little reliable indication of the motive of the *alu* formula itself. In the bracteate tradition *alu* is perhaps juxtaposed to *laukaR* three times. The comb of Setre (KJ 40) may also contain a restricted use of *alu* juxtaposed to a personal or divine name — a pattern which is attested eight times in the corpus. The most significant restricted attestation is on the Lindholm amulet (KJ 29) — with its apparent curse-like, or malificent formulas (VI.31; 48) clearly terminated by **alu**. The amulet's function or motive may be apotropaic but its mode is apparently one of aggression.

The three attestations in elaborated code (KJ 52; 58; 101) — all of which were probably originally connected to graves — could also have some negative or malificent connotations, e.g., *alu missyrki*: '*alu* to the wrong-doer (who would disturb the grave?).'

It appears most likely that *alu*, although perhaps etymologically identical with ON *ǫl*: 'ale,' retained some of its previously abstract quality in the older runic tradition, and that it was used as a generic "word of power" as a way to infuse operative potency into a formula. *Medu* on the Undley bracteate provides a semantic parallel to the use of a name of an intoxicant for operative purposes.

As opposed to *alu*, the word-formula *laukaR* is used in a more limited context — although it also appears outside the bracteate genre at least once on the Fløksand tanning knife (KJ 37). *LaukaR* only occurs in restricted code forms, but its motivational sphere is clearly that of fertility, increase, wealth, and good health. This interpretation is based on its use on tanning knives (cf. its possible logographic representation of Gjersvik, KJ 38), on the lore of the leek in Germanic tradition (V. 9), and on its formulaic combination with *līna*: 'flax, linen' in the Fløksand inscription and in the verse contained in the *Vǫlsapáttr* (VI.37).

If Lundeby's (1982) etymology of *salu* (IK 105) is correct, this formula may have been executed with a motivation similar to that of *laukaR-līna*. This etymology would make *salu* (cf. ON *sǫl*: 'the samphire, red algae') a concrete word-symbol for vitality and health, since this plant was used as a medicinal herb and a potent diet supplement in times of famine, etc.

The larger frame of reference of the concept embodied in the possible runic formula(s) **ehwaR/*ehwō* complicate the interpretation of this bracteate word-formula. It occurs on perhaps as many as 13 bracteates in restricted code forms — all of them runologically problematic (VI.39). Based purely on the medium-typology of the bracteate genre, and the general meaning of the horse in Germanic lore, we are left to speculate that the formula is intended to convey an apotropaic force (through the aggressive instrumental power of the horse?),(17) or to have a more general meaning of wealth, fertility, and well-being. The only elaborated form (IK 11) seems to have an almost cultic, dedicatory function — *ehē*: 'to the horse.' In fact, it may be that the **ehw-* formula has this more "religious" function — as an extended symbol of a divine entity (**Wōðanaz?*). This would fit with Hauck's (1981a) interpretation of the bracteates as primarily "*Devotionalien*" of the Odinic cult in Denmark.

Of all the word-formulas, *lapu* is the most difficult for which to determine a concrete motive. Like *alu*, it seems to be used in a general sense — and to appear either at the beginning or at the end of a complex restricted-code formula; often connected to a PN. The clearer meaning of *lapu* as a 'summons, invitation, or invocation' (here: to the god[s]), or the "loading" of some dynamistic force into the medium, at least makes its function more obvious. Therefore the primary motivation seems to be the provision of the medium with an extraordinary force which supplements the operative motive expressed through other (runic, and/or pictographic) elements. As a word expressing an originally vocal concept, *lapu* may be fundamentally comparable to *rūnō*, and be used in a way similar to that in which the singular form *rūnō* is sometimes found (VI.5-6). This is made clearer when we compare the semantically parallel elaborated-code formulas with *laþu* (e.g., N. *fahide laþoþ*, IK 70) with those which have *rūnō* (e.g., N. *rūnō fāhido*, KJ 63).

Motivationally, the *auja* formula is one of the most clear. It obviously carries the intention of imparting luck or good fortune to the wearer of the bracteate. The restricted-code formula on IK 161: *auja* (*Alawin*) seems to operatively wish good luck for *Alawin*,(18) while the elaborated code formula on IK 98: *gibu auja* is straightforwardly a performative in which the rune-master gives good fortune to the wearer of the bracteate. In both cases, the motive of *auja* is the attraction of beneficial influences.

The *nomen agentis* spear head names (VI.41) stand somewhat apart from the other word-formulas, but their motive is clearly an aggressive communication with the enemy, and with their protective weapons. The rune-master attacks the protective forces of the enemy through the inscribed form on the weapon, and thereby weakens their defences and perhaps frightens away their protective entities (i.e., beings analogous to the ON *valkyrjur, landvættir*, etc.).

This idea would lend support to Düwel's (1983: 124) interpretation of the Illerup spear heads' **ojingaR** as 'the terrorizer,' i.e., 'the one that frightens away the protective entities of the enemy.' Of course, a secondary benefit of this effective form of magical attack would be the ultimate defence of one's own forces.

Rune-Formulas

4. The essentially two types of rune-formulas (i.e., series of runic characters without apparent semantic content) are 1) sequential (i.e., according to **fuþark** order) and 2) non-sequential or random. These formulas have often been referred to in a somewhat off-handed way as "magical," without specifying *how* they are supposed to be magical — i.e., how they are supposed to affect objective or subjective reality. These sequences have sometimes been viewed as strings of ideo- or logographs,(19) or simply as graphemes (III.4). For purposes of this study, we will only concentrate on the runic characters as graphemes and as elements of an *a priori* organized system subject to manipulation. In the course of this interpretative analysis of data presented in ch. VI. 43-49, perhaps more questions are raised than problems solved, but it is hoped that some new avenues for the consideration of these problematic sequences will be opened. Certain suggestions are admittedly speculative. This is, however, to a large extent determined by the ambiguous nature of the data.

Sequential Formulas

Sequential formulas seem to be of three types: 1) complete, or nearly so, fuþarks (also perhaps apparent attempts to represent a series of 24 characters?),(20) 2) abbreviated versions of the **fuþark** order,(21) and 3) apparently random sequences somehow affected by the **fuþark** order (i.e., IK 153): Skåne II-C, and KJ 154. Of the 14 inscriptions which belong to one of these types, only two (KJ 5 and perhaps KJ 6) would seem to have non-operative functions.

Mode

Whether or not the graphemes in question are to be understood as logograms, they unquestionably represent the ideas of *entirety* or completeness, and *order*. This is the primary meaning, which I think can be ascribed to the **fuþark**-formulas. These then act as graphic symbols of wholeness and order itself, that through the same kind of contagion used in the word-formula inscriptions impart this quality to the medium upon which they are carved. Could the **fuþark** then be a channel for the communication of the idea of a certain order in subjective or objective reality? If this is true, then the **fuþark** (or its abbreviated forms) would qualify for a metaphorical meaning: "completeness, order," and work on the same modality as the word-formulas.

Motives

Besides the rather vague (but common) magical motive generally to restore or maintain an order of some kind, what might be more specific motives for **fuþark**-formulas? For a solution to this question, we must explore the runic and archeological contexts of the formulas. Eight of the twelve probably operative formulas are on bracteates, which may be amuletic (i.e., apotropaic or beneficial), or cultic in nature. The only runic contexts on these are the possible *ephesion grammaton* **luwatuwa** (see below) and conjecturally *salu*: 'the samphire.'(22) Two brooch formulas, KJ 7: Aquincum (with a problematic byname) and KJ 154 Herbrechtingen, also seem to have been worn by living persons, and are thus possibly amuletic. Their primary motive could be the maintenance of a beneficial (and natural) order, which might include fertility and good health in the life of the wearer.

Another only rarely attested context for **fuþark** inscriptions is the grave. The most famous example is the Kylver st. (KJ 1) which also bears the palindrome **sueus** = 'horse'(?).(23) (1981b: 77-79) has convincingly shown that KJ 8: Beuchte brooch was carved just prior to its placement in the grave, so it too must be considered a funderal inscription. The underlying motive for both of these would be the holding of the dead in the grave — again as a function of the modality of the ordered **fuþark** as a maintainer of natural order. At least this gives a plausible explanation as to how the fuþark could be used for both beneficial amulets and binding formulas.

An additional function of the **fuþark** order may have been an expression of a sort of intellectual, anlaytical ordering in the subjective reality of the rune-master. This is also a feature of alphabetic magic in other cultures (see Dornseiff 1922). That this system provided a framework for ordering extra-lingusitic data is likely further indicated by the enduring features of the runic system itself (IV.11).

Non-Sequential Formulas

The variations of this kind of formula, and the problems in any attempt to interpret them, are discussed in VI.46-48. Phonologically, they may be divided into pronounceable and unpronounceable sequences, and runological and archeological data may be brought to bear on their possible motivations. Since the great majority of these formulas (at present count ca. 47 of ca. 61) are on bracteates, and since the majority of these (ca. 39) are without any other runic context, we must assume that most of these *ephesia grammata* are probably random repetitions of runic (and rune-like) characters by analphabetic bracteate-masters.(24) These may, or may not, have been intentionally devoid of semantic content. Basically, we are left with four formula types:

  I. random/unpronounceable forms in isolation
  II. random/unpronounceable forms in runic contexts
  III. pronounceable forms in isolation
  IV. pronounceable forms in runic contexts

It is tempting to think that in some instances the unpronounceable forms are *graphic* in nature (i.e., represent a randomized sequence of graphs), while the pronounceable ones are possibly *phonetic* (i.e., represent a vocalized formula of some kind).

Modes

Non-sequential rune-formulas seem to work in two distinct modes. Based upon analogy with the symbolism of order represented by the sequential **fuþark** formula, random, graphic unpronounceable formulas could be an operative symbol for disorder and confusion. But how might this symbolism of disorder be interpreted? If our interpretation of the mode of the sequential formulas is to any degree correct, we might suppose that the disordering effect of non-sequential formulas is to work toward some dynamic change, i.e., to alter some existing detrimental condition, or to prevent some feared maleficence. Such a formula might also act as a "graphic riddle" meant to confuse a threatening malicious entity.(25) In any event it would represent the communication of confusion and disorder to the subjective or objective environment.

Quite independent of the graphic symbolism of the **fuþark** order, non-sequential, pronounceable formulas might work on the level of phonetic symbolism transferred to, or reinforced by, graphic form for operative purposes. But the important question remains as to how these "sound-formulas" might function. The most plausible, and at the same time meaningful, explanation of these relatively rare phonetic forms might be found in the concept of *glossolalia*.(26) These formulas could be understood as examples of purely *emotive*(27) utterances (perhaps first spoken in shamanic trance states, etc.) which might have been perceived as "divine speech" or direct communication from the gods, etc. These would then represent words in the magical language of the gods, which might be endowed with some profound, but strictly emotive, non-semantic, non-etymological significance through a secondary process of stereotyping and eventual inclusion in the runic lexicon. Ultimately, these "words" would act on the same level as the word-formulas — but their traditional meanings (if any) are now virtually untraceable.

Motives

If the isolated random graphic formulas present almost exclusively on bracteates(28) have any operative motive (beyond perhaps making them more attractive to buyers?), it may have been to confuse potentially malicious entities and thus act apotropaically. But we must generally classify these as unknown or doubtful as to motive.

Once similar random formulas are attested in runic and more varied archeological contexts, a certain amount of motivational interpretation must be ventured. The most remarkable of these is the Lindholm amulet (KJ 29) with its repetitive, non-sequential, partially random rune-formula (see VI.48), which is reflected in later tradition as both a curse and an amatory curse formula.(29) We can be certain that this formula had some degree of aggressive intent or mode, but its motive may have been apotropaic. Three various kinds of inscriptions seem to be intended to pin the dead in their graves. The Beuchte brooch (KJ 8, see above) perhaps contains the randomized formula **Rj**, which might have helped hold the dead in the grave in which it was found. Two stones may have had similar motives, i.e., the Krogsta *bauta*-st. (KJ 100), with its pictographic representation of a man holding his hand out with widely splayed fingers (an apotropaic gesture?),(30) which is standing in a grave field,(31) and the By st. (KJ 71), the archeological context of which is unsure. All three of these bear what is probably the rune-master's name in various types of formulas —but the motive of the *ephesia grammata* is perhaps to confuse potential *draugar* and to prevent them from becoming animate. Complex formulas of this kind are also found on bracteates — which we can only assume had a beneficial function. Allesø-B (IK 13) may be specifically intended as a fertility charm if r. 1-4 can be reconstructed *lau(ka)R*. What follows that has been reconstructed as other word-formulas (cf. Krause 1966: 250), but it may be an extended *ephesion grammaton*. The Halskov-C and Maglemose III-C bracteates both contain probable rune-master names juxtaposed to random formulas. The Aquincum brooch (see above), with its random two-rune formula **jl** between a **fuþark** and appellative, remains conjecturally a beneficial formula.

Isolated pronounceable formulas are as obscure as the apparently purely graphic ones. Among the most intriguing of this type are Norway-A **anoaṅa**, the Illerup spear shaft plane **afilaiki**,(32) and if we ignore sometimes questionable reconstructions, the bracteate formulas of Lellinge-B: **salusalu** and Faxe-B: **foslau** could easily belong to this category. Beyond our conjectural interpretation of such utterances being direct ("spiritual") communication with animate entites (to attract them or to ward them off?), little more can be ventured without further context.

Runic and archeological contexts for these pronounceable non-sequential formulas provide a limited motivational typology. Apparently intended as formulas for holding the dead in the grave are Noleby (KJ 67) and Kylver (KJ 1), both of which were probably barrow-stones. The Noleby *ephesion grammaton*: **suhurah:susi**... is especially remarkable because it is embedded in a complex syntactic formula (VI.50), while the Kylver formula: **sueus** is actually most probably a palindrome for Gotlandic *eus*: 'horse'— but as it stands, could be read as a "magical word" *sueus* juxtaposed to a complete **fuþark**. The dedicatory cultic formula on the spear shaft of Kragehul (KJ 27) contains the curious g̃a g̃a g̃a *ginu* g̃a (see VII.50), which is usually read as an abbreviation of some lexemic formula,(33) may also be left as g̃ag̃ag̃a *ginu* g̃a: i.e., a magical-emotive intensifier of the semantic formula. Of apparent beneficial motivation are the three(34) bracteates: Vadstena-C, Fyn I-C, and the more recently found Anglo-Saxon bracteate of Undley. The Vadstena phonetic formula: **ḷuwatuwa**, prefixed to a complete **fuþark**, and the Fyn sequence, embedded between the fairly clear word formulas *laþu*, seem to be unambiguously intentional. The Undley bracteate appears to bear a formula similar to that on the Kragehul spear shaft: [g̃o] g̃a g̃o g̃a.

Two repetitive formulas which seem clearly logographic are contained on the (KJ 38) Gjersvik tanning knife (perhaps *laukaR* x 10 — or — *[ina-laukaR* x 5), and the triple f-runes (*fehu*) on the Gummarp st. (KJ 95) — both of which seem to be operative wishes for increase and prosperity.

By their very nature, these rune-formulas are the most difficult to interpret. But on a basic level, it seems that with the **fuþark**-formulas we are dealing with the rune-master's desire to order, to give structure and organization to his subjective and objective reality; while with the non-sequential formulas we are faced with the rune-master's need to confuse or disorganize some detrimental aspect, or perhaps to express a special magical channel of communication between these realities.

Syntactic Operative Formulas

5. These inscriptions somehow make explicit an operative motive, and usually give some indication of the mode of that operation. The structures of these formulas are complex in that they often contain more than one formulaic element. For example, eight of the sixteen inscriptions dealt with in detail here include a rune-master formula, and four or five of them seem to have prosodic qualities. In general; however, these complex formulas are too few and formally too diverse to be reduced to a simplified typology. Each must be approached to some degree on its own terms.

Vocabulary

Due to the complexity of these formulas, they are not dominated by a restricted lexicon. There is a considerable number of PNs (nine); mainly due to the fact that rune-master formulas are often included. Also, it is noteworthy that the material medium upon which the runes are carved is stated or implied in the text a total of eight times. It is made explicit on Eggjum (KJ 101): **stAin**: 'stone,' Vetteland (KJ 60): **staina**: 'stone,' Strom (KJ 50): **hali**: 'stone,' Strand (KJ 18): **sikli**: 'jewel,' and Westeremden B (AZ 38): **ïwi**: 'yew (dat.).' It has been reconstructed on the Kragehul spear shaft (KJ 27): **g[aiRa]**: 'to the spear,' and it is implied by a demonstrative on the stones of Stentoften and Björketorp (KJ 96;97): **þAt**: 'this (monument, stone?).' This is a feature that we might have expected based on the naming of the medium in later formulaic literary accounts of rune-carving (see V.15).

Composition

Because of the explicit nature of the formulas, their composition often gives insight into the actual mode of operation as well. Various phrases in these complex formulas conform to one of five categories (outlined in VI.50-52): 1) performatives (which would include all explicit rune-master formulas, cf. KJ 101; 96; 97; 18; 27; 50[?]; 60; 61; 102; 67; 95; AZ 38; and IK 98, 2) imperatives, cf. KJ 62; 76(?); 165(?); and Oetting[?], 3) juridics, cf. KJ 101; 96; and 97,(35) 4) analogies (mythic/epic paradigms used analogically), cf. KJ 101; 96(?); and AZ 38, and 5) prayer/invocation, cf. KJ 67[?], Whitby comb [M. p.134]).(36)

Possible prosodic qualities are contained in perhaps five of these formulas. Simple rhythmic alliteration is present in the main text on the Stentoften st. (KJ 96): *Niuha-būrumR / niuha-gestumR // HaþuwolfR gaf jāra / HariwolfR. . .'s nū hlē*, and on part of KJ 67: Noleby, e.g., *rūnō fāhi ragina-kundo. . .* The rhythmic work-song style of KJ 50: Strøm is well known (cf. Krause 1966: 112; Antonsen 1975b). While the Eggjum st. (KJ 101) appears to be a poetic masterpiece of the rune-master's craft, which not only displays metrical sophistication (cf. e.g., Owen 1927/28 *passim*), but also demonstrates the possible use of *kenningar* (e.g., II.b *land gotna*?) and *heiti* (e.g., *hæriọss*: 'lord-god [= Óðinn],' cf. also H. Schwarz (1956: 229). The Westeremden B yew stave (AZ 38) also seems to contain some sophisticated poetic features.

Mode

By means of syntactic formulas, the rune-master is in a position to communicate in a more refined way with the numinous reality — be it conceived of as animistic or dynamistic. He may directly communicate his operative message in an elaborated code, that is, save for its execution in rune-staves, often a representation of an oral formula in natural speech.

Each of the various formal elements that we have identified in these syntactic formulas works in its own way. Performatives (II.1) essentially "do the thing" (to paraphrase Austin 1962) by carving the formula (and by performing other actions in proper context). This type of action is most clearly subjective with regard to the rune-master, as he is the independent authority for setting the process in motion. Although that process might include activity by other animistic or dynamistic forces. Imperative formulas also work on the authority of the rune-master to command the objective reality in order to have some effect on the environment. Juridical forms are more complicated in that they presuppose a legal structure with which the formula and the will of the rune-master interacts. Nevertheless, the chief power which resides in these formulas seems to be that of the rune-master and of the runes themselves (cf. KJ 96/97). The analogical formulas, although poorly represented in the tradition,(37) work in a more indirect way by effectively linking a present situation with a paradigmatic one which has an outcome analogous to the one desired by the rune-master. There are no clear examples of supplicative prayer-type formulas in the older runic corpus,(38) although there is evidence to show that animistic beings were perhaps called upon to carry out certain functions, cf. e.g., KJ 101; 60; 38(?), and the underlying significance of the formula *laþ-* (see VI.40).

All of the formulaic elements act as channels for the communicative will of the rune-master; channels which seem to be enhanced by various features, i.e., that they are carved in runes, that they are often carefully composed in particular rhythms, and that they were perhaps accompanied by auxiliary ritual actions (see V.15-16).

Motives

The complex motives for these inscriptions are made more or less explicit by their linguistic interpretations presented in VI.50-52. However, a summary of the corpus arranged according to a motivational typology may yield some additional information.

Protection of a (sacred/juridical?) locality from malicious outsiders seems to be the motivation for the Björketorp and Stentoften sts., while a similar protection of the grave from howebreakers appears the most likely motive for the Vetteland and Eggjum sts. On the other hand, the Noleby, Kalleby, and Tørvika B sts., and the brooch of Strand seem to be apotropaics intended to hold the dead in their graves, or perhaps to prevent them from being used by malefactors.

More aggressive motives may be behind the stone of Roes if we interpret the horse-symbology as indicative of a curse formula. An equally dangerous curse formula would be presented by the Gjersvik tanning knife if we accepted Olsen's (*NIæR*: II, 640ff.) reconstruction *dís fioþ iRwiR*: 'a dís hates you...' — which we would not necessarily expect on a tanning knife.

Theultimate motive of the Kragehul spear shaft (VI.51) is most probably a kind of cultic curse placed on the military enemies of the runemaster in which he formally dedicates — or consecrates — the enemies' defensive weapons (symbolized by the helmet) to the aggressive weapons (symbolized by the spear?), i.e., he foredooms the enemy with his cultic formula to be sacrificed (to *Wōðanaz?).

The Westeremden B yew stave (AZ 38) would seem to have as its motivation the stilling of stormy seas, which is quite practical for trips in the North Sea. This particular motive was apparently common enough, cf. the ON term *brimrúnar*: 'surf-runes' (see V.14).

Generally beneficial motives lie behind the *gibu auja*: 'I give good fortune' formula on the Sjælland II-C bracteate (although the whole works rather apotropaically). The logographic f(*ehu*) runes of the Gummarp st. would indicate that wealth and prosperity were its ultimate aims. A similar motivation (also with a logographic rune, see sect. 7) appears to underly the main text on the Stentoften st. (KJ 96): 'To the new (or nine?) farmers, to the new (or nine?) foreigners, Haþuwolf gave good harvest. (See V.50)

Some amatory motivation may be present on the Bülach brooch, although it is unclear for whom it is meant. Since it was worn by a woman, and it bears a masc. PN followed by an imperative formula: *ðū f(a)t(o) mik*: 'embrace thou me:' — we could formally consider that either the woman was wishing for the man's embrace (in which case we would have a fem. rune-master, see VI.32), or if the PN is that of the rune-master, the subject of imperative would be the woman who wore the brooch.

Auxiliary Elements

Concealment

6. In runic literature, the apparent hiding of inscriptions (e.g., *in* graves, on the *backs* of brooches, etc.) has been the subject of comment. While the older literature viewed this simple physical concealment as "proof" of "magic," some later investigators have doubted this. Certainly, taken alone such evidence, without any supporting theoretical framework, is usually not convincing.(39)

However, the fact that the whole idea of concealment seems to form a theme in the thinking of the rune-master and in the "ideology" of the runes, gives us reason to reconsider the evidence in a larger context.

The use of the verb **felhan* (ON *fela*: 'to hide, conceal') in connection with the runes, e.g., *rūnō. . felheka* (KJ 96, cf. also KJ 97), and the ON phrase *vel fólgit í rúnum*: 'well concealed, in secret or obscure words,(40) might indicate that this had a special runo-technical sense, which perhaps had to do with an operative function. Placement of the inscriptions (especially of operative portions of the text, cf. e.g., the younger Tryggevælde st., DR 230) in locations invisible to human eyes also remains a point to be considered.

Physical concealment is only one way in which runic messages might be made obscure to the unknowing observer. The most remarkable of these are the runic codes (see IV.11), which in the Middle Ages seem to have had little intrinsic operative force. But they may have had a certain magical function in earlier times, cf. e.g., the possible encoded forms of *alu* on the Körlin ring (KJ 46) and on the Ellestad st. (KJ 59).

The operative mode of such practices could work on the simple analogical thought of: what is hidden (i.e., unseen) becomes effective in the hidden or unseen realm with which one is trying to communicate. But no more concrete conclusions are forthcoming.

Runic Logographs

7. Another form of operative concealment may be behind the practice of runic logographs, i.e., the use of single runes as abbreviations for some word (usually the traditional rune name). Krause (1966: 320-23) in his index to the runic inscriptions lists 45 possible attestations of *Begriffsrunen* (see III.2). Not all of these would meet Düwel's (1974) criteria for consideration as ideographic runes, but nevertheless the tradition does

appear to be well established. Among the clearest examples are the Gummarp st. (KJ 95) with three f(*ehu*)-runes, the Stentoften st. (.KJ 96) and the Skadborg-B bracteate (IK 161) with j(*ēra*)-runes in syntactic contexts, and the Nebenstedt-I-B bracteate with a final l(aukaR)-rune. One of the most intriguing examples would be the apparent ǥa bind-rune on the Kragehul spear shaft (KJ 27) — which with little real justification has been identified with the *gibu auja* formula (cf. IK 98), along with the ǥa ~ ǥo bind-runes on the Undley bracteate. The operative mode of such abbreviations is perhaps related to that of runic cryptography. In fact, they might be considered another form of code — the decipherment of which is dependent upon the reader's degree of familiarity with the extra-linguistic features of the "runic system."

Number Patterns

8. As noted in III.3, attempts to determine more or less complex numerical patterns according to various systems (many times *ad hoc*) have dominated the discussion of "rune-magic" at least since the time of Olsen's (1917) study. None of these methods are entirely convincing, especially when applied to actual runic inscriptions. A systematic survey of the inscriptions in the older fuþark made by the author in 1981-82 yielded no consistent patterns in the corpus. It is, however, suspected that if the latest inscriptions and the younger inscriptions were similarly treated as a corpus, different results might emerge, if only simple rune counts (i.e., totals of the number of runic characters in a text) were taken into account. A systematic attention on the part of the rune-master to such a detail would not be unlike the poet's attention to the syllable-count in verse. In fact, this very correspondence was noted in Morgenroth's (1961) critical review of Olsen's theories. The possible operative effect of such a practice would then be analogous to that of *poetry*, i.e., the establishment of an empathetic form of communication with higher powers.

Ideographic Signs

9. Non-runic ideographic signs (see V.10), the genealogies of which are more or less known, occur with some regularity in the environment of older runic inscriptions. Among the North Germanic inscriptions, the sign ᛋ (41) is found in the ductus of the runes at least five times (KJ 11, IK 13, 129, 302, 326), and it is closely juxtaposed to the inscription on the Åsum

bracteate (IK 11), cf. Krause (1932: 58ff.). This swastika symbol is also common on other (runic and non-runic) bracteates, but as a part of the internal pictographic iconography, which can not be directly correlated to the runic formulas. Furthermore, the sign appears (along with *tamga*-signs) on two of the East Germanic spear heads (KJ 32: Dahmsdorf and KJ 33: Kovel), and on one of the triangular panels of the ring of arlin (KJ 46). A tree-like sign appears in the ductus of KJ 1: Kylver st. and IK 98: Sjælland II-C (⍟). Also, there are two curious non-runic signs (✤ and ᛭) on the stone of Skåäng (KJ 85) directly appended to PNs. South Germanic inscriptions also bear a number of unique non-runic symbols cataloged conveniently by Arntz (1939: 480).(42) The bracteate corpus is liberally sprinkled with inscriptions which consist entirely or in part of rune-like (but non-runic) signs, i.e., rune-imitations,(43) and inscriptions which appear to be attempts to imitate Latin capitals.(44)

It is highly probable that well-known signs such as the swastika, the triskelion (KJ 32), and the Sarmatian *tamgas* were placed on the objects in question for some operative purpose, but the motive is far from clear. On comparative evidence it has been generally assumed that the ⌘ had an apotropaic function, or had the sense of "good fortune." (See V.10.) The nature of the evidence and the lack of contemporary corroborating evidence leaves us in no position to analyze this question further. It is most likely that the various rune- and Latin capital-imitation inscriptions are botched or careless efforts on the part of bracteate-masters. The only possible operative mode they could have would be analogous to the non-sequential, unpronounceable formulas (see sect. 4).

Pictographic Signs

10. Apart from the bracteate tradition, pictographic (or iconic) iconography that appears intentionally juxtaposed(45) to a runic inscription is relatively rare. Equine symbolism dominates the corpus. In addition to the C-type bracteates,(46) a horse and rider (surrounded by dogs?) appears on the Mjöbro stone (KJ 99), while a horse is portrayed in isolation on the Eggjum (KJ 101) and Roes (KJ 102) stones. A fish-like or serpentine figure appears on the Lindholm amulet (KJ 29), and on the reverse side of the fishing weight(?) of Førde (KJ 49). A crude anthropomorphic and zoomorphic figure is depicted on the Krogsta st. (KJ 100). Miscellaneous anthropomorphic and zoomorphic figures were portrayed on the unique horn of Gallehus B (KJ 43) and on the ring of Körlin (KJ 46) — both now lost.

Of these attestations, it seems that several could have operative motives. The magical symbology of the horse has been discussed several times in the foregoing chapters, but its direct operative function in pictographic form is only apparent on the stones of Eggjum and Roes — where an aggressive formula is juxtaposed to it. The C-type bracteates, which are more beneficial in function, may be best interpreted in the realm of cultic iconography. It is also attractive to view the serpentine shape and head of the Lindholm amulet as corroborative of the interpretation of the inscription as an aggressive, perhaps even malicious, one.(47) The unique human figure on Krogsta has been suggested to be apotropaic in function, cf. Krause (1966: 227).

Color

11. We can be certain that most inscribed runic texts were also colored with some form of pigment — probably red in hue. Traces of this material have even been detected in some younger inscriptions (cf. Jansson 1963: 158-64). Of course, linguistic evidence also shows this procedure to have been fundamental to the runic technology, i.e., the verb *faihjan, ON fá: 'to color,' which became synomymous with 'to carve' in the runo-technical terminology, and the later term rjóða: 'to redden' (cf. Ebel 1963: 30ff.). Literary evidence perhaps gives us the key to the original operative symbology of this coloring when we read of the coloring of the runes with blood (cf. *ES* ch. 44, *Gret. s.* ch. 79), and other references to blood and runes. (See V.14.) The magical function of the substance of blood is well known (V.9), and the red pigment (probably ochre or minium) would be a symbolic substitution for this vivifying substance — especially in more elaborate inscriptions. However, it must be noted that once the use of this color became traditional, the practice of dyeing the runes red could have been carried on with no particularly operative motive. But at its most archaic level, there seems to be little doubt that this procedure had a magical significance, i.e., that of lending some kind of "life" to the runes.

Notes for Chapter VII

1. For our purposes, features which compose this linguistic-formulaic level are: phonology, semantics, and syntax (prosody).

2. This is the level at which elements (perhaps lexemes, or perhaps graphs in the case of rune-formulas) are *ordered* and juxtaposed to other elements in a complex formulation.

3. For some general treatments of these formulas, see Olsen (*NIæR*: II, 623ff.), Feist (1922), Sierke (1939: 107-09), Jacobsen-Moltke (1942: 645), Marstrander (1952: 106), and Andersen (1961: 93-97 *et passim*).

4. This is later reinforced in the younger tradition with formulas such as: **iak sata runar rit** — *iak sæta rūnar rētt*: 'I set the runes rightly' (cf. DR 239: Gørlev).

5. The idea of the ritual power of "pastness" or as Eliade (e.g., 1971) calls it *in illo tempore*, is superbly developed for Germanic cosmology by Bauschatz (1976; 1982). It may be that on an operative level, such a concept could work on the basic conception: 'what was, shall be.'

6. Cf. van Baal (1971: 264). Marstrander (1952: 106) emphasizes this aspect as well. Solid paradigmatic textual evidence would seem to be offered by Háv. 142: (*Rúnar*). . ./ *er fáði Fimbulþulr // oc gorðo ginregin // oc reist Hroptr rǫgna*. (See V.14.) See also Flowers (2006: 76).

7. Examples of this group, which would also include third-pers. formulas, are KJ 13a; 16; 17a; 30; 39(?); 53; 55; 56; 63; 69; and IK 42; 70; 156(?); 241,1-2; 340; 341 (?).

8. See Düwel (1979a: 233ff.). Other inscriptions which might belong to this group include: KJ 96: Stentoften, and KJ 97: Björketorp.

9. See the discussion of the etymology and meaning of *þirbijaR* in ch. VI, note 116.

10. See V.9, VI.37, and cf. Krause (1946/47) and Düwel (1977).

11. This motive has often been ascribed to runic inscriptions. The question has been examined by Düwel (1979a). We are tempted to suspect that many of the (buried and concealed) barrow-stone inscriptions, which consist merely of a single PN in the nom. or gen., refer to the dead and have the motive of *holding* the dead in the grave by force of attraction or attachment to that *name*. (See V.3. on the force of the name in Germanic traditions.) Examples of this type might be: KJ 74; 75; 76; 78; 79; 80; 81; 82; 83; 84; 89; 90; 93; and 94.

12. See VI.50. for a full reading of the Noleby text, and see sect. 5 below for a complete analysis of the magical modalities and motives contained in the complex formula.

13. This may have developed from an originally abstract concept, "ecstasy → magic," which was at least partially transferred to a substance, see V.9, and VI,34.

14. *Salu* could also be interpreted in the abstract class if we read it with Grienberger (1906: 138ff.) as *traditio*: 'transfer (of property, etc.),' cf. ON *sala*: 'sale.'

15. This term is used in a way parallel to socio-linguistic terminology (cf. e.g., Edwards 1976: 90-95).

16. Cf. the ideas concerning a special "sacred" or poetic vocabulary outlined by Watkins (1970; 1982) and Campanile (1977).

17. Cf. the use of the horse image in Germanic curse formulas, see VI note 289, and IV.39.

18. The identity and importance of *Alawin* remains obscure. It is most probably a common PN, and thus the inscription could represent an unusually personalized bracteate formula.

19. Especially most recently by K. Schneider (1956; 1968).

20. Cf. IK 110: Lindkær-C, IK 140: Overhornbæk IK 295: Lundeborg-A, and IK 339: Småland-C.

21. This is usually done with the first few runes of the normal sequence, but perhaps the Alpha-Omega-type interpretation of IK 101: Faxe-B, cf. Krause's (1966: 258) reading: f-o *salu*, would qualify it in this category.

22. But this whole formula foslau may be another *ephesion grammaton*.

23. See VI.48 for a full reading of this palindrome.

24. Certain repeated elements and runic combinations would suggest that these artisans were at least to some degree cognizant of runic practice.

25. Cf. the suspected magical function of the riddle-like *ephesia grammata* (Moltke 1938: 129).

26. For linguistic and/or non-Judeo-Christian cross-cultural discussions of this phenomenon, cf. Samarin (1968), Eliade (1964: 93ff, *et passim*), Mauss (1972: 57-58), Goodman (1972: 121ff.), and Williams (1981: 169ff. *et passim*).

27. These utterances are devoid of any semantic content. Cf. Goodman's (1972: 123-25) intriguing but unproven theory that the glossolaliac vocalization behavior is produced in a state of arrested conscious cortical control in the brain, with a reconnection of the speech center with some subcortical structure.

28. The only possible exception is the runologically questionable Frøslev wand (KJ 36), which is certainly a palindrome for the formula *liR or *lim in the older or younger fuþark respectively.

29. Cf. *Galdrabók* no. 46 and Árnason (1954: I, 435), and see VI.48.

30. Cf. Krause (1966: 227).

31. Because the Krogsta st. is not connected to any one mound, it may have been intended to hold the dead in the vicinity in general. Although it may have been directed toward grave robbers, this seems less likely.

32. Both of these would violate Goodman's "rule" of glossolaliac units never beginning with a vowel (1972: 121ff.).

33. Cf. e.g., Olsen (*NIæR*: II, 625ff.) *gibu auja*, etc., or Krause (1966: 66) with rune name logographs *g(ebu) a(nsuR)*: 'gift to the gods.'

34. A fourth could be added, IK 149: Skåne I-B, but its *possible ephesion grammaton* gakaR is most satisfactorily reconstructed as *ga(u)kaR*: 'cuckoo.' (See VI.42.)

35. These are formulas which actually contain or imply the structure if x is done, then y will follow as punishment. Three other inscriptions seem to bear declarative legalistic formulas, i.e., KJ 59: Ellestad (with encoded *alu*?), KJ 72: Tune, and KJ 77: Mykklebostad.

36. This is a somewhat misleading category since prayerful supplication does not seem to be present in the tradition, while an impersonal subjunctive may be present in KJ 50: 'Let the horn wet the stone, etc.' (but see VI.51) and divine or demonic beings may be invoked in imperative or performative formulas in KJ 38(?); 60; 101; and Oetting(?).

37. They are better represented in the younger tradition, see VI.53.

38. The reading of part of the Noleby st. (KJ 67) as *hwatin Haukoþu*: 'may they (i.e., the runes of the formula?) make *HaukoþuR* sharp' is far from certain. (See VI.50.)

39. Notable exceptions would be the barrow-stones (those hidden within the mound, or as part of a burial chamber), but many of these were called into question by Bæksted (1951).

40. See VI.50.

41. Cf. e.g., Olsen (*NIæR*: III, 204ff.), Krause (1932: 58-62; 1966: 34 *passim*), and Düwel (1981b: 75).

42. Cf. also Op. 26; 27; and Eichstetten (Opitz 1981: 26ff.). Opitz tends to interpret these as Christian signs with an apotropaic motive. This could certainly be correct given the social context of the South Germanic runic corpus.

43. Cf. e.g., IK 9, 91, 151, 154, 165, 198, 215, 231, 238, 239, 295, 312-1, 323, 329, 339, 343, 345, 357, 358, 362, 364.

44. Cf. e.g., IK 25, 31, 47, 59, 85, 107, 145, 174, 183, 193, 323, 354, 213, 246, 254, 256, 282, 302, 326, 346, 351, 361, 384.

45. Two inscriptions, KJ 53: Kårstad and KJ 54: Himmelstalund, have been placed within the context of pre-existing Bronze Age rock carvings.

46. Bracteates are classified according to their iconography, e.g., A: human head in profile, B: mixture of various anthropomorphic and zoomorphic figures, C: horse and rider, F: highly stylized zoomorphic figure.

47. It is noteworthy that Óðinn is the only Germanic god positively connected to snakes or serpents, cf. his (in the guise of Bǫlverkr:) transformation into a serpent to gain access to the poetic mead (Háv. 106; *ESS*, *Skalds*. ch. 2), and his *heiti*: Ófnir: 'the instigator,' and Svávnir: 'the killer' — both identified as serpents (*ESS*, *Gylfa*. ch. 16; *Skalds*. ch. 57), cf. Falk (1924: 23; 26).

Chapter VIII

Summary

Over the past generation, there has been a tendency to downplay the importance of "magic" in the runic tradition. This was perhaps necessary to some extent — when it was not accompanied by close-minded attitudes. In this work, I seek to place the study of runes and magic within the framework of the most recent academic or scientific theories concerning "magic" as a system of operative acts of communication based on a semiotic model. Through this system, the human magician may effectively interact with his environment and bring it into accordance with his will by means of performative acts analogous to, or symbolic of, the desired result. Through performative linguistic acts, the magician is virtually able to "converse" with his environment in an effective way. Since this kind of magical theory is based on linguistic models, it is well suited for application to the runic corpus.

One of the most important aspects of this semiotic theory of magic is the existence of a certain cultural "frame of reference," of which the symbolic system is a part, and of which it (and the magician) take advantage. For the runic tradition, it is essential to show the degree to which the runes, and those who were able to use them, were part of a special social structure. Because of the way the runes were so quickly and systematically taken up over such a wide geographical area by a previously illiterate population, I suspect that some network — based on cultic leagues or socio-economic associations — pre-existed the introduction of the runes. When the early history of the tradition is viewed from this perspective, we see that the rune-masters most likely composed a network of persons who, by traditional (oral) means, were able to transmit knowledge of the runic system, with all its systematic extra-linguistic features, from generation to generation over a period lasting at least 800 years. The gradual, but apparently systematic, transformation from the 24-rune **fuþark** to the 16-rune **fuþark** would be a further indication of the continuing existence of such a network of individuals who shared a common tradition. The fact that this systematic transformation was effected so thoroughly would also suggest that the network was bound by at least some institutional features.

Since no primary literary evidence contemporary with the inscriptions (lst-8th cent.) exists, we are dependent upon corroborative evidence from later textual sources and from contemporary archeological data. Both of these pose particular difficulties and must be dealt with cautiously. Archeological material is inexact and open to widely divergent interpretations, while the written evidence usually dates from several hundred years after the end of the older runic period. However, the written data has the decided advantage of being roughly contemporary with younger runic traditions which seem to be in large measure a continuation of older practices. This is especially true when we focus on the extra-linguistic features of the "runic system," i.e., *ætt*-division, set number, order, names, etc. For our purposes, the most important body of written evidence is that which indicates the technical aspects of the execution of a runic inscription which is unambiguously operative in motive, i.e., it is done to have some effect on the environment. This form of magic — which essentially consists of writing a performative formula in runes accompanied by certain ritualistic auxiliary actions — is so unique in the annals of European magic at the time of these recordings that any possibility of these reports being based on Mediterranean models is easily ruled out.

The fundamental reality with which any would-be interpreter of the magical aspects of runic inscriptions must come to terms is the runic corpus itself. For this reason, a great deal of space is devoted to the formal interpretation, analysis, and classification of the runic material. Due to a variety of factors, e.g., physical condition, runological variation, lack of linguistic contexts, etc., individual inscriptions pose significant difficulties. It has been noted that not one of the older runic inscriptions is completely free of interpretative difficulty. Therefore, I have tried to base such interpretative conclusions on the level of formulaic typology rather than on (supposedly paradigmatic) individual examples. In other words, I have tried to analyze the data within the context of similar examples rather than looking at individual inscriptions in isolation.

A total of four types of formulaic elements were identified in the older runic corpus. (1) Rune-master formulas, which may be transformative, lend the force of the special personality of the rune-master to the medium upon which the runes are carved. The formula can be considered transformative to the extent that the rune-master name or byname seems to be a *functional* or religio-cultic one with which the carver identifies for operative purposes. (2) Word-formulas, by a process of symbolic contagion, transfer the metaphorical qualities of the word-symbol to the medium that it may "act" in accordance with the characteristics of that (magical) substance, quality, or entity, e.g., *alu, laukaR, salu, laþu, auja, *ehwaR*. (3) Rune-formulas have two distinct types. The first is sequential (i.e., **fuþark**-formulas) and is most logically seen as lending the quality of (natural) order to the communicative channel, while the second is non-sequential (i.e., *ephesia grammata*) and seems to impart an element of disorder — perhaps as a way of confusing detrimental influences. In addition, there is a possibility that in this corpus there exists a tradition of non-semantic, emotive "words" akin to glossolaliac utterances which became stereotyped and eventually represented in graphemic form. (4) Semantic formulas are the most elaborate type of runic operation in which the rune-master is able to carry out a complex form of "interreality communication."

For reasons outlined in the introduction, it may not be possible to arrive at a comprehensive and universally agreed upon theory of how runes were used for operative purposes. However, based on what the present study has shown, it is possible to refine further the theory of the way in which runes were utilized for magical operations. The runes themselves, i.e., the whole "runic system," were probably considered to be originally "of the gods" (cf. *ragina-kundo*), perhaps a gift of the god *Wōðanaz. They were part of a complex of features probably common at some point to a specific, self-conscious social group (i.e., *erilōR*?). Because the runes are from the gods (or of a numinous quality) it is natural that they could be considered as symbols intelligible to that "other reality" inhabited by these entities. In order to communicate operatively by means of runes, it seems that the rune-master would first have to identify himself in some ritualized way with the god(s), and then (by means of a traditional ritual format) execute the message (encoded in runes), into a medium — all of which *objectifies* the subjective code. This code, objectified in speech and in physical reality (i.e., the inscription itself), is communicated to a numinous objective reality (animistic and/or dynamistic), which is able to decode it due to the level of systemic empathy or similarity between the source of the communication and the receiver. The numinous receiver then responds with the "feedback" appropriate to the message, e.g., prosperity or protection is granted, evil-doers are destroyed. The ultimate degree of communicative effectiveness may be in direct proportion to the level of empathy, which the magician is able to generate between himself and the receiver. Presumably, this would be effected through the composition of the formula and its correct and traditional performance by the rune-master (in his transformed, more god-like, persona). It is not being suggested that this structure necessarily underlies *all* the older inscriptions, but primarily those that appear to be "magical" based on formulaic and/or archeological data.

REFERENCES

Aakjær, Svend.
1927. "Old Danish Thegns and Drengs." *APS* 2: 1-30.
Agrell, Sigurd.
1927a. *Runornas Talmystik och dess antika Förbild*. (Skrifter utgivna av Vetenskaps-Societen i Lund 6) Lund: Gleerup.
1927b. "Der Ursprung der Runenschrift und der Magie." *ANF* 43: 97-109.
1928a. *Zur Frage nach dem Ursprung der Runennamen*. (Skrifter utgivna av Vetenskaps-Societen i Lund 10) Lund: Gleerup.
1928b. "Studier i senantik Bokstavmystik." *Erannos* 26: 1-51.
1931. *Senantik Mysteriereligion och nordisk Runmagi*. Stockholm: Bonnier.
1931-32. *Die spätantike Alphabetmystik und die Runenreihe*. (Kungl. Humanistiska Vetenskapssamfundet i Lund: Arberättelse 1931-1932) Lund: Gleerup.
1934. *Lapptrummor och Runmagi*. Lund: Gleerup.
1936. *Die Pergamenische Zauberscheibe und das Tarokspiel*. (Kungl. Humanistika Vetenskapssamfundet i Lund. Arberättelse 1935-36, IV) Lund: Gleerup.
1938. *Die Herkunft der Runenschrift*. (Kungl. Humanistiska Vetenskapssamfundet i Lund. Arberättelse 1937-1938, IV) Lund: Gleerup.
Almgren, Oscar.
1909. "Symboliska Miniatyryxor fran den Järnaldern." *Fv*.: 39-42.
1934. *Nordische Felszeichnungen als religiöse Urkunden* (tr. S. Vrandken) Frankfurt/Main: Diesterweg.
Almqvist, Bo.
1965. *Norrön Niddiktning: traditionshistoriska studier i versmagi. I. Nid mot furstar*. (Norska Texter och Undersökningar 21) Stockholm: Almqvist & Wiksell.
1974. *Norrön Niddiktning: Traditionshistoriska studier i versmagi II:1-2. Nid mot Missionärer*. (Norska Texter och Undersökningar 23) Stockholm: Almqvist & Wiksell.
Altheim, Franz.
1938. "Neue Felsbilder aus der Val Camonica: Die Sonne im Kult und Mythos." *Wörter und Sachen*. N.F. 1:1: 12-45.
Altheim, Franz and Trautmann, E.
1939. *Vom Ursprung der Runen*. Frankfurt/Main: Vittorio Lostermann.
1942. *Kimbern und Runen: Untersuchungen zur Ursprungsfrage der Runen*. Berlin-Dahlem: Ahnenerbe-Stiftung Verlag.
Aly, Wolf.
1934/35. "Name." *HDA* VI: 950-67.
Andersen, Harry.
1946. "Runedansk ailti." *ANF* 61: 171-81.
1947. "Det yngre Runalfabets Oprindelse." *ANF* 62: 203-227.
1961. "Guldhornindskriften (Gallehus)." *ANO*: 89-121.
1964. "Einang-stenens Runeindskrift." *ANO*: 93-114.

1967.	"Til Kårstad-Ristningen." *APS* 28: 54-59.
1968.	"Runica." *ANF* 83: 175-83.
1971.	Runologica. Copenhagen: Akademisk Forlag.

Antonsen, Elmer.

1972.	"The Runic Inscription from Opedal." In: Firchow, E. *et al.* (eds.) *Studies for Einar Haugen.* The Hague: Mouton: 46-52.
1975a.	*A Concise Grammar of the Older Runic Inscriptions.* Tübingen: Niemeyer.
1975b.	"The Inscription on the Whetstone from Strøm." *Visible Language* 9: 123-32.
1980a.	"On the Typology of the Older Runic Inscriptions." *SS* 52: 1-15.
1980b.	"Den ældre fuþark: en gudernes gave eller et hverdagsalfabet?" *MM*: 129-43.
1980c.	"Linguistics and Politics in the 19th-century: The Case of the 15th Rune." *Michigan Germanic Studies* 6: 1-16.

Árnason, Jón.

1954-56.	*Islenzkar Þjóðsögur og Æfintyri.* Reykjavík: Bokaútgáfan Þjóðsaga Prentsmiðjan Hólar, 4 vols., 2nd ed.

Arntz, Helmut.

1935a.	*Handbuch der Runenkunde.* Halle/Saale: Niemeyer.
1935b.	"Das Ogom." *BGDSL* 59: 321-413.
1938.	"Christliche deutsche Runendenkmgler?" *Archiv für Religionswissenschaft* 35: 35-60.
1939.	(with contributions by H. Zeiss) *Die einheimischen Runendenkmäler des Festlandes.* Leipzig: Harrassowitz. (cited as AZ).
1944a.	*Handbuch der Runenkunde.* Halle/Saale: Niemeyer, 2nd ed.
1944b.	"Runen and Runennamen." *Anglia* 67-68: 172-250.

Arntz, Helmut and Zeiss, Hans.

1936.	"Ein bajuwarischer Sax mit Runen von Steindorf." *Germania* 20: 127-32.

Askeberg, Fritz.

1944.	*Norden och kontinenten i gammel tid.* Uppsala: Almqvist & Wiksell.

Austin, J. L.

1962.	*How to do things with Words.* (The William James Lectures 1955) Oxford: Clarendon Press.

Avalon, Arthur (John Woodroffe)

1913.	*Tantra of the Great Liberation.* New York: Dover 1972.

Baal, J. van.

1971.	*Symbols for Communication: An introduction to the anthropological study of religion* (Studies of Developing Countries 11) Assen: Van Gorrcum.

Bach, Adolf.

1952-56.	*Deutsche Namenkunde.* Heidelberg: Winter, 2nd ed.

Bæksted, Anders.

1942.	*Islands Runinskrifter.* (Bibliotheca Arnamagnæana II) Copenhagen: Munksgaard.
1943.	*Runerne, deres Historie og Brug.* Copenhagen: Nytt nordisk Forlag.
1945.	"Værløsa Runefibula." *ANO*: 84-91.

1947. "The Stenmagle Rune Box and the Golden Horn Inscription." *Acta Archeologica* 18: 202-10.
1951. "Begravede Runestene." *ANO*: 63-95.
1952. *Måruner og Troldruner: Runemagiske Studier* (Nationalmuseets Skrifter. Arkæologisk-Historisk Række 4) Copenhagen: Nordisk Forlag.

Baesecke, Georg.
1934. "Die Herkunft der Runen." *GRM* 22: 413-17.
1940. *Vorgeschichte des deutschen Schrifttums*. Halle/Saale: Niemeyer, vol. I.

Baetke, Walter.
1942. *Das Heilige im Germanischen*. Tübingen: Mohr.
1964. *Yngvi and die Ynglingar: Eine quellenkritische Untersuchung über das nordische Sakralkönigtum*. (Sitzungsberichte der sächsischen Akademie der Wissenschaften zu Leipzig, Phil.-Hist. Kl. 109, Heft 3) Berlin: Akademie Verlag.

Bammesberger, Alfred.
1969. "Zur Runeninschrift auf dem Sax von Steindorf." *Münchner Studien zur Sprachwissenschaft* 25: 7-10.

Barlau, Stephen.
1975. "Germanic Kinship." Diss. University of Texas at Austin.

Barner, W.
1957. "Von Kultäxten, Beilzauber und rituellem Bohren." *Kunde* N.F. 8: 175-86.

Barnes, Michael and R. I. Page
2006 *The Scandinavian Runic Inscriptions of Britain*. (= Runrön 19) Uppsala universitet: Uppsala.

Bately, J. M. and Evison, V. I.
1961. "The Derby Bone Piece." *Medieval Archeology* 5: 301-05.

Bauschatz, Paul.
1975. "Urth's Well." *JIES* 3: 53-86.
1976. "The Germanic Ritual Feast." In: Weinstock, J. M. (ed.) *The Nordic Languages and Modern Linguistics III*. Austin: University of Texas Press: 289-94.
1982. *The Well and the Tree: World and Time in Early Germanic Culture*. Amherst: University of Massachusetts Press.

Becker, Alfred.
1973. *Franks Casket: Zu den Bildern und Inschriften des Runenkästchens von Auzon*. (Regensburger Arbeiten zur Anglistik 5) Regensburg: Hans Carl.

Behn, Friedrich.
1966. "Der reitende Mitras." In: Rudolf, K. et al. (eds.) *Festschrift Walter Baetke*. Weimar: Böhlaus: 46-49.

Benveniste, Emile.
1973. *Indo-European Language and Society*. (Miami Linguistics Series 12) (tr. E. Palmer) Coral Gables, FL: University of Miami Press.

Berlo, David K.
1960. *The Process of Communication: An Introduction to Theory and Practice*. New York: Holt Rinehart & Winston.

Bertholet, Alfred.
   1926/27.   "Das Wesen der Magie." *Nachrichten von der Gesellschaft der Wissenschaften zu Göttingen*: 63-85.
   1942.   "Der Sinn des kultischen Opfers." *Forschungen und Fortschritte* 18: 17/18: 167.

Beth, Karl.
   1914.   *Religion und Magie bei den Naturvölkern*. Leipzig: Teubner.

Betz, Hans Dieter.
   1991.   "Magic and Mystery in the Greek Magical Papyri" In: Christopher A. Faraone and Dirk Obbink (eds.) *Magika Hiera*. Oxford: Oxford University Press.

Betz, Werner.
   1957.   "Die altgermanische Religion." In: Stammler, W. (ed.) *Deutsche Philologie im Aufriss*. Berlin: Schmidt, vol. III, 2nd ed.: 1547-1646.
   1979.   "Dän. AUJA bei den Alemannen um 575? Zur Inschrift der neugefundenen Oettinger Scheibenfibel." *Archiv* 216: 214-45.

Birkeli, Emil.
   1938.   *Fedrekult i Norge: Et forsøk på en systematisk-deskriptiv fremstilling*. Oslo: Dybwad.

Birkhan, Helmut.
   1965.   "Gapt und Gaut." *ZDA* 94: 1-17.
   1970.   *Germanen und Kelten bis zum Ausgang der Römerzeit*. Vienna: Böhlaus.

Blau, Ludwig.
   1898.   *Das altjüdische Zauberwesen* (Jahresbericht der Landes-Rabbinerschule in Budapest für Schuljahr 1897-98) London: Gregg 1970.

Blomfield, J.
   1942.   "Runes and the Gothic Alphabet." *Saga-Book of the Viking Society* 12: 177-94; 209-31.

Bø, Olav.
   1960.   "Gand." *KHNM* V: 183-85.

Bonfante, Larissa.
   1981.   *Out of Etruria: Etruscan Influence North and South* (BAR International Series 103) Oxford: B.A.R.

Bonnet, Hans.
   1952.   *Reallexikon der ägyptischen Religionsgeschichte*. Berlin: de Gruyter.

Bosworth, Joseph and Toller, T. Northcote.
   1898.   *An Anglo-Saxon Dictionary*. Oxford: Oxford University Press.

Brate, Erik.
   1898.   "Fyrunga-stenen." *ANF* 14: 329-51.
   1911-18.   *Östergölands Runinskrifter*. Stockholm: Kungl. Vitterhets Historie och Antikvitets Akademien. (cited Ög.)
   1925.   *Svenska Runristare*. (Kungl. Vitterhets Historie och Antikvite Akademiens Handlingar 33:3) Stockholm: Akademiens Förlag.

Brate, E. and Wessén, E.
1924-36. *Södermanlands Runinskrifter*. Stockholm: Kungl. Vitterhets Historie och Antikvitets Akademien. (Cited Sö.)
Braune, Wilhelm and Ebbinghaus, Ernst A.
1969. *Althochdeutsches Lesebuch*. Tübingen: Niemeyer, 15th ed.
Brix, Hans.
1927. "Runemester-Kunsten." *Tilskueren* 2: 231-40; 317-24.
1928. *Studier i nordisk Runemagi*. Copenhagen: Nordisk Forlag.
1929. *Nye Studier i nordisk Runemagi*. (*ANO* 1929: 1-188).
1932. *Systematiske Beregninger i de danske Runeindskrifter*. Copenhagen: Gyldendal.
Brønsted, Johannes.
1960. *Danmarks Oldtid III. Jernalderen*. Copenhagen: Gyldendal.
Bruce-Mitford, Rupert.
1978. *The Sutton Hoo Ship-Burial*. London: British Museum, 2 vols.
Bruder, Reinhold.
1974. *Die germanische Frau im Lichte der Runeninschriften und der antiken Historiographie*. Berlin: de Gruyter.
Buchholz, Peter.
1968. "Schamanistische Züge in der altisländischen Überlieferung." Diss. Münster.
Bugge, Sophus.
1874. "Om Runeskriftens Oprindelse." *Forhandlinger i Videnskapsselskapet i Christiana 1873*: 485-89.
1881-89. *Studier over de nordiske Gude- og Heltesagans*. Christiana: Cammermeyer.
1900. "En nyfunden Gotlandsk Runesten." *Svensk Fornminnesforeningens Tidskrift*. 11: 109-13.
1902. *Et benstykke med Runeskrift fundet i Trondhjem*. (Det kgl. Norske videnskaps-Selskap. Skrifter 1901, nr. 4). Trondhjem.
1908. "Das Runendenkmal von Britsum Friesland." *ZDP* 40: 174-84.
Bugge, Sophus and Olsen, Magnus.
1891-1924. *Norges Indskrifter med de ældre Runer*. Christiana: Brøgger. Introduction and 3 vols. (Cited *NIæR*)
Buisson, Ludwig.
1976. *Der Bildstein Ardre VIII auf Gotland* (AAWG Phil.- Hist. Kl. 111.102) Göttingen: Vandenhoeck & Ruprecht.
Buma, W. J.
1951. "Das Runenstäbchen von Britsum." *BGDSL* 73: 306-16.
1966. "In runefynst ut Rasquert." *Us Wurk* 15:4: 85-90.
Buti, Giangabriella.
1982. *Glossario Runico*. Bologna: Editrice Club.
Cahen, Maurice.
1921. *Études sur le vocabulaire religieux du vieux-scandinave: La libation*. (Collection Linguistique publée par la societe linguistique de Paris 9) Paris: Champion.

1925. "L'Etude du Paganisme Scandinave au XXe siecle." *Revue de l'histoire des religions* 92: 33-107.
Campanille, Enrico.
1977. *Ricerche di Cultura Poetica Indoeuropea*. (Orientamenti Linguistici 2) Pisa: Giardini.
Cannon, Walter B.
1942. "'Voodoo' Death." *American Anthropologist* N.S. 44: 169-81.
Chadwick, H. M.
1899. *The Cult of Othin*. London: Clay & Sons.
Chadwick, Nora.
1970. *The Celts*. Harmondsworth: Penguin.
Chaney, William A.
1970. *The Cult of Kingship in Anglo-Saxon England*, Berkeley: University of California Press.
Chao, Yuen Ren.
1968. *Language and Symbolic Systems*. Cambridge: Cambridge University Press.
Chisholm, James.
2002. *Grove and Gallows*. Smithville: Rûna-Raven.
Christiansson, Hans.
1959. *Sydskandinavisk Stil*. Uppsala: Almqvist & Wiksell.
Čiževskij, Dmitrij.
1956. "Magische Speerwurf." In: Chyzhevs, Cmytre (ed.) *Aus zwei Welten* (Slavistic Printings and Reprintings 10) 's Gravenhage: Mouton: 17-28.
Cleasby, Richard, and Vigfusson, Gudbrand.
1957. *An Icelandic Dictionary*. Oxford: Clarendon Press, 2nd ed.
Clemen, Carl.
1928. *Fontes Historiae Religionis Germanicae*. Berlin: de Gruyter.
1937. "Mithramysterien und germanische Religion." *Archiv für Religionswissenschaft* 34: 217-26.
1938. "Alterklassen bei den Germanen." *Archiv für Religionswissenschaft* 35: 60-65.
Clodd, Edward.
1920. *Magic in Names and Other Things*. Detroit: Singing Tree Press 1968.
Closs, Alois.
1936. "Die Religion des Semnonenstammes." In: Koppers, W. (ed.) *Die Indogermanen- und Germanenfrage* (Wiener Beiträge zur Kulturgeschichte und Linguistik 4) Salzburg: Pustet: 549-674.
1952. "Das Versenkungsopfer." In: Koppers, W. *et al.* (eds.) *Kultur und Sprache* (Wiener Beiträge zur Kulturgeschichte und Linguistik 9) Vienna: Herold: 66-107.
1961. "Die Religion der Germanen in ethnologischer Sicht." In: König, F. (ed.) *Christus und die Religionen der Erde*. Vienna: Herder, vol. II: 267-366.
Cockayne, Oswald.
1864-66. *Leechdoms, Wortcunning, and Starcraft of Early England*. London: Longmans, Green, Render, and Dyer. 3 vols.

Codrington, R. H.
 1891. *The Melanesians.* Oxford: Clarendon Press.
Conant, Jonathan B.
 1973. "Runic Alu - A New Conjecture." *JEGP* 72: 467-73.
Cook, R. M.
 1959. "The Diffusion of the Greek Alphabet." *American Journal of Archeology.* 63: 175-78.
Cumont, Franz.
 1911. *Oriental Religions in Roman Paganism.* London: G. Routledge.
Daviðsson, Óláfur.
 1903. "Isländische Zauberzeichen und Zauberbücher." *ZfV* 13: 150- 67.
Derolez, René.
 1954. *Runica Manuscripta.* Brugge: Rijksuniversiteit te Gent.
 1959a. "Die 'Hrabanischen' Runen." *ZDP* 78: 1-19.
 1959b. Rev. Schneider K. *Die germanischen Runennamen.* In: *English Studies* 40: 180-83.
 1965. "Scandinavian Runes in Continental Manuscripts." In: Bessinger, J. B. and Creed, R. P. (eds.) *Franciplegius.* New York: New York University Press: 30-39.
 1968. "La divination chez les Germains." In: Caquot, A. and Leibovici, M. (eds.) *La divination.* Paris: Presses Universitaires de France: 257-302.
 1981. "The Runic System and its Cultural Context." *Michigan Germanic Studies* 7: 19-26.
Dickins, Bruce.
 1915. *Runic and Heroic Poems of the Old Teutonic Peoples.* Cambridge: Cambridge University Press.
 1935. "Runic Rings and Old English Charms." *Archiv* 167: 252.
Diehl, C. G.
 1956. *Instrument and Purpose: Studies in Rites and Rituals in South India.* Lund: Gleerup.
Dieterich, Albrecht.
 1901. "ABC-Denkmäler." *Rheinisches Museum für Philologie* 56: 77-105.
Dietrich, Franz.
 1867. "Drei altheidnische Segensformeln. Nebst einigen jüngeren auf Runendenkmälern und in Hss. aufgefundenen." *ZDA* 13: 193-217.
Dillmann, Francois-Xavier.
 1976. "Les runes dans la littérature islandaise ancienne." Diss. Caen, 2 vols.
 1981. "Le Maître des Runes: Essai de détermination socio-anthropologique: quelques réflexions methodologiques." *Michigan Germanic Studies* 7: 27-36.
 1982. "Katla and her Distaff: An Episode of Trifunctional Magic in the Eyrbyggja Saga?" In: Polomé, E. (ed.) *Homage to Georges Dumézil (JIES* Monograph no. 3) Washington: Institute for the Study of Man: 113-124.
Dinkier, Erich.
 1962. "Kreuzzeichen und Kreuz." *Jahrbuch für Antike und Christentum* 5: 93-112.

Dornseiff, Franz.
1922. *Das Alphabet in Mystik und Magie* (Stoicheia 7) Leipzig: Teubner.
Düwel, Klaus.
1968. *Runenkunde* (Sammlung Metzler 72) Stuttgart: Metzler.
1970a. "Die Runen des Brakteaten von Hitsum." In: Hauck, K. *Goldbrakteaten aus Sievern.* Munich: Fink: 284-87.
1970b. "Germanische Opfer und Opferriten im Spiegel altgermanischer Kultworte." In: Jankuhn, H. (ed.) *Vorgeschichtliche Heiligtümer und Opferplätze in Mittel-und Nordeuropa* (AAWG Phil.-Hist. Kl. 74) Göttingen: Vandenhoeck & Ruprecht: 219-39.
1971. *Das Opferfest von Lade und die Geschichte vom Völsi: Quellenkritischen Untersuchungen zur germanischen Religionsgeschichte.* Habilitationsschrift, Göttingen.
1972. "Die Runeninschrift auf der silbernen Scheibe von Liebenau." *Die Kunde* 23: 134-41.
1974. "Begriffsrunen." *RGA*^{2} 2: 150-53.
1975. "Runische Zeugnisse zu 'Bauer'." In: Wenskus, R. et al. (eds.) *Wort und Begriff 'Bauer'* (AAWG Phil.-Hist. Kl. III. 89) Göttingen: Vandenhoeck & Ruprecht: 12956.
1976. "Beuchte 2." *RGA*^{2} 2: 321-22.
1977. "Die 15. Rune auf dem Brakteaten von Nebenstedt I." In: Hassler, H. (ed.) *Studien zur Sachsenforschung.* Hildesheim: Lax: 89-96.
1978. "Grabraub, Totenschutz und Platzweihe nach dem Zeugnis der Runeninschriften." In: Jankuhn, H. et al. (eds.) *Zum Grabfrevel in vor- und frühgeschichtliche Zeit* (AAWG Hist.-Phil. K. III. 113) Göttingen: Vandenhoeck & Ruprecht: 229-43.
1979. Rev. W. Hartner *Die Goldhörner von Gallehus* and H. Klingenberg *Runenschrift-Schriftdenken-Runeninschriften.* In: *GGA* 231: 224-50.
1981a. "Runeninschriften auf Waffen." In: Schmidt-Wigland, R. (ed.) *Wörter und Sachen im Lichte der Bezeichnungsforschung.* Berlin: de Gruyter: 128-67.
1981b. "Runes, Weapons, and Jewelry: A Survey of some of the Oldest Runic Inscriptions," *MQ* 22: 69-91.
1981c. Rev. Buisson, Ludwig. *Der Bildstein Ardre VIII auf Gotland. BGDSL* 113: 110-115.
1981d. "The Meldorf Fibula and the Origin of Runic Writing." *Michigan Germanic Studies* 7: 8-14.
1982. "Runen und interpretatio christiana. Zur religionsgeschichtlichen Stellung der Bügelfibel von Nordendorf I." In: *Tradition als historische Kraft.* Kamp, N. and Wellasch, J. (eds.) Berlin: de Gruyter: 78-86.
1983. *Runenkunde.* (Sammlung Metzler 72) Stuttgart: Metzler, 2nd ed.
1988. "Buchstabenmagie und Alphabetzauber: Zu den Inschriften der Goldbrakteaten und ihrer Funktion als Amulette." *Frühmast.* 22, pp. 70-110.
1992. "Runen als magische Zeichen." In: *Das Buch als magisches und als Representationssobjekt.* Eds. Peter Ganz and Malcom Parkes. (= Wolfenbütteler Mittelalter-Studien 5) Wiesbaden, pp. 87-100.

1997a	"Magische Runenzeichen und magische Runeninschriften." In: *Runor och ABC*. Ed. Staffan Nyström. (= Runica et Mediævalia *Opuscula* 4) Stockholm: Medeltidsmuseum, pp. 23-42.
1997b	"Zeichenkonzeptionen in germanischen Altertum." In: *Semiotik*. Ed. Roland Posner, et al. Berlin: de Gruyter, pp. 803-822.
1997c	"Neufunde 1996." *NoR*: 12: 18-19.
2008.	*Runenkunde*. (Sammlung Metzler 72) Stuttgart: Metzler, 4th ed.

Düwel, K. and Gebühr, M.
1981. "Die Fibel von Meldorf und die Anfänge der Runenschrift." *ZDA* 110: 159-76.

Düwel, K., Willer, G., and Hauck, K.
1975. "Zu Ikonologie der Goldbrakteaten. IX. Die philologische und ikonographische Auswertung von fünf Inschriftenprägungen." *Frühmast*. 9: 143-85.

Düwel, K. and Roth, H.
1977. "Die Runenfibel von Donzdorf." *Frühmast*. 11: 409-13.

Düwel, K. and Tempel, W.
1971. "Knochenkämme mit Runeninschriften aus Friesland." *Palaehistoria* 14: 354-91.

Dow, Sterling.
1954. "Minoan Writing." *American Journal of Archeology* 58: 77-129.

Dumézil, Georges.
1929. Le probleme des Centaures. Étude de mythologie comparée indo-européenne. Paris: Geuthner.
1939. *Mythes et dieux des Germains*. Paris: Leroux.
1970. *The Destiny of the Warrior*. (tr. A. Hiltebeitel) Chicago: University of Chicago Press.
1973. *Gods of the Ancient Northmen*. Haugen, E. (ed.) Berkeley: University of California Press.

Durkheim, Émile.
1912. *Les formes elementaire de la vie religieuse*. Paris: Alcan.

Ebel, Else.
1963. "Die Technologie der Runentechnik." Diss. Göttingen.

Eckhardt, Karl A.
1937. *Irdische Unsterblichkeit: Germanischer Glaube an die Wiederverkörperung in der Sippe*. Weimar: Böhlaus.

Edwards, Anthony D.
1976. *Language in Culture and Class*. London: Heinemann.

Egger, Rudolf.
1959. "Die Inschrift des Harigasthelmes." *Anzeiger der phil.-hist. Klasse der österreichischen Akademie der Wissenschaften* nr. 5: 79-91.

Eggers, Hans J.
1932. *Die magischen Gegenstände der altisländischen Prosaliteratur*. Leipzig: Eichblatt Verlag.
1951. *Der römische Import im freien Germanien*. Hamburg: Hamburgisches Museum für Völkerkunde and Vorgeschichte.

1968. "Wikinger-Runen aus Pommern." *Baltische Studien*. N.F. 54: 7-13.
Egilsson, Sveinbjörn and Jónsson, Finnur.
    1931.   *Lexicon Poeticum*. Copenhagen: Moller.
Ehnmark, Erland.
    1956.   "Religion and Magic — Frazer, Söderblom, and Hägerström." *Ethnos* 21: 1-10.
Einarsson, Stefán.
    1957.   *A History of Icelandic Literature*. New York: Johns Hopkins Press.
Elgqvist, Eric.
    1952.   *Studier rörande Njordkultens spridning bland de norska folken*. Lund: Olins Antikvariat.
Eliade, Mircea.
    1958.   *Rites and Symbols of Initiation*. (tr. W. Trask) New York: Harper and Row.
    1964.   *Shamanism: Archaic Techniques of Ecstasy* (Bollingen Series 76) (tr. W. Trask). Princeton: Princeton University Press.
Elliott, Ralph W. V.
    1957.   "Runes, Yews, and Magic." *Speculum* 32: 250-61.
    1989.   *Runes: an Introduction*. Manchester: Manchester University Press, 2nd ed.
Ellis (Davidson), H. R.
    1941.   "Fostering by Giants in Old Norse Sagas." *Medium Ævum* 10: 70-85.
    1943.   *The Road to Hel*. Cambridge: Cambridge University Press.
    1973.   "Hostile Magic in Icelandic Sagas." In: Newell, V. (ed.) *The Witch Figure*. London: Routledge and Keagan Paul: 20-41.
Erben, Johannes.
    1966.   "Der Schluss der zweiten Merseburger Zauberspruchs." In: Rudolf, K. et al. (eds.) *Festschrift Walter Baetke*. Weimar: Böhlaus, 118-121.
Evans, E. Ellis.
    1981.   "Celts and Germans." *Bulletin of the Board of Celtic Studies* 29: 230-55.
Falk, Hjalmar.
    1914.   *Altnordische Waffenkunde* (Videnskapsselskapets Skrifter II. Hist.-Filos. Kl. 6) Kristiana: Dybwad.
    1924.   *Odensheite*. (Videnskapsselkapets Skrifter II. Hist.-Filos. Kl. 101) Kristiana: Dybwad.
    1926.   "Sjelen i Hedentroen." *MM*: 169-74.
Falk, H. and Torp, A.
    1960.   *Norwegisch-dänisches etymologisches Wörterbuch*. Oslo: Universitetsforlaget, 2 vols., 2nd ed.
Feist, Sigmund.
    1919.   "Runen and Zauberwesen im germanischen Altertum." *ANF* 35: 243-87.
    1922.   "Die religionsgeschichtliche Bedeutung der ältesten Runeninschriften." *JEGP* 21: 602-11.
    1939.   *Etymologisches Wörterbuch der gotischen Sprache*. Leiden: Brill, 3rd ed.
Ferguson, Samuel.
    1887.   *Ogham Inscriptions in Ireland, Wales, and Scotland*. Edinburgh: David Douglas.

Finnegan, Ruth.
1969. "How to do things with words: Performative Utterances among the Limba of Sierra Leone." *Man* N.S. 4: 537-52.

Fleck, Jere.
1971a. "Óðinn's Self-Sacrifice — A New Interpretation. I. The Ritual Inversion." *SS* 43: 119-42.
1971b. "Óðinn's Self-Sacrifice — A New Interpretation. II. The Ritual Landscape." *SS* 43: 385-413.

Flom, George.
1917. "Alliteration and Variation in Old Germanic Name-Giving." *Modern Language Notes* 32: 7-17.

Flowers, Stephen E.
1983. "Toward an Archaic Germanic Psychology." *JIES* 11: 117-38.
1993 "Magic" In: *Mediveal Scandinavia*. Ed. Phillip Pulsiano. New York: Garland.
1999 *A Concise Edition of Old English Runic Inscriptions*. Smithville: Rûna-Raven.
2000 "A Semiotic Theory of Rune-Magic." In: *Studia Germanica*. Smithville: Rûna-Raven, pp. 1-7.
2002 *The Rune-Poems*. Smithville: Rûna-Raven.
2003 "The Malt Stone." *Woodharrow-Letter* I: 1: 3-8.
2005 *The Galdrabók*. Smithville: Rûna-Raven.
2006 "How to Do Things with Runes: A Semiotic Approach to Operative Communication." In: *Runes and their Secrets*. Eds. Marie Stoklund, et al. Copenhagen: Museum Tusculanum Press.

Foerste, William.
1950. *Untersuchungen zur westfälischen Sprache des 9. Jahrhunderts* (Münstersche Forschungen 2) Marburg: Simons Verlag.

Förstemann, Ernst.
1900. *Altdeutsches Namenbuch I. Personennamen*. Bonn: Hanstein, 2nd ed.

Foster, George M.
1944. "Nagualism in Mexico and Guatemala." *Acta Americana* 2: 85-103.

Frazer, James.
1890. *The Golden Bough*. London: MacMillan, 2 vols. (cited from the 1917 edition.)

Friesen, Otto von.
1904. *Om Runskriftens Härkomst* (Språkvetenskapliga sällskapets Forhandlingar) Uppsala: Akademiska boktryckeriet, E. Berling.
1915. *Runorna i Sverige* (Forntima 1) Uppsala: Bonnier.
1916. *Lister- och Listerbystenarna i Blekinge*. (Uppsala Universitets Årskrift 1916, nr. 2) Uppsala: Almqvist & Wiksell.
1918-19. "Runenschrift." *RGA*[1] 4: 5-51.
1924a. *Rö-stenen i Bohuslan och Runorna i Norden under Folkvanderingstiden* (Uppsala Universitets Arskrift 1924) Uppsala: Almqvist & Wiksell.
1924b. "Runstenarna i Altuna." *Upplands Fornminningsförenings Tidskrift* 39: 339-64.

1933. *Runorna* (Nordisk Kultur 6) Stockholm: Bonnier.
Fritzner, Johan.
1886. *Ordbog over det gamle norske Sprog.* Kristiana: Norske Forlagsforening, 3 vols.
Fuchs, Harald.
1951. "Die Herkunft der Satorformel." *Schweiz. Archiv für Volkskunde* 47: 28-54.
Gager, John G.
1992. *Curse Tablets and Binding Spells from the Ancient World.* Oxford: Oxford University Press.
Ganzlin, Dr.
1902. *Sächsische Zauberformeln.* Bitterfeld: R. Schencke.
Gebühr, Michael.
1979. "Das Kindergrab von Winbeby: Versuch einer 'Rehabilitation.'" *Offa* 36: 75-107.
Gelb, I. J.
1958. *Von Keilschrift zum Alphabet.* Stuttgart: Kohlhammer.
Gelling, Peter and Ellis Davidson, H. R.
1969. *The Chariot of the Sun.* New York: Praeger.
Gennep, Arnold van.
1960. *The Rites of Passage.* (tr. M. Vizedom and G. Caffee) Chicago: University of Chicago Press orig. 1909.
Genzmer, Felix.
1952. "Die Geheimrunen der Egilssaga." *ANF* 67: 39-47.
Gering, Hugo.
1917. "Zur Runenschrift des Weberkammes von Drontheim." *ANF* 33: 63.
Goessler, P.
1938. "Germanisch-christliches an Kirchen und Friedhöfen Südwestdeutschlands." *Archiv für Religionswissenschaft* 35: 65-92.
Gonda, Jan.
1960. *Die Religionen Indiens: I. Veda und älterer Hinduismus.* Stuttgart: Kohlhammer.
Goodman, Felicitas.
1972. *Speaking in Tongues: a Cross Cultural Study of Glossolalia.* Chicago: University of Chicago Press.
Goody, Jack.
1968. "Introduction." In: Goody, J. (ed.) *Literacy in Traditional Societies.* Cambridge: Cambridge University Press: 1-26.
1977. *The Domestication of the Savage Mind.* Cambridge: Cambridge University Press.
Goody, Jack and Watt, Ian.
1968. "The Consequences of Literacy." In: Goody, J. (ed.) *Literacy in Traditional Societies.* Cambridge: Cambridge University Press.

Gough, Kathleen.
1968a. "Implications of Literacy in Traditional China and India." In: Goody, J. (ed.) *Literacy in Traditional Societies*. Cambridge: Cambridge University Press: 70-84.
1968b. "Literacy in Kerla." In: Goody, J. (ed.) *Literacy in Traditional Societies*. Cambridge: Cambridge University Press: 133-60.
Gimbutas, Maria.
1971. *The Slavs*. New York: Praeger.
Graebner, Fritz.
1911. *Methode der Ethnologie*. Heidelberg: Winter.
Grambo, Ronald.
1975. "Models of Magic." *Norveg* 18: 77-109.
Green, D. H.
1965. *The Carolingian Lord*. Cambridge: Cambridge University Press.
Grein, Christian W. M. and Wülcker, R. P. (eds.)
1881. *Bibliothek der angelsächischen Poesie*. Kassel: Wigand, 3 vols.
Grienberger, Theodor.
1900. "Neue Betrāge zur Runenlehre." *ZDP* 32: 289-304.
1906. Rev. S. Bugge. *Norges Indskrifter med de ælder Runer*. Ind., I-II. In: *GGA* 170: 373-426.
1907. "Neue Beiträge zur Runenlehre." *ZDP* 39: 50-100.
1908. "Neure runische Literatur." *GGA* 170: 373-426.
1924. "Runensachen." *ZDP* 50: 274-83.
Grimm, Günter.
1969. *Die Zeugnisse ägyptischer Religion und Kunstelemente im römischen Deutschland*. Leiden: Brill.
Grimm, Jacob.
1875-78. *Deutsche Mythologie*. Berlin: Dammler, 3 vols., 4th ed
Grønbech, Vilhelm.
1931. *The Culture of the Teutons*. London: Oxford: Oxford University Press.
Grønvik, Ottar.
1981. *Runene på Tune-Stenen*. Oslo: Universitetsforlaget.
Güntert, Hermann.
1921. *Von der Sprache der Götter und Geister*. Halle/Saale: Niemeyer.
Gustavson, H. and Brink, T. S.
1979. "Runfynd 1978." *Fv*: 228-50.
1981. "Runfynd 1980." *Fv*.: 186-202.
Gutenbrunner, Siegfried.
1936/37. "Beiträge zur Deutung einiger Runendenkmäler." *APS* 11: 162-73.
Gutenbrunner, S. and Klingenberg, H.
1967. "Runenschrift, die älteste Buchstabenschrift der Germanen." *Studium Generale* 20: 432-48.
Hachmann, Rolf.
1970. *Die Goten und Skandinavien*. Berlin: de Gruyter.
1971. *Die Germanen*. Geneva: Nagel Verlag.

Hachmann, R., Kossak, G., and Kuhn, H.
1962.   *Völker zwischen Germanen und Kelten.* Neu Münster: Wachhotz.
Hälsig, Friederich.
1910.   *Der Zauberspruch bei den Germanen bis um die Mitte des XVI. Jahrhunderts.* Leipzig: Dr. Seele.
Hageberg, Ulf Erik.
1970.   "Religiongeschichtliche Aspekte des Moorfundes vom Skedemose auf Öland." In: Jankuhn, H. (ed.) *Vorgeschichtliche Heiligtümer und Opferplätze in Mittel- und Nordeuropa* (AAWG Phil.-Hist. Ki. III. 74) Göttingen: Vandenhoeck & Ruprecht: 167-71.
Halsall, Maureen.
1981.   *The Old English Rune Poem: A Critical Edition* (McMaster Old English Studies and Texts 2) Tornoto: University of Toronto Press.
Hammarström, Göran.
1976.   Linguistic Units and Items. Berlin: Springer.
Hammarstöm, M.
1930.   "Om Runskriftens Härkomst." *Studier i Nordisk Filologi* 20: 1-67.
Hampp, Irmgard.
1961.   *Beschwörung, Segen, Gebet. Untersuchungen zum Zauberspruch aus dem Bereich der Volksheilkunde* (Veröffentlichungen des staatlichen Amtes für Denkmalpflege Stuttgart Reihe C. 1) Stuttgart: Silberburg.
Harder, Hermann.
1931.   "Eine angelsächsische Runeninschrift." *Archiv* 160: 87-89.
1936.   "Inschriften angelsächsischen Runenringe." *Archiv* 169: 224-28.
1943.   "Wunsch- und Zahlenmagie in Runenritzungen." *Germanien* Heft 9-10: 255-64.
Hartmann, Hans.
1943.   *"Heil" und "Heilig" im nordischen Altertum.* Heidelberg: Winter.
Hauck, Karl.
1957.   "Germanische Bilddenkmäler des frühen Mittelalters." *Deutsche Vierteljahresschrift für Literatur und Geschichte* 31: 349-79.
1969.   "Vom Kaiser- zum Götter-Amulett. Die Bildforme in der Inschriften Brakteaten." *Frühmast.* 3: 27-46.
1970a. *Goldbrakeaten aus Sievern.* Munich: Fink.
1970b. "Völkerwanderungszeitliche Bilddarstellungen des zweiten Merseburger Spruchs als Zugang zu Heiligtum und Opfer." In: Jankuhn, H. (ed.) *Vorgeschichtliche Heiligtümer und Opferplätze in Mittel- und Nordeuropa* (AAWG Hist.-Phil. Kl. III. 74) Göttingen: Vandenhoeck & Ruprecht: 297-319.
1972.   "Zur Ikonologie der Goldbrakteaten. IV: Metamorphosen Odins nach dem Wissen von Snorri und von Amulettmeistern der Völkerwanderungszeit." In: Bandle, C. et al. (eds.) *Festschrift für Siegfried Gutenbrunner.* Heidelberg: Winter: 47-70.
1976.   "Ein neues Buch zu 'Franks Casket.'" *Frühmast.* 10: 362-66.

1977.	"Zur Ikonologie der Goldbrakteaten, XIV: Die Spannung zwischen Zauber- und Erfahrungsmedizin, erhellt an Rezepten aus zwei Jahrtausenden." *Frühmast.* 11: 414-510.
1980.	"Gemeinschaftstiftende Kult der Seegermanen. Zur Ikonologie der Goldbrakteaten XIX." *Frühmast.* 14: 463-617.
1981a.	"Germanische Bildtradition im christlichen Mittelalter. Zur Ikonologie der Goldbrakteaten XXII." *Frühmast.* 15: 1-8.
1981b.	"Die bildliche Wiedergabe von Götter- und Helderwaffen im Norden seit der Völkerwanderungszeit." In: Schmidt-Wiegland, R. (ed.) *Wörter und Sachen im Lichte der Bezeichnungsforschung.* Berlin: de Gruyter: 168-269.

Hauck, Karl, et al.
1983-89. *Die Goldbrakteaten der Völkerwanderungszeit. Ikonographischer Katalog.* (Münstersche Mittelalter-Schriften 24) Berlin: de Gruyter. [Cited as *IK*]

Haugen, Einar.
1976. *The Scandinavian Languages.* Cambridge, Mass.: Harvard University Press.

Hedeager, Lotte.
1978a. "A Quantitative Analysis of Roman Imports in Europe North of the Limes (0-400 A.D.), and the Question of Roman-Germanic Exchange." In: Kristiansen, K. and Paludan-Muller, C. (eds.) *New Directions in Scandinavian Archeology.* Copenhagen: National Museum: 191-216.
1978b. "Processes towards State Formation in Early Iron Age Denmark." In: Kristiansen, K. and Paludan-Muller, C. (eds.) *New Directions in Scandinavian Archeology.* Copenhagen: National Museum: 217-223.

Hegedüs, L.
1958. "Beiträge zum Problemen des sprachlichen Tabu und der Namenmagie." *Orbis* 7: 79-96.

Heiermeier, Annie.
1934. *Der Runenstein von Eggjum: Ein Beitrag zu seiner Deutung.* Halle/Saale: Niemeyer.

Hellmuth, Leopold.
1975. *Die germanische Blutbruderschaft* (Wiener Arbeiten zur germanischen Altertumskunde und Philologie 7) Vienna: Halosar.

Helm, Karl.
1913. *Altgermanische Religionsgeschichte I.* Heidelberg: Winter.
1937. *Altgermanische Religionsgeschichte: Die nachrömische Zeit II. 1. Die Ostgermanen.* Heidelberg: Winter.
1946. *Wodan: Ausbreitung und Wanderung seines Kultes* (Giessener Beiträge zur deutschen Philologie 85) Giessen: Schmitz.
1953. *Altgermanische Religionsgeschichte: Die nachrömische Zeit II. 2. Die Westgermanen.* Heidelberg: Winter.

Hempel, H.
1928. "Hellenistisch-orientalisches Lehngut in der germanischen Religion." *GRM* 16: 185-202.

Henning, Rudolf.
1889. *Die deutschen Runendenkmäler.* Strassburg: Truebner.

Hepding, Hugo.
   1924.   "Kleine Beträge zu magischen Formeln." *Hessische Blätter für Volkskunde* 23

Hermann, Paul.
   1928   *Altdeutsche Kultbräuche*. Jena: Diederichs.

Heusler, Andreas.
   1894.   "Über germanischen Versbau." Berlin: Weidmann.
   1918/19. "Stabreim." *RGA*[1] 4: 231-40.
   1925.   *Deutsche Versgeschichte I*. (Grundriss der deutschen Philologie 8,1) Berlin: de Gruyter.
   1926.   *Die altgermanische Dichtung*. Wildpark-Potsdam: Akademische Verlagsgesellschaft Athenaion.

Hills, C. M.
   1974   "A Runic Pot from Spong Hill, North Elmham, Norfolk." *Antiquaries Journal* 54: 87-91.

Höfler, Otto.
   1934.   *Kultische Geheimbunde der Germanen*. Frankfurt/Main: Diesterweg.
   1952.   *Germanisches Sakralkönigtum I. Der Runenstein von Rök und die germanische Individualweihe*. Tübingen: Niemeyer.
   1970.   Rev. W. Krause. *Die Runeninschriften im älteren Futhark*. In: *GGA* 222: 109-43.
   1971.   "Herkunft und Ausbreitung der Runen." *Die Sprache*. 17: 134-56.
   1972.   "'Sakraltheorie' und 'Profantheorie' in der Altertumskunde." In: Bandle, O. et al. (eds.) *Festschrift für Siegfried Gutenbrunner*. Heidelberg: Winter: 71-116.
   1973a.   "Abstammungstraditionen." *RGA*[1]: 18-29.
   1973b.   "Zwei Grundkrafte im Wodan Kult." In: Mayrhofer, M. et al. (eds.) *Antiquitates Indogermanicae* (Gedenkenschrift für Hermann Güntert). Innsbruck: Institut für Sprachwissenschaft der Universitat: 133-44.

Høst, Gerd.
   1952.   "Til Sigtuna og Canterbury Formelene." *NTS* 16: 342-46.
   1954.   "Om innskriften på den yngre Runehellen fra Torvika." *NTS* 17: 454-83.
   1960.   "To Runestudier." *NTS* 19: 418-554.
   1976.   *Runer. våre eldste norske runeinnskrifter*. Oslo: Aschehoug.
   1977a.   "Runer og hedenskap i gamle Norge." *Samtiden* 86: 437-47.
   1977b.   Rev. Antonsen, E. *A Concise Grammar of the Older Runic Inscriptions*. In: *NTS* 31: 151-56.
   1980.   "'Trylleordet' alu." *Norske Videnskaps-Akadamis Årbok*: 35-49.

Honko, Lauri.
   1959.   *Krankheitsprojektile. Untersuchungen über eine urtümliche Krankheitserklärung* (Folklore Fellow Communications 178) Helsinki: Academia Scietiarum Fennica.

Hoops, Johannes.
   1905.   *Waldbäume und Kulturpflanzen im germanischen Altertum*. Strassburg: Trübner.

1911-19. *Reallexikon der germanischen Altertumskunde.* Strassburg: Trübner, 4 vols. (Cited as RGA[1])
Horton, Robin and Finnegan, Ruth.
1973. *Modes of Thought: Essays on Thinking in Western and Non-Western Societies.* London: Faber & Faber.
Hunger, Ulrich.
1984. *Die Runenkunde im Dritten Reich.* Frankfurt: Lang.
Hunter, David E. and Whitten, Phillip.
1976. *Encyclopedia of Anthropology.* New York: Harper & Row.
Ilkjær, Jørgen and Lønstrup, Jørn.
1977a. "Illerup ådal. Udravningen 1976." *Kuml*: 105-15.
1977b. "Mosefundet fra Illerup ådal." *Convivium*: 144-68.
1981. "Runefundene fra Illerup ådal: En arkæologisk vurdering af vore ældste indskrifter." *Kuml* : 49-65.
Jacobsen, Lis.
1931. *Eggjum-stenen.* Copenhagen: Levin & Munksgaard.
1935. *Forbandelses-Formularer i nordiske Runeindskrifter* (Kungl. Vitterhets Historie och Antikvits Akademiens Handlingar 39:4) Stockholm: Akademiens Forlag.
Jacobsen, L. and Brøndal, V.
1935. "Runekammen fra Setre." *ANO*: 58-78.
Jacobsen, L. and Moltke, E.
1942. *Danmarks Runeindskrifter.* Copenhagen: Munksgaard, 2 vols. (Cited as DR.)
Jänichen, Hans.
1951. "Eine neue Runeninschrift von Schretzheira." *Germania* 29: 226-30.
Jaide, Walter.
1937. *Das Wesen des Zaubers in den primitiven Kulturen und in den Islandsagas.* Lepizig: Noske.
Jankuhn, Herbert, Nehlsen, Hermann, and Roth, Helmut (eds.)
1978. *Zum Grabfrevel in vor- und frühgeschichtlicher Zeit* (AAWG Hist.-Phil. K. III. 113) Göttingen: Vandenhoeck & Ruprecht.
Jansson, Sven B. F.
1963. *Runinskrifter i Sverige.* Stockholm: Almqvist & Wiksell.
1969. "Runristare." *KHNM* 14: 486-505.
Jansson, S. B. F. and Wessen, E.
1962. *Gotlands Runinskrifter I.* (Sveriges Runinskrifter XI) Stockholm: Almqvist & Wiksell.
Jarausch, Konrad.
1930. "Der Zauber in den Isländersagas." *ZfV*. N.F. 1: 237-68.
Jeffery, L. H.
1961. *The Local Scripts of Archaic Greece.* Oxford: Oxford University Press.
Jensen, Adolf E.
1950. "Gibt es Zauberhandlungen?" *Zeitschrift für Ethnologie* 75: 3-12.
1951. *Mythos und Kult bei den Naturvolkern.* Wiesbaden: Steiner.

Jensen, Hans.
   1958.   *Die Schrift in Vergangenheit und Gegenwart*. Berlin: Deutscher Verlag der Wissenschaften, 2nd ed.
Jente, Richard.
   1921.   *Die mythologische Ausdrücke im altenglischen Wortschatz* (Altanglistische Forschungen 56) Heidelberg: Winter.
Jóhannesson, Alexander.
   1951-56. *Isländisches etymolgisches Wörterbuch*. Bern: Francke.
Johansen, Erling and Liestøl, Aslag.
   1977.   "Jellingsteinen: Steinhogger og Runerister." *Kuml*. 65-84.
Johnsen, Ingrid Sanness.
   1968.   *Stuttruner i vikingtidens innskrifter*. Oslo: Universitetsforlaget.
   1969.   "Kan runeinnskrifter bidrå til å belyse kvinnens stilling i det førkristne Norden?" *ANF* 84: 38-55.
Jónsson, Finnur.
   1908.   *Den Norsk-Isiandske Skaldedigtning*. Copenhagen: Gyldendal, 2 vols.
   1910.   "Runerne i den norsk-islandske Digtning og Literatur." *ANO*: 283-308.
Jungandreas, Wolfgang.
   1935.   "Die germanische Runenreihe und ihre Bedeutung." *ZDP* 60: 105-21.
   1936   "Zur Runenreihe." *ZDP* 61: 227-32.
   1981.   *Sprachliche Studien zur germanischen Altertumskunde*. Wiesbaden: Steiner.
Jungner, Hugo.
   1924.   "Västergötlands äldsta runinskrifter." *Festskrift tillägnad H. Pipping*. Helsingfors: Mercator: 230-50.
   1936.   "Högstena-Galdern. En västgötsk runbesvärjelse mot gengångare." *Fv*.: 278-304.
Jungner, H. and Svärdström, E.
   1940-58. *Västergötlands Runinskrifter*. Stockholm: Kungl. Vitterhets Historie och Antikvitets Akademien. (Cited Vg.)
Kålund, Kristian.
   1907.   *Den islandske lægebog*. Copenhagen: Bianco Luno.
Kabell, A. A
   1967.   "Periculum Runicum." *NTS* 21: 94-126.
   1977.   "Das schwedische Amulett aus Hedeby." *ANF* 92: 64-69.
   1978.   "Die Inschrift auf dem Schädel fragment aus Ribe." *ANF* 93: 38-47.
Kahle, B.
   1895.   "Krankheitsbeschwörungen des Nordens." *ZfV*. 5: 194-95.
Kapteyn, J. M. N.
   1933.   "Zwei Runeninschriften aus der Terp von Westereroden." *BGDSL* 57: 160-226.
Kaufmann, Henning.
   1968.   *Altdeutsche Personennamen. Ergänzungsband*. Munich: Fink.
Keil, Max.
   1931.   *Altisländische Namenwahl*. (Palaestra 176) Leipzig: Mayer & Müller.

Kiessling, Edith.
1941. *Zauberei in den germanischen Volksrechten.* (Beiträge zur mittelalterlichen, neueren und allgemeinen Geschichte 17) Jena: Fischer.
Kiil, Vilhelm.
1953. "Rune-rimet på Straums-brynet." *ANF* 68: 30-96.
1955 "Runesteinen fra Eggjum i Sogndal." *ANF* 70: 129-81.
1964. "Nye kommentarer til Eggja-runene." *ANF* 79: 21-30.
Kippenberg, Hans G.
1978. "Einleitung 'Zur Kontroverse über das Verstehen fremden Denkens.'" In: Kippenberg, H. G. and Luchesi, B. (eds.) *Magie: Die sozialwissenschaftliche Kontroverse über das Verstehen fremden Denkens.* Frankfurt/Main: Suhrkamp: 9- 51.
Kjaer, A.
1914. "Nogle Stedsnavne." *MM*: 204-23.
Klare, Hans-Joachim.
1933/34. "Die Toten in der altnordischen Literatur." *APS*: 1-56.
Klingenberg, Hainz.
1969. "Möglichkeiten der Runenschrift und Wirklichkeit der Inschriften." In: *Frühe Schriftszeugnisse der Menschheit.* Göttingen: Vandenhoeck & Ruprecht: 177-211.
1972. "Havamal: Bedeutungs- und Gestaltenwandel eines Motivs." In: Bandle, O. et al. (eds.) *Festschrift für Siegried Gutenbrunner.* Heidelberg: Winter: 117-44.
1973. *Runenschrift-Schriftdenken-Runeninschriften.* Heidelberg: Winter.
1974. "Eucharistischer Runenlöffel aus alamannischer Frühzeit." *ZDA* 103: 81-94.
1976. "Runenfibel von Bulach, Kanton Zurich: Liebesinschrift aus alamannischer Frühzeit." *Alamannisches Jahrbuch* 1973/75: 308 - Brühl: Konkordia: 308-25.
Klingenberg, H. and Koch, U.
1974. "Ein Ringschwert mit Runenkreuz aus Schretzheim, Kr. Dillingen a. d. Donau." *Germania* 52: 120-30.
Kluge, Freidrich and Mitzka, Walter.
1957. *Etymologisches Wörterbuch der deutschen Sprache.* Berlin: de Gruyter, 17th ed.
Knirk, James.
2004 "Nyfunn og nyregistrering 2003." *NoR* 19: 16-18.
Knudsen, Anne M. and Dyvik, Helge J. J.
1980. "Et runekors fra Sogn of Fjordane." *MM*: 1-22.
Krause, Wolfgang.
1932. *Beiträge zur Runenforschung I.* (Schriften der Königsberger Gelehrten Gesellschaft 9:2), Halle/Saale: Niemeyer.
1934. *Beiträge zur Runenforschung II.* (Schriften der Königsberger Gelehrten Gesellschaft 11:1) Halle/Saale: Niemeyer.
1935. *Was man in Runen ritzte.* Halle/Saale: Niemeyer.

1937.	*Runeninschriften im älteren Futhark.* (Königsberger Gelehrten Gesellschaft 13: 4) Halle/Saale: Niemeyer.
1938.	"Die Runen als Begriffszeichen." In: Schottig, K. (ed.) *Beiträge zur Runenkunde und Nordischen Sprachwissenschaft.* (Neckel Festschrift) Leipzig: Harrassowitz: 35-53.
1939.	"Runenmacht." *Geistige Arbeit.* 6: 19: 1-2.
1943a.	*Was man in Runen ritzte.* Halle/Saale: Niemeyer, 2nd ed.
1943b.	"Zum Stand der Runenforschung." *GGA* 205: 231-68.
1946/47.	"Untersuchungen zu den Runennamen I: Die Lauch-Rune." NAWG 1946/47: 60-63.
1948.	"Untersuchungen zu den Runennamen II. Runennamen und Götterwelt." NAWG 1948: 93-108.
1948/50.	"Herkunft und Namen der Runen." *Selskab for nordisk Filologi, Årsberetning for 1948/50:* 33-35.
1961.	"Runica III." NAWG 1961: 225-80.
1964.	Rev. Kuhn, Hans. *Edda: Die Lieder des Codex Regius nebst verwandten Denkmälern.* In: *Anzeiger für deutsches Altertum und deutsche Literatur* 75: 145-56.
1966.	*Die Runeninschriften im älteren Futhark.* (AAWG Hist.-Phil. K. III. no. 65) Göttingen: Vandenhoeck & Ruprecht, 2 vols. (With archeological contributions by H. Jankuhn, also cited KJ.)
1968.	*Handbuch des Gotischen.* Munich: Beck, 3rd ed.
1969.	"Zur Herkunft von finn. *runo* 'Lied.'" *Finnisch-ugrischen Forschungen* 37: 91-97.
1970.	*Runen.* (Sammlung Göschen 1244/1244a) Berlin: de Gruyter.
1971.	*Die Sprache der urnordischen Runeninschriften.* Heidelberg: Winter.

Kriss, Rudolf.
1968.	"Zum Problem der religiösen Magie und ihre Rolle im volkstümlichen Opferbrauchtum und Sakramentalien-Wesen." *Österreichische Zeitschrift für Volkskunde* N.S. 22: 69-84.

Krogmann, Willy.
1962.	"Die Runeninschrift von Kårstad."*PS* 25: 151-60. Krüger, Bruno (ed.).
1976.	*Die Germanen.* Berlin: Akademie Verlag, vol. 1.

Kuhn, Adalbert.
1864.	"Indische und germanische Segensprüche." *Zeitschrift für vergleichende Sprachforschung* 13: 49-73.

Kuhn, Hans.
1956.	"Die Grenzen der germanischen Gefolgschaft." *Zeitschrift der Savigny-Stiftung für Rechtsgeschichte. Germanische Abteilung* 73: 1-83.
1968a.	"Kämpen und Berserker." *Frühmast.* 2: 218-27.
1968b.	*Edda: Die Lieder des Codex Regius nebst verwandten Denkmälern II. Kurzes Wörterbuch.* Heidelberg: Winter, 3rd ed.
1978.	"Der Todesspeer: Odin als Totengott." In: Hoffmann, D. (ed.), *Kleine Schriften IV.* Berlin: de Gruyter: vol. IV, 247-58.

Lange, Wolfgang.
1957.	Rev. Schneider, K. *Die germanischen Runennamen.* In: GGA 211: 72-89.

Laur, Wolfgang.
1981. *Runendenkmäler in Schleswig-Holstein.* (Schleswig-Holsteinisches Landesmuseum für Vor- und Frühgeschichte in Schleswig 9) Neumünster: Wachholz, 3rd ed.
Leake, Jane A.
1967. *The Geats of Beowulf.* Madison: University of Wisconsin Press.
Legeza, Laszlo.
1975. *Tao Magic,* New York: Pantheon.
Lehmann, F. Rudolf.
1966. "Versuche die Bedeutung des Wortes 'Mana' im Bereiche der Sprachen der polynesischen Inselwelt festzustellen." In: Rudolf, K. et al. (eds.) *Festschrift Walter Baetke.* Weimar: Bohlaus.: 215-40.
Lehmann, Winfred P.
1955. "*Lín* and *Laukr* in the Edda." *The Germanic Review* 30: 163-71.
1956. *The Development of Germanic Verseform.* Austin: University of Texas Press.
Lehmann-Filés, M.
1898. "Volkskundliches aus Island." *ZfV* 8: 154-62; 285-91.
Liberman, Anatoly.
1978. "Germanic *sendan* 'to make a sacrifice.'" *JEGP* 77: 473-88.
Lid, Mils.
1921. "Um Finnskot og alvskot." *MM*: 37-66.
1927. "Gand og tyre." In: *Festskrift til Hjalmar Falk* (various eds.): 331-50 (cited from Lid 1950).
1944. "Gandfuge og Gandfugl." *MM*: 201-20. (cited from Lid 1950).
1950. *Trolldom.* Oslo: Cammermeyer.
Lidén, Hans-Emil.
1969. "From Pagan Sanctuary to Christian Church: The Excavation of Meere Church in Trødelag." *Norwegian Archeological Review* 2: 3-32.
Liestøl, Aslak.
1963. "Runer fra Bryggen." *Viking*: 5-52.
1965. "Runeinnskrifta på Eikelandspenna." *Fra Haug ok Heiðni* 4: 155-58.
Lincoln, Bruce.
1981. *Priests, Warriors, and Cattle: A Study in the Ecology of Religions.* Berkeley: University of California Press.
Linderholm, Emanuel.
1918. *Nordisk Magi. I. Urnordisk Magi.* (Svensk Landsmal och svensk-Folkliv 20) Stockholm: Norstedt.
Lindow, John.
1975. *Comitatus, Individual and Honor.* Berkeley: University of California Press.
Lindqvist, Ivar.
1923. *Galdrar.* Göteborg: Elander.
1932. *Religiösa Runtexter I. Sigtuna-Galdern.* (Skrifter utgivna av Vetenskaps-Societen i Lund 15) Lund: Ohlsson.

1940. *Religiösa Runtexter II. Sparlösa-stenen.* (Skrifter utgivna av Vetenskaps-Societeten i Lund 24) Lund: Ohlsson.
1947. "Oversikt över de äldsta skandinaviska Personnamen, med huvudvikten på de urnordiska." In: Janzen, A. (ed.) *Personnamen.* (Nordisk Kultur 7) Stockholm: Bonniers.
Lindqvist, Nat.
1921. *En islandsk Svartkonstbok fran 1500-talet* (= Galdrabók). Uppsala: Appelberg.
Lindqvist, Sune.
1941-42. *Gotlands Bildsteine.* Stockholm: Wahlstrom & Widstrand, 2 vols.
Losemann, Volker.
1977. Nationalsozialismus und Antike: *Studien zur Entwicklung des Faches. Alte Geschichte 1933-1945.* (Historische Perspektiven 7) Hamburg: Hoffmann & Campe.
Loth, J.
1895. "Le sort chez les germains et les celtes." *Revue Celtique* 16: 313-14.
Lundeby, Einar.
1982. "Urnordisk *salu*." *MM*: 33-40.
Mackeprang, Mogens B.
1952. *De Nordiske Guldbrakteater.* (Jysk Arkaeolgisk Selskaps Skrifter 2) Aarhus: Universitetsforlaget.
McKinnell, John and Rudolf Simek (with Klaus Düwel)
2004 *Runes, Magic and Religion.* (Studia Medievalia Septenrionalia 10) Fassbinder: Vienna.
MacLeod, Mindy and Bernard Mees.
2006 *Runic Amulets and Magical Objects.* Woodbridge: Boydell.
McManus, Damien.
1991 *A Guide to Ogam.* Maynooth: Ar Sagart.
Markey, Thomas L.
1974. "Drinking at Funerals: the Germanic Funerary Libation." *Frühmast.* 8: 60-70.
Marold, Edith.
1974. "Thor weihe diese Runen." *Frühmast.* 8: 195-222.
Marquardt, Herta.
1941. Rev. Sierke, Sigurd. *Kannten die vorchristlichen Germanen Runenzauber?* In: *Deutsche Literaturzeitung*: 13-14.
1961. *Bibliographie der Runeninschriften nach Fundorten I. Die Runeninschriften der britischen Inseln* (AAWG Phil. Hist. Kl. III. 48) Göttingen: Vandenhoeck & Ruprecht.
Marstrander, Carl J. S.
1928. "Om Runene og Runenavenes Oprindelse." *NTS* 1: 85-188.
1929a. "De gotiske runeminnesmerker." *NTS* 3: 25-157.
1929b. "Opedalstennen." *NTS* 3: 158.-96.
1929c. "Germanische Waffennamen aus römischer Zeit." *NTS* 3: 218-35.
1929d. "Myklebostadstenen." *NTS* 3: 197-217.

1930. "Ein neues Perfektopräsens." *NTS* 4: 245-50.
1937. Rev. Krause, W. *Runeninschriften im älteren Futhark.* In: *NTS* 8: 494-97.
1938. "Barmeninnskriften." *NTS* 10: 361-70.
1939. Rev. Arntz, H. *Die einheimischen Runendenkmäler des Festlandes. NTS* 11: 280-337.
1946. "Vettelandsstenen." In: *Stavanger Museums Årbok* 1946: 13- 42.
1951. *Rosselandssteinen.* (Universitetet i Bergen Årbok 1951. Hist.-Antik, rekke 3) Bergen: Grieg.
1952. "De nordiske Runeinnskrifter i eldre alfabet I. Danske og Svenske Innskrifter." (*Viking* 16, pp. 1-277) Oslo: Arkeologisk-Selskap.

Marzell, H.
1930/31. "Hasel." *HDA* 3: 1527-42.

Mauss, Marcel.
1952. *A General Theory of Magic.* (tr. R. Brain) New York: Norton.

Meissner, Rudolf.
1934. "Das Blutopfer in der Inschrift von Eggjum." *ZDA* 71: 189-200.

Mentz, Arthur.
1936. "Die Urgeschichte des Alphabets." *Rheinisches Museum für Philologie.* N.F. 85: 347-66.
1937. "Die Notae der Germanen bei Tacitus." *Rheinisches Museum für Philologie.* 86: 194-205.

Meyer, Richard.
1899. "Der Begriff des Wunders in der Edda." *ZDP* 31: 315-27.
1919. "Zahlensystem." *RGA*[1] 4: 576-77.

Miedema, H. T. J.
1974. "Dialect en Runen van Britsum en de oudste anglofriese Runeninscripties." *Taal en Tongval* 26: 101-28.

Mildenberger, Gerhard.
1972. *Sozial- und Kulturgeschichte der Germanen.* Stuttgart: Kohlhammer.

Miller, Patricia Cox.
1986. "In Praise of Nonsense." In: *Classical Mediterranean Spirituality* ed. A. H. Armstrong. London: Routledge and Kegan Paul, pp. 481-505.

Moeller, Walter.
1973. *The Mithraic Origin and Meaning of the Rotas-Sator Square.* Leiden: Brill.

Mogk, Eugen.
1919. "Runenzauber." *RGA*[1] 4: 51-52.
1925. "Nordgermanische Gotterverehrung nach den Kultquellen." In: *Germanica Festschrift Eduard Sievers.* Halle/Saale: Niemeyer: 258-72.

Moltke, Erik.
1927. "Graverus suedois de runes." *APS* 2: 186-90.
1928. Rev. Agrell, Sigurd. "Runornas Talmystik och dess antika Forbild." *APS* 3: 90-96.
1929/30. "Bidrag til Tolkning af Gørlev-Stenen." *APS* 3: 172-85.

1932/33.	"Glavendrup-stenen og de nyfundne runer." *APS* 7: 83-96.
1934.	"Runetrolddom." *Nordisk Tidskrift för Vetenskap, Konst och Industri.* 10: 427-39.
1936a.	"Runologiske Meddelelser IV. Rister- og Mesterformler." *ANO*: 238-59.
1936b.	"Greenland Runic Inscriptions." *Meddelser om Grønland* 88: 223-32.
1936/37.	"Runologiske Bidrag." *APS* 11: 252-62.
1938a.	"Medieval Rune Amulets in Denmark." *Acta Ethnologica*: 116-47.
1938b.	"Runestenen paa Einang." *Viking*: 111-19.
1940/43.	"Hvad er meningen med en meningløs brakteatindskrift." *Fra Ribe Amt* 10: 545-55.
1947.	"Hvad var Lægæst, Guldhornets Mester, Magiker, Præst eller Guldsmed?" *Fv.*: 336-42.
1956-58.	*Jon Skonvig og de andre Runetegnere* (Bibliotheca Arnamagn Supplementum I) Copenhagen: Munksgaard, 2 vols.
1960.	"Runepindene fra Ribe." *Nationalmuseets Arbeidsmark*: 1-16.
1961.	"En grønlandsk runeindskrift fra Erik den Rødes tid: Narssaq-Pinden." *Tidskrift Grönland* Nov.: 401-10.
1963.	"Runeindskriften på rosetfibula fra Nøling." *Kuml*: 37-41.
1976a.	*Runerne i Danmark og deres Oprindelse.* Copenhagen: Forum.
1976b.	"Runeninschriften aus der Stadt Schleswig." *Ausgrabungen in Schleswig* (Beiträge zur Schleswiger Stadtgeschichte 20): 76-88.
1981a.	"The Origin of the Runes." *Michigan Germanic Studies* 7: 3-7.
1981b.	"Järsbergstenen en maekelig värmlandsk runesten." *Fv.*: 81-90.
1985	*Runes and Their Origin: Denmark and Elsewhere.* Copenhagen: National Museum.

Moltke, E. and Jacobsen, L.
    1928.   "Troldtal." *Tilskueren*: 155-173.

Moltke, E. and Stoklund, M.
    1981.   "Runeindskrifterne fra Illerup mose." *Kuml*: 67-79.

Morgenroth, Wolfgang.
    1961.   "Zahlenmagie in Runeninschriften. Kritische Bemerkungen zu einigen Interpretationsmethoden." *Wissenschaftliche Zeitschrift der Universität Greifswald* 10: 279-83.

Motz, Lotte.
1973a.	"New Thoughts on Dwarf-Names in Old Icelandic" *Frühmast.* 7: 100-117.
1973b.	"Withdrawal and Return: A Ritual Pattern in the *Grettis saga.*" *ANF* 88: 91-110.
1973/74.	"Of Elves and Dwarfs." *Arv* 29-30: 93-127.
1981a.	"Giantesses and their Names." *Frühmast.* 15: 495-511.
1981b.	"Aurboða-Eyrgjafa: Two Old Icelandic Names." *MQ* 22: 93-105.

Mowinckel, Sigmund.
    1953.   *Religion und Kultus.* Göttingen: Vandenhoeck & Ruprecht.

Mookerjee, Ajit and Khanna, Madhu.
    1977.   *The Tantric Way: Art, Science, Ritual.* Boston: New York Graphic Society.

Much, Rudolf.
1967. *Die Germania des Tacitus.* Heidelberg: Winter, 3rd ed.
Müller, Günter.
1976. "Zur Heilkraft der Walküre: Sondersprachliches der Magie in kontinentalen und skandinavischen Zeugnissen." *Frühmast.* 10: 350-61.
1988. "Von der Buchstabenmagie zur Namenmagie in den Brakteateninschriften." *Frühmast.* 22, pp. 111-157.
Müller, Martin.
1901. *Über die Stilform der altdeutschen Zaubersprüche.* Gotha: Perthers.
Mulder, J. W. F.
1972. *Theory of the Linguistic Sign.* The Hague: Mouton.
Mundal, Else.
1974. *Fylgjamotiva i Norrøn Literatur.* Oslo: Universitetsforlaget.
Murdoch, Brian.
1983. *Old High German Literature.* Boston: Twayne.
Musset, Lucien.
1965. *Introduction à la Runologie* (Bibliotheque de Philologie Germanique 20) Paris: Aubier Montaigne.
Neckel, Gustav.
1925. *Altgermanische Kultur.* Leipzig: Harrassowitz.
1926. "Regnator omnium deus." *Ilbergs neue Jahrbücher für das klassische Altertum* 2: 139-50.
1928. "Runische Schmuckformen." *Jahrbuch des deutschen Vereins für Buchwesen und Schrifttum*: 31-38.
1933. "Die Herkunft der Runenschrift." *Neue Jahrbücher für Wissenschaft und Jugendbildung.* 9: 406-17.
1938. "Die Runen." *APS*: 102-15.
1944. *Vom Germanentum.* Leipzig: Harrassowitz.
Neckel, Gustav and Kuhn, Hans.
1962. *Edda: Die Lieder des Codex Regius nebst verwandten Denkmälern.* Heidelberg: Winter.
Neff, Mary.
1980 "Germanic Sacrifice: An Analytical Study using linguistic, archeological, and literary data." Diss. University of Texas at Austin.
Neu, Erich.
1974. *Der Anitta-Text* (Studien zu den Bogazköy-Texten 18) Wiesbaden: Harrassowitz.
Newcome, Theodore M.
1950. *Social Psychology.* New York: Dryden Press.
Niederhellmann, Annette.
1981 "Heilkundliches in den Leges: Die Schädel Verletzungen und ihre Beziehungen." In: Schmidt-Wiegand, R. (ed.) *Wörter und Sachen im Lichte der Bezeichnungsforschung.* Berlin: de Gruyter.
Nielsen, Karl Martin.
1940. "Guldhorninskriften." *ANO*: 57-69.
1954. Rev. Bæksted, Anders. *Måruner og Troldruner.* In: *ANF* 69: 221-32.

1970. *Om Dateringen af de Senurnordiske Runeindskrifter* (Institut for nordisk Filologi Studier 2) Copenhagen: Akademisk Forlag.
1985. "Runen und Magie." *Frühmast.* 19, pp. 75-97.
Nielsen, Niels Åge.
1968. *Runestudier* (Odense University Studies in Scandinavian Languages 1) Odense: Odense University Press.
1969. "Freyr, Ullr, and the Sparlösa Stone." *MScan.* 2: 102-28.
Nielsen, Ulla and Vitus, and Moltke, Erik.
1976. "Pikhammeren — kan man ogsa skrive med den?" *Hikuin* 6: 7-16.
Nilsson, Bruce E.
1976. "The Runic 'Fish Amulet' from Öland: A Solution." *MSca.* 9: 236-45.
Nilsson, M. P.
1941-50. *Geschichte der griechischen Religion.* Munich: Beck, 2 vols.
Nordén, Arthur.
1934a. "Från Kivik till Eggjum I. De gravmagiska bildristningarna." *Fv.*: 35-53.
1934b. "Från Kivik till Eggjum II. Runristningar med gengangårbesvärjelse." *Fv.*: 97-117.
1936. "Från Kivik Till Eggjum III. Fågel-fisk-magien- och vattnet som gengårskydd." *Fv.*: 241-48.
1937a. "Magiska Runinskrifter." *ANF* 53: 147-87.
1937b. "Söderköpingsstenen: En Nyfunnen Runsten med Magiskt Syfte från Övergångstiden." *Fv.*: 129-56.
1941. "Felszeichnungen und Runenschrift." *Runenberichte* 1 Heft 2-3: 51-75.
1943. *Bidrag till svensk Runforskning I. Magiska runinskrifter. Runblecken.* (Kungl. Vitterhets Historie Akademiens Handlingar 55:1) Lund: Gleerup: 143-231.
1960. "Sibberyd, Röks Prästgard och Sibbe Helgedomsvårdare." *Fv.*: 260-79.
Nordland, Odd.
1951. "Det vonde haglet og runeteignet hagall." *MM*: 90-128.
Noreen, Adolf.
1903. "Suffixablaut im Altnordischen." *IF* 14: 396-402.
1923. *Altisländische und altnorwegische Grammatik.* Halle/Saale, 4th ed.
1927. "Inscription runique des bracteates de Äsketorp et de Väsby." *APS* 1: 151-55.
Odenstedt, Bengt.
1983. "The Inscription on the Meldorf Fibula." *ZDA* 112: 153-61.
Oberg, Herje.
1942. *Guldbrakteaterna från Nordens Folkvanderingstid.* Stockholm: Wahlstrom & Widstrand.
Okasha, Elisabeth.
1971. *Handlist of Anglo-Saxon Non-Runic Inscriptions.* Cambridge: Cambridge University Press.
Olsen, Björn Magnusson.
1883. *Runerne i den Oldislandiske Literatur.* Copenhagen: Gyldendal.
Olsen, Magnus.
1907a. "Runeindskriften paa en Goldbrakteat fra Overhornbæk." *ANO*: 19-44.

1907b.   *Valby amulettens runeindskrift*. (Christiania Videnskabs-Selsabs Forhandlinger for 1907: 6) Christiana: Dybwad.
1908.   *Tryllerunerne paa et vasvspjeld fra Lund i Skaane*. (Christiania Videnskabs-Selskabs Forhandlinger for 1908: 7) Christiana: Dybwad.
1911.   "Runerne paa to Middelalderske Blykors fra Bru i Ryfylke." *Stavanger Museums Årshefte*: 3-21.
1914/15.   "En indskrift med ældre runer fra Gjersvik (Tynesøen) i Nordhordland." *Bergens Museums Årbok* 4: 14-33.
1916.   "Om Trollruner." *Edda* 5: 225-45. (Cited from *Norrøne Studier*, Oslo: Aschehoug 1938 : 1-23.)
1919.   *Eggjum-stenens Indskrift med de ældre runer* (*NIæR*: 111:3) Christiana: Brøgger.
1927.   "Magie et Culte dans la Norvege Antique." *Revue de l'Histoire des Religions* 48: 1-38.
1930.   "Runebudskapet i Atlamal." *ANF* 46: 161-70.
1932a.   "Rúnar er ristu rýnastir menn." *NTS* 5: 167-88.
1932b.   "Kingigtorsoak-Stenen og Sproget i de grønlnlandske Runeinnskrifter." *NTS* 5: 189-257.
1934.   "Þundarbenda." *MM*: 92-97.
1935.   "Le prêtre-magicien et le dieu-magicien dans la Norvège ancienne." *Revue de l'Histoire des Religions* 111-112: 177-221; 5-49.
1936.   "Runestenen på Barmen i Nordfjord." *Bergens Museums Årbok*: 3-40.
1940.   *Sigtuna-Amuletten: Nogen Tolkningsbidrag* (Avhandlinger utgitt av det Norske Videnskaps-Akademi i Oslo II. Hist.-Filos. Kl. 1940:3) Oslo: Dybwad.
1943.   *Grimhilds og Gudruns runeinnskrifter* (Avhandlinger utgitt av de Norske Videnskaps Akademi i Oslo II. Hist.-Filos. Kl. 1943:1) Oslo: Dybwad.
1954.   "Runic Inscriptions in Great Britain, Ireland, and the Isle of Man." In: Shetelig, H. (ed.) *Viking Antiquities in Great Britain and Ireland VI*. Oslo: Aschhoug, vol. 6: 152-233.

Olsen, Magnus and Shetelig, Haakon.
1909.   "En indskrift med ældre runer fra Fløksand i Nordhordland." *Bergens Museums Årbok* 1909: 7: 35-79.
1933.   "Runekammen fra Setre." *Bergens Museums Årbok* 1933: 2: 1-92.

Olsen, Magnus et al.
1941-60.   *Norges Innskrifter med de yngre Runer*. Oslo: Bokcentralen. (Cited as *NIyR*)

Olsen, Olaf.
1965.   *Hørg, Hov og Kirke*. (= ANO 1965) Copenhagen: Lynge.

Olson, Emil.
1908.   "Benplatta med runinskrift." *Fv.*: 14-27.

Ong, Walter.
1982.   *Orality and Literacy*. London: Routledge.

Oomen, Hans-Gert.
1971. "Lateinisch-christliche Inschriften aus alamannischen Gräbern." *Zeitschrift für württembergische Landesgeschichte* 30: 404-07.
Opitz, Stephan.
1977. *Südgermanische Runeninschriften im älteren Futhark aus der Merowingerzeit.* Kirchzarten: Burg Verlag.
1981. "Runeninschriftliche Neufunde: Das Schwert von Eichstetten/Kaiserstuhl und der Webestuhl von Neudingen/ Baar." *Archeologische Nachrichten aus Baden* 27: 26-31.
Otto, Rudolf.
1917. *Das Heilige.* Breslau: Treuedt & Granier.
Owen, Francis.
1927/28. "Alliteration in the Runic Inscriptions." *Modern Philology* 25: 397-408.
Page, R. I.
1964. "Anglo-Saxons, Runes, and Magic" *Journal of the Archeological Association* 27: 14-31.
1968. "The Old English Rune, *Eoh*, *Íh*, 'Yew Tree.'" *Medium Ævum* 37: 124-34.
1973. *An Introduction to English Runes.* London: Methuen.
1999 *An Introduction to English Runes.* Boydell: Woodbridge, 2nd ed.
Parsons, Talcott.
1966. *Societies: Evolutionary and Comparative Perspectives.* New York: Prentice Hall.
Pauli, Ludwig.
1975. *Keltischer Volksglaube.* München: Beck.
Pedersen, Holger.
1920-25. "L'origine des runes." *Memoires de la Societé Royale des Antiquaires du Nord* 1920-25: 88-136.
Petersen, Henry.
1876. *Om Nordoernes Gudedyrkelse og Gudetro i Hedenold.* Copenhagen: Reitzel.
Pettersson, Olof.
1957. "Magic-Religion: Some Marginal Notes to an Old Problem." *Ethnos* 22: 109-119.
Philippson, Ernst Alfred.
1929. *Germanisches Heidentum bei den Angelsachsen* (Kölner anglistische Arbeiten 4) Leipzig: Tauchnitz.
1938. "Runenforschung und germanische Religionsgeschichte." *PMLA* 103: 321-32.
Pipping, Hugo.
1911. *Rök-studier.* (Studier i Nordisk Filologi 2:1) Helsingfors: Svenska Literatursällskapet i Finland.
1912. *Nytt om Röksteninskriften* (Studier i Nordisk Filologi 3:8) Helsingfors: Svenska Literatursällskapet i Finland.
1919. *Om Runinskriften på Rökstenen* (Acta Societatis Scientiarum Finnicae 49:1) Helsingfors: Svenska Literatursällskapet i Finland.

1921. *Röksteninskriften ännu en gang* (Acta Societatis Scieniarum Fennicae 49:3) Helsingfors: Svenska Literatursällskapet i Finland.
1929/30. "Zur Deutung der Inschrift auf dem Runenstein von Rök." *APS* 4: 247-69.
1933. *Sigtuna-amuletten* (Studier i Nordisk Filologi 23:4) Helsingfors: Svenska Literatursällskapet i Finland.
1935/36. "Bokstavsräkning i runskrift." *APS* 10: 81-88.

Pizarro, Joachin Martinez.
1978/79. "On *Níð* against Bishops." *MScan.* 11: 149-53.

Ploss, Emil.
1958 "Der Inschriftentypus 'N.N. ME FECIT' und seine geschichtliche Entwicklung bis ins Mittelalter." *ZDP* 77: 25-46.

Plutzar, Friedrich.
1924. *Die Ornamentik der Runensteine.* Stockholm: Akademiens Forlag.

Pokorny, Julius.
1959. *Indogermanisches etymologisches Wörterbuch.* Bern: Francke.

Polomé, Edgar C.
1950. "Reflexes de la laryngales en arménien." *Annuaire de l'Institut de Philologie et d'Histoire Orientales et et Slaves* 10: 539-69.
1953. "L'étymologie du terme germanique *ansuz 'dieu souverain.'" *Etudes Germanique* 8: 36-48.
1954. "Notes sur le vocabulaire religieux du germanique 1. Runique *alu*." *La Nouvelle Clio* 6: 40-55.
1969. "Some Comments on Völuspá Stanzas 17-18." In: Polomé, E. (ed.) *Old Norse Literature and Mythology: A Symposium.* Austin: University of Texas Press: 265-90.
1970. "The Indo-European Component in Germanic Religion." In: Puhvel, J. (ed.) *Myth and Law among the Indo-Europeans.* Berkeley: University of California Press: 55-82.
1974. "Approaches to Germanic Mythology." In: Larson, G. (ed.) *Myth in Indo-European Antiquity.* Berkeley: University of California Press: 51-65.
1975. "Old Norse Religious Terminology in Indo-European Perspective." In: Dahlstedt, K. (ed.) *The Nordic Languages and Modern Linguistics II.* Stockholm: Almqvist & Wiksell : 654-65.
1984. "Initial PIE *gh- in Germanic" [To have appeared in *Festschrift for Henri Hoenigswald*.]
1991. "The Names of the Runes." In: A. Bammesberger (ed.) *Old English Runes and their Continental Background.* Heidelberg: Winter.
1996. "Beer, Runes and Magic." *JIES* 24:1-2, pp. 99-105.

Preisendanz, Karl and Henrichs, Albert.
1973-74. *Papyri Graecae Magicae: Die griechischen Zauberpapyri.* Stuttgart: Teubner, 2 vols, 2nd ed.

Quak, Arend.
1978. "*ybiR risti runaR* Zur Sprache eines upplandischen Runenmeisters." *Amsterdamer Beitrage zur alteren Germanistik* 13: 35-67.
1982. "Zur Entstehung der sogenannten jüngeren Futharks." *Amsterdamer Beiträge zur älteren Germanistik* 17: 129-44.

Reichborn Kjennerud, I.
 1923. "Laegeradene i den eldre edda." *MM*: 1-57.
 1924a. "Eddatidens Medisin." *ANF* 40: 103-48.
 1924b. "Navnets og ordets makt i Norsk folkemedisin." *MM*: 158-91.
Reichardt, Konstantin.
 1936. *Runenkunde*. Jena: Eugen Diederichs Verlag.
Reier, Herbert.
 1952. "Der Eggjumstein — Ein Schandstein." *APS* 21: 73-86.
Rice, Tamara.
 1957. *The Scythians*. New York: Praeger.
Rischel , Jörgen.
 1966/67. *Phoneme, Grapheme, and the Importance of Distinctions: Functional Aspects of the Scandinavian Runic Reform*. Stockholm: Research Group for Quantitative Linguistics.
Ristow, Gunter.
 1974. *Mithras im römischen Köln* (Études preliminaires aux religions orientales dans l'Empire Romain 24) Leiden: Brill.
Roth, Helmut.
 1981. "New Chronological Aspects of Runic Inscriptions: The Archeological Evidence." *Michigan Germanic Studies* 7: 62-68.
Saal, Walter.
 1979. "Ein Amulettstein mit Vortragekreuz und Runen aus Osterburg, Ot. Krumke." *Ausgrabungen und Funde* 24: 274- 77.
Salberger, Evert.
 1959. "An Ideographic Rune on the Skodborg Bracteate." *APS* 24: 18-32.
 1978. *Runsvenska Namnstudier* (Stockholm Studies in Scandinavian Philology 13) Stockholm: Alqvist &Wiksell.
Salin, Bernhard.
 1903. "Heimskringlas tradition om asarnas invandring i Norden." In: Salin, B. (ed.) *Studier tillägende O. Montelius*. Stockholm: Norstedt: 133-41.
Samarin, William T.
 1968. "The Linguisticality of Glossolalia." *Hartford Quarterly* 8: 49-75.
Saraṇa, Gopāla.
 1975. *The Methodology of Anthropological Comparisons* (Viking Fund Publications in Anthropology 53) Tuscon, AZ: University of Arizona Press.
Saxo Grammaticus.
 1931. *Saxonis Gesta Danorum*. Copenhagen: Levin & Munksgaard.
Schlottig, Kurt H.
 1938. "Sind die Inschriften der EHU-Brakteaten undeutbar?" In: Schlottig, K. (ed.) *Beiträge zur Runenkunde und nordischen Sprachwissenschaft* (Neckel Festschrift) Leipzig: Harrassowitz: 74-77.
Schmidt, Ludwig.
 1910-18. *Geschichte der deutschen Stämme bis zum Ausgange der Völkerwanderung*. Berlin: Weidemann, 2 vols.

Schmidt, Wilhelm.
1912. *Die Bedeutung des Namens in Kult und Aberglauben.* Darmstadt: Otto.
Schmidt, Wilhelm.
1931. *The Origin and Growth of Religion: Facts and Theories,* (tr. H. J. Rose) New York: Cooper Square. 1972.
Schneider, Karl.
1956. *Die germanischen Runennamen: Versuch einer Gesamtdeutung.* Meisenheim: Anton Hain.
1968. "Six Old English Inscriptions Reconsidered." In: Orrick, A. (ed.) *Nordica et Anglica: Studies in Honor of Stefán Einarsson.* The Hague: Mouton: 37-52.
1980. "Zu einem Runenfund in Trier." *ZDA* 109: 193-201. Schnippel, Emil.
1929. "Lein und Lauch im Runenzauber." *ZfV.* N.F. 1: 65-68.
Schönaich-Caroiath, Isa von.
1924. *Runendenkmäler.* Mühlhausen i. Thüringen: Urquell.
Schönfeld, M.
1911. *Wörterbuch der altgermanischen Personen und Völkernamen.* Heidelberg: Winter.
Schöttler, Wolfgang.
1948. "Die Runenstrophen der Edda: Runenkundliche Untersuchungen über den Quellenwert der eddischen Runenstrophen." Diss. Göttingen.
Scholem, Gershom.
1974. *Kabbalah.* New York: New American Library.
Schröder, Edward.
1893. "Über das Spell." *ZDA* 37: 241-68.
Schröder, Franz Rolf.
1922. "Neuere Runenforschung." *GRM* 10: 4-17.
1924. *Germanentum und Hellenismus.* Heidelberg: Winter.
1929a. *Die Germanen.* Tübingen: Mohr.
1929b. *Altgermanische Kulturprobleme.* Berlin: de Gruyter.
Schurtz, Heinrich.
1902. *Altersklassen und Männerbünde: Eine Darstellung der Grundformen der Gesellschaft.* Berlin: Reimer.
Schwarz, Ernst.
1956. *Germanische Stammeskunde.* Heidelberg: Winter.
Schwarz, Hans.
1956. "Über skaldische Wortwahl." *Wirkendes Wort* 6: 257-62.
Seabrook, William.
1940. *Witchcraft: Its Power in the World Today.* New York: Harcourt & Brace.
See, Klaus von.
1972. *Kontinuitätstheorie und Sakraltheorie in der Germanenforschung: Antwort an Otto Höfler.* Frankfurt/Main: Anthenaum.
Seipp, Horst.
1968. *Entwicklungszuge der germanischen Religionswissenschaft: Von Jacob Grimm zu Georges Dumézil.* Berlin: Dissertations Druckstelle.

Shamastry, R.
    1906.   "The Origin of the Devangari-Alphabet." *The Indian Antiquary* 35: 253-58.
Siebs, Benno-Eide.
    1959.   "Stal-Roland-Rosengarten: Zur magischen Bedeutung der Gerichtsstatten." *Zeitschrift der Savigny-Stiftung für Rechtsgeschichte. Germanische Abteilung* 76: 246-66.
Sierke, Sigurd.
    1939.   *Kannten die vorchristlichen Germanen Runenzauber?* (Schriften der Albertus-Universität Geisteswissenschaftliche Reihe 24) Königsberg: Ost-Europa Verlag.
Simon, Karl.
    1928.   "Die Runenbewegung und das arianische Christentum." *ZDP* 53: 41-48.
Simpson, Jacqueline.
    1973.   "Olaf Tryggvason versus the Powers of Darkness." In: Newell, V. (ed.) *The Witch Figure*. London: Routledge & Kegan Paul: 165-87.
    1975.   *Legends of the Icelandic Magicians*. Cambridge: Brewer.
Skorupski, John.
    1976.   *Symbol and Theory: A Philosophical Study of Theories of Social Anthropology*. Cambridge: Cambridge University Press.
Söderberg, A. and Brate, E.
    1900-06.   *Ölands Runinskrifter*. Stockholm: Kugl. Vetterhets Historie och Antikvitets Akademien.
Solheim, Svale, et al.
    1958.   "Draug." *KHNM* 3: 297-99.
Soustelle, Jacques.
    1964.   *Daily Life of the Aztecs on the Eve of the Spanish Conquest*. Harmondsworth: Penguin.
Steblin-Kaminskij, M. I.
    1973.   *The Saga Mind* (tr. K. Ober) Odense: Odense University Press.
Steinhauser, Walter.
    1968a.   "Die Runeninschrift von Rubring an der Enns und der Eisreise Iring." *Archeologica Austriaca* 44: 1-28.
    1968b.   "Die Wodansweihe der Nordendorfer Runenspange A." *ZDA* 97: 1-29.
Steinmeyer, Elias von.
    1963.   *Die kleineren althochdeutschen Sprachdenkmäler*. Berlin: Weidmann, 2nd ed.
Steinsland, Gro., and Vogt, Kari.
    1981.   "'Aukin ertu Volse ok upp tekinn:' En religions-historisk analyse av Vǫlsaþattr i Flateyjarbók." *ANF* 96: 87-106.
Stenberger, Martin.
    1962.   *Sweden*. New York: Praeger.
Stephens, George.
    1866-1901. *The Old-Northern Runic Monuments of Scandinavia and England*. London: John Rüssel Smith, 4 vols.
    1884.   *Handbook of the Old Northern Runic Monuments of Scandinavia and England*. London: Williams and Norgate.

Stoklund, Marie.
1990 "Arbejdet ved Runologisk-Epigrafisk Laboritorium." *NoR* 5: 4.
1995 "Nyfund fra Danmark i 1994 (og 1993)." *NoR* 10: 4-5.
Storm, Gustav.
1893. "Vore Forfædres Tro paa Sjælevandring og deres Opkaldelesessystem." *ANF* 9: 199-222.
Storms, G.
1948. *Anglo-Saxon Magic*. The Hague: Martinus Nijhoff.
Ström, Åke.
1966. "Die Hauptriten des wikingerzeitlichen nordischen Opfers." In: Rudolf, K. et al. (eds.) *Festschrift Walter Baetke*. Weimar: Böhlaus: 330-42.
Ström, Åke and Biezais, Haralds.
1975. *Germanische und Baltische Religion*. Stuttgart: Kohlhammer.
Ström, Folke.
1947. *Den döendes make och Odin i tradet*. Göteborg: Elander.
1948. *Den egna Kraftens Män: En Studie i forntida irreligiositet*. (Göteborgs Hogskolas Arskrift Liv 1948: 2) Göteborg: Elander.
1954. *Diser, Nornor, Valkyrjor: Fruktbarheitskult och Sakralt Kungadome i Norden*. Stockholm: Almqvist & Wiksell.
1974. *Níð, ergi and Old Norse moral attitudes*. London: Viking Society.
Ström, Folke, et al.
1960. "Gengångare." *KHNM* 5: 551-55.
Strömbäck, Dag.
1935. *Sejd*. Stockholm: Geber.
1975. "The Concept of the Soul in Nordic Tradition." *Arv* 31: 5-22.
1976/77. "Ein Beitrag zu den älteren Vorstellungen von der *mara*." *Arv* 32-33: 282-86.
Stroheker, Karl Friedrich.
1965. *Germanentum und Spätantike*. Zürich: Artemis.
Strutynski, Udo.
1975. "Germanic Divinities in Weekday Names." *JIES* 3: 363-84.
Sturtevant, Albert M.
1916. "A Study of the Old Norse word *Regin*." *JEGP* 15: 251-66.
Sulimirski, T.
1970. *The Sarmatians*. New York: Praeger.
Svärdström, Elisabeth.
1967. "Högstena-bleckets rungalder." *Fv.*: 12-21.
Tambiah, Stanley J.
1968a. "The Magical Power of Words." *Man* N.S. 3: 175-208.
1968b. "Literacy in a Buddhist Village in North-East Thailand." In: Goddy, J. (ed.) *Literacy in Traditional Societies*. Cambridge: Cambridge University Press: 85-131.
1973. "Form and Meaning of Magical Acts: A Point of View." In: Horton, R. (ed.) *Modes of Thought*. London: Faber & Faber: 199-229.

Tavenner, Eugene.
   1916.   *Studies in Magic from Latin Literature.* New York: Columbia University Press.
Thamdrup, Ole.
   1981.   "...og gjorde disse mindesmærker..." *Kuml*: 7-12.
Thompson, Claiborne.
   1972a.   "Öpir's Teacher." *Fv.*: 16-19.
   1972b.   "Nonsense Inscriptions in Swedish Uppland." In: Firchow, E. S. *et al.* (eds.) *Studies for Einar Haugen.* The Hague: Mouton: 522-34.
   1975.   *Studies in Upplandic Runography.* Austin: University of Texas Press.
   1977.   "'Rune' and 'Runic.'" *Scandinavica* 16: 23-28.
Thorpe, Benjamin.
   1868.   *Analecta Anglo-Saxonica.* London: John Rüssel Smith.
Thrane, H. *et al.*
   1973.   "Amulett." RGA^2 1: 268-74.
Titiev, Mischa.
   1960.   "A Fresh Approach to the Problem of Magic and Religion." *Southwestern Journal of Anthropology* 16: 292-98.
Tollenaere, F. de.
   1967.   *De Harigasti-Inscriptie op Helm B van Negau.* (Mededelingen der koninklijke Nederlandse Akademie van Wetenschappen 30: 11) Amsterdam: Noord-Hollandsche Uitgevers Maatschappij.
Turville-Petre, E. O. G.
   1963.   "A Note on the *Landdísir.*" In: Brown, A. and Foote, P. (eds.) *Early English and Old Norse Studies.* London: Methuen: 196-201.
   1964.   *Myth and Religion of the North.* New York: Holt, Rinehart & Winston.
Turville-Petre, E. O. G. and Ross, A.
   1936.   "Agrell's 'magico-numerical' Theory of the Runes." *Folklore* 97: 203-13.
Tylor, Edward.
   1871.   *Primitive Culture.* New York: Appleton.
Ulansey, David.
   1989   *The Origins of the Mithraic Cult.* Oxford: Oxford University Press.
Ulff-Møller, Jens.
   1993   "Remnants of Medieval Symbolic Number Usage in Northern Europe." In: Surles, Robert, ed. *Medieval Numerology.* New York: Garland.
Vigfusson, Guðbrandr and Unger, C. R.
   1860-68. *Flateyjarbók.* Christiana: Mailing, 3 vols. (cited *Flb*)
Vries, Jan de.
   1930/31. "Ginnungagap." *APS* 5: 41-66.
   1935-37. *Altgermanische Religionsgeschichte.* Berlin: de Gruyter, 2 vols.
   1944.   "HagustaidaR." *ANF* 58: 93-104.
   1956-57. *Altgermanische Religionsgeschichte.* Berlin: de Gruyter, 2 vols., 2nd ed.
   1960.   *Kelten und Germanen.* Bern: Francke.
   1961a.   *Altnordisches etymologisches Wörterbuch.* Leiden: Brill.
   1961b.   *Keltische Religion.* Stuttgart: Kohlhammer.
   1964-67. *Altnordische Literaturgeschichte.* Berlin: de Gruyter, 2 vols., 2nd ed.

Wähle, Ernst.
1962. *Deutsche Vorzeit*. Darmstadt: Wissenschaftliche Buchgesellschaft, 3rd ed.
Watkins, Calvert.
1970. "Language of Gods and Language of Men: Remarks on Some Indo-European Metalinguistic Traditions." In: Puhvel, J. (ed.) *Myth and Law among the, Indo-Europeans*. Berkeley: University of California Press: 1-17.
1982. "Aspects of Indo-European Poetics." In: Polomé, E. (ed.) *The Indo-Europeans in the Fourth and Third Millennia* (Linguistic Extranea, Studia 14) Ann Arbor: Karoma: 104-20.

Wax, Murray and Wax, Rosalie.
1962. "The Magical Worldview." *Journal for the Scientific Study of Religion* 1: 179-88.
1963. "The Notion of Magic" *Current Anthropology* 4: 495-518.
Webster, Hutton.
1948. *Magic: A Sociological Study*. Stanford: University of Stanford Press.
Weiser, Lily.
1927. *Altgermanische jünglingsweihen und Mannerbünde*. Bruhl : Konkordia.
Wenskus, Reinhard.
1961. *Stammesbildung und Verfassung: Das Werden der frühmittelalterlichen gentes*. Köln: Bohlau.
Wesche, Heinrich.
1940. *Der althochdeutsche Wortschatz im Gebiete des Zaubers und der Weissagung*. Halle/Saale: Niemeyer.
Wessén, Elias.
1924. *Studier till Sveriges hedna mythologi och fornhistoria* (Uppsala Universitets Arskrift 1924: 6) Uppsala: Almqvist & Wiksell.
1958. *Runstenen vid Röks Kirka* (Kungl. Vitterhets Historie och Antikvitets Akademiens Handlingar 5) Stockholm: Almqvist & Wiksell .
Wessen, E. and Jansson, S. B. F.
1940-58. *Upplands Runinskrifter*. Stockholm: Kungl. Vitterhets Historie och Antikvitets Akademien.
West, Stanley E.
1983. "Gold bracteate from Undley, Suffolk." *Frühmast*. 17: 459.
Whatmough, Joshua.
1933. *The Prae-Italic Dialects of Italy*. Cambridge, Mass.: Harvard University Press, vol. II.
Wiegelmann, G.
1967. "Bier." In: *RGA*[2] 2: 533-37.
Wipf, K. A.
1975. "Die Zaubersprüche im Althochdeutschen." *Numen* 22: 42-69.

Fuþark Figures
I. The Older Fuþark

Form	Transcription	Name PGmc.	PNor.	Translation
ᚠ	f	*fehu →	*fehu	"cattle"
ᚢ	u	*ūruz →	*ūruR	"aurochs"
ᚦ	þ	*þurisaz →	*þurisaR	"giant" (þurs)
ᚨ	a	*ansuz →	*a(n)suR	"god" (áss)
ᚱ	r	*raiðō →	*raidu	"ride; wagon"
ᚲ	k	*kauna- →	*kauna	"sore"
		*kēnaz →	*kānaR	"torch"
ᚷ	g	*gebō →	*gebu	"gift"
ᚹ	w	*wunjō →	*wunju	"joy"
ᚺ	h	*hagala- →	*hagla	"hail"
			*hagalaR	
ᚾ	n	*naudiz →	*naudiR	"need"
ᛁ	i	*īsa- →	*īsa	"ice"
			*īsar	
ᛃ	j	*jēra- →	*jāra	"year; harvest"
ᛇ	ï	*ī(h)waz →	*īwaR	"yew"
ᛈ	p	*perþrō (?) →	*perþu	"gaming piece"(?)
ᛉ	z/R	*algiz →	*algiR	"elk" (?)
ᛋ	s	*sowilō →	*sowilu	"sun"
ᛏ	t	*tīwaz →	*tīwaR	"the god Týr"
ᛒ	b	*berkanō →	*berkana	"birch-twig"
ᛖ	e	*ehwaz →	*ehwaR	"horse"
ᛗ	m	*mannaz →	*mannaR	"man"
ᛚ	l	*laguz →	*laguR	"water"
		*laukaz →	*laukaR	"leek"
ᛜ	ŋ	*ingwaz →	*ingwaR	"the god Ing"
ᛞ	d	*dagaz →	*dagaR	"day"
ᛟ	o	*ōþila →	*ōþila	"ancestral land"
		*ōþala →	*ōþala	

Figure I.A.

I.B Older Fuþarks

1. Standardized Older Fuþark (see Düwel 2008: 7-8)
fuþarkgwhnijïpRstbemlŋdo

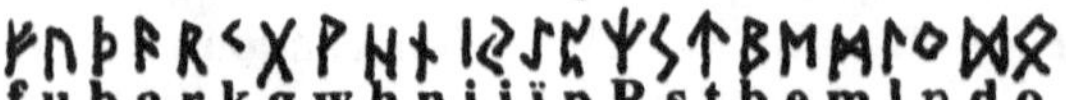

2. KJ 1 Kylver st., ca. 400
fuþarkgwhnijpïRstbemlŋ do

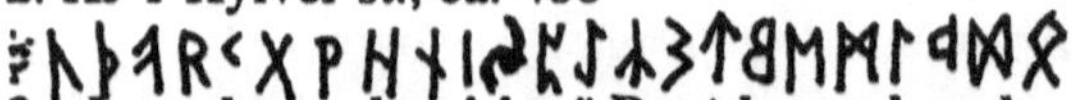

3. IK 377, 1-2 Vadstena/Motala brs. 450-550
fuþarkgw:hnijïpRs:tbemlŋod:

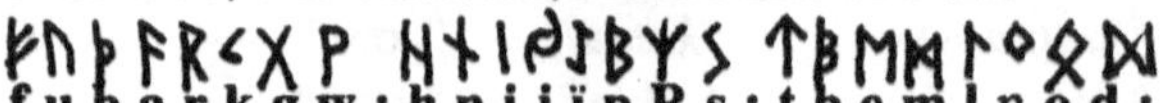

4. IK II.31 Grumpan br. 450-550
fuþarkgw........hnijïp[Rs]....tbemlŋod

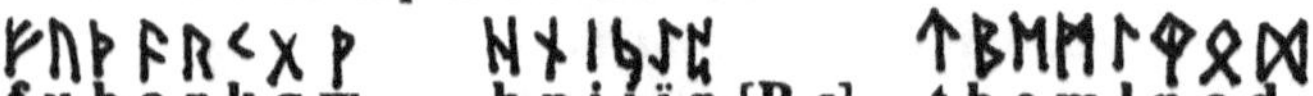

5. KJ 8 Beuchte brooch, 450-600
fuþarRj

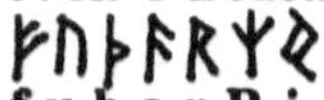

6. KJ 5: Breza marble column, ca. 550
fuþarkgwhnijïpRsteml...

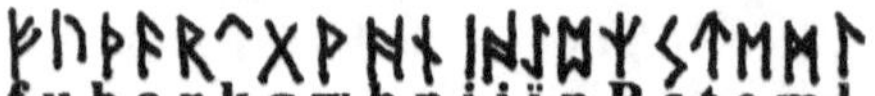

7. KJ 6: Charnay brooch, 550-600
fuþarkgwhnijïpRstbem

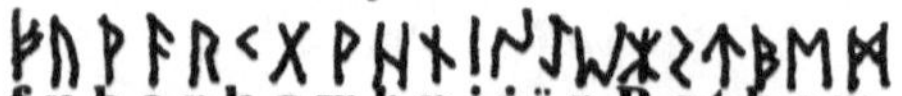

8. KJ 7: Aquincum brooch, ca. 530
fuþarkgw

Figure I.B.

II. The Old English Epigrapical Fuþorc

Form	Transcription	Name	Translation
ᚠ	f	*feoh*	"cattle"
ᚢ	u	*ūr*	"aurochs"
ᚦ	þ	*þorn*	"thorn"
ᚩ	o	*ōs*	"mouth" or "god"
ᚱ	r	*rād*	"a ride"
ᚳ	c	*cēn*	"torch"
ᚷ	g	*gyfu*	"gift; generosity"
ᚹ	w	*wynn*	"joy"
ᚺ	h	*hægl*	"hail"
ᚾ	n	*nȳd*	"need"
ᛁ	i	*īs*	"ice"
ᛄ	j	*jēra*	"(fruitful) year"
ᛇ	3	*ēoh*	"yew-tree"
ᛈ	p	*peorþ*	"chess-piece (?)"
ᛉ	x	*eolhx*	"sedge-grass(?)" (*eolh-secg*)
ᛋ	s	*sigel*	"sun"
ᛏ	t	*tīr*	"glory(?)"
ᛒ	b	*beorc*	"birch-tree(?)"
ᛖ	e	*eoh*	"horse"
ᛗ	m	*mann*	"man"
ᛚ	l	*lagu*	"water"
ᛝ	ŋ	*Ing*	"(the god) Ing"
ᛞ	d	*dæg*	"day"
ᛟ	œ	*œþel*	"ancestral home"
ᚪ	a	*āc*	"oak-tree"
ᚫ	æ	*æsc*	"ash-tree"
ᚣ	y	*ȳr*	"yew-bow"
ᛠ	ea	*ēar*	"earth-grave(?)"

Figure II.

III. The Younger Fuþąrk

Form	Transcription	Name	Translation
ᚠ	f	*fé*	"wealth, gold"
ᚢ	u	*úr(r)*	"slag" or "drizzle"
ᚦ	þ	*þurs*	"giant, thurs"
ᚨ	ą	*ąss*	"god (*Áss*)"
		óss	"estuary, mouth"
ᚱ	r	*reið*	"a ride, riding"
ᚴ	k	*kaun*	"sore, ulcer"
ᚼ	h	*hagall*	"hail"
ᚾ, ᚿ	n	*nauð(r)*	"constraint, distress"
ᛁ	i	*íss*	"ice"
ᛆ ᛅ	a	*ár*	"good harvest, plenty"
ᛋ ᛌ	s	*sól*	"sun"
ᛏ ᛐ	t	*Týr*	"the god Týr"
ᛒ	b	*bjarkan*	"birch-tree"
ᛘ ᛉ	m	*maðr*	"man"
ᛚ	l	*lǫgr*	"water(-fall)"
ᛦ	R/y	*ýr*	"yew; yew-bow"

<u>Figure III.A</u>

The Gørlev Fuþąrk

ᚠᚢᚦᚨᚱᚴᚼᚾᛁᛆᛋᛏᛒᛘᛚᛦ
f u þ ą r k h n i a s t b m l R

Figure III.B

IV. Ætt-Arrangement of the Runes

A. Older:

ᚠ ᚢ ᚦ ᚨ ᚱ ᚲ ᚷ ᚹ
ᚺ ᚾ ᛁ ᛃ ᛇ ᛈ ᛉ ᛊ
ᛏ ᛒ ᛖ ᛗ ᛚ ᛝ ᛞ ᛟ

B. Younger:

ᚠ ᚢ ᚦ ᚨ ᚱ ᚴ
ᚼ ᚾ ᛁ ᛅ ᛋ
ᛏ ᛒ ᛘ ᛚ ᛦ

C. Altered Arrangement for Cryptographic Practices:

ᛏ ᛒ ᛘ ᛚ ᛦ
ᚼ ᚾ ᛁ ᛅ ᛋ
ᚠ ᚢ ᚦ ᚨ ᚱ ᚴ

Figure IV.

V. Runic Alphabets

A Norwegian (from mid-13th century)

ᛆᛒᛍᛑᚦᛂᚠᚵᚼᛁᚴᛚᛘᚿᚮᛔᚱᛌᛐᚢ(x)ᛦᛆᛨ
a b c d ð e f g h i k l m n o p r s t u (x) y æ ø

B. Danish (from ca. 1300)

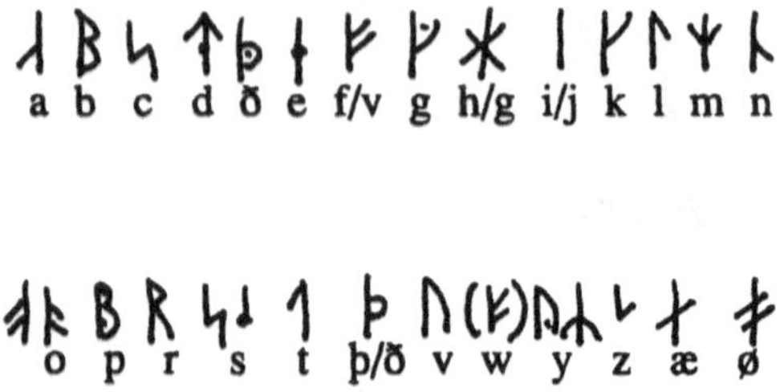

ᛆᛒᛍᛐᚦᛂᚠᚹᚼᛁᚴᛚᛘᚿ
a b c d ð e f/v g h/g i/j k l m n

ᚮᛔᚱᛌᛐᚦ(ᛑ)ᚡᚥᛦᛎᛅᛨ
o p r s t þ/ð v w y z æ ø

C. Swedish (from the early 13th century)

ᛆᛒᛍᛑᛂᚠᚵ✳ᛁᚴᛚᛘᚿ
a b c d e f/v g h/3 i/j k l m n

ᚮᛔᛩᚱᛌᛐᚦᚢᛦᛎᛅᛨ
o p q r s t þ/ð u/w y z æ ø

Figure V

MAPS

Map I. Older Runic Inscriptions before ca. 250 CE

Map II. Older Runic Inscriptions between ca. 250 and 350 CE

Map III. Older Runic Inscriptions between ca. 350 and 450 CE

Map IV. Older Runic Inscriptions between ca. 450 and 550 CE

Map V. Older Runic Inscriptions between ca. 550 and 650 CE

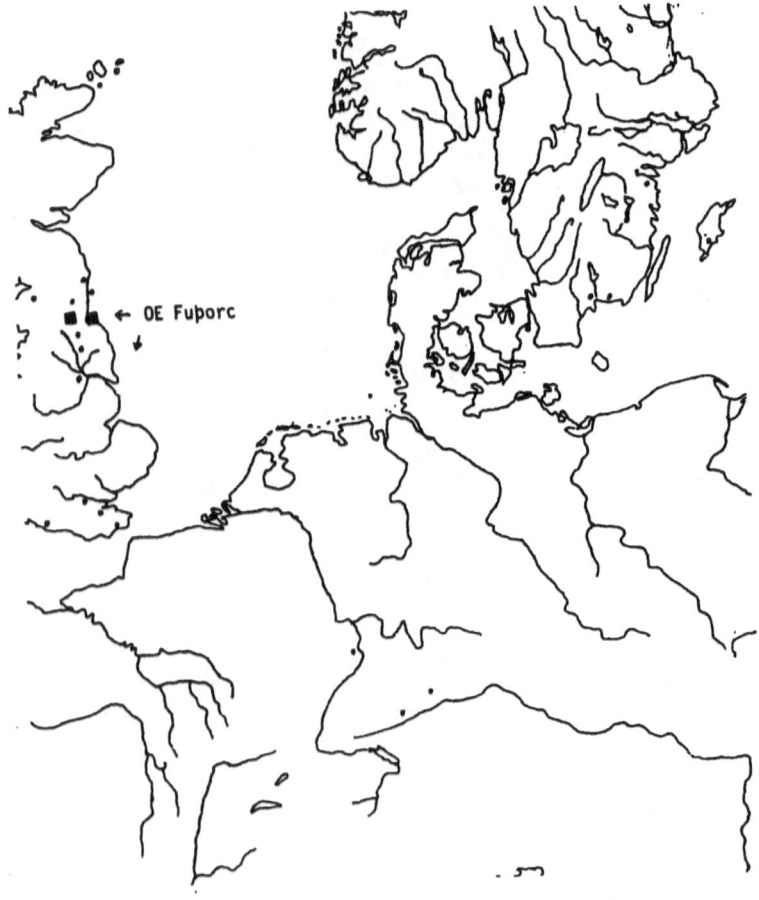

Map VI. Older Runic Inscriptions after ca. 650 CE

Map VII. Areas of Early Germanic Cultic Leagues

1. Ingvaeones-group (Nerthus)
2. Swabian-group (Semnones-grove)
3. Vandali-group (Alcis)
4. Sugambri-group (Tanfana)
   Approximate site of the cultic center

www.ingramcontent.com/pod-product-compliance
Lightning Source LLC
Chambersburg PA
CBHW021832220426
43663CB00005B/221